BEHIND THE HEADLINES

A parallel universe

ARROGANCE, CORRUPTION, DITHER, DELAY

SUE WOOD

The Conservative Government 2021 - 2022

First published in Great Britain as a softback original in 2022

Typeset in TheAntiquaB

Design, typesetting and publishing by UK Book Publishing

www.ukbookpublishing.com

ISBN: 978-1-915338-53-2

I dedicate this book to all those who believe in democracy, freedom of speech and independent journalism.

CONTENTS

CONTENTS

PREFACE

Having finished my book, **'Beneath the Bluster'** in June of 2021 I decided that I had no energy or enthusiasm left, to care about this incompetent and uncaring government any more. The headlines were shrieking at Boris Johnson's shambolic lack of leadership, the debacle over the withdrawal of Afghanistan, the shuffling of the inadequate cabinet, the lack of hauliers, the empty supermarket shelves, the cuts in Universal Benefit, and the end of the furlough scheme, so that I thought their unsuitability for government was absolutely obvious.

But then today, the 28th of September 2021, I read two stories which make me so angry that I have to write once more. I need to bring them to your attention because I know that you, and in fact most people, do not have the time to search for them yourselves. These stories do not make the headlines today, mainly because people are worrying about getting fuel in their cars and food on their tables.

But before I write about today I have to go back to the couple of stories I read two days ago in *The Observer*. The first one concerns women and prisons and it is one of the most disturbing articles I have ever read.

****

2021

26TH SEPTEMBER

A vulnerable young woman who is just 18 years old is in prison on remand for alleged robbery. She is pregnant. She goes into labour and calls for help but none is forthcoming. She calls again and again but eventually gives birth on her own without any medical assistance whatsoever. Her baby is purple and not breathing and she has to bite through the umbilical cord and then wraps the baby in a towel. 12 hours later, after two prisoners called for help, prison staff entered her cell to find the place covered in blood and her under the duvet with her dead baby.

These details were buried in a report last week by a prison watchdog, but I also read that the prison officers who failed to give help have been offered counselling and are still in their jobs. However, would it surprise you to know that the 18 year old woman has not received any of the routine bereavement or practical support or counselling that should normally be provided for a case such as this?

What am I writing here? A case such as this? How many cases such as this have there been? **Indeed how many pregnant women are there in prison?** And who, I would like to know, are the judges who deem it imperative for the safety of the community that a vulnerable pregnant young woman should be locked away?

But just read this: Mrs. A, as she was called, was regarded as having a "bad attitude" and she was viewed as a "difficult woman". So that's OK then ....just treat her like dirt...........she will be used to that.

I speak to the Howard League for Penal Reform this morning and they are conducting a three-year programme to reduce the arrests of women and stem the flow of women into the criminal justice system.

So Mr. Dominic Raab, our 8th new Justice Minister in 11 years, how are you planning to reform the prison system exactly? We would all very much like to know. Oh but I forgot. The Minister of Justice is viewed as a demotion from Foreign Secretary. I doubt if you have even started to look at your brief. But you look extremely smart in your robes of state.

****

And that brings me straight on to the other story I read about.

Peers in the House of Lords are really angry. Oh my goodness that is such good news I thought. What is it about? Is it about lack of affordable child-care, or lack of reform for the NHS, or cuts in the education budget, or the scrapping of the £20 uplift for Universal Credit or even the treatment of women in our prisons?

Well I was in for disappointment.

They are very angry that a decision has been made *without a vote* to abolish full uniform and horsehair wigs for their Parliamentary clerks, except for ceremonial occasions. Lord Cormack said, "I don't think decisions of this sort should be taken without consulting the view of the House. There should have been a vote on this and the House should have decided."

So this is the big story in the Lords at the moment.

****

But on to today. Let us turn to the Commons and see what is happening here, in particular with Rishi Sunak and Boris Johnson.

28TH SEPTEMBER
More cuts in education. Having rejected the £15 billion over the next three years asked for by Sir Kevan Collins, the education Tsar appointed by the government in order to bring education standards up to scratch, the Department of Education is going to get between

£1 and £2 billion for catch-up funding. The Department of Education are up in arms at this. To add insult to injury they are being accused of not getting their application for the money in by the required date. They are incensed by this accusation as they say they got it in well before the reshuffle took place.

Well we all know what that means. It means that it went to Gavin Williamson. I need say no more.

****

And then in the very next article I read about Boris and **"galactic Britain"**. Apparently space ports from Cornwall to the Shetlands will launch rockets into orbit next year as Boris promises to create "galactic Britain". These will spy on hostile powers, help forecast the weather and look for power grid outages. The trouble is, that with the education cuts in funding there will be no-one sufficiently educated to interpret the results. So the large amounts of tax-payers money spent on this programme will be a complete waste.

This might be a little simplistic but it just does not make any sense to me.

****

At the close of my last book I said, *"Please look out for U turns, resignations, weasel words and lies by this government, improper uses of our taxes, the extent of poverty in the UK, and the proper and lawful use of Parliament. But more important than any of all of that, please, please, please keep a sharp look out for **our children**. From birth, to students in further education, they must be everyone's top priority. Wraparound affordable childcare from birth, an extended curriculum which involves music, sport, drama, creative arts, outdoors adventure; a curriculum of excellence, free of paranoid testing and unnecessary exam; but an array of subjects taught by dedicated teachers who love the children they teach and who are respected and properly paid."*

And so here we are. It is all still happening and I am upset, angry and shocked all over again. This will not be an easy book to read but we owe it to all those whose lives and livelihoods have been damaged and destroyed beyond repair by the actions of this Conservative government, to read and remember.

****

WORDS, WORDS, WORDS

2021

October has been a big political month which opened with the party conferences and closed with the budget and spending review. In-between those events the topics that need discussing are, as ever, the NHS, education, the cost of living, child care, the vaccination programme and the pandemic, the criminal justice system, Nazanin Zaghari-Ratcliffe, climate change, the retail sector, fishing, farming, asylum seekers and the words and speeches of our Prime Minister. If you have read my previous book you will be familiar with all of these topics. But on they go and I wouldn't say that any of them have been satisfactorily resolved.

****

I forced myself to listen to the PM's speech at the **Tory party conference on October 6th in Manchester.** It was terrible. He was like a sub- standard stand-up comedian trying to make joke, after joke, after joke and I honestly could not understand a single word that came out of his mouth. This was partly because he jabbered at such high speed that many of his words were lost. He began with a tasteless joke about Jeremy Corbyn. Now I am no Corbyn fan but this was not the sort of thing we expect from a Prime Minister making a speech in such serious times, or ever actually. He said they had sent, **"that corduroy Communist cosmonaut into orbit where he belongs."**

Then of course he has to have a dig at the Leader of the Opposition and called Sir Keir Starmer a **"seriously rattled bus conductor"** and like **"the skipper of a cruise liner that has been captured by Somali pirates."**

Then he goes on to try to show how clever he is by talking about Greek mythology. When he was very ill with Covid, he said, NHS nurses **"pulled my chestnuts out of the Tartarean pit."** Tartarus was the underworld abyss, beneath even Hades, but I think this only goes to show that a knowledge of Greek mythology does not necessarily mean intelligence, wisdom or literary elegance.

Then he starts talking about North London when he says that local schools favour no competition and they have races in which pupils do not win. There is tolerance for drugs, he says, in "the powder rooms of the north London dinner parties" and, here we go again, he talks about "lefty Islington lawyers". **You just might remember that Johnson spent a number of years living in Islington, where his then-wife was a lawyer.**

Now you might find this next bit difficult to believe but I actually heard it, although I found it difficult to fathom as I don't tend to watch reality shows on television. But he did use the words **"kangaroo testicles."** Definitely no words you would normally hear in a speech by a British Prime Minister.

In a segment in which he bemoaned people having more control over voting on celebrity reality shows than they did with Parliament, he suggested that, "If Parliament were a reality TV show the whole lot of us would have been voted out of the jungle by now". (If only).

But, he added: "At least we could have watched the Speaker being forced to eat a kangaroo testicle". In 2017, Johnson's own father, Stanley, appeared in the ITV show "I'm A Celebrity ... Get Me Out Of Here!" declaring before he went into the jungle, that he did not "know that a lamb's testicle is different from a kangaroo testicle". What, please, is he talking about?

And then again Johnson tried other so-called jokes about the **'build back better'** slogan which I have always thought to be grammatically clumsy.

Referring to nature and wildlife initiatives, Johnson pledged to **"build back beaver"**, and to the renewal of UK beef imports to the US, to **"build back burger"**. Who on earth does he think he is talking to?

In a section addressing the UK's energy usage, Johnson said there were some days when wind and solar power were delivering more than half of the UK's energy needs. He explained this was in defiance of the sceptics who had once said that **"wind farms couldn't pull the skin off a rice pudding."** But that quote is what **he** said when he was a journalist for *The Telegraph* in 2013.

As Wes Streeting (Shadow Health Minister) says **"The more he speaks the less he says."** There was no detailed mention in his speech of fuel shortage, the supply chain, empty supermarkets or food shortages. Ed Davy (leader of the Lib Dems) said, "Boris Johnson might as well have made that speech in a **parallel universe**. Nothing for struggling families facing universal credit cuts and soaring bills, nothing for businesses on the brink of bankruptcy and nothing for our nation's carers. Totally out of touch."

Well the Tory faithful loved that bumbling speech but I am afraid it didn't get a smile out of me.

And at the end of this so called speech he didn't wait for the customary standing ovation but dashed off the podium in an unseemly hurry. But we now know why. He was going off to pack for a week in Marbella with Carrie and Wilfred. And if you think, "well he really deserves a break," then maybe this book is not for you.

****

Throughout this month there seems to be more and more criticism of the Prime Minister. Manufacturing bosses have told the PM and his ministers to **stop treating business as "the enemy within".**

The criticism by 'Make UK' is a first in recent times and ratchets up the war of words between British business and the government during the crisis in energy, logistics and labour.

They also say that the government's abandonment of an industrial strategy meant that it must set out a long term vision for the economy and industry and its transition to a digital and green future if the UK was to retain the confidence of investors.

But you will have noticed the word "vision" in there which is not a word we associate with this government unfortunately. Manufacturing bosses have been increasingly upset by the **PM blaming business for dragging down wages because of what has been called an addiction to cheap labour**. 'Make UK' says that "manufacturing is a high skill sector that invests in its workforce and already pays above the national average for the economy overall."

****

But this headline should be a real worry to Boris. James Forsyth writes in *The Times* **on October 15th** the headline "**Face it prime minister, you're not in control".**

He goes on to say: "As he returns from his holiday in Marbella, three factors will play a huge role in determining what the next few months will be like: inflation, energy shortages and geopolitical tensions. Johnson has little to no control over any of these forces. And he is loath to admit it."

His whole attitude to any difficulties seems to be a breezy indifference. When he said at the conference that **inflation fears were unfounded** a minister said, "I can't believe he just said that," and another one said that he thought the Prime Minister's views are, "out of sync with reality."

"Take back control" was the Brexit slogan. But James Forsyth ends his column by saying that, **"for good or ill much of the country's fate is out of Johnson's control."**

****

There is another disturbing headline the very next day from Matthew Parris of *The Times*. **"We're about to wake up to the mess we're in".**

"We're going to the dogs" he says. Well we have all been saying that for the last couple of years. But we have just been watching a television programme about Blair and Brown which has been fascinating and Mr. Parris highlights a particular sentence voiced by Peter Mandelson. **"The single most important thing for a political party" he says, "is for the dominating agenda to be the one you set."** He goes on to say that if you get that wrong voters will start looking around and begin to add things up for themselves.

Well there is a great deal for us to see, as Matthew Paris says, which makes us lose trust in the government's ability to govern.

Fuel shortages, ships and containers lined up at Felixstowe, groceries, farmers, factories, the courts, retailers, hospitality, gas prices, the Northern Ireland protocol, delayed operations, the crisis in our care homes, and now the dispute with France over fishing and the "impending failure of Cop 26 in Glasgow." **"There is a vacuum at the heart of our politics"** says Matthew Parris and Boris is a "giggling impediment to the unifying sense of political momentum that Mandelson describes."

He finishes this brilliant and pertinent article by saying, "'**Watch this space' is often a lazy way of ending a column, but this time there really is a space. Watch it."** We certainly will Matthew. We certainly are.

****

So what are other ministers saying this month? Well Oliver Dowden said on the **14th October** that there will certainly **be enough toys for children to have this Christmas. Don't worry, he says, Santa WILL come!** However retailers are worried about the delays in supply chains and do advise people to do their Christmas shopping early.

And on the **24th October** we hear that there might be a **bin collection strike at Christmas** as drivers are quitting their jobs to get better pay working for supermarkets and food hauliers. In Johnson's conference speech he said he was aiming to turn the UK into a **"high wage, high skilled, high productivity economy"** which is all very well but actually there are no realistic plans for it and Brexit will clobber it.

Surely we can foresee that higher wages will mean higher costs and prices and no-one left to do the more menial jobs that do need doing? So higher pay for hauliers will mean no-one left to drive the bin lorries unless the pay for those drivers goes up as well.

****

27TH OCTOBER
Graeme Dear chairman of the British Poultry Council said there was a "likelihood" of a shortage of UK produced turkeys and that produce may have to be imported from France and Poland. Brexit again. **He said that these turkeys will probably have been raised by some of the European workers we trained and who left to go back to their homelands.**

Tom Bradshaw, vice-president of the National Farmers Union, said that the government's prediction that the end of furlough would lead to a pool of unemployed people to fill the roles had not materialised and urged them to authorise another 31,000 visas for migrant workers. But I have yet to see any evidence of this government thinking anything through.

It is all words, words, words. I am with the Queen here, as she was overheard at a reception talking about Cop 26 when she said, "we only know about those not coming.............. **and it's really irritating when they talk but don't do."**

****

COP 26

2021

So we get onto the hot air that is **Cop 26.** Of course it is really good that so many countries are getting together to discuss the dangers of climate change and we really hope that something good and positive will come from it.

But as Mr. Andrew Rawnsley points out in *The Observer* on the 17th October in his headline he says, **"The host of Cop 26 needs to be a master of diplomacy. Unfortunately, it's Mr. Johnson".**

Indeed maybe the PM should have been spending the last few weeks zooming other presidents and nurturing them and talking to them in the lead up to this conference instead of holidaying in Marbella. Just a thought.

But there are so many other things which puzzle me.

One is the trade deal Liz Truss did with Australia which was only achieved because we allowed them to scrub out key pledges on climate change. And can anyone explain to me how it is better for the carbon footprint to get beef from Australia rather than from Europe?

Then there is still a debate going on about a new coal mine in Cumbria.

And in the recent budget, air taxes on British internal air flights have been abolished.

There is also confusion and criticism about the plan to replace gas boilers with heat pumps. By the time you have added on the cost of upgrading to larger radiators or to fan convectors the overall cost per household could be as much as £16,000. At the moment the government is saying that households can apply for a grant of £5,000 but 'Friends of the Earth' are saying that the overall budget will only support 90,000 pumps in total, which won't meet the PM's ambition of 60,000 a year by 2028.

One other pertinent announcement in the budget relating to all of this, was that foreign aid will be restored to the 0.7% GDP levels by 2024. This is of course far, far too late. The damage has been done. **Scientific programmes on climate change in African countries have already been stopped due to lack of funding.**

Then we heard about all **the raw sewage being pumped into our seas and rivers** as there was a vote in Parliament **against** an amendment to the Environment Bill to stop private water companies dumping raw sewage into rivers and coastlines.

Well as you can imagine there has been a huge backlash about this. The government has done a sort of U-turn and under new rules there will be a duty on water companies to reduce the impact of sewage discharges from storm overflows. This means the organisations will be required by law to show a reduction in sewage overspills over the next five years. So no urgency there then.

Well regarding the pouring of untreated sewage into our rivers today **(May 16th 2022,)** there is a report out from the government saying that actually it is going to be too difficult and too expensive to use volume monitors which have actually been recommended by MPs. So without these, **the volume of raw sewage being dumped in our rivers will go unchecked**

But back at the conference we hear Johnson talking about the melting ice-cap. He said that there **are "opportunities" for the UK from melting ice caps as "the retreat of ice towards the North Pole" could open up new sea routes that would benefit Scottish ports.**

It really is a worry and a great cause of concern that anyone could say something like that, let alone a Prime Minister, let alone a Prime Minister at a conference about climate change. But that is what he said and if you don't remember him saying that then the media and the opposition parties are not doing their job.

****

14TH NOVEMBER

So, Cop 26, in Glasgow, ended yesterday. It was a mammoth task and was chaired by Alok Sharma who actually did a sterling job. Disappointment at the end though when India insisted on watering down the final words by changing the use of fossil fuels to **be "phased down" and not "phased out."** But at least, they are saying, coal and fossil fuel are mentioned for the first time. A lot has been achieved but nevertheless many people are very unhappy about it all. I will just quote Peter Stone who is Britain's Nobel prize-winning climate scientist when he says, **"The task ahead is not impossible but it is now much harder than if humanity had acted sooner. For that the climate change deniers bear a heavy responsibility."** We have also ignored for too long what science was telling us.

Interesting to note though, that at a press conference today about Cop 26 our Prime Minister talked about being in Edinburgh. Just a slip of the tongue you might think **but not only does he seem not to know whether he is coming or going, he doesn't even know where he is when he is there.**

****

16TH NOVEMBER

In *The Guardian* today there is a brilliant article by John Crace, who slams Johnson and his appearance in Parliament yesterday. He comments on the fact that Johnson did actually really know that it took place in Glasgow and not Edinburgh. (Well it is all just Scotland isn't it?!) But he then goes on to mention everything I have mentioned in my previous book. How are we able to help other countries when their climate change programmes have been stopped due to our cuts in foreign aid? What about the coal mine in Cumbria? Why had the trade deal with Australia ignored climate commitments and why was the climate crisis not mentioned in the budget?

I honestly do not know how this Prime Minister can remain in the highest office of the land when articles are written about him, such as this one, every single day.

****

2022

4TH MARCH

I mention a few climate change problems in various other chapters but this news deserves to be written here.

Friends of the Earth are proceeding with a legal challenge against the government and there will be a judicial review heard in the High Court very shortly. It will examine both the government's Net Zero Strategy and its Heat and Buildings Strategy. They believe that the government has breached the Climate Change Act 2008 and also the Equality Act 2010.

"Principally" they say, "we hope to prove just how woefully inadequate the government's Net Zero Strategy is, the same policy framework that is supposed to be the UK's roadmap to a safer, greener future."

They contend that the **complete lack of any detail** as to how and when the government's policies will be achieved means that it is entirely theoretical and so unlawful. It means that it cannot be held accountable by Parliament or the public.

So far as the Equality Act is concerned, they say that the Heat and Buildings Strategy has not considered the effects of its policies on protected groups in order to have a fair energy transition.

As so often, we see this government being accused of being all talk and no action. We wait to see the outcome of this judicial review.

****

15TH MARCH

Last night Conservative MPs voted down a law, 286 to 179, that would have named and shamed water companies **that kill animals by dumping raw sewage into our lakes and rivers. Lake Windermere is now so polluted that dog owners do not let their dogs swim there.**

Following the defeat of the plan, Liberal Democrat rural affairs spokesperson Tim Farron, who proposed the amendment, said Conservative MPs, "should hang their heads in shame. Yet again they have let water companies off the hook whilst our precious rivers and waters are being pumped full of raw sewage," he said.

"Enough is enough, we need to name and shame water companies which are being found to destroy precious wildlife habitat. It is scandalous that animals are swimming in filth and seeing their habitats become sewage traps."

Water companies apparently made £2.8 billion in operating profits in 2020/2021 but have been underinvesting in infrastructure in order to boost their profits.

How can the government allow this to carry on? We still have Victorian sewers which are not fit for purpose and yet instead of welcoming this amendment they turn it down. Who or what are they afraid of?

Rejecting the amendment in the Commons, environment minister Jo Churchill said: "It is important that we do not dictate the committee's work plan. Its members are the experts, not us, and are best placed to know where they can add value."

I don't even know what on earth she means. They speak gobbledygook and have no idea what they are talking about. Meanwhile water animals are killed and our once beautiful rivers and lakes stink.

****

2ND JUNE
So what has been happening in the six months since the COP 26 conference in Glasgow?

Well not nearly enough apparently. The three living former directors of the 'UN Framework Convention on Climate Change' have said that the policies currently in place to tackle the climate crisis around the world will lead to "catastrophic" climate breakdown, **as governments have failed to take the actions needed to fulfil their promises.**

For the first time they have written an article together for *The Guardian* in order to convey the seriousness of the situation.

There is a stark gap, they say, between what governments promised to do to protect the climate, and the measures and policies needed to achieve the targets.

I wish I could say that this really surprises me but sadly I can't.

"The myriad reports of extreme weather we have witnessed in 2022 suggest there is no time to waste," they write. "The further climate change progresses, the more we lock in a future featuring more ruined harvests, and more food insecurity, along with a host of other problems including rises in sea level, threats to water security, drought and desertification. Governments must act against climate change while also dealing with other pressing crises."

"Actions by developed countries have so far been 'disappointing', in their failure to reduce emissions fast enough, and in **not making finance available to poorer countries to help them cope with the impacts of climate breakdown,**" they add.

This is a damning indictment on governments around the world and our government is, of course, not exactly leading the way.

We know that reductions in our foreign aid have meant many poorer countries having to suspend work they have been involved with on climate change but the government does not seem capable of thinking their actions through to any logical conclusion. We can only hope that someone is listening and thinking and maybe even doing.

****

22ND JUNE

Sky news reports today that **traces of polio have been found in London sewage,** and health officials have declared a national incident. Well yes hardly surprising if you dump raw sewage into the rivers.

Severn Trent Water Company, who have recently increased their average household bills by 7.1%, were recently fined £1.5 million for dumping 800,000 gallons of raw sewage into Worcestershire waterways.

****

25TH JUNE

Sir Chris Whitty, the chief medical officer, has warned that **river sewage is becoming a serous public health concern.** He demands that water companies do more to keep effluent out of Britain's waterways. He said that river bathers and other recreational users could become seriously ill by ingesting bacteria from human faeces.

****

28TH JUNE

The recently formed Office for Environmental Protection warned earlier this year that there **is not a single river or lake in England which currently has a clean bill of health.**

They will probe whether Environment Secretary George Eustace, the Environment Agency and the water services regulator Ofwat have failed in their duties in the management of water quality.

Well I would have thought it was absolutely obvious.

****

16TH JULY

The Met Office has just issued its first ever 'red alert' for the forthcoming heat- wave when temperatures in parts of the UK are forecast to reach 40 degrees.

****

19TH JULY

We won!! If you look back at my entry on March 14th you will see that **the 'Good Law Project' launched a legal challenge stating that the Government's strategy for getting to Net Zero is inadequate and unlawful.**

Well the High Court has just concluded its review and has held that the proposals for achieving Net Zero approved by the Secretary of State were too vague to enable him to be satisfied that the statutory targets would be met. And that the report placed before Parliament lacked the specificity necessary to meet the Secretary of State's duty to inform Parliament and the public of his plans.

So this is the shout at the top of the email I have just received from them.

The illegality of its landmark climate change strategy is a huge political embarrassment to the Government. The Court has ordered that the existing strategy be fleshed out with the detail necessary for Parliamentary and public scrutiny within the next eight months. The Government has also been ordered to pay all costs.

'Client Earth' and 'Friends of the Earth' joined with the 'Good Law Project' in this challenge and we owe them a huge debt for calling this government to account.

Especially as today the Mayor of London has declared a major incident as fires break out across the city and temperatures break all records.

****

20TH JULY
Is climate change at the top of anyone's agenda?

I don't think so.

There was a Cobra meeting two days ago to discuss the forthcoming heatwave and the unprecedented temperatures, but guess who wasn't there. No, after hosting a lavish bash at Chequers our Prime Minister, in all but name, rummaged around in his dressing-up box, found an airman's flying suit, and went up in a typhoon air craft. We have a photo of him in the cockpit whilst it is being re-fuelled in mid-air.

So Boris Johnson, our Prime Minister, fiddles while the country burns.

It is a very worrying situation and someone needs to galvanise the government into action.

****

So now let us look, in detail, at the different areas of our society, and let us look also at the people in positions of authority and power who are endeavouring to lead this country into a future of peace and prosperity.

****

THE NHS

2021

13TH NOVEMBER

The NHS continues to be overwhelmed by anyone's standards as we hear of 15 hour waits for ambulances after 999 calls, staff leaving care homes as they do not comply with mandatory vaccinations, one in ten of the population in need of important hospital procedures still waiting for treatment and of course continual under-funding.

Cases of the pandemic are increasing all over Europe and we cannot be far behind.

It has to be only a matter of time before new restrictions are imposed on us as we remember Boris Johnson's words about Christmas being perfectly safe.

****

15TH NOVEMBER.

A new report issued by the Royal College of Nursing says staff are facing a unique series of challenges. They say that conditions have become "unsustainable" and "untenable" and have highlighted 10 major pressures in the system. They are:

1. NHS bed occupancy rate

2. Sickness absence amongst nurses
3. NHS nursing vacancy rate
4. High Covid infection rate
5. NHS hospital waiting times
6. NHS community waiting times
7. Social care workforce vacancies
8. International recruitment in NHS and social care
9. Insufficient domestic NHS and social care nursing supply
10. Increased demand for social care services.

They also say that an increase in **"corridor care,"** or time spent on trolleys in hospital corridors before being admitted to a bed, is, "clearly a symptom of an unsustainable system," according to RCN members.

"We are clear that delivery of care in inadequate environments, such as that commonly referred to as 'corridor care' or **'corridor nursing,' is fundamentally unsafe and must not be normalized,"** the nursing chiefs said.

The wait for ambulances in an emergency is also at dangerous levels and some people are being driven to hospital by family members as the waiting times mount up. Many people are waiting in ambulances before being transferred to A and E again for many hours.

The RCN says that it is imperative that the government invests in number of ways to develop   nursing workforce supply which will meet the present needs of the NHS.

And so let us hear from the **Department of Health and Social Care**.

A spokesperson said:

"There are now a record number of doctors and nurses working in the NHS and we are on track to deliver 50,000 more nurses by the end of this Parliament. Our record investment is helping to tackle the backlog and recover NHS services with an extra £2 billion this year plus £38 billion more over the next three years to deliver an extra nine million checks, scans, and operations for patients across the country.

To ensure this funding makes a lasting impact the NHS is deploying more efficient, innovative ways of working and the latest technology to provide more appointments and treatments. This includes dedicated surgical hubs and community diagnostic centres to ramp up routine surgery."

They appear to be on **a parallel universal** as it sounds as though, so far as they are concerned, there is not a problem.

****

16TH NOVEMBER.

But today we hear again that it really is a huge problem. Kat Lay, Health Editor of *The Times*, reports that twenty times more people are waiting for more than six weeks longer for **vital heart scans** than before the pandemic. Tens of thousands of people are living with **chronic obstructive pulmonary disease** according to the British Lung Foundation. And widespread disruption to the availability of **echocardiograms** causes considerable disruption to health care that ultimately puts lives at risk. And the delay in ambulance handovers at hospitals has reached crisis point.

A damning report revealed up to 160,000 patients each year may be affected due to the long periods waiting to be admitted. Of these, about 12,000 suffer 'severe harm', according to a document written by NHS ambulance bosses in England. **Everyone in the NHS is concerned about the coming winter.** Nurses and doctors are facing 'burn out' they are so exhausted.

It really does not sound as though all is well to me.

****

Jeremy Hunt, our former Health Secretary, says that any money the government throws at the NHS will be wasted on the salaries of locum doctors and agency nurses without an **official plan to increase staffing levels**. He told the BBC *Radio 4 Today* programme "**The argument about money has poisoned intelligent debate about the NHS.** The system is geared up to say to ministers, 'give us more money and we'll give you the things you want', when in reality, unless you expand the capacity of the system to do things, **principally by training up and recruiting more doctors and nurses,** it doesn't matter how much extra money you throw at it, you won't get the improvements you're looking for".

They really need to listen to him.

NHS England was estimated **to be short of up to 100,000 staff heading into the pandemic, including 44,000 nurses and 9,000 doctors in nearly every specialty**. So why does this government not understand what everyone else does?

****

18TH NOVEMBER.
NHS social care reform bill.

There is huge concern about changes to the payment system for **social care** that has just been announced by the government. The government has been accused of **watering down key reforms** in order to save money and that these reforms will hit the poorest the most. At present there is a cap of £86,000 for all pensioners to pay for social care after which the government takes over. So hopefully no-one needs to sell their house in order to fund their care. For poorer pensioners the weekly fees they and the government paid were added up and once this reached £86,000 the pensioners paid no more. **Now only the element paid by the pensioner counts towards the £86,000 meaning they pay for longer and have much higher bills.** This will affect those in the north more, of course, and many of them will have to sell their house. **So now that we see the details this looks like another broken promise.**

****

19TH NOVEMBER.

The Infrastructure and Projects annual report 2020-2021, says that Boris Johnson's pledge to **build 40 new hospitals by the end of the decade is "unachievable".**

Well I could have told them that as I thought it was ridiculous from the very first moment I heard him announcing it. He was in a cabinet meeting and he did a pantomime act by saying, "How many hospitals?" and they all shouted back **"40"**.

It looked and sounded absolutely stupid at the time. Later of course we hear that many will be just new wings or refurbishments which are, of course, very much needed. But we were told **"40 new hospitals"**.

But to quote the report word for word, just in case you missed it, it says, **"There are major issues with project definition, schedule, budget, quality and /or benefits delivery, which at this stage do not appear to be manageable or resolvable. The project may need re-scoping and/or its overall viability reassessed."**

In other words someone with a degree of intelligence and specialist knowledge needs to re-write this report.

The initial cost was said to be £3.7 billion but early criticism of the plan by experts said it could be over £24 billion and no-one knew where the money would come from. *The i* reports that the roof in the Queen Elizabeth Hospital in King's Lynn is being supported by more than 200 props to prevent it from collapsing. They are hoping to be one of the eight new builds but fear that a decision has been put off till next spring.

So are we all set to hear of another manifesto promise broken? And of course many existing hospitals need repair and renewal but when oh when will this government understand that we need more medical staff? Have they learnt nothing from the Nightingale hospitals?

****

22ND NOVEMBER

As we continue to hear the government insist that there are record numbers of doctors and nurses working in the NHS, we continue to read disturbing headlines in the media.

Yesterday, 'March with Midwives', a campaign group, held demonstrations across the UK and attended a vigil in Parliament Square opposite Westminster. Sarah Muggleton, a midwife in London for six years said, **"We have to have improvements. We are burnt out and crying for help now."**

A spokesman for the Department of Health said, "There are more midwives in the NHS now than at any other time in its history."

A parallel universe.

****

The Test and Trace Service.

Well we hear that this service is now being wound down. Apparently in June, Dr Jenny Harries, chief executive of the UK Health Security Agency, and who is responsible for the service, said that there was a **"very detailed ramp-down plan" to cut the number of consultants.**

Well good because not only do these consultants cost an inordinate amount of money, but a report by the public accounts committee concluded that the service had "**not achieved its main objective**" which was to enable people to return to a more normal way of life.

But wait a minute. Ben Ellery in *The Times* today highlights a report in *The Guardian* which states that multi-million pounds contracts are still being awarded to private consultants firms despite promises to limit their use. **The government has agreed to at least seven new NHS test and trace deals, together worth more than £17 million.** £1 million a day is being spent on these consultants and many MPs are saying that it is an **"eye-watering" waste of tax-payers money.** Figures for October show it employed 1.230 consultants. The average daily contractor rates of £1,100 equate to potentially £1,353,000 a day.

But a UK health Security Agency spokesman said, "We are working to reduce the number of consultants in a constructive and planned way without it having a detrimental effect on our health protection services."

Hmmm. These spokespeople certainly enable this book to live up to its subtitle! And I know many people in the NHS who would be very happy to see some of this money.

****

23RD NOVEMBER.

Last night was the debate and vote on the second reading of the **bill on social and health care reform**. The reform bill itself was published in September but this amendment about the cap on payments was only inserted last week. MPs were saying that there had not been enough time to study it properly. It was a long and tedious debate and the phrase that I remember was the one **"Robin Hood in reverse!"**

However much they skirted around the issue they could not say that the new cap on payments was fair. The final vote was a majority of 26 in favour of the bill down from a working majority of 77. 19 Conservatives voted against and some abstained. It now goes to the Lords and they have said that they will study it **"line by line!"**

****

But not a particularly good look as we hear that Tory MPs had to be bussed back from the **Tory winter ball** at 9.30pm in order to vote. This was a fund-raising ball where there was an auction for people to pay vast sums of money for really exciting things.

One donor paid £35,000 to play cricket for an hour with Rishi Sunak. Another paid £30,000 for a "Get Brexit Done" sign from the 2019 election. Dinner with Michael Gove went for £25,000 **(I promise you it does get worse)**. Karaoke with Liz Truss raised £22,000. There you go! Then they go back to vote on the bill which will make the already poor even poorer. A **parallel universe** indeed.

****

26TH NOVEMBER

It is interesting to note an amendment to the Health and Social Care Bill tabled by the former health secretary Jeremy Hunt. This amendment would strengthen workforce planning of the NHS **and increase transparency and accountability in whether we are training enough people now to meet future demands. The amendment is supported by over 60 health and care organisations** including The Royal College of Physicians, NHS Providers, the Health Foundation, MacMillan Cancer Support, the BMA and the Royal College of Nursing. To me it sounds an absolutely excellent plan and one that is long overdue.

At the moment there are around 100,000 NHS staffing vacancies advertised in England. Currently the NHS pays around £6 billion a year in locums to fill the gaps. The Health Foundation predicts an extra 4,000 doctors and 17,000 nurses will be required to clear the backlog. Richard Murray, Chief Executive of the King's Fun, said, **"years of poor planning and short-term thinking has left health and care services struggling to cope with chronic staff shortages."**

So what a good idea to have to show the long term planning that will help to cope with a workforce that is at the moment burnt out and exhausted. So please tell me why, oh why, oh a hundred times why

did this government vote this amendment down and reject it by 280 votes to 219 just three days ago?

Patricia Marquis director of the Royal College of Nursing in England said: "A broad coalition of professional, political and public support has been overlooked by a Government still unwilling to solve the staffing crisis in the NHS and care system." She goes on to say, "**There is wide-spread disappointment this evening. When vacancy levels are so high the move is short-sighted at best and wilfully reckless at worst.**"

The danger this government is inflicting on us all is beyond belief.

****

28TH NOVEMBER

A new variant of the pandemic has been discovered in South Africa which is being called the Omicron variant and is sending everyone, except the government, into panic mode. Two cases have been discovered in England and six in Scotland.

Mr. Johnson gave a press conference today but it was so vague and inarticulate that he might just as well not have bothered. I think he said that we should all wear masks in shops and on public transport but it took a question from a journalist to find out whether this is mandatory or not. I think the answer is yes, from Tuesday. But people are questioning why is it not going to be mandatory in the hospitality sector, in cinemas and theatres and all inside spaces with large gatherings? Why are people not being encouraged once again to work from home? The NHS yet again is really worried about what all this is going to mean for their overstretched hospitals.

****

2ND DECEMBER

We see the details of the white paper, long promised, at last. Whilst it is a ten year plan and provides information on funded proposals that will be implemented over the next three years, would it surprise you to hear that many people think that it hasn't gone far enough? As Simon Bottery, senior fellow in social care at 'King's Fund' puts it: **"Even with the measures already announced, the WP is far more a 'whimper' than a 'bang.'"**

Cllr David Fothergill, Chairman of the Local Government Association's Community Wellbeing Board, said: "While councils share the Government's ambition and want nothing more than to deliver it, they will need a substantially bigger share of the new Health and Social Care Levy for that to happen."

He goes on to point out that much more needs to be done to tackle the problem in retaining and recruiting hard working care staff **and more investment is needed in prevention in all areas in order to bolster the core services.**

There are approximately 100,000 vacancies for carers at the moment and it is this which needs urgent help and support. **So once more it would appear that the government is lacking and unable to deliver what is required.**

****

3RD DECEMBER
The poor old NHS is really suffering and are so upset at the fact that so many beds in ICU are taken up with unvaccinated patients. Everyone is being encouraged to get their booster jabs and the six month gap from the second vaccination is being reduced to three in order to beat this new vaccine called Omicron.

****

7TH DECEMBER.
It has been reported that the government **is selling off the Harwell Vaccination Manufacturing Innovation Centre, which has received more than £200m in taxpayers' money,** and which was

commissioned in the wake of the West African Ebola epidemic to develop a state-run vaccine manufacturing network to better prepare the country for future outbreaks of infectious diseases.

Many eminent people are saying what a dreadfully short-sighted decision this is.

Professor Adrian Hill, director of the University of Oxford's Jenner Institute, compared the sale of VMIC to "having been in a terrible war and you suddenly cut your defence budget substantially".

Professor Dame Sarah Gilbert, delivering the prestigious Richard Dimbleby Lecture, said the scientific advances made in research against fighting deadly viruses "must not be lost".

Labour's Wes Streeting, the new Shadow Health Secretary, said it, "would be unbelievably short-sighted and complacent" to sell off VMIC during a pandemic that was still raging. "We are not out of the woods yet, as the emergence of the Omicron variant has reminded us all too well," he said. **"This stinks of the Tories putting ideology ahead of Britain's safety against Covid and future pandemics."**

****

8TH DECEMBER

This afternoon Boris Johnson announces that **Plan B is being put in place**. This means that you should work from home if you can, there is more mandatory mask- wearing and vaccine passports are needed for entry to certain places. We feel that this was announced in rather a hurry, having previously denied the necessity for it and maybe it is hoped that it will be a distraction from the **Christmas party story. (see the chapter on Johnson.)**

The message seems to be **work at home but party at work** as Boris said don't cancel Christmas parties. The presenter on the *Today* programme was trying to get our Health Secretary to explain the logic here but he was unable to do so.

****

13TH DECEMBER

Yesterday evening we had an address to the nation from the Prime Minister. He said that new data has just shown that the rate of transmissibility of the new variant is so rapid that he has decided that the booster vaccination programme is going to be boosted (!) so that every adult over the age of 18 will get their booster jab by the end of this month. That will require a million people to be jabbed each day.

Well this was the first that the NHS had heard of it. Everyone has to step up and give vaccines even if it means that other appointments have to be postponed. The NHS are saying that this will not be possible. The government seem to be saying now that everyone will be **offered** a jab by the end of the month which is of course slightly different.

The NHS booking site crashed this morning as so many people tried to book. The lateral flow tests were unavailable to book and there were queues of up to seven hours long at walk-in centres.

Dominic Cummings says in a tweet today that this data was known weeks ago and **Johnson needs to go before he is responsible for the deaths of 1000s more people**. This could all have been put in place much earlier. So there you have it: **Danger, Dishonesty, Dither and Delay**.

****

19TH DECEMBER

The Mayor of London yesterday declared a **major incident in London** due to the rise in Omicron cases. London was the UK region with the largest number of Covid cases. There have been more than 26,000 new cases in the last 24 hours. There is a Cobra meeting this weekend and everyone is wondering what new restrictions will be introduced just before Christmas. Interesting to note that the majority of patients in hospital are unvaccinated.

Where is the vaccine minister I wonder? Do you even know the vaccine minister's name? It is Maggie Throup. **Never seen, never heard, never anywhere**. It is not looking good for Johnson.

****

23RD DECEMBER
Savid Javid our Health Secretary says there will be no restrictions before Christmas in spite of the fact that the infections rates are nearly doubling every week. However Northern Ireland, Wales and Scotland have all brought in further restrictions.

****

27TH DECEMBER
Well we made it through Christmas but we are all being urged to be cautious and to take lateral flow tests before we celebrate the New Year.

Yes, well that is a good idea. So we all go on-line or to pharmacies to get the tests only to find that they have run out due to high demand and there are no tests to be had. No forward planning there then.

****

30TH DECEMBER
So if, because of the lack of tests or restrictions, the record number of Covid-19 infections leads to a surge in admissions in hospitals and therefore outstrips existing capacity, the government have announced that the NHS will build eight temporary Nightingale hubs at various hospitals throughout England to take in the excess.

You may remember the Nightingale hospitals that were built in the previous lockdowns and that were never used. Why were they not used? For exactly the same reason as these will not be used. **Because in an already under-staffed and now increasingly sick NHS there** will not be any spare doctors, nurses or support staff available to work in them.

****

2022

3RD JANUARY

The New Year begins with an explanation for the lack of lateral flow tests. Apparently there is just one wholesaler who has been given the job of doling out all lateral flow tests to pharmacies around the country. This does seem to be a bit short sighted and indeed Leyla Hannbeck, chief executive of the Association of Independent Multiple Pharmacies thought so too and wrote to the health secretary to suggest that they used more than one. She never got a reply.

The distributer **Alliance Healthcare took delivery of 2.5million tests on Christmas Eve................. and then immediately closed for four days**. These were the very days that we were all told to test, test, test.

****

4TH JANUARY

Johnson gives a press conference today and he announces that although we still have to be very cautious there will be no further restrictions and he thinks that we can just ride this one out. This is despite the fact that Covid infection rates have reached record levels. But he is desperate to appease his right wingers and also to keep the economy going.

****

6TH JANUARY

Boris Johnson was at a vaccination centre today and whilst he acknowledged that the NHS was under "huge pressure" at the moment, **he said it was "not true" that the health service does not have enough staff to cope with the pressures it is facing**. How can he say that?

****

7TH JANUARY

For then we hear this. The army is called in and 200 armed forces personnel are to be deployed in London as staff struggle in situations that are unprecedented. They are on stand-by for the rest of the country.

The Royal College of Nursing said that NHS workers in England had been reduced to tears with exhaustion and that this deployment **means that the government can no longer deny that there is a staffing crisis in the NHS.**

A top GP, Dr Chaand Nagpaul, Chairman of the British Medical Association, told *Sky News*, **"We have never known this level of staff absence before"** amid the continuing spread of the Omicron variant of Covid 19.

As of yesterday **17 hospital trusts in England have declared critical incidents**, signalling there are fears that priority services cannot be safely delivered.

"I'm a GP, I've never known it this bad" he said.

He warns the government that it cannot "just wait to ride this out" and must do three things to relieve unprecedented pressure on the NHS.

The first thing, he says, is to bring down the levels of infections in the community urgently, by which I think he means that there must be further restrictions.

He goes on to say that, "The second thing is we need to ensure that those of us who are working on the front line who are mixing with patients who are infectious, need to be properly protected.

"And one of the things we've been **calling for is higher grade masks** that can filtrate the airborne spread of COVID-19 and Omicron as opposed to the normal paper surgical masks that don't.

"The third thing is to actually make sure we do have ready access to lateral flow tests, because of course it's having that negative test on day six and seven that has allowed healthcare staff to return to work after seven days of isolation rather than 10 days."

And he then says how difficult it still is to get hold of lateral flow tests.

I cannot believe what I am reading here.

High grade masks for the NHS, enough lateral flow tests available, restrictions on large gatherings, and no lies about the number of NHS staff that are working at the moment. Is that really too much to expect? That a GP has to speak like this to our government is a disgrace.

Yes our NHS used to be the envy of the world but after a decade of Conservative governments and two years of a Boris Johnson Premiership it is on its knees. **The medical staff and all frontline staff are the best in the world but the support from the government is non-existent to the point of negligence.**

****

13TH JANUARY.

Today in *The Guardian* we hear that Sajid Javid has ordered the boss of the health service to **give private hospitals up to** £270m, even though they may not treat any NHS **patients in return**.

Amanda Pritchard is very concerned about this instruction and has deep misgivings about it. She has been asked to hand private hospitals £75m to £90m a month **from NHS England funds** for the next three months, in case they are needed to help manage a new Omicron-driven surge in Covid cases. Operators of the facilities will receive the money as a "minimum income guarantee" simply for being on standby until the end of March to receive NHS patients, **even if they treat none.**

She also raised grave doubts about a deal under which her organisation would have to pay independent hospitals up to £525m if they **did** end up treating any NHS patients.

She requested a "direction" from Javid – an order in effect – on whether or not to conclude a deal with the private sector, given her fear that it would prove a waste of valuable NHS funding and that she might be in breach of her legal duty, as NHS England's accountable officer.

In her letter to the health secretary she said that either deal would leave the health service **"exposed financially" and involved "a material risk that the NHS pays for activity that is not performed".** Either scenario represented poor value for money for the NHS because private hospitals' lack of staff meant they could not be relied upon to treat many NHS cases, even if asked to do so, she said.

In his reply Javid overrode Pritchard's concerns and ordered her to conclude the deal. "I recognise the managing public money issues that these arrangements cause for you as the accounting officer," he wrote. "However ... I believe the need to protect NHS services and prevent a further reduction in NHS capacity are compelling reasons to justify their introduction."

Sid Ryan, a researcher at the Centre for Health and the Public Interest, a think tank, says, "There are real concerns not just on value for money, but on the industry's ability to deliver too, so it's not clear why this deal is necessary, especially at this late stage in the Omicron wave. The National Audit Office and the Public Accounts Committee must look into this deal urgently, **and we expect the department [of health and social care] and NHSE to publish a full account of what the private providers actually deliver under this deal."**

I find this absolutely extraordinary. They just seem to have shed loads of money to give away on non- essential projects when this sort of money could be very helpful to the NHS.

****

16TH JANUARY

In *The Observer* today in an article by Chaminda Jayanetti we hear that there are nearly **9,000 people in England waiting for home care services**. Caroline Abrahams, charity director of Age UK, says that it is tempting for the policy makers to place all the blame on the pandemic but she blames it on the fact that **"there has been no effective workforce planning over many years".**

Jane Townson, chief executive of the Home Care Association blames "inadequate government investment in social care." Many staff leave for better paid jobs.

The staff problem is in crisis and is getting worse.

But you will be happy to hear that a spokesman for the Department for Health and Social Care, who as you already are aware is in a parallel universe, said "We are committed to delivering **world-leading social care** across the country and that is why we're investing an additional £5.4 billion over three years to reform adult social care."

Why does everything have to be world beating? Look at what happened to Test and Trace. **Basic competence would be a good start.**

****

20TH JANUARY

All plan B restrictions will be lifted on the 27th January. This seems a bit sudden but could have something to do with the possibility of the imminent departure of the PM. Is this another bit of 'red meat'? Covid numbers are still high and the NHS is still coping with unprecedented demands and is under enormous stress. But it pleases the backbenchers no end.

****

27TH JANUARY

All plan B restrictions are lifted today including the mandatory wearing of masks which many people are not happy about including the NHS. No big announcement in the Press room by the PM. I wonder why? That room is becoming a bit of a white elephant. How much did it cost again? Oh yes £2.6 million.

****

30TH JANUARY

On April 20th 2021 in **'Beneath the Bluster'** I reported on the critical understaffing of maternity units and the pressure on midwives to provide a safe service.

Last summer the Care Quality Commission's chief inspector of hospitals told a Parliamentary inquiry that inspections had found that **38% of NHS maternity services "require improvement for safety" – more than any other medical speciality. Staff numbers, they say, are the most important building block in providing safe care and progress is urgently needed.**

If you read the stories of mothers in these maternity units it is heart breaking. Just one: "On my first night on the ward, a nurse came and said, "I apologise in advance in case you feel abandoned, but it's just me and one assistant." They all blame staffing levels not the staff.

But it is not just this government that is to blame. Jon Skewes, executive director for external relations at the Royal college of Midwives said "The RCM has been raising concerns about this for decades, **yet successive governments have chosen not to listen.**"

Yet an NHS spokesperson (him again) said that, **"the NHS remains one of the safest places in the world to give birth, and services have continued to see women and their babies throughout the pandemic."** (Please remember this sentence and keep it burning in your mind throughout the rest of this chapter.)

I have to repeat what I said in my previous book on page 36 when Dr Peter Green, chairman of the National Network of Designated Healthcare Professionals for Children said, "**If all the infants born in the UK in 2017 had been born in Finland, as many as 1,500 more would have survived.**" He also said that, "**when assessed over the past decade the statistics indicate well over 10,000 excess UK infant deaths in that time.**"

I just do not understand how any government can ignore this situation over and over again. Are they all in a **parallel universe**? Do they just not care? Do they not have ears to listen or eyes to see? How can they keep on saying that the NHS is the envy of the world?

So here is something you can do. Next time you hear anyone say that, please write to your MP.

****

31ST JANUARY.

The government had decided that vaccinations for all staff in the NHS should be mandatory. However that apparently would mean that an enormous number of nurses and consultants would have to leave an already understaffed health service.

So today there is a Cabinet meeting to discuss all of this and it is looking very likely that there will be a U-turn. This will be justified on the basis that the Omicron strain of Covid has been less severe than the Delta strain.

Obviously it is more desirable to use powers of persuasion and education to get people to accept vaccinations and obviously we do not want to decimate our NHS of staff even further, but if I go into hospital I want to be treated by fully vaccinated staff. Their freedom to choose should not compromise my freedom to choose.

****

6TH FEBRUARY.

Today we are hearing that the **hundreds of beds** bought for the Nightingale hospitals at a cost of £13million cannot be used for patients on any other hospital wards. The NHS said that the beds do not meet the required standard. They say that these were bespoke beds for field hospitals.

So there we go. I can't hear an apology at all and maybe these were the only options at the time. Who knows? But the whole exercise of the Nightingale hospitals has cost the tax payer over £530 **million**. Yes it was difficult to know how the pandemic was going to evolve. But before you even think of building new hospitals you must think about how you are going to be able to staff them and also buy equipment that can be used elsewhere.

Tim Spector, a professor of epidemiology at King's College London, said that he was "surprised and shocked" by the decision, given the high prevalence of the Omicron variant in the UK.

Other experts raised concerns saying it **could prove to be a "very stupid" move.**

****

14TH FEBRUARY

Yet another diary is about to be published. **This one is by a nurse and she relates in shocking detail her time working throughout the pandemic at St George's hospital in Tooting.** Next time you hear Boris Johnson shouting at us that the NHS has more staff than ever before you need to remember that he is an inveterate liar. Then you need to read this book and then you need to write to your MP. Then, please send the book to whoever is the PM at the moment

The book is called **"Life, Death and Biscuits"** and it is by Anthea Allen and published by HarperCollins. I have ordered my copy.

****

17TH FEBRUARY

As I have already reported, maternity services are the most severely underfunded speciality in the NHS.

Today a petition, which was signed by 123,000 people, was handed to the Health secretary, Sajid Javid, by the chief executive of the Royal College of Midwives, Gill Walton, demanding that urgent action be taken to stem the tide of staff leaving the NHS.

Despite promises to increase the workforce, the number of midwives has actually fallen from 27,272 last year to 26,901 today.

Ms Walton said: "Maternity services have been at the bottom of the list for investment for far too long and we're now seeing what that means in practice.

Midwives are being spread too thinly across the service because there are just too few of them. That's compromising the level of care they want to give to pregnant women and it's driving many of them out of the profession.

"It is absolutely within the Government's gift to change this, by putting proper investment in maternity services and by demonstrating that they value the work that midwives do. We've been saying this for years, and I'm so grateful to everyone who signed this petition for adding their voices to ours."

She goes on to say that, **"My hope is that the Government listens to the call for support** so that we can move forward with a strong midwifery profession that is able to provide safe and effective care, improving outcomes for women and families."

But, as she says, this has been the case for years, many of them during a Tory government, and no-one has listened. **And no-one is listening now**.

****

22ND FEBRUARY

And so we hear last night at a press conference, what we had been expecting for a while which is that Boris Johnson is abandoning all Covid restrictions from this coming Thursday the 24th. There will be no free lateral flow tests from April 1st, and there is no need to self-isolate even if you have symptoms. Covid is not completely over but we really do need to **learn to live with it.**

You still need to be cautious says the PM and you need to take personal responsibility. So a question then of "doing as I say and not what I do" from a Prime Minister who shows no personal responsibility whatsoever.

Well a lot of people are not too happy about all of this.

But of course the people who were delighted were the Conservative back benchers who all whooped with euphoria when he announced it all in the Commons yesterday afternoon. Even folk like David Davis who previously had told him to go, stood up and cheered. So that is all right then. **They** must be kept happy at all cost.

But everywhere else we read about problems and deep concern.

Keir Starmer said yesterday that he thought it was reckless to throw off all protection especially as we see cases still rising.

He said that he would have gone for a balanced approach with mask wearing, ventilation in schools and proper financial support for those who do need to self-isolate.

And **the Editorial in *The Times*** today says, "There needs to be a proper plan to live with Covid."

Answers to many questions were "conspicuously absent from yesterday's plan." More advice is needed, they write, for "protecting the immunocompromised, on when to stay at home and on further guidance for employers."

They go on to say, "The reality is that what was billed as a plan to live with Covid **looked more like a plan to cut the costs of dealing with Covid** to create fiscal space for Mr Sunak's ambition to cut taxes."

I think we could all agree with that.

There is very real concern for those who are immunocompromised and who are still vulnerable and who still need to shield.

Apparently Sajid Javid lost an argument with the chancellor and the PM yesterday morning when he was asking for more money in order to provide free testing for the over 50s who had Covid symptoms. He was told he would have to take the money out of the Department of Health's annual budget.

By the evening press conference Boris Johnson was a bit more circumspect, possibly because he had **Sir Chris Whitty and Sir Patrick Vallance** each side of him. They were both very cautious in their approach and said over and over again that we need to be **prepared to put restrictions back in place very quickly if new variants appear which could happen**. They also said that vulnerable people should still be able to have access to free tests. This was a major concern of so many.

And others were quick to criticise these inadequate plans.

They were blasted by the BMA who said that removing all restrictions was 'premature' and 'completely illogical'

"**Dr Stephen Griffin, a virologist** at Leeds University said, "I am dumbfounded by the majority of these announcements."

The head of the NHS Confederation — which represents hospital trusts — Matthew Taylor, urged the Government to 'reconsider' its plans.

He called for 'dedicated funding for continued access to Covid tests for all NHS workers in patient-facing roles.'

And Julia Faulconbridge, the **vice-chair of the British Psychological Society**, said: '**Living with Covid does not mean consigning groups of our society to living in isolation, and it does not mean we have to put vulnerable people at risk of damage to their physical and mental health."**

It really does seem crazy to do this when, as the leader of the opposition says, a more balanced approach would have been safer.

Time will tell.

****

[Russia invades Ukraine]

24TH FEBRUARY
All Covid restrictions are lifted as from today.

****

The ongoing failures in our maternity services are blown wide open with the *Panorama* programme broadcast last night about the Ockenden Report. This is a report about maternity care at Shrewsbury and Telford NHS Trust. The initial review was of 23 families, but this rapidly increased to 1,862 cases between 2000 and 2019.

It was a very harrowing programme and it is astounding that such dangerous practice has been able to carry on for so long.

We saw the families who have been fighting for answers for so long and who are still grieving. It was a letter to the Secretary of State for Health written in 2020 by Donna Ockenden which has helped to bring some transparency and accountability to this whole trauma. It is a long letter and it produces seven recommendations. I have to include a very small part here but you can google it if you want to read it all. But please read this slowly and carefully. It is so important.

She writes:

"We have met face to face with families who have suffered as a result of the loss of brothers and sisters or, from a young age, have also been carers to profoundly disabled siblings. We have met many parents where there have been breakdowns in relationships as a result of the strain of caring for a severely disabled child, the grief after the death of a baby or resultant complications following childbirth.

"Following the review of 250 cases we want to bring to your attention actions which we believe need to be urgently implemented to improve the safety of maternity services at The Shrewsbury and Telford Hospital NHS Trust as well as learning that what we recommend be shared and acted on by maternity services across England.

"Between June 2018 and the summer of 2020 a further 900 families directly contacted the review team raising concerns about the maternity care and treatment they had received at the Trust. These included a number of maternal and baby deaths and many cases where

babies suffered brain damage possibly as a result of events that took place around the time of their birth.

"It is likely that, when completed, this review of 1,862 families will be the largest number of clinical reviews undertaken relating to a single service, as part of an inquiry, in the history of the NHS. The majority of cases are from the years 2000 to 2019"

Then in the report we hear about the individual experiences of many women. I will just quote three.

"A woman was considered appropriate for birth in a remote stand-alone birth centre despite developing known risk factors in the weeks leading up to her delivery. There were then errors in the foetal monitoring in labour. After birth the baby was not monitored appropriately despite clear warning signs, and was transferred, too late, to a specialist unit where the baby died. (2009)"

"A woman who laboured at the birth centre was not adequately monitored as 'the unit was busy. When problems were eventually identified in labour there was a delay in transferring the mother to the labour ward, where her baby was delivered in a very poor condition having suffered a brain injury. The baby subsequently died. (2012)"

"A woman who delivered in a stand-alone birth centre suffered a catastrophic haemorrhage requiring transfer to the consultant unit, where she died. Her family stated that there had not been an explanation of the risks of birth in a midwifery led unit, nor information on the need for transfer if complications arose. (2017)"

Over and over again we hear that the voices of the mothers were not being listened to. One of the recommendations says that mothers and their families must be heard.

Then of course, it is the ongoing culture, which says that **caesarean sections must be done very sparingly.**

The report, referring to, the Shrewsbury Trust says:

"A typical quote during interviews was that 'they didn't like to do caesarean sections'. The review team observed that women who accessed the Trust's maternity service appeared to have little or no freedom to express a preference for caesarean section or exercise any choice on their mode of delivery.

The review team have the clear impression that there was a culture within The Shrewsbury and Telford Hospital NHS Trust to keep caesarean section rates low, because this was perceived as the essence of good maternity care in the unit. "

If you look back at my entry on the 30th January you will be reminded of the appalling state throughout the maternity services in this country generally.

Women continue to be let-down, ignored, unheard, dismissed, uncared for and inadequately treated, often with fatal consequences for them and their babies.

****

25TH FEBRUARY

We hear that the government have proposed a **3% pay rise for nurses**, when writing to the NHS review body which advises on salary increases.

With inflation at an all-time high at 5.5% this will in effect be a pay cut.

Well that should sort out the severe nursing staff shortages and prevent them leaving the NHS in droves.

****

27TH FEBRUARY

Except of course that it won't. In an article by Michael Savage, policy editor of *The Observer*, we hear that a record number of **400 NHS workers left every week during the past year.**

This is obviously affecting the quality of care being given to patients.

Jeremy Hunt told the government it had "missed an opportunity" to alleviate the workforce crisis in the NHS and social care, after rejecting the health select committee recommendation to overhaul the work force plan. **Staff shortages were the main driver of worker burnout, he said.**

But with the greatest of respect we all know that. That has been the case for years and it is getting worse. Nothing is done and nothing is ever done. You can have reports and reviews and discussions until you are blue in the face but it is all in vain. **The will is not there to transform our NHS.**

****

13TH MARCH

Covid cases are rising again especially in the over 55s and hospitals are seeing more and more patients with Covid. But, so far as the government is concerned, the pandemic is over. All travel restrictions are to be scrapped shortly in time for the Easter holidays.

And the one thing that we **did** do well, **our infection-tracking capability, is having all future funding cancelled.** This decision has been met with dismay among leading scientists and researchers world-wide who have questioned the UK's ability to respond to future Covid threats.

The React Study (Real-Time Assessment of Community Transmission) and also the Zoe Covid app, which tracks people's symptoms, will be defunded with only a few weeks' notice.

Professor Tim Spector who leads the research for Zoe says, **"We strongly believe that decision is a really bad mistake."**

I will also quote the last two sentences from a book called "**Spike**" by Jeremy Farrar with Anjana Ahuja when it says, "Two years after the Covid -19 outbreak was declared a pandemic, we are not yet ready to call an end to it. **And we remain terrifyingly unprepared for the next crisis."**

Professor Sylvia Richardson, President of the Royal Statistical Society praised the research programmes and said that we should be proud of them.

"**The government says we have to learn to live with Covid, but to learn to do that we need data which is agile enough and trustworthy enough**," she says.

She goes on to say that, "I would like to see strategic plans for preparedness in terms of what type of studies and resources they are going to keep."

She says that neither she nor other experts have been consulted and "there seems to be a lack of strategy. We don't know how they are going to monitor new variants, for example"

So once again the government does not understand value for money, does not understand the words 'strategic plan', and does not understand the importance of consulting with experts. But this all defines our present government and so long as they remain in power our lives and livelihoods continue to be in danger.

****

18TH MARCH
All Covid restrictions involving foreign travel are lifted today.

****

23RD MARCH

Two years ago today we entered our first lockdown.

And today in PMQs we hear our Prime Minister saying what he always says when being criticised which is that, "we got all the big calls right."

Well with the greatest of respect Prime Minister that is a lie.

And in *The Guardian* today there is an article written by the author of a book called 'Breathless'. Her name is **Rachel Clarke** and she works in the NHS as a consultant in palliative care. Looking at her book and reading this article is like having a dose of turgid realism chucked into my face.

At the beginning of her article she is critical of the fact that **people are trying to rewrite the grim realities of the state of the NHS two years ago and she asks if truth is the first casualty of a pandemic.**

She quotes Boris Johnson speaking in April 2020 when he said, "We succeeded in the first and most important task", because, "at no stage has our NHS been overwhelmed. No patient went without a ventilator. No patient was deprived of intensive care ... **We avoided an uncontrollable and catastrophic epidemic."**

But on that very day the death toll reached 26,771.

She says that the NHS did **not** cope with Covid; **it is damaged and drowning**.

"The truth is, Covid caused a collapse of healthcare as we know it – in both the first and subsequent waves. **The NHS was overwhelmed**."

She is also critical of the fact that the lockdown was not enforced much sooner. And we have heard this point of view time and time again from so many.

But, as she says, hospitals were literally beginning to run out of oxygen before the PM finally decided to act.

She is scathing about a certain section of society who are now saying that lockdowns were a blight on our freedom and must never happen again. This is completely wrong and whilst accepting they must be a last resort she says that if we had not had lockdowns we would have seen corpses in the hospital car parks.

I think most of us are aware that staff morale is at an all-time low. Over 400 NHS employees are quitting their jobs every week. How on earth is it surviving? And yet I hear from friends and family the amazing things they still keep doing in order to look after their patients.

She concludes her article by saying that, **"False narratives about the NHS 'coping' are unhelpful and damaging"** and she accuses our political leaders, and much of the media, of air brushing and sanitising the world in which she is working on a daily basis. They all just seem desperate to move on and ignore it.

As I keep saying if they don't even realise that there is a problem, and in so many cases they don't, then they are never going to be able to fix it. With the present government I am afraid they just don't get it. They are on **a parallel universe** and the **only thing that interests them is their ability to stay in power.** It is dangerous and incompetent on so many levels.

****

30TH MARCH

The final report of the Ockenden review was published today. We hear again of the traumas suffered by so many mothers as they were treated with cruelty and incompetence which **resulted in the death of 201 babies and 9 mothers at the Shrewsbury and Telford NHS Trust.**

Shrewsbury MP Daniel Kawczynski said: "The accounts of the parents are truly heart breaking and the brave staff members who came forward gave very concerning accounts.

"One of the central issues surrounding the failures of the Shrewsbury and Telford hospital is that there was a drive by the NHS, the Royal College of Midwives (RCM), Royal College of Obstetricians and Gynaecologists (RCOG), and National Childbirth Trust **for mothers to have a natural birth, seemingly at all costs.** The lowest percentage of caesarean deliveries by the Shrewsbury and Telford Hospital was incorrectly applauded and regarded as a laudable achievement. **This was accompanied by a grave lack of empathy for mothers, a pattern of consistent disregard for the families' concerns and, when there was medical intervention provided, it was often tragically too late.**

"I mention the staff who came forward and characterise them as brave. It is very concerning that it has been reported that staff members often felt afraid to voice their concerns or were worried of being reprimanded for giving accounts to Ms Ockenden and her team."

It breaks my heart to read this report.

****

31ST MARCH

But this news is just completely incomprehensible. A proposed amendment to the Health and Care Bill – which would have made it compulsory for the Government to publish regular, independent assessments of how many doctors and nurses the NHS needs based on projected patient demand – was defeated again in the Commons last night. As I have mentioned before this is something that Jeremy Hunt has been pushing for, for years now.

Something like this is absolutely vital but the government is disagreeing.

Why?

As the Royal College of Physicians says "**This is poor planning. All successful organisations rely on long-term workforce planning to ensure that they can meet demand – as we have said many times, the NHS and the social care system should be no exception.**

And it is particularly disappointing that this decision comes in the same week as the Nuffield Trust and King's Fund report that public satisfaction with the NHS is at an all-time low and the NHS Staff Survey highlights how demoralised heath care professionals are. **In both cases, staff shortages are given as the reason, with the public also very concerned about inadequate government funding.**"

I read a letter written to the PM by over **100** health and care organisations urging him to support this amendment. It was a long and detailed letter and as I read it I just knew that the PM would not have given it more than a cursory glance, if that.

And the reply to last night's vote from the RCP concluded with this paragraph.

*"Last night's vote in the House of Commons has removed a foundation from which we could have begun to put the NHS and social care workforce back on a sustainable footing. As the bill progresses I hope MPs look to 2040 as we do, when a quarter of the population will be over 65 and needing significant amounts of care, and realise we can't carry on like this. **Without this amendment, the Health and Care Bill will fail to address the biggest challenge facing the NHS and social care system: staffing shortages**. The money from the National Insurance rise this April to help reduce pressure on the NHS and support social care reform will only go so far if there are not enough staff to deliver care to those on waiting lists or accessing social care services. **Workforce is the limiting factor in your government's plans for health and care. We urge you to carefully consider the intention of amendment 29 and ensure it stands part of the final Act.**"*

This Tory government seems to look at something, anything, and then do the absolute opposite from what every sane, professional and experienced person advises.

They have to go.

****

1ST APRIL
From today all NHS staff will have to start paying to park their car in a hospital car park again.

****

Also from today nearly everyone will have to pay for their lateral flow tests.

****

5TH APRIL
And now we hear about the dreadful state of affairs with the NHS gynaecology specialism in the UK. **The waiting list here has risen by 60% during the pandemic, more sharply than any other speciality.** Problems with gynaecology did not start with the pandemic but obviously it made things much worse.

The Royal College of Obstetricians and Gynaecologists said that patients were "consistently deprioritised and overlooked".

Why? Apparently across the UK more than 570,000 women are waiting for treatment. More than 1,300 have been on the waiting list for two years.

Dr Edward Morris, the RCOG president, said he felt helpless not being able to speed up access to care for women and people on his waiting lists. **"There is an element of gender bias in the system.** I don't believe that we are listening to voices of women as well as we should be. The priority they urgently need is not being given to them," he said.

Well surprise, surprise. **When have vulnerable women's voices ever been listened to?**

Many of the conditions these women have are progressive and if left untreated will possibly need more radical and invasive surgery. Conditions like endometriosis and fibroids can affect fertility. Many women are in excruciating pain and have been for years which is affecting their mental health. Obviously.

I've said it before and I will say it again and I will no doubt go on saying it: Don't be a vulnerable woman or child or young person or old person in Britain today. Nobody in government cares.

****

AstraZeneca is criticising the government for delays in ordering a life- saving drug called Evusheld. This drug can reduce the chances of vulnerable patients getting Covid-19 by 77%. There are more than 500,000 clinically extremely vulnerable people with blood cancers or who are immunocompromised who would benefit from this drug.

Around 20 countries, including Australia, the US and some European countries have already begun to roll it out or are planning to do so.

More than 5,000 people have signed a petition to fund it and Lib Dem health spokesperson Daisy Cooper said, "The window of opportunity the Government has to order it is shrinking fast -- we need to see swift action now."

Yes, well, I am sorry to say this, but the words "swift" and "action" do not sit well with this government in any shape or form.

The Department of Health says it is still carrying out tests to see how effective it is. But it was authorised by the Medicines and Healthcare Regulatory Agency for Covid-19 prevention on the 17th of March.

This decision was endorsed by the government's independent expert scientific advisory body, the Commission on Human Medicines, after carefully reviewing the evidence. For goodness sake what more do they need?

But then I see the name of the vaccine minister Maggie Throup in there somewhere and I just despair.

****

6TH APRIL

The Covid infection **rates are now the highest they have ever been which means that the NHS pandemic recovery plan is already behind**. They are saying that one in every 16 people has Covid.

We have no guidance from the PM and people are wanting to know the where-abouts of Chris Whitty and Patrick Vallance.

We have been told we have to **learn to live with Covid,** but on the first few days of the Easter holidays people are not too happy as they realise that it means chaos at airports as planes are cancelled and delayed, due to staff shortages due to Covid. There have been **78 cancelled flights at Heathrow, and 30 at Gatwick** today and the Managing Director at Manchester airport resigned earlier this week when holiday makers faced lengthy queues.

But living with Covid also appears to mean trying to ignore it which is actually impossible. The NHS is facing more and more unsustainable pressure and indeed some hospitals are heading for another crisis. **Yesterday, the South Central Ambulance Service Trust declared a critical incident due to extreme pressures across their services.**

So leaving everything to common sense is not working and the country seems to be grinding to a halt. And then we have our Health Secretary, Sajid Javid, telling us all is well with the NHS this morning,

****

11TH APRIL

The headline in *The Times* today is:

"Almost half of NHS maternity services in England are unsafe"

It goes on to say that of the 193 maternity services in England, 80 are rated as "inadequate" or "requires improvement", meaning they do not meet basic safety standards. Eleanor Hayward, health correspondent, writes a damning article.

But then, I find a report from the Health and Social Care committee titled The Safety of Maternity Services in England which was ordered by the House of Commons to be published on the 29th June 2021 and was actually published on the 6th July 2021.

It is 66 pages long so I just pick out one paragraph.

In the summary and recommendations section they say that:

It is deeply concerning that maternity units appear to have been penalised for high Caesarean Section rates. **We recommend an immediate end to the use of total Caesarean Section percentages as a metric for maternity services, and that this is replaced by using the Robson criteria to measure Caesarean Section rates more intelligently.** *NHS England and Improvement must write to all maternity units to ensure that they are aware of this change.*

Of course this is a long and detailed report and there are many excellent recommendations, but here we are **nearly a year later,** and still we have articles in the media like the one in *The Times* today.

I would also add here that it is not safe to give birth in prison. You will have seen evidence of this in my preface and I also write about this in detail in the chapter entitled "Women".

****

Another article by Eleanor Hayward today is also disturbing. She writes that health bosses are desperate for the government to introduce new measures to curb the spread of coronavirus. **They're saying that hospitals face a "brutal Easter as bad as any winter.**

The NHS Confederation accuses Downing Street of "abandoning any interest in Covid whatsoever" as hospitals struggle with record infections.

The National Statistic figures show that one in thirteen people in England have Covid.

3% of NHS staff are off sick with Covid so adding to the staff shortages.

Matthew Taylor Chief Executive of the confederation said **"NHS leaders' report a clear disconnect between the Governments' Living with Covid plan and the realities of the NHS front line."**

That is the problem of this government in a nutshell. They are on another planet.

He goes on to say that, **"NHS leaders and their teams feel abandoned and they deserve better."**

Of course they do Mr Taylor. It is shocking to hear this sort of criticism over and over again. Where is this government and the Health Secretary? Oh wait. They are all defending each other from scandal after scandal and are spouting hot air from inside their Westminster bubble.

****

And an article in *The Guardian* by Denis Campbell reports that the number of **GPs in England has fallen every year since the government first pledged to increase the GP workforce by 5,000**. In September 2015 there were 29,364 fulltime GPs and this number has now fallen to 27,920.

No that doesn't look like an increase to me.

The main problem seems to be that more and more GPs are retiring early due to heavy workloads, excessive bureaucracy, and a lack of other health professionals working alongside them in their surgeries. They fear making mistakes under undue pressure and they want to get out.

Prof Martin Marshall, the chair of the Royal College of GPs has said that, "Good progress is being made recruiting more doctors into general practice but, if more GPs are leaving the profession than entering it, we're fighting a losing battle."

"There are many support packages and incentives which could be put in place in order to stop the early retirement of GPs and I think the government should be looking at these and acting on them as soon as possible."

Now that would be a novel approach.

****

16TH APRIL

The number of people in hospital with Covid and the ambulance logjams have reached new heights, a paramedic was saying this morning. He highlighted the problem with social care **because there were people ready to leave hospital yet can't because social care is not fit for purpose**. Staff were leaving care homes in droves in order to take on work which is more financially beneficial.

So two years after the PM said he would transform social care it continues to be the Cinderella of our health system.

****

23RD APRIL

The problems of staffing care homes are highlighted again today. About 410,000 staff resigned last year in order to go into higher paid jobs such as retail and hospitality. **This has the knock-on effect of severe bed-blocking in hospitals, as a record of 13,000 patients a day cannot be discharged.** This is costing lives as there are fewer vacant hospital beds now than at any time since the start of the pandemic.

Where are the convalescence homes? They were a good idea.

Social care staff do not feel as valued in the same way as NHS staff. They are being paid £9 an hour and one in four are on zero-hours contracts.

And of course we all remember Boris Johnson standing on the steps of Downing Street in his first speech as Prime Minister in 2019 and **promising to fix social care "once and for all."** Just to remind you we are **now one third** of the way through 2022.

The final paragraph in the editorial of *The Times* today says, "The government's reforms barely address this crucial issue. Workers in social care must be properly valued and paid, or the costs to the NHS and the tax payer will expand remorselessly."

We all know what needs to be done, but this particular government will not be doing it.

****

27TH APRIL

The High Court has just ruled that the government policies on discharging patients from hospitals to care homes without first testing them for Covid was unlawful.

Two women took Matt Hancock and Public Health England to court as they both lost relatives due to this practice

I first mentioned this on May 30th in my first book on page 44.

The whole way this was handled was a disgrace. Many lives were lost because of this practice but Matt Hancock said he had "put a protective ring around care homes."

Even then Helen Wildbore of the Relatives and Residents Association said it was "complete nonsense". And all of us could see that it was.

Many, many avoidable deaths were the result of absolutely no infection controls being put in place.

Matt Hancock is now saying that it was the fault of Public Health England who did not give them the correct advice. Always blame others.

Both women have said Boris Johnson should resign because of this ruling.

****

29TH APRIL

The Norfolk and Suffolk NHS Foundation Trust is a mental health Trust that has been found to be completely inadequate and unsafe. More than 100 patients died unexpectedly in a two year period and the Care Quality Commission has said it must improve. **The latest inspection downgraded the trust from "requires improvement" to "inadequate."**

Some of the findings of the report were:

- 115 "unexpected or potentially avoidable" deaths reported over a two-year period
- 15 people in contact with trust services were "thought likely" to have taken their own lives in the previous three months
- The long stay unit for adults had one consultant psychiatrist working half a day per week when patient reviews took place, and a locum junior doctor was shared between this service and another
- A patient's carer shared concerns about illegal substances on a ward with staff not always taking appropriate action
- A huge rise in referrals within children and adolescent community services - from 95 in August 2020 to 2,547 in July 2021

It really is heart-breaking to read this.

Under-staffed, under-valued and under-resourced, yet another hospital trust fails in its duty of care to patients.

Where does any funding go? It goes to administration, to bureaucracy, and to the Chief Executives but never to the front line.

What is the government doing about it? Nothing but spouting lies saying that we have more doctors and nurses than ever before and the NHS is alive and well and the envy of the world.

****

1ST MAY

The Prime Minister continues to say that they did not know that Covid 19 was asymptomatic and therefore they did not know that it was possible for patients being discharged from hospitals to care homes to transmit the disease to others. However this is **proving to be an absolute lie** as we hear a radio interview by Sir Patrick Vallance, the government's chief scientific adviser, as early as **13th March 2020** saying that there was indeed a risk of asymptomatic transmission.

We also see a video clip of Matt Hancock saying the same thing on the same day. **They lie and lie and lie and lie and lie.**

There were over 20,000 avoidable deaths between March and June 2020 because of the practice of discharging untested patients into care homes.

No responsibility, no remorse, no apology, no accountability, no consequences. Shocking.

****

3RD MAY

The PM says that they are going to build 48 new hospitals. That has gone up from 40. But I want to know what he is going to do about the existing hospitals. In a report by Eleanor Hayward in *The Times* today it says **that patient's lives are being put at risk because NHS hospitals have been allowed to fall into a dreadful state of disrepair.** It makes shocking reading. Ceilings are falling down and power cuts are occurring in operating theatres. In one hospital there was a massive leak of roof water into a unit for new-born babies and there are many, many reports of equipment failures.

Official figures show that the crumbling infrastructure of the NHS estate does "not meet the demands of a modern health service." Some parts date back to the Victorian era.

Nigel Edwards Chief Executive of the Nuffield trust health think-tank said that without urgent investment, waiting lists for routine operations and scans now at 6.2 million would continue to rise.

So when you do actually get into an operation theatre for your over-due operation, on top of everything else just keep an eye on the ceiling. It will take your mind off the fact that you will be awake anyway due to the shortage of anaesthetists.

****

5TH MAY

Well today we hear that yesterday, NHS England bosses have written to hospital trusts to urge them to coax elderly doctors out of retirement and to persuade others to stay on.

There is a shortage of 110,000 NHS staff at the moment and about 21,000 doctors over the age of 65 are due to retire this year. **So surgeons will be encouraged to work extra hours and the cap on the amount that surgeons can work per week will be removed.** Vaccine volunteers will be deployed "on a longer term basis" and medical students will staff certain wards.

Well I don't know about you but that sounds unethical, unsafe and unworkable. NHS staff are leaving in droves due to burn-out and exhaustion. Jeremy Hunt keeps talking about the long-term workforce plan that is needed and Chris Hopson, chief executive of NHS Providers, which represents hospitals says, **"We cannot disguise the fact that the NHS simply doesn't have enough staff."**

No you can't. We, the general public, have known this to be the case for years. No-one does anything to rectify this situation. Not now. Not ever.

****

9TH MAY

There is a really worrying report today saying that drug shortages are at their worst on record and that **500,000 people are affected by medicine shortages.** Pharmacies are pushing the government to allow them to be able supply substitute prescriptions instead of having to refer people back to their GPs. They say this would help the situation enormously. I don't believe anything has happened yet.

****

15TH MAY

If you are in need of a physiotherapist and you manage to get an appointment then you are very lucky indeed. Physiotherapists are at their wits end because of a bureaucratic nightmare. The Health and Care Professions Council decided not to send out any reminder letters to physios on their register and so they **have just de-registered 5,311 physios who forgot to re-register on time.**

Their distress is enormous. One turned up in tears at the HCPC's headquarters but no-one would see her. So many are suffering a loss of income but obviously it is the enormous detriment to patients that is the main concern.

Yes you could say that people should remember things like this but for goodness sake it is a momentary lapse in paper-work in what are very stressful times, and some common sense and humanity should prevail.

****

19TH MAY

The BMA has just published the first two reports out of five, which concludes that **the UK Government failed in its duty of care to protect doctors and other health care workers from avoidable harm and suffering in its management of the Covid-19 pandemic.**

It makes shocking reading and it will form part of the BMA'S submission to the UK Covid-19 Public Inquiry. It is a scathing attack on the government as they interviewed thousands of medics across the UK.

Page after page details the devastating impact of the pandemic on medical professionals as individuals, and on the NHS as a whole, and it shows mistake after mistake – errors of judgement and policy made by the UK Government - **which amount to a failure of a duty of care to the workforce.**

The chief complaint appears to be about the **lack of PPE** in the early stages of the pandemic. **81% of doctors did not feel fully protected during the first wave of the pandemic.**

There was no PPE availability. Consultants tell how they had to make their own and buy their own when they could. Many were initially told not to wear masks as it could frighten the patients. **What?**

A GP in Northern Ireland said: "*We were sent six pairs of gloves and six aprons in an envelope, approximately three weeks after the start of lockdown.*"

Many of them say that they saw levels of illness and death they were never trained for and they often had to hold phones up to dying patients so they could say goodbye to their loved ones. Their mental health was severely impacted and there was no proper risk assessment carried out at any time.

They say that the evidence presented in their reports, **"demonstrates, unequivocally, that the UK Government failed in its duty of care to the medical profession."**

They go on to make seven key recommendations for future governments. Well it won't be acted upon by the present government that's for sure.

****

22ND MAY
Six NHS Trusts have set up food banks in their hospitals for nurses and other staff. I write that again: **Six NHS Trusts have set up food banks in their hospitals for nurses and other staff.**

****

24TH MAY

The British Dental Association are saying that due to the 'unprecedented lack **in NHS commitment'** and the **lack of government funding**, over half of all high street dentists are threatening to withdraw from all ties with the NHS.

3,000 dentists have left the NHS since the beginning of the pandemic. Analysis suggests that only 33% of adults and less than 50% of children have access to an NHS dentist. Patients in poorer areas are worst affected and some schools are being forced to call in charities to treat pupils who are crying in pain with tooth decay.

There has also been insufficient planning by the government for investment in the British dental schools to discover the number of dentists needed to work in the NHS because of the decline in numbers even before the pandemic as a result of Brexit. Many EU qualified dentists used to come to the UK to live and work here but this is now no longer the case.

Is there anyone in government working to resolve this issue?

****

28TH MAY

Yet another NHS Trust has been found to have an unsafe maternity department. Nottingham University Hospital Trust has been told to make "significant and immediate improvement" to its maternity services where more than 500 babies died or their mothers may have suffered harm whist in their care.

I think there can be no doubt that mothers suffered harm as I listen to one young woman say that **her bladder was removed by mistake**. There is to be an inquiry led by Donna Ockenden.

I just remind you once again what the government said in answer to the Health and Social Care Committee's report published on the **6th July 2021** on 'The safety of maternity services in England.'

They said that, **"The government welcomes the HSCC report. Maternity safety is a priority for the government and the government remains committed to making the NHS one of the best places in the world to have a baby."**

****

7TH JUNE

47% of GPs plan to retire before the age of 60 according to a poll by *Pulse* the general practitioners' magazine.

One GP said, "The sooner I leave this mess the better. I don't recognise the job anymore and I wouldn't recommend it to anyone pursuing a career in general practice".

****

11TH JUNE

The price of a litre of petrol has just reached £2. It can therefore cost up to £100 to fill up your car. Nurses and health workers are finding it impossible to afford and many are considering phoning in sick rather than pay this exorbitant amount.

The government pays 56p a mile for NHS workers who drive to work and although it is reviewed every six months **it has not been increased since 2014.**

****

12TH JUNE

Just one story out of thousands. When a young man called for an ambulance for his father who was complaining of chest pains he was told it would take three to four hours for an ambulance to reach him. They said it would be great if he was able to drive his father to hospital. So this is what he did, all the while desperately hoping that his father wouldn't have a cardiac arrest on the way.

They arrived at hospital at 8pm and he was not triaged by the emergency staff until after midnight. He was not seen by a doctor until 4am. This was a total wait of 8 hours after a car journey rather than an ambulance.

Yet just a week ago our Prime Minister claims that "record numbers" of doctors and nurses are in place and the NHS now has "unprecedented" funding. **"We will continue to make sure patients receive world-class care whenever they need it," he says.**

Parallel Universe and Another Planet.

****

18TH JUNE
The government has just spent £54 million on a new fleet of ambulances. The only trouble is they are very uncomfortable for taller paramedics who say the pedals are too close together and they are impossible to drive.

****

28TH JUNE
Doctors are demanding a 30% pay rise over the next five years as some medics say they may have to go on strike. **Mid-term pay cuts since 2008 have accumulated to 30% loss in earnings.**

****

30TH JUNE
New Covid infections are increasing at an alarming rate. And today nurses are told by the government that their Covid related sick pay is to be discontinued. Access to Covid special leave for the purpose of self- isolation will also be scrapped.

The Royal College of Nursing said **the decision indicates "how little the UK government values its nursing staff."**

****

5TH JULY

Hospitals are reintroducing mandatory face masks and social distancing as they deal with the highest number of Covid patients since April.

****

9TH JULY

The Royal College of Emergency Medicine has warned that rising numbers of infections mean three in four A and Es are experiencing significant staffing shortages as doctors and nurses go off sick. **They said this is disrupting care with some patients having to wait more than three days to be admitted to a ward from overcrowded A and E units.**

A man was told to wait 14 hours for an ambulance and it was suggested that it might be better to take a taxi. This was a medical emergency.

****

19TH JULY.
"The NHS is dying of Covid." I end the chapter on the NHS with this chilling headline.

In a rare joint editorial by the editors of the BMJ and the Health Service Journal, they say "The NHS is not living with covid, it is dying from it." They warn that at no time in the past 40 years had so much of the NHS been so close to collapse.

They criticised the government's response, questioning the contention that the link between infections and hospital admissions had been broken.

New waves appear to be getting more frequent and more transmissible. And new variants are better at re-infecting those already vaccinated.

****

So what is the future of our NHS?

There needs to be a sharp scalpel to rip out the top-heavy and eye-wateringly expensive bureaucracy, a full and complete overhaul of the pay and salaries of all NHS staff, a serious commitment to increases in numbers training for the medical profession in every speciality, a long term plan to establish what work force is going to be needed and no more complete and absolute rubbish spoken about 40 new hospitals when there are no staff or new funding available.

The medical staff are working themselves to a standstill and need proper investment financially and in staffing levels.

Is that too much to hope for? Sadly, and certainly until we get a change in government, I think it is. I just ask you to look back at the entry on the 15th November and you will realise that there has been no progress whatsoever.

****

So now let us see where all the money is going.

****

THE BUDGET AND LEVELLING UP

2021

27TH OCTOBER

Well there many interesting words of course in **the budget**! And much to the disgust of the Speaker many of them were 'leaked' days before it was to be presented to the Commons. In the good old days this would have been a cause for resignation but this appears to be normal practice with this government.

Well this was Mr. Sunak's big moment but we are not happy. Normally the party of low tax, the 'Resolution Foundation' has calculated that the average household will be £3,000 a year worse off. **Tax relative to the economy will surge to the highest level since the early 1950s, when the Attlee government had been rebuilding Britain after six years of a world war.**

Of course as we have seen a load of cash will be thrown down the black hole that is the NHS when what it is in desperate need of is total reform and more training and investment in doctors, nurses, midwives, anaesthetists and all medical staff.

A few pounds will be spent on education but nothing like the amount asked for by Sir Kevan Collins the education Tsar. The best-case analysis sees the spending per pupil get back just about to where it was in 2010. Many head teachers are worried that they will have to make cuts in order to pay wage rises for teachers. As Christina McAnea, the Unison general secretary said, "Anything less than the rate of inflation is, effectively, a pay cut."

The real term funding for local authorities will still be far less than it was before the Tories came into office in 2010. In fact the Treasury has made it quite clear that the money for all pay rises will have to be found from existing departments which are unlikely to rise above 3% a year which is below the current rate of inflation of 4.2%. With the scrapping of Universal Credit there was a tapering approach for people as they get into work but of course nothing for those who are disabled or unable to work. There was an increase in the minimum wage which could in itself fuel inflation but the prospect of a high-wage economy is a complicated practice and a high bar for Johnson and Sunak to set themselves. I hope they have thought it through (pardon?) but I think this is going to be a hard winter for a lot of people.

****

16TH NOVEMBER

The Prime Minister is expected to confirm on Thursday of this week that the **Eastern route of HS2 and the new Leeds to Manchester rail line via Bradford are to be scrapped.** They are likely to approve improvements to existing infrastructure rather than a new line between Manchester and Leeds. And I do not think Bradford will get a look-in at all.

Well everyone, including the new northern Conservative MPs, are jumping up and down in horror.

It is interesting to go back a few years and note what Boris said in a **speech in Manchester on the 27th July 2019.**

He gave his backing to the Trans-Pennine transport link to **"turbo-charge the economy."** (This is always how he talks). The Northern Powerhouse rail project was part of Mr Johnson's wider commitment to deliver a high-speed railway link across the north of England, which would cost about £39 billion.

Leeds City Council leader Judith Blake said: "Northern Powerhouse Rail is key to our vision for a modern, reliable transport network that delivers faster journey times, additional capacity and greater reliability and **I hope the government will now work with us to accelerate delivery of this project."**

And this is a sweet touch don't you think**? Mr Johnson wore a badge saying "Northern Powerhouse" during the speech.**

Well I am not sure that this will be sending a strong signal about levelling up, but some are saying that in view of the cost of the pandemic perhaps this is a sensible compromise. Well we will wait until Thursday 18th and see what transpires.

****

17TH NOVEMBER

There is an interesting article in *The Times* today by David Smith about the latest productivity readings. He says that, "without improvements in regional productivity there can never be a meaningful levelling up of prosperity." He goes on to say that, "while we like to think of ourselves as tech-savvy, this country has invested less in information and communication technology than its competitors since the early 1990s and has seen a decline since 2017, while others have shown a rise."

A report by the 'Resolution Foundation' says that, "There are troubling patterns of attainment across generations: **literacy and numeracy skills of the young in the UK have slipped relative to previous cohorts."**

That is an absolutely dreadful thing to read. And with the present neglect of our education system by this government things are not going to improve.

In fact David Smith ends his column by saying, "When the government talks about creating a high productivity economy **it has not even scratched the surface."**

****

19TH NOVEMBER

So the new plans for the northern rail system were indeed announced yesterday and today we see that what has in fact transpired is an almighty backlash and fury from northern MPs and Mayors and the general public. **Manifesto promises are broken as the PM does what he does best which is overpromise and under-deliver.**

They are trying to sell the upgrading of part of the Northern Powerhouse Rail line as a fantastic investment but people are seeing through this for what it is: a broken promise and a kick in the teeth for Leeds and Bradford. "Levelling up" is just an empty slogan and as the editorial in *The Times* today says that with all the manifesto broken promises, "come the next election no matter what Mr. Johnson puts in his manifesto, voters won't believe a word of it".

Actually, Mr Witherow, Editor of *The Times*, come the next election, mark my words, Mr. Johnson will not be anywhere to be seen.

****

21ST NOVEMBER

The rail debacle is all over the press today as you would expect.

"The great train robbery"

"2nd class ticket to the north"

"A slap in the face" are a few of the headlines.

It really is an own goal for Johnson I think, as for all his talk of levelling up this will do the exact opposite. He is trying to sell it as a fantastic opportunity and indeed nearly £100 billion sounds amazing but people are not fooled. The Northern Powerhouse Rail Project needs much more than just a bit of upgrading and listening to those people who will be most affected by this downgrade I have to say they are not at all happy. Apparently at the moment it takes **just over an hour to travel the 35 miles between Manchester and Leeds** and the long-promised high speed link was due to cut this time to 25 minutes. People feel that the gap between the north and the south is getting wider.

And so we have more criticism of the incompetence of this government as David Olusoga of *The Observer* says that we should look to Germany to see how they have managed reunification.

Oh goodness they won't like that! But he writes that, "Germany's historic act of political will was achieved through the imposition of serious policies and the making of tough and often unpopular decisions, not through slogans and gestures. **After last week's events can anyone seriously imagine such commitments and serious-mindedness emanating from Downing Street?"**

Well I presume that that is a rhetorical question but I will answer it just the same! **NO MR. OLUSOGA, I CAN'T.**

****

28TH NOVEMBER

In today's *Times* David Smith is not happy again. Everyone is asking the PM if he is OK after his abysmal Peppa Pig speech to the CBI and he says that you do have to wonder. He is concerned about the 'levelling up 'agenda and whether it really exists. **The white paper on levelling up has yet to make an appearance.** He has been told it is "forthcoming." Oh yes.........we've heard that one before. A lot of times actually.

David Smith is concerned about **our big cities**. As he says, we tend to think of 'left behind' places as being smaller communities such as former pit villages. However he says that analysis by the Centre for Cities show us that regional cities compare very badly with counterparts on the Continent. Even in France, which like the UK is dominated by its capital, regional cities contribute far more to the economy and to productivity than the UK's regional cities. He says that "cities have attracted low-productivity 'non-tradeable' activities such as hospitality, the arts, entertainment and leisure. These bring a liveliness to city centres but they do not bring innovation and lasting prosperity."

He goes on to criticise the relocation of central government in this country as a "branch office mentality" compared to the more genuine regional autonomy across European countries. The Centre for Cities makes six recommendations for fixing the problems but the government also needs to invest in struggling city centres through a city centre productivity fund to make them more attractive places to do business. **He cites Birmingham, Manchester and Glasgow but also includes London, whose productivity growth has been dismal, he says, since the pandemic.**

****

5th December Lisa Nandy, the new shadow secretary for levelling up, is tackling Michael Gove, the government levelling up secretary and criticising his department for being in complete "disarray". She said that the news that the government's **white paper on levelling up has been delayed until next year** because of disagreements over strategy and the definition of the term showed that they have never been serious about plans to make the UK more equal in the first place. **Dither, dither, dither, delay, delay, delay.**

****

2022

3RD JANUARY

Today we hear that the **white paper on levelling up is being delayed yet again**! It was apparently hoped that this document of over 100 pages would be the first big government announcement of the year. But no, it has been pushed towards the end of the month. Not sure why. There are some big policies in there it seems and Gove was discussing it with Johnson at Chequers over the Christmas holidays. So we continue to wait with interest to find out what is meant exactly by "levelling up."

****

10TH JANUARY

Well just a bit of light relief which we could all do with. This morning Michael Gove was due in the *Today* studios. He **will** be here actually, face to face they were saying, rather than on a telephone line. Except they then had to report that **he was stuck in a BBC lift!** When they did manage to get him out he brushed aside their apologies and said no, no please don't worry I've just had a bit of levelling up! Always polite Michael Gove.

Apparently there was an instant hash tag which was saying "free Michael Gove". He did have the grace to say to that there were probably more people saying leave him there!

****

16TH JANUARY

An article in *The Observer* today by Julian Coman, points out that far from levelling up beginning to occur after two years of talk by this government, the **north south divide is actually getting worse**. There is a report out tomorrow by the northern branch of the Institute for Public Policy Research and called **"State of the North 2021"**.

It compares the levels of public investment in London and the south east with that in the north. The authors estimate that in the five years leading up to 2019-2020 London received £12,147 per person whilst in the north it was only £8,125. Jonathan Webb, one of the authors, said, "It's clear that central government simply hasn't put its money where its mouth is... **Levelling up will be consigned to the list of hollow promises** made to people in regions like the north for a long time now, if it isn't underpinned by investment and crucial fiscal development."

Well, let us hope that Michael Gove has it all under control and the rabbit will be pulled out of his hat when the levelling up white paper is published at the end of the month.

.

****

19TH JANUARY

In an article by Alice Thomson in *The Times* today she writes that we are entering a **new age of inequality**. The ten richest men in the world doubled their wealth during the pandemic according to Oxfam. At the same time according to the Legatum think-tank, **nearly 900,000 people in the UK have been pushed into poverty over the last two years**.

Income inequality has increased for the first time in a decade despite the PM's insistence this month that it has shrunk. But then even today in PMQs he was shouting that our economy was absolutely fantastic.

So it is all the more galling to hear that £4.3 **billion of public money lost to fraud during the pandemic is just going to be written off** and not pursued and so never recovered. The anti-fraud task force says that it has reached "a point of diminishing returns" in tracking down the fraudsters which sounds a bit pathetic to me. Especially as the Treasury announced in practically the next breath that they are going **to retrospectively pursue mothers who may inadvertently**

have been given too much child benefit. As Alice Thomson says, "an easy target."

As we know only too well this government with Johnson at the head neither thinks about nor cares about women or children. And that would appear to be the case for the Treasury as well.

****

UK households are feeling an enormous pressure with their finances as the **cost of living reaches 5.4%, its highest level in almost 30 years.** Clothes, food, footwear and energy prices have all risen considerably and there is more hardship to come in April when energy prices will go up again.

****

21ST JANUARY
It is reported in the media today that MPs have accused the government of presiding over a **"shameful shambles" for failing to tackle pension underpayments dating back as far as the 1980s.** It is reported that an estimated 134,000 state pensioners have not received what they are owed due to long-standing errors totalling more than £1 billion, which mostly affects **widows, divorcees and women who rely on their spouse's pension contributions for some of theirs**.

Unknown numbers of people have died before the mistakes could be fixed but there is no plan for contacting the next of kin.

The failures have led to significant losses to taxpayers as staff costs in correcting mistakes by the end of 2023 are expected to **reach more than £24 million.**

The Public Accounts Committee said that there was a risk that the errors which led to underpayments in the first place, could be repeated in the correction programme, the ninth such exercise since 2018.

More and more incompetence and waste.

****

23RD JANUARY

Miranda Bryant writes in *The Times* today that, according to a report by 'Covid Realities', a two year study by the universities of York and Birmingham and the Child Poverty action group, **Britain's welfare state is "unfit for purpose" and in urgent need of reform.** Experts warn that millions more families will struggle to make ends meet with the dual pressures of the pandemic and the spiralling cost of living.

Ruth Patrick, senior lecturer in social policy at York University and leader of this research programme said that many are being faced with "**impossible" choices of either sitting in the dark to conserve electricity or saving the heating for when the children come home**. "People are experiencing stress, anxiety and insecurity about how they'll manage now and in the future." she said.

Research by the Resolution Foundation think-tank found that the number of households spending at least 10% of their budget on energy bills, **will almost triple overnight in April to 27% affecting an additional 4 million households.**

They are calling for the government to increase Universal Credit, or to expand the warm home discount, or face "catastrophe".

Parallel Universe: A government spokesperson says in effect it is all OK, don't worry, "we're providing extensive support for those on low incomes." So that's OK then. This Conservative Government under the leadership of Boris Johnson, will look after you. I do hope that everyone is assured.

****

28TH JANUARY

The rise in National Insurance is proving to be a difficult problem for the PM. The Chancellor needs this money to fund social care but many Tory MPs have warned the PM that the rise must be delayed as a condition of their support. Earlier today he refused to say what he was going to do either one way or the other.

However, later today we have just heard that he has said he will stand by his Chancellor and **the rise will definitely go ahead "no ifs, no buts".**

****

30TH JANUARY

A press release has just been released in advance of the Levelling Up white paper due to be published this week after many delays. It is causing a lot of concern. When *The Observer* contacted the Treasury to ask if its ministers had indeed signed off on the promised £1.5 billion, Michael Gove's department back-tracked and confessed that the **"new" fund was not new money at all but would be made up from funds that had been announced in the spending review last autumn.**

They are accusing this of being a "stunt to save Johnson's job". We wait to see exactly what is in the white paper.

****

2ND FEBRUARY

The white paper is published today at last and the Secretary of State for Housing, Communities and Local Government says, "Our 12 new national levelling up missions **will drive real change in towns and cities across the UK so that where you live will no longer determine how far you can go."**

It is being said, however, that there are a lot of words with very little detail. It lacks ambition and the money available will barely scratch the surface. The disparity between places in the UK and the poverty gap are just too enormous to be solved by such a thin statement.

We heard on the radio this morning from someone who lives in Wakefield in Yorkshire bemoaning the fact that bus services have been cut to a bare minimum. She said that it was easier to get to London than to the other side of the town.

We already know about the dreadful cuts in the northern rail scheme.

And a new report looking into levelling up schemes that are already in progress – such as the towns and levelling up funds – has offered a damning assessment, saying billions of pounds spent in both may have been wasted because ministers are picking projects too small to revive poorer areas and failing to analyse "what works."

In response to the 'no new money' accusation Michael Gove says that the strategy was not aimed at providing new funding but ensuring it is spent effectively on local priorities.

But The National Audit Office says that grants issued from the funds are not being "based on evidence". It comes after criticism **that allocations from the two funds, favoured Conservative areas – for voter-friendly improvements such as libraries and leisure centres.**

Gove also acknowledges **that most of the missions are existing policies with funds already allocated to them but he says they will be enshrined in law for the first time.**

All very inadequate.

There will be more local mayors but they will need more local powers.

****

3RD FEBRUARY

Well there is huge criticism over this white paper from Michael Gove's department.

Apparently it looks as though parts of it have been copied from Wikipedia! It talks about ancient cities such as Jericho, Rome and Constantinople.

Is this Gove trying to be clever and comparing ancient cities with cities in the UK? It is being said that it has been cobbled together in a rush and a lot of it shows signs of "copy and paste." The sentences about Constantinople are identical to sentences on Wikipedia and appear twice in the document which contains glaring publishing errors – **with entire paragraphs repeated wholesale.** It had obviously not been proof read!

In terms of policy substance, **eight of the document's 12 "missions" are also the same as those included in Theresa May's industrial strategy, which was released four years ago and then scrapped by the government.**

They really are not up to the job and they treat us all as fools.

****

And today is the day when some 20 million households will have an enormous spike to their energy bills. Ofgem will lift its cap on prices with the effect that they will rise by about 50%.

And it is being forecast that **households will experience the biggest fall in their living standards since records began**. The Bank of England warns people that take home pay would fall by five times the amount it did during the financial crises of 2008. They also **urged workers not to ask for pay rises** in an attempt to keep a lid on inflation which is predicted to hit 7.25 per cent in April.

The Chancellor is expected to announce billions of pounds in state backed loans to give a discount of £200 to all households. But as loans of course they will have to be paid back in future years when it is hoped energy prices will have fallen which is highly doubtful. Also people are saying that £200 is not nearly enough when the bills will go from 1,000 to £2,000 a year.

The Chancellor will also commit to giving households in council tax bands A to C rebates funded by government grants. However council tax bands were set in 1991 which will mean that many of the people who will benefit, particularly in London and the South East will be relatively wealthy because property prices have increased significantly since then.

VAT might be cut from energy bills for one year and the Warm Homes discount might be increased for some.

So some help available but not nearly enough especially with the cost of living generally rising at the fastest rate for 30 years.

The 'Resolution Foundation' think-tank said that even with state support the number of people living in fuel poverty would double to five million.

There are so may heart breaking stories from people who have to make choices between heating and eating and have to use food banks more and more.

And it is just interesting to note that just weeks before this Chancellor cut the £20 uplift to Universal Credit in July last year, **he asked for planning permission to build a swimming pool, gym and tennis court at his Grade 11 listed Yorkshire manor house.**

Now I personally do not begrudge him or anyone else who has enormous wealth, and I am very happy for them to use it for their personal advantage, but I just think that it must be very difficult for some, and I include our Chancellor, to really understand what it means to live in absolute poverty. **I really think that they and their family should try to live in a high rise two bedroom flat on the minimum wage for a month.**

****

4TH FEBRUARY

There was a press conference yesterday afternoon in the lovely new blue press room. We haven't seen this for a while. How much did it cost again? Oh yes, £2.6 million. (You **will** remember this fact by the end of this book!)

Sunak did indeed announce a £9 billion package of loans and council tax rebates but said that Britain would just have to get used to higher energy prices in the long term.

The Bank of England confirmed that interest rates would rise from 0.25 % to 0.5%.

But there is a lot of disquiet about the small and inadequate support from the government.

The future looks bleak.

****

9TH FEBRUARY

David Smith writes a very worrying article about the "drifting economy" in *The Times* today. He states that the projections from the Bank of England says that "the UK will have very slow growth of only 1.25% this year and a dismal 1% next year. **The latter feels less like growth, more a kind of stagnation."**

He goes on to describe how this compares badly with the Eurozone and even worse with America.

He quotes the Oxford Economic Consultancy Assessment which says, "The levelling-up white paper contains nothing to cause us to revive our forecasts for the UK's various nations and regions, let alone the UK as a whole. While it contains many fine sentiments, there's little that is new or significant."

David Smith finishes his article by saying that, **"We are drifting with 1% growth in sight. And it is not good enough."**

****

13TH FEBRUARY

In a report by the 'Intergenerational Foundation' think-tank which is due out tomorrow it is being said that **young people will bear the brunt of the costs of social care reform and the pandemic**. They accuse the government of imposing a "tax by stealth" with the freeze on income tax brackets, the student loan threshold and April's national insurance rise. **Those under 30 will be the hardest hit.**

Researchers calculate a graduate earning £27,000 a year will see their deductions rise by about 20% over the next four years – from 18% of their pay to 22%. They predict their disposable income will drop by almost 30%.

'The Institute for Fiscal Studies' published a report on Thursday that accused the government of using high inflation to **"quietly tighten the financial screws"**.

There are so many heart-breaking stories about young people never seeing a future where they can afford to live away from their parents and they accuse the government of specifically targeting young people.

****

22ND FEBRUARY

There are huge concerns at the moment about possible future plans by the government to **reduce bus funding** as authorities around the country have warned of severe cuts to come. Almost one in three services are at risk. At the moment the Treasury is refusing to confirm if it will continue to grant funding to support operators whose bus revenues have yet to recover to pre-pandemic levels. The improvement fund has been reduced to just over £1.2 billion, with the government counting emergency support grants to the industry as part of the total figure.

Manchester's Metrolink, Tyne and Wear and the West Midlands are all at risk, as are country services in rural areas.

And as a short term Covid deal with TFL expired on the 18th February, **bus services in London are now under pressure, as an agreement was not reached with the government for a new funding settlement.**

We will know more details tomorrow.

But it does look as though everyone will have to forget about climate change and carbon footprints, ignore the severity of the devastating and life-threatening storms we have just experienced and get into their cars.

Or.................. maybe constituents around the country can lobby their MPs and just ask them to do their utmost to get rid of this PM and this government and let them know in no uncertain terms that they will not be voting for them in the future. I live in hope but not in any expectation.

****

[24th February Russia invades Ukraine]

27TH FEBRUARY

More news about buses! You might not remember this pledge (promise) from Boris Johnson, which he made in February 2020, exactly two years ago, when he said that his government would provide **4,000 new zero-emission British built buses** by the end of 2024. The trouble is that, as yet, UK manufacturers **have not received any orders**. They are saying that if everything is left to the last minute and funds are not forthcoming they will have to look over-seas for quicker and cheaper options.

****

1ST MARCH

Train passengers in England and Wales have been hit with the largest fare rise in nearly a decade today, with ticket prices increasing by up to 3.8%. This hike is the biggest jump in nine years.

And also today there is a tube strike. People think of London as being full of the wealthy but as a letter from London businesses to the Chancellor points out there is widespread poverty across the capital and **access to public transport is depended on by many for vital jobs, education and services.**

Hang on, wait a minute. MPs have just been awarded a 2.7% pay rise which on their salary means an extra £2,000 a year. But I thought they were telling people not to ask for any pay rises.

****

9TH MARCH

There is an article in *The Guardian* today by Frances Ryan in which she emphasises the upcoming hardships that many people are set to endure. Of course we are aware that the conflict in Ukraine will affect us all and my goodness none of us are complaining about that. But those on benefits are going to be hit hard and in this article she calls for more understanding and support from the government.

The 'Joseph Rowntree Foundation' says 9 million families on benefits due to low incomes will be £500 worse off on average from April. About 400,000 people could be pulled into poverty.

The 'Resolution Foundation' says the conflict in Ukraine will further push gas and oil inflation in UK to above 8% this spring – the biggest hit to households since the 1970s.

Bear in mind that benefit rates are already at a 30 year low and of course the £20 week uplift has recently been axed.

As Frances Ryan says so powerfully in this article, **the present government look upon those seeking benefits as the lowest of the low.** They want to make life even harder for them than it already is. We already know that they are now forced to travel miles to get any job however unsuitable.

"Until we challenge it," she writes "this country is destined to repeat the same old mistakes, becoming an ever meaner society, one that is ill-equipped to provide even the most basic essentials for millions of its citizens."

****

18TH MARCH
Cultural Levelling Up.

I am indebted to Richard Morrison of *The Times* today for letting us know about the **removal of £75 million of arts funding from London** to the regions by Nadine Dorries our present culture secretary. **I say our 'present culture secretary' because if she is in this post for much longer there will be no culture left for her to mess up.**

He mentions four completely misconceived ideas that she seems to display.

Here they are in brief:

1. The 14 million population of London is exactly 25% of the entire population so it is reasonable to give London 25% of the funding.

2. Offering London based arts organisations to re-locate their offices to the regions will frustrate and demean the existing regional art companies.

3. And, as he says, this is absolutely against the spirit of levelling up. It should be up to the elected local councillors to decide what sort of cultural activities they need in their areas and it is their budgets that should be boosted in order to do this.

4. Of course, he says, this would mean that Dorries would lose some control over how the money is spent. She wouldn't like that. And is all this really about getting cheap headlines in order to persuade the voters in the north to vote Tory?

He looks back with nostalgia to a time when the Arts Council was fiercely independent and ministers took a pride in not interfering in artistic matters.

I actually find it difficult to remember such a wonderful, democratic and sensible time as that.

****

24TH MARCH

Yesterday the Chancellor presented his **spring statement** to the House. It has been met with huge disappointment and much criticism.

There is not nearly enough there to help the poorest in our society, those on benefits, the disabled, or pensioners, at a time when inflation is at the highest for 30 years at 6.2%. And the **Office for Budget Responsibility** said yesterday that **inflation would hit a 40-year high of 8.7% in October, fuelling the biggest fall in living standards in any single year since records began in 1956.**

The chief measures were a cut of 5p off a litre of petrol, a £3,000 increase in the threshold for paying national insurance and at the end of this Parliament in May 2024 income tax would drop by 1p to 19p which would, surprise, surprise, be just before a general election.

For goodness sake that is just ridiculous. And some are saying that petrol in their local petrol stations went up by 5p last week so it is just back to what it was then.

The 'Resolution Foundation' said it was the first time there would be such a large increase in the number of people falling into poverty outside of a recession.

1.3 million people, **including half a million children**, will be pushed below the poverty line next year as taxes will be at the highest level since the Second World War. Their think-tank calculates that the poorest fifth of families got £136 out of our Chancellors package, and the richest got £475.

As they say, **"the outcome is so eye-poppingly at odds with what the times demand.........as to be baffling."**

Of course the trick question that journalists like to ask politicians, especially those in the Treasury, is **do you know the price of a loaf of bread?** On being asked this question Rishi Sunak replied that he thought it was about £1.20 and it used to be £1 from memory. But he went on to say that whilst he has a sort of seedy Hovis type of bread, they had a whole range of different breads in his house. A degree of healthiness he said between him, his wife and his kids.

Well aren't they lucky. There are so many people in the UK who can only get bread from a food bank.

****

27TH MARCH

Unions are predicting a **mass exodus of key workers** unless public sector employees receive pay rises that at least match the spiralling rate of inflation. Believe me there is a massive tsunami of employment problems coming our way and there are some very black days ahead. Workers in education, the NHS, and social care are already leaving in droves, burnt out, exhausted and not appreciated and how the government doesn't understand this I do not know. I can't see sufficient pay rises on the horizon at all...........unless you are an MP of course.

****

1ST APRIL

From today tax, energy, phone and council tax bills will surge with average households experiencing a rise of more than £1,000. Water companies and travel insurance will also go up. The Office for Budget Responsibility has forecast that disposable incomes will fall by 2% this tax year which is the largest decline since records began.

The latest analysis by the 'Resolution Foundation' predicts that 1.3 million more people will be plunged into absolute poverty by 2023. Including the 700,000 who fell into poverty during the pandemic, that's around 16.5 million people.

Many ministers feel that the Chancellor must do more. One said that, "It's not enough. It doesn't even touch the sides for a lot of families. It feels unsustainable."

Statistics are one thing but I listened to a single mother of three children on *LBC* this morning talking to James O' Brien. She was talking through her tears for most of the time about the difficulties she is in. She works full-time but gets a very low wage and with these increases today she is in despair. James O'Brien was brilliant. He was compassionate, and encouraging and gave her time to talk. He told her she was a brilliant mother as her only thoughts were for her children.

It was so upsetting to listen to and she is just one of thousands. What do people like her think of the entire Conservative government going out to a plush hotel for a four-course meal with wine this week just so they could have time to talk to each other.

As she kept saying they just don't understand.

****

And today they have all started a three week recess and our Chancellor has gone to his mansion in California with his family.

****

We also hear that MPs who have second homes in order to be near their constituents get a heating allowance. In fact looking into this a bit more I discover that MPs are getting as much as £22,000 a year in expenses designed to help towards the cost of owning another property. Maybe that is fair enough if they live a long way from London and need to be living in their constituency but some who live only an hour's commute from London also claim this allowance.

****

3RD APRIL
Almost 300,000 disabled people are to **lose their Warm Home Discount of £140 this winter.**

Disability Rights UK called the move "appalling" and its chief executive Kamran Mallick said, "Disabled people often need more hot water, more heating and more energy to run specialist equipment."

****

We also hear that the **government is dropping another bill** which was expected to be in the Queen's speech in May and which was promised in their 2019 election manifesto. This is a bill in which the

Conservatives promised to 'encourage flexible working and consult on making it the default unless employers have a good reason not to'.

Calls for the Employment Bill grew after anger about the working conditions and pay in factories and warehouses across the country. Coupled with the emerging 'fire and rehire' practice, as well as fears of dwindling workers' rights post-Brexit, **Johnson promised to revamp workers' rights back in December 2019.**

Flexible working has been campaigned for by so many charities including 'Pregnant then Screwed' and they are all so angry at this new set back.

Not enough space in the Queen's speech apparently. Looks like another U-turn or, if you prefer, another broken promise.

****

6TH APRIL

The National Insurance tax hike comes into force today as contributions will rise by 1.25%. Well you will be relieved to know that the PM says that he has no problem with this at all as it will help to pay for the NHS and social care.

We will all just have to put on an extra jumper, turn down the heating and buy cheaper food.

The other person who will have no problem with this is our Chancellor. Well of course it was his idea.

But it has also been revealed today that his **billionaire wife is classed as a 'non- dom.'** As she was born in India of an Indian father she can declare it as her domicile of origin on a tax return. There is absolutely nothing illegal in this but it is interesting to note that it is her choice. Although India does not recognise dual nationality, if you state on your tax form that your intention is to live in the UK and not go back to your country of origin then you will be considered British for tax purposes and will lose your domicile of origin.

Of course it is up to her but it is just not a good look as her husband pushes more and more people into poverty.

****

7TH APRIL

It has also been disclosed that Rishi Sunak had a Green Card until last October. They are very difficult to come by but it means that you can work in the US. Well he used to work in New York but it is still a bit strange that he kept it for so long.

****

10TH APRIL
Things are really not looking good for the Chancellor.

The removal lorries have been spotted outside No 11 Downing Street. His family will now live in their London mews house which is nearer to their daughter's primary school and he will work at No 11 during the week, going to their house at the weekends.

Any support he had from the public or fellow MPs has nose-dived. Apparently he nearly resigned over disagreements with the PM over the funding of social care and at the moment his future looks decidedly uncertain.

****

12TH APRIL
I have to congratulate the BBC on the *Panorama* programme which was shown last night.

They followed three families in three different parts of the UK who are struggling with the rise in the cost of living.

It was heart- breaking. The government keep saying that the best way out of poverty is to get a job. This is their answer to everything. However the adults in all of these families were all in employment.

One mother was working in the NHS. One mother owned a shop and her husband was in a good job. The third mother was also working. At different points during the programme they were all close to tears.

The NHS worker worked just three days a week because of the difficulty in affording child care.

The husband worked about 50 miles away so the cost of fuel every week was exorbitant.

They were all struggling to pay the bills and the recent price increases were the last straw. They all had lovely children and one teenager was heard saying to her mother that she really was not hungry and **she wanted her mother to have her supper.**

They were all trying so hard to provide for their families that it was painful to watch. And this must be multiplied a thousand times up and down the country.

As usual it was the kindness of so-called ordinary people that made one weep. The neighbour who was given too much food so she brought some round to her friend and was given a huge, warm hug in thanks.

The man who filled boxes with food every week and did 15 drop-offs every day completely voluntarily.

This programme did not try to be sensational. It just talked to the families and recorded the facts and, as I say, made me weep.

****

13TH APRIL

Inflation rises to 7%, the highest in three decades and the Bank of England is forecasting a rise to 8% by the end of the month and to 10% later this year.

Rishi Sunak has just had a fixed penalty notice from the police for illegally attending a party in Downing Street during lockdown but has decided, like Johnson, not to resign.

****

22ND APRIL

I hear today that the **cost of living work group has not met for 6 months**. So just to be crystal clear about this, when the PM says he needs to be left to get on with the job he is actually not doing it anyway.

Liberal Democrat Treasury spokesperson Christine Jardine said, **"This is all the proof you need that the Government is asleep at the wheel during the worst cost of living crisis in a generation."**

****

27TH APRIL

There needs to be much more transparency over who benefited from the coronavirus loans. Ministers are apparently spending tens of thousands of pounds fighting to prevent the public from knowing. George Greenwood in *The Times* today writes that the British Business Bank, which handled Covid bounce-back schemes has been refusing for over a year now to publish its records of who got the money and is fighting transparency campaigners in the courts.

So obviously, to me anyway, they have something to hide.

The government has also refused a *Times* request for information on where nearly £1 billion went in Sunak's scheme **Eat Out to Help Out** and they have also resisted calls to issue the identity of all businesses that borrowed a combined £1.14 billion via Sunak's **Future Fund** scheme for technology start-ups.

The British Business Bank says that more transparency could lead to greater fraud. I don't understand this. When *The Times* asked for evidence to back up this claim the bank declined to comment.

So when the government says it has no more money to spend on, for example children's education, you need to know and remember that figures released to 'Open Democracy' under freedom of information laws show that **the cost to the government departments when fighting tribunal cases against transparency can be as much as £130,000 with most costing tens of thousands of pounds in legal fees.**

****

Last night there was a dinner at the InterContinental Hotel in Park Lane. It was a fund-raiser for the Conservative party aimed at encouraging city fat cats to part with their money. Rishi Sunak was the "guest of honour". It cost £1,000 a head for the event. Other Tories there were Dominic Raab, Kit Malthouse, Nadine Dorries and my MP Oliver Dowden.

Then today in an interview with the Mums-net forum he tells struggling families that it would be **"silly" to give them more financial help** with energy bills "when we don't know what the situation in the autumn is going to be."

Thank you Mr Sunak for your understanding and compassion.

****

30TH APRIL

Money Box, which is an excellent programme on Radio 4, has uncovered that the Chancellor's pledge that councils in England would make £150 payments towards domestic energy bills **"in April"** has been broken in some areas. The guidance has now been changed to "**from April**". The deadline for these payments is September but many councils have not even started. The Department for Levelling Up did not answer a direct question about why the guidance had been changed or when that change happened.

Just a further example of dishonesty and incompetence.

****

2ND MAY

Apparently Ben Wallace, the defence secretary, **called for an increase in defence spending before the Chancellor's spring budget.** The Chancellor never replied to his letter and did not increase the budget for defence. Treasury officials apparently put pressure on the MoD to withdraw the letter, leading to tensions within the cabinet.

One Whitehall source said, "MoD officials are still flabbergasted they were barred from engaging with the Treasury on this matter and **the letter appeared to have gone in the bin at No 11."**

****

3RD MAY

But today we hear that Boris Johnson has promised **a £300 million package of support for Ukraine** with equipment which includes electronic warfare, a counter battery radar system, GPS jamming equipment and thousands of night vision devices.

"In the coming weeks" says Johnson, "We in the UK will send you Brimstone anti-ship missiles and Starmer anti-aircraft systems. We are providing armoured vehicles to evacuate civilians from areas under attack and protect officials."

He has just given a "This is your finest hour" speech on zoom to Ukraine so he is being all Churchillian at the moment, and of course anything that helps Ukraine is to be applauded.

I just hope he has cleared this with the Treasury.

****

8TH MAY

In today's *Sunday Times*, David Smith looks at the "**Build Back Better**" document which was published a year ago. He asks "Was it, like a lot from this government, **an extended soundbite from which it would be naive to expect anything meaningful?**"

That puts it in a nutshell.

He goes on to say that actually it would appear that we are building back a lot worse with the worst inflation for 30 years, a reduced workforce and labour shortages. Although employment rate is high, productivity remains low. He says that "any strategy designed to improve the long- term performance of the economy has to start with protecting and improving on those areas in which the UK is strong –some of which are under threat, not least from Brexit."

He also goes on to write about the banks and writes "As things stand they look terrible. **The Bank's new forecast is a horror story.**"

Inflation could reach 10% by the end of the year. He thinks that we are looking at the best of three years of stagnation.

It does make very dismal reading.

****

9TH MAY

Today we hear that the fire brigade is being called out to pensioners who have had fires in their homes because **they were trying to cut their heating costs by burning timber in their living rooms**. They are worried that the rise in energy bills could result in a surge of fires as people resort to alternative methods to heat their homes.

But wait what is this?

Our Education Secretary Nadhim Zahawi MP has just apologised, and promised to repay the part of his £5,822.27 expenses claim for second home energy bill that relates to the electricity heating supply to **his stables**. This is tax-payers money that we are talking about here. **This is heating for horses.**

It has also been reported that some 340 MPs, including government ministers, have used the parliamentary system to recoup the cost of heating their homes.

They really are in a parallel universe.

****

The National Institute of Economic and Social Research estimates that 1.5 million British households-- one in twenty of the total-- **will soon face bills for food and energy which will exceed their disposable income after household costs. It also forecasts that the UK will fall into a recession in the second half of this year.**

And 'The Resolution Foundation' said 1.3 million people would fall into absolute poverty next year, and not be able to afford basic necessities.

Labour asks for a windfall tax: the Treasury says there is no more money until 2024.

****

The boss of Scottish Power, Keith Anderson, has called for ten million households to have their energy bills reduced by £1,000 this October. Energy bills are expected to rise to nearly £3,000 a year.

The 'Food Foundation' think-tank reports that already more than 2 million adults in the UK have gone without food for a whole day over the past month because they can't afford to eat.

Caring Britain.

******

11TH MAY

The Mayor and Mayoress of Dartford have opened a new ……….. hospital? school? playground?……..er, no it was new foodbank. They cut a red ribbon, laughed at some jokes and then ate a buffet of sandwiches and cakes inside the food bank. Photos everywhere.

Lee Anderson, a Tory MP has said in Parliament that there isn't a massive need for food banks in the UK it's just that people "cannot cook properly, they cannot cook from scratch, they cannot budget."

It needs reminding that this MP claimed £223K in expenses on top of his salary of £84,000 and also eats subsidised meals in the House of Commons.

He says people should be able to cook a meal from scratch for 30p a day. Perhaps he would like to show us how it's done. Their understanding and compassion knows no bounds.

****

Breaking news is that government data from the ONS reports that Brexit costs Britain around £173m a week, about £25m a day, or just over £1m every single hour.

****

It has also just been revealed that at the start of the pandemic, taxpayers' money was given to a club of newspapers known as **the News Media Association.**

Brian Cathcart of the *Byline Times* has written a long report which relates how a scheme called '**All in, All Together'** was the result of some intense lobbying by the NMA. They argued that they had to be able to continue their valuable work of informing the public especially at such a crucial time. Advertising was dropping so please could they be given some financial help?

But of course, says the Prime Minister and he gave them £35 million of our money for the first three months which is still continuing now in its 23rd month.

Brian Cathcart says it has been difficult to get information about it but it would be likely that the money went to the Mail group, the Murdoch group, the Telegraph group and the Mirror group. But when asking for details it was as though it was top secret. He was sent all round the houses and back again.

And of course all these groups are owned by billionaires of, as he says, dubious tax status, whereas it was, and still is, the smaller local independent publications who needed help but who were completely cut out of the 'All In, All Together' deal.

At the moment it is impossible to find out how much of our money was spent here as even under the Freedom of Information Act he was told that it would be too difficult to separate it from the rest of the money spent.

So now we know why the press keep letting Johnson off the hook. He is their friend.

****

15TH MAY

Oh dear what is this? The £500m household support fund which the government launched last year to help with the cost of living crisis and which was meant to last until the end of March, **ran out of money** in some local authorities by last December.

Not only that, but apparently the bureaucracy involved was so complicated that it also meant that many councils, which still had funding available, rejected more than a quarter of all applications.

Can we believe this? Yes we can.

****

As I am not a financial whizz kid (anything but, I hear my family cry) I look to those who are the financial experts and so once again I read David Smith in *The Sunday Times*. **Well it worries me, it should worry you and it should definitely be worrying the government.**

He begins his column today with the words, **"The economy is not so much falling off a cliff as entering a deep freeze, which unintentionally rhymes with one of the main causes, the cost-of-living squeeze."**

Consumer spending is down, business investment is now 9.1 % below pre-pandemic levels, government spending fell by 1.7% in the first quarter of this year and although investment spending by the government is up, as he says, "you cannot grow an economy on infrastructure alone."

But then he goes on to strike terror into our hearts when he says, **"I have left the worst until last and it is something of a horror story."**

"Export-led growth" he says "is the holy grail, the golden ticket for our economy. But it is not happening."

Exports are 19.9% down on pre-pandemic levels.

And whilst there are other factors involved, **Brexit, he says, is the main cause.**

"Whatever your views on Brexit, and I have made it clear over the years what I think of it, we should be able to agree that this was a terrible time to do it, let alone threaten a trade war now, which would compound one of the great political errors of our time."

He finishes this part of his column by saying, **"we are not going anywhere fast."**

Actually I do disagree with this last sentence. We are heading into oblivion at the **speed of lightning**. With plenty of thunder along the way.

****

16TH MAY

Did I say the government had no plan to ease the cost-of-living crisis? I was incorrect and I apologise. They do.

This is it:

Rachel Maclean, Tory MP for Redditch, **says that if you are poor you should work more hours or get a better job.**

Oh my goodness why did we not think of that?

I do find it interesting to note however that between 1st June 2020 and the 31st May 2021 **she claimed over £220,000 in expenses.**

And I also make no apologies for repeating a quote that I mentioned in '**Beneath the Bluster**'. You might have missed it.

It is by Nelson Mandela and he said, "Overcoming poverty is not a task for charity, it is an act of justice. Like slavery and apartheid, poverty is not natural, it is man-made and it can be overcome and eradicated by the actions of human beings."

I leave you to decide whose words you want to go with.

****

19TH MAY

Inflation reaches 9%, its highest point for 40 years. And according to the Bank of England's Monetary Policy Report published this month, it will only get worse.

In a speech to the CBI yesterday the Chancellor said that he is working on a plan (there isn't one). He said that a windfall tax, which they all voted against this week, would not be sensible (believe me they will U-turn on this any minute now) and he also said that the next few months will indeed be tough (but not, of course, for him).

Everyone is telling him that people need help NOW. But this government is completely bereft of ideas.

Indeed at PMQs yesterday, as Keir Starmer asked his six questions about the cost of living, the PM had nothing to say. He continues to bluster and shout and just accuses the opposition of being the party which puts up taxes which is such a lie.

John Crace of *The Guardian* agrees with me as he says the PM was completely bereft of ideas. He goes on to say, "This was deranged. Johnson is decomposing before our eyes. Being Prime Minister is something beyond his shallow talents. He can no longer cope. He was only ever in it for the good times. The parties. The status. The Being There. A tanking, stagflating economy and an imminent recession is beyond his compass."

He absolutely tells it as it is.

But listen to this:

The Chief Inspector of Constabulary, Andy Cooke, has said that the cost of living crisis will trigger an increase in crime. He had previously said that, "The impact of poverty, and the impact of lack of opportunity for people, does lead to an increase. There's no two ways about it."

He has said that officers should use their "discretion" when deciding whether to prosecute people who steal to eat.

I cannot believe I am writing these awful words.

But the policing minister, Kit Malthouse, has said these views are "old-fashioned thinking" and officers must not let shop-lifters off if they are caught stealing food out of desperation during the cost of living crisis.

So what does he advise? Bring them to the House of Commons and give them a slap up subsidised meal? No, I presume he means arrest them and let them and their families starve.

****

22ND MAY

Rishi Sunak is about to spend £500,000 of taxpayers' money for researchers to carry out two focus groups for him and one national online poll each week until February 2023. He is sparking a claim that he is trying to **"repair his image."**

I will just remind you of what he said a few days ago: 'He tells struggling families that it would be **"silly" to give them more financial help** with energy bills.'

****

23RD MAY

We are hoping that Johnson has spent the weekend at Westminster working out how to address the cost-of-living crisis. Windfall tax or no windfall tax? But no. We hear that he has been at his country estate Chequers working out how to save his skin when the Sue Gray report on Partygate is published as expected this week.

At the same time we hear today that the E.ON CEO called for the government to take action to support families on the knife edge of the cost of living crisis, although he stopped short of calling for a windfall tax.

He called for the "broadest shoulders" to bear the burden, telling the BBC: "The most important thing is that the government intervenes – it is up to the government to decide how they fund that."

Mr Lewis said the annual energy price cap could reach as high as £3,000 in the autumn, compared with the £1,277 that families were paying before April.

But as *The Independent* says, "Whether it's the windfall tax or a different measure, with the war in Ukraine continuing to impact food prices, the government will find little room to hide from implementing an emergency package to support struggling Britons."

****

26TH MAY

The Lib Dems and Labour have been calling for a **windfall tax** on energy companies for months now but when they forced a debate on it a few week ago **every single Tory MP voted against it**. They said that the enormous profits made by these companies were needed for further investment although the companies have actually said that they could cope with a tax such as this.

There is going to be a statement from the Chancellor later today when everyone is expecting a **screeching U-turn and a windfall tax to be implemented.** It just happens to be the day after the Sue Gray report and they so need to look like the good guys. (This report is discussed in the chapter on Johnson.)

But once again David Smith writing in *The Times* makes horrific reading. Basically he says that a windfall tax would give only temporary relief and would give the impression that Britain has become a less attractive place to do business. He says that they should borrow more instead and, as 'The Resolution Foundation' advises, increase Universal Credit and the employment and support allowances. They could also increase the pensioners' winter fuel allowance and give more generous warms homes discount. This would target those most in need.

Mind you I think the pensioners' winter fuel benefit should be means tested.

We hope that the sharpest minds in the government are working on this but it is a little bit worrying to read that one suggestion from a Downing Street source was to cut VAT on food. I think we all know that food is zero-rated.

Worrying, but sadly not surprising.

****

We have just heard the Chancellor's statement to the House. Would you believe it? **He has announced a 25% windfall tax on the energy companies.** Exactly what we all predicted.

He doesn't call it that mind you. He calls it a **"temporary targeted energy profits levy."** So a screeching U-turn about a week after the entire party voted against it saying it was "un-conservative". Amazing what some questions about parties can do.

Some Tory MPs are not happy about this as they say they were marched up the hill to vote against it and are now being marched down the hill.

He has also announced that the twice yearly £200 forced loan scheme initially promised, has been abandoned and will be a £400 grant to **every** household.

Why every household? I don't understand. It doesn't make sense to me. Surely this should have been targeted to those most in need. I also understand that if you have 2 or even 3 houses you will get £200 for each one. The Chancellor says he will be giving his to charity and urges all who can afford to, to do the same. Why? Is it a vote bribe to wealthy Tories do you think?

For 8 million people on lowest incomes there will be a one-off payment of £650.

For all pensioners there will be a one-off payment of £300 and for the disabled £150. What? £150 for the disabled? Defend that if you can.

So nothing much specifically targeted and mostly ideas that the Lib Dems and Labour have been asking for, for months.

Nothing about Universal Credit.

Far too little and far, far too late. Johnson managed to stay in the Commons for the Chancellor's statement looking dishevelled and unkempt but then dashed off before listening to the fiery reply from the Shadow Chancellor.

As she says the government are now implementing Labour policies.

****

27TH MAY
An interesting analogy by the Channel 5 television presenter, Marina Purkiss:

£400 for all households + £650 for the poorest = £1,050

Universal Credit cut of £20 a week.

£20 x 52 weeks = £1,040.

There you go. **You have £10 extra to spend.**

As she says....... don't spend it all at once.

****

30TH MAY

The Federation of Small Businesses say that they are facing a crisis unless more financial support from the government is forthcoming. Figures from The Office for National Statistics show that about 40%, that is 2 million of the UK's small business **have less than three months' worth of cash left. Some have only weeks left.** Their chairman, Martin McTague, said that without further support, the expensive emergency assistance used to keep businesses afloat through the Covid-19 pandemic would effectively be wasted.

"The chancellor spent approximately £45 billion making sure those businesses survived the Covid crisis," the chairman said. "Are we seriously expecting him now to abandon them just as they've managed to get through one crisis and effectively lose that money for the taxpayer?"

****

Swimming pools are also in trouble as, with the soaring price in energy levels, some will have to close.

Many are going to reduce opening hours, turn down the water temperature and ask swimmers to spend less time in the showers. Bu they are saying that unless there is government intervention many can't see a way through.

I just wish I could say that I am sure the government has all of this under control.

****

6TH JUNE

Labour MP, Siobhain McDonagh, asked some very pertinent questions of the Chancellor at a Treasury Committee meeting today. She was very concerned about the £400 which is going to every single household in the country.

She asked if he thought it was right that the 772,000 households who have second homes should receive £800 which altogether will cost the tax payer £620 million. **She also mentioned the £73 million that would be going to the 61,000 people who had three homes as they will get £1200 each.**

But I think that is a very good question. It is ridiculous to give all this money to people who do not need it when there are so many who do. He really did not answer the question.

****

7TH JUNE

The HS2 link to Scotland has just been scrapped but you might have missed this because everyone has been concentrating on the vote of confidence in Boris Johnson.

This link was designed to connect the existing west coast main line from Manchester to Glasgow and Edinburgh.

Engineers have warned against cancelling this link saying it "hobbles the value" of the HS2.

So whatever you think of the HS2 it would appear that this part would have been good value especially for the people of Scotland.

****

12TH JUNE

Rishi Sunak has been accused **of wasting £11billion of tax payers' money** by paying too much in interest on the government's debt. The National Institute of Economic and Social Research said that he had failed to insure against interest rate rises of £900 billion of reserves created through the quantitative easing programme.

Wow! Just think what our schools could have done with that.

Oh wait a minute. It has just been announced that the government is giving some money to schools as part of a new government food strategy to be announced tomorrow. It is designed to teach healthy eating and it is calling it a "school cooking revolution". But that is marvellous.

Until you look at the detail.

The overall budget is £5 million which works out at £250 per school.

Just in order to be helpful I have looked up the prices of some kitchen equipment as I am sure the school kitchens will be busy preparing the lunches with their new equipment.

I have no details but just to say that a five pan saucepan and frying pan set can cost up to £249.99.

But will there have to be new kitchens? How will it work exactly?

****

12TH JUNE

It has just been announced that a planned speech by the Chancellor and the Prime Minister about the economy has been delayed until next month. There is to be a series of international summits at the end of this month, including meetings of the G7 and NATO, and they want to leave this speech until after that.

They were all set to share with us their plans to boost the economy, which actually would be very welcome because the economy appears to be tanking at the moment. I acknowledge that this is not a very technical term and that I am not an economic statistician so let us see what the Office for National Statistics has to say.

Well they had been expected to confirm a slight rise in GDP in April but in actual fact the UK economy contracted by 0.3%.

Apparently a big drop in the health sector, due to the winding down of the test and trace scheme, pushed the economy into negative territory in April. Also some manufacturing companies suffered as they were affected by rising fuel and energy prices.

This is really serious and the CBI have demanded "vital actions" from the government in order to prevent an inflation driven recession. They call for measures to include steps to alleviate labour and skills shortages.

The trouble is that as we all know, and as Tony Danker director general of the CBI says most succinctly, "You have Conservative politicians pushing for their own ideological favourites in return for supporting the PM".

There is some supposition that the Chancellor and the PM have fallen out over all this but this has been strongly denied so ....it could be true. (It was!)

******

20TH JUNE

This evening the Tories held their annual summer ball at the Victoria and Albert museum. Tickets cost £2,000 per head. There were auctions for fabulous prizes in order to swell the Tory coffers. Here are some of them:-

- £30,000 for a wine tasting.
- £37,000 for a shooting weekend.
- £65,000 for a safari.
- £120,000 for a dinner with May, Cameron and Johnson. That one sounds fun.

Let us just remind ourselves that the budget for free school meals, at a time when the cost of living has rocketed through the roof and inflation has just reached a record high of 9.1%, has been increased by 7p. This means smaller portions and fewer ingredients.

Enjoy your meal Prime Minister.

****

22ND JUNE

There is a national train strike today with nurses, doctors, teachers, postal workers, criminal barristers and other key public sector workers also threatening strike action. This, at a time when Rishi Sunak is saying that there will have to be real pay cuts as soon as next month for all public sector workers. However the government is planning to relax control on City bosses' pay in order to reduce the overall burden in business and so 'attract more companies to the UK following Brexit.'

So as Sir Keir Starmer said in PMQs today we have a "pay rise for City bankers and a pay cut for district nurses."

****

27TH JUNE

Levelling up not going well. The 'Resolution Foundation' think-tank says that in order for levelling up to be successful it requires investment "far beyond anything currently being contemplated by the government."

****

28TH JUNE

Councils are going to be forced to rip up 'financial plans' as cost of living inflation adds £800 million to their cost so putting vital public services at risk.

James Jamison chair of the body representing local authorities says we must expect cuts to all of the following: bin collections, the filling of pot-holes, care for older and disabled people, the early intervention years, support for those on low incomes and homelessness prevention.

Carl Les, the financial spokesman of the County Council network says we "face a winter of difficult decisions."

Levelling up going well? Or do I keep saying that??

This is such a difficult time for so many people and all we hear about are arguments between the Treasury and other Ministers.

****

So let us take a close look at the Ministers in charge at the moment. Are they all at the top of their game? Who are they and what exactly are they doing?

******

SHUFFLE, SHUFFLE, SHUFFLE

2021

30TH NOVEMBER

You might have noticed that, unlike in my previous book, I have not been jumping up and own in exasperation at Gavin Williamson any more. That is because on the 15th September Boris Johnson reshuffled his cabinet and shuffled him well and truly out of the cabinet, to the relief of all concerned with education.

So how did the rest of the reshuffle go? Well it was really a game of musical chairs. Same suspects, new positions.

Robert Buckland, Justice Secretary had to go to make way for Dominic Raab our inadequate Foreign Secretary, who is now our inadequate Justice Secretary.

Liz Truss is now our Foreign Secretary replacing Dominc Raab. You may remember her, as, when she was Justice Secretary (for less than a year), she called our judges "the enemy of the people." If you don't remember that then please store it in your memory now, as she is one of the politicians that the Tories would like to replace Boris Johnson.

Oliver Dowden was moved from being Culture Secretary to party co-chairman and Minister without Portfolio.

Meanwhile Nadine Dorries was moved to Culture. In November 2012 she was temporarily suspended from the Conservative party after taking part in the reality TV programme "I'm A Celebrity Get Me Out Of here" without getting parliamentary approval.

She won't be a disappointment to all of us music and theatre lovers as we have absolutely zero expectations.

So an abysmal reshuffle and all goes on as before.

However today, Sir Keir Starmer has had a reshuffle of his own. Hooray, Yvette Cooper is on the shadow front bench at last. Also David Lammy and two young rising stars, Wes Streeting and Bridget Phillipson. These are all excellent politicians with brilliant debating skills and ideas and policies which I can relate to. Together, with people like Chis Bryant and Jess Phillips on the back benches, the disparity between them and the Conservatives is obvious.

****

2022

8TH FEBRUARY

Another mini- shuffle today in order to try to shore up the premiership of Boris Johnson. So many staff have just resigned from No.10 that others need to be brought in quickly from somewhere.

Jacob Rees-Mogg who was leader of the House has been made Minister for Brexit opportunities. **What**? What opportunities are those exactly? This is a non-job; a poisoned chalice. Quote: **"It will take 50 years to feel the benefits of Brexit,"** he said some time ago. As people are saying it might have been a good idea to have explored the opportunities before we voted.

And we know that he was able to benefit from Brexit by **relocating his City firm SCM to Dublin** due, he said, to Brexit causing "considerable uncertainty."

He has now **written to *The Sun* newspaper** asking readers to write in and tell him about "Any petty old EU regulations that should be abolished."

Well the backlash on social media has been fast and furious. I quote just two: Brendan May says "Congratulations to Jacob Rees-Mogg who has secured the only job so far created by Brexit".

Marinna Purkiss says: "1st day on the job as new Minister for Brexit Opportunities and Jacob Rees-Mogg has opted to delegate his entire role to ......*The Sun* readers."

You really couldn't make it up.

Chief whip **Mark Spencer** has been moved to Rees-Mogg's old job! But he is **undergoing an investigation** at the moment for his behaviour to a Muslim MP.

This shake-up was triggered by Mr Johnson's decision to appoint **Stephen Barclay** as chief of staff in No 10 as part of his promise to show that Downing Street was changing in the wake of the Partygate affair.

The appointment of a minister to a role normally held by a civil servant sparked concern that Mr Barclay would be unable to combine his new duties with the wide-ranging responsibilities of his other job of Chancellor of the Duchy of Lancaster. The civil servant job is usually very full time.

Chris Heaton – Harris, a Foreign office minister, is now Chief Whip. He is a flag waver for the Prime Minister and a firm Brexiteer.

Guito Harri (no I have no idea either) has been appointed as the new director of communications. Apparently he and Johnson go back a long way. He worked for Johnson when he was Mayor of London. But it is a very strange appointment because Harri has become very critical of Johnson recently.

He told Johnson to make a "grovelling apology" to the public over the Partygate scandal and he said that Downing Street needed to "get a grip" of the "toxic" affair. He also said that the public had a right to be angry about it all.

But there he is, in Downing Street, presumably because the PM thinks he can help him to stay there.

Labour's deputy leader Angela Rayner accused Johnson of **"reshuffling the deckchairs when he's already hit an iceberg,"** while ignoring debates called by Labour in the Commons today on the cost of living crisis and mental health.

In fact in the House today for this debate there were only 11 Conservative MPs.

This is the real scandal in my opinion. They are all so busy trying to defend the indefensible that they have no time to do the job they were elected to do which is to debate the important issues relating to the general public.

SNP deputy leader in Westminster, Kirsten Oswald said: **"No amount of shuffling the deckchairs on the Titanic can stop Boris Johnson's sleaze-ridden government from sinking further into chaos."**

And one MP told a BBC reporter that, "No 10 promised change. **Nothing has changed. The PM just makes it worse."**

Indeed the main change we need is a change of Prime Minister.

****

10TH FEBRUARY

There has been no attempt to unite the Conservative Party in this mini shuffle says Andrew Grice in a long article for *The Independent*. He writes **"Boris Johnson is in his bunker surrounded by the noisy Eurosceptics– and the end is nigh."** What a wonderful headline! But it is very true. No 'One Nation' former Remainers brought in, but then, sadly, we never expected that.

****

Richard Morris, the Arts critic in *The Times*, writes a whole article about **Nadine Dorries** today and it makes abysmal reading. As he so rightly says there has not been a minister for culture in living memory who has shown any interest in the arts whatsoever.

But Nadine!!!! She is beyond belief. "Scarcely a day passes" he writes, **"without another dotty Dorries decree lurching onto Twitter like a drunk staggering towards a bar-stool."** (I love his turn of phrase.)

He cites her announcement about the BBC licence fee last month when she tweeted that the next BBC licence fee settlement "will be the last."

So what would replace it? Oh goodness she hadn't thought of that. When confronted by MPs asking difficult question she frantically back-pedalled and said this was only about "discussion and debate".

Then she denounced nepotism in the arts appearing to forget that she had used £80,000 of public money to employ her own daughters in her parliamentary office.

And then this week she flew to Saudi Arabia to sign a "memorandum of understanding" intended to "strengthen ties" between the UK and Saudi Arabia in sports, tourism and the arts.

Richard Morrison asks **"what part of the Saudi mind-set does Dorries think is worth 'understanding?' Dismembering troublesome** journalists? Locking up intellectuals and campaigners for reform? Repressing women? Censoring the internet? Persecuting gay people? Public executions?"

He says we should enjoy this Dorries disaster show for as long as it lasts for like most of her predecessors she won't be around for long.

Please, please let it stop as soon as possible.

****

16TH MAY

The next reshuffle is likely to be just before the summer recess on the 21st July. The best move of course would be the downfall of Boris Johnson. Oh goodness I have been forecasting this for months.

I must be the worst forecaster in the world. But surely one day I could be right?

****

27TH JUNE

The PM is saying that there will not be another re-shuffle until the autumn.

I shan't say another word!

****

7TH JULY

I don't need to! Two have just resigned.

****

I think we need to find out how some of these ministers are settling in to their new roles. The criminal justice system is on its knees so

how is Dominic Raab, the new Justice Secretary working to improve things there I wonder?

****

THE CRIMINAL JUSTICE SYSTEM

More uncertainty and more underfunding and more ignorance and more neglect is to be found in our criminal justice system. This was once the gold standard for the rest of the world, but it continues its downward spiral, causing untold hardship to many barristers.

2021

18TH OCTOBER

In a report in *The Times* today by Jonathan Ames we hear that hundreds of barristers have left the criminal courts since 2016. He says that, "senior lawyers have told *The Times* that low legal aid rates, which means some defence barristers being paid below the minimum pay wage, and court delays because of Covid-19, have led to an exodus, particularly of young lawyers."

Well this is certainly not news to me. **Criminal barristers have been leaving the Bar in droves years before Covid 19 raised its ugly head.** I know because my son was one of them. In order to become a barrister you have to put in years of hard work, take loads of exams and suffer some disappointments along the way. But when you succeed in joining a Chambers it is a very rewarding and interesting career. You certainly do not give all this up lightly. But cast your minds back to one of the 8 Ministers of State for Justice that we have had over the last 12 years and you will come up with the name Chris Grayling. It was indeed he who began the devastating cuts to legal aid so started destroying the best criminal system in the world as my letters to *The Times* over the years would indicate.

The following letter was published on December 27th **2013**

Legal Jeopardy

Sir, You say ("Barrister say 'no' and put fraud trials in jeopardy", Dec 23rd) that 17 chambers have refused to provide barristers for a very complicated fraud case. What a disgraceful state of affairs. And how has this been allowed to happen? Cut after cut in legal aid, and a government and Justice Secretary who refuse to listen to genuine concerns from the legal profession. There has just been a vote of no confidence in the chief executive and president of the Law Society by the solicitors, and criminal barristers will be 'on strike' on January 6th. This from a profession who never normally get together to protest. What more do they have to do to underline the seriousness of their concerns that the best legal system on the world is now under threat?

And then there was this one published on 8th August **2014.**

Crisis at the Bar

Sir, We really do need to tell young people not to do a law degree at all if they think it is going to lead to employment at the Bar.

It will indeed be a waste of money. Defence barristers are leaving the Bar in droves, because it is such a shambles. Cuts in legal aid, late payment for work done years ago, inefficiency by the CPS, all contribute to a profession in crisis.

It is becoming impossible to make a living at the Bar unless you are one of the very few at the top.

Well of course I can't put all this at Johnson's door but it has been a Conservative government, for the last 12 years and the Tories continue to look upon the Justice Secretary as a really unimportant job.

Dominic Raab is now the 10th Justice Secretary since Lord Falconer in 2007. The longest any politician who has been in the job since then was the Labour MP Jack Straw at 2 years and 10 months. Liz Truss was there for just over 10 months and David Liddington was there for just over 6 months. Dominic Raab was **demoted** to the position from Foreign Secretary just over a month ago.

This is one reason why our prisons are the most appalling prisons in Europe and are the most in need of complete reform.

No-one has the time to even think about that.

There is now a backlog of over 60,000 criminal cases in the crown courts.

It really is a disgrace. You should be warned that if you are ever a victim of a crime or if you are ever arrested by the police for something that you didn't do, just be prepared to defend yourself in court. **There will not be an available barrister to represent you.**

****

22ND NOVEMBER

Dominic Raab, has been accused of **neglecting the problems in the criminal courts,** of which there are many, as it would appear that up to **20 percent of criminal law barristers have left the profession since the beginning of the pandemic.**

A member of the Bar council said that, "The shrinking of the profession is making it very difficult to service criminal trials."

So where exactly is our justice secretary in all of this? Well he is no-where to be seen. A council member said that Raab **continued "not to respond"** to requests for a meeting. Then at the Bar Council's Annual conference at the weekend he did **not bother to show up at all.** Instead, he sent a recorded video message which failed to address what many lawyers are saying is a growing crisis.

****

25TH NOVEMBER

Today we hear that there has been a **rise in prosecution cases of sexual offences** and of other violence against the person. However experts warn that not all the money put in recently was new funding and the rise in prosecutions was the result of the current figures being compared with the situation during lockdown last year. Rebecca Hitchen of the 'End Violence Against Women Coalition' says that, "while these increases in prosecutions are welcome, they cannot be seen as a success, given they fall well below the level of prosecution we saw in 2016, which the government and the CPS have set as targets for prosecution sexual offences. **In this context we see declining numbers across the board.**"

And Jo Sidhu QC Chairman of the Criminal Bar Association points to recent data from the Ministry of Justice showing that just because a prosecution begins does not mean that it concludes. **In the three months to last June 1st, 307 trials concluded but 1,479 were postponed.**

He goes on to refer Dominic Raab to a recent annual report from Lord Burnett of Maldon, the Lord Chief Justice which said that, **"the courts are not a service like any other. They do not exist simply to provide a service to those who use them. They are one of the foundations of the rule of law and one of the building blocks on which civil society and economic activity rests."**

Sadly I do not think that Dominic Raab, or many people in our present government, understand this sort of language.

******

2022

3RD JANUARY

The year begins with Dominic Raab displaying yet again his unsuitability for the role of Justice Secretary. Last month Raab, said in the Commons that it was "widespread practice" for defence lawyers to encourage their clients to wait until being in court before pleading guilty or not guilty. This was absolutely rejected by lawyers with one accusing Raab of, "an attempt to play to the anti-lawyer gallery". And a letter in *The Times* today from a circuit judge emphasises the point that **what Raab says is completely untrue.**

Raab needs to get a grip with this new role and try to understand the workings of the criminal justice system, and come to terms with the fact that due to extensive cuts in legal aid we now have a criminal justice system which is not fit for purpose.

Junior barristers have left in droves, many court buildings are crumbling away and the backlog of cases is at an unprecedented high. I am afraid it is obvious though that there is no-one in the present government, and least of all Mr. Raab, who has any idea of the way in which our criminal justice system works. **It used to be considered the gold standard of the world but now it is stumbling along with no funding, no support, no interest and absolutely no concern.**

****

7TH JANUARY

A report in *The Times* today by the Home Affairs editor Matt Dathan, states that the **Ministry of Justice wasted £160 million of tax payers money** last year. This is 14 times the amount for the previous year. The ministry's annual accounts show that losses were driven by an expenditure of £98.2 million to develop an electronic tagging system that the Prison and Probation Service eventually scrapped.

A further £14 million was paid to companies that used local probation services after their contracts were broken early, even though they failed to meet targets to reduce re-offending.

The Courts and Tribunals Service spent a further £18 **million** on a digital case management system for court staff which has led to strike threats over its poor performance.

I hope you are keeping up with all of this.

But I have to quote a spokesman from the **parallel universe of the Ministry of Justice** when he says, "Achieving value for money for tax-payers is a key consideration in all decision making."

Not according to the annual accounts it's not. He goes on to say, "We have improved public safety by bringing forward reforms designed to help protect the public by reducing re-offending, cutting crime and providing swift access to justice."

What???? There are about 60,000 crown court cases waiting to be heard nationally at the moment. There is certainly no swift access to justice. Who **are** these people I would like to know?

****

18TH JANUARY

Our Justice Secretary has just come up with a new idea. He will announce today that magistrates will be given new powers to hand out tougher sentences and be able to send offenders to prison for a year rather than just 6 months. This is in order to try to reduce the appalling backlog of cases in the crown courts. (Which they continue to deny.)

Well at first glance you might think that that could be a good idea. But then you might think, perhaps we should explore it in a bit more detail because it is Dominic Raab we are talking about here.

And indeed campaigners are saying that it is the height of irresponsibility and will stretch the prison population to breaking point.

Jo Sidhu QC, said: "Increasing magistrates' sentencing powers will do nothing to unplug the existing massive backlog of trials stuck in the crown court pipeline. This is distraction politics at its worst. The government seems wilfully blind to the stark reality **that hundreds of criminal barristers have left the field in despair due to a quarter century of falling real incomes**. That is the reason why victims of serious crime are being denied justice in our crown courts."

Indeed many are saying that it is the **draconian cuts in legal aid** that is the basic cause of backlogs and it has just been exaggerated by the pandemic.

And Jo Sidhu goes on to say, "Fiddling with magistrates' sentencing powers is a betrayal of victims of crime. **This is a cynical means of depriving those accused of serious crime from being judged by their peers in our long-established jury system.**

"It is also quite possible that the changes may prompt more defendants to elect trial in the crown court, increasing the trial backlog. This would damage the interests of complainants and victims and be **counterproductive to everything we are trying to achieve to deliver timely and fair justice.**"

Magistrates are obviously excellent in what they do and apparently have been campaigning for this change for a while. But it is thought that many defendants will prefer to be tried by their peers with a jury.

But time will tell what the outcome will be here.

****

21ST JANUARY

Well Mr. Raab is trying hard to do things but it is difficult to know if they are going to work or not. His department has just introduced new x-ray scanners in prisons to detect and prevent drugs, weapons and phones being smuggled in. The trouble is that according to an analysis of the MoJ figures by the Labour party they are only detecting a quarter of the number of contraband items being found in **manual checks** by prison officers. **They have spent £100 million on them so they really do need to make sure that they work.**

Money is no object here obviously.

****

30TH JANUARY

I have been a member of the Howard League for Penal Reform for over 25 years. I first became interested and concerned about the way we treat our children in Young Offenders Institutes after seeing a television programme about Feltham YOI. The way these children, for that is what they were, were being treated was appalling. The physical and verbal abuse from the officers in charge was frightening. So when I see an article in *The Observer* today by Nick Cohen about an 18 year old committing suicide whilst in prison and awaiting trial it reminded me of another case many years ago of a 16 year old committing suicide whilst also on remand.

Obviously the pandemic has had a serious effect on all those in prison. Being kept in cells for 23 hours a day slowed the spread of the virus but it caused severe mental health problems. Many inmates have been pushed to the edge and over it. **The authorities apparently don't keep decent records because they know that the public doesn't care.**

But Nick Cohen relates the story of Charlie and it makes very disturbing reading. Charlie was awaiting trial for burglary and a more serious wounding charge. Prosecutors later dropped the wounding allegation so the chances were that he wouldn't have been charged and so wouldn't have received a custodial sentence. Charlie's mother described "a handsome, loving boy who loved to tell a story and would put a smile on the face of anyone who met him."

As Nick Cohen says the prisons are full of inmates like him **on remand or serving pointless and dangerous short sentences.** He goes on to quote Rory Stewart, who, as prison minister, with his then boss David Gauke, tried to limit the abuse that he saw in the prison system. **Rory Stewart said that nothing he had seen in Afghanistan or Iraq was "so screwed" as the prison system he saw here.** "Violence had tripled to 30,000 assaults a year, every institution was over crowded, filthy and rat and drug infested." He went on to say that in the poor world, prisons were relatively open. Inmates could leave cells. Their families could bring food. **Here he found only neglect.**

Of course we remember that Stewart and Gauke, two really good politicians who wanted to work hard on prison reform, were driven out of Parliament by our Prime Minister because they were not in favour of Brexit.

And as Nick Cohen goes on to say, "Johnson has a reverse Midas touch, however: everything he touches turns to dirt".

Well in all my writings for this book I have to agree.

Nick Cohen wants to make you care and so do I. So I am including a poem I wrote some years ago. Johnson was not PM of course but it was a time of Tory rule.

A 16 year old boy commits suicide whilst in prison on remand

NOBODY'S CHILD

I warn you, don't try to push me around,
Others have done it, but I've always found
That they soon back down when I kick and I bite
When I throw things and swear and I shout and I fight.
I know I'm aggressive, I know that I'm wild
But I'll stand on my own; for I'm nobody's child.

*

One day they tell me, someone out there
Will want me, and love me, and tell me they care.
Meanwhile, they threaten, they plead and they frown
Now just you conform they say - just you calm down.
They have to be joking; I'm not meek and mild
I'm me - and I'm scared, for I'm nobody's child.

*

The bang of the door, the turn of the key
The mind doesn't function, this cannot be me.
Someone will come, it's a game, it's not real
I'll try not to show the panic I feel
For I'm locked up in prison, hated, reviled,
I'm lonely, alone, and I'm nobody's child.

*

I'm beaten, exhausted, I feel sick with fear,
I'm cornered, confused, for there's nobody here
Who will hug me and hold me and give me some hope.
This place is hell, I don't think I can cope -
I feel filthy and tainted, disgusting, defiled,
No-one will love me; I'm nobody's child.

*

I'm finished with anger, aggression and strife
There's nothing to live for, I've hated my life
I've no more bravado, no tears left to cry.
I'm only sixteen and I now want to die.
They will close my case-history --- all neatly filed
And no-one will mourn; for I'm nobody's child.

*

Please care.

****

3RD FEBRUARY

Well, well this Tory government is really scared of Sir Keir Starmer. **They are presenting lie after lie in order to try to discredit him.** And the interesting thing is, that the more they do this the more we hear of the brilliance of Sir Keir and of the amazing things he did whilst Director of Public Prosecutions.

On the *Today* programme two days ago Dominic Raab said:

"I think it is quite right to look at Keir Starmer's record between 2008 and 2010 "Conviction rates for sexual offences and rape fell between 2008 and 2010."

Well he really needs to think very carefully before he says such monstrous untruths.

He has been fiercely criticised by women's campaigners. Harriet Wistrich, who is an award-winning human rights lawyer and director of the 'Centre for Women's Justice,' told *The Independent*: "The important point to make is Keir Starmer did a huge amount of work to **improve prosecution of rape and sexual offences.** He was quite revolutionary as a Director of Public Prosecutions in that respect. **He did far more than other DPPs to improve the prosecution approach to rape and sexual offences."**

And in June last year the government apologized to rape victims for declining conviction levels, with senior Cabinet ministers saying they're "deeply ashamed" by the downward trend in bringing sexual offenders to justice.

Only 1.6 per cent of rapes recorded by the police are currently prosecuted in England and Wales – the lowest proportion for any crime.

Indeed it is all documented in '**Beneath the Bluster'** on page 106. I write that **"only 1.4% of rape cases in England and Wales recorded by the police resulted in a suspect being charged."**

Meanwhile, Jess Phillips, Shadow Minister for Domestic Violence and Safeguarding, also hit out at Raab's comments on Twitter.

"You have a serious nerve trying to use falling rape conviction when your government has basically overseen total degradation of rape charging," the Labour MP said. "Since you have been justice secretary sexual violence conviction has fallen. More rapists left on our streets. Cheers."

How does he think he can get away with telling blatant lies like this and not be held to account by some very angry people?

****

And then also today we hear that **Boris Johnson and Priti Patel are being reported to the head of the Official Statistics Watchdog for falsely claiming that crime has fallen.** The PM actually said in the House on Monday that "we have been cutting crime by 14 per cent."

However this does not include crimes of fraud which when they are included **overall crime has actually increased by 14 per cent.**

I think I have run out of words!

****

4TH FEBRUARY
Oh no I haven't!!

It is reported this morning that the UK Statistics Authority **concluded that both Johnson and Patel had presented figures in a "misleading way".**

Alistair Carmichael the Liberal Democrats' home affairs spokesman said that "it was a damning verdict" and one which warranted an apology from the PM.

Well that won't happen.

****

11TH FEBRUARY
Oh my goodness what on earth is this I am seeing? There is an article in *The Times* today by the Education Secretary Nadhim Zahawi and, wait for it, Dominic Raab our Justice Secretary. And credit where credit is due it looks like good news. Well we really are in need of that just now.

They say that they are working to offer apprenticeship to offenders who are out on day release or nearing the end of their sentence so that they are job-ready when they leave prison. They also say that new prisons are being built with in-cell technology and modern workshops to equip offenders with skills they need and which businesses want.

Fantastic. I don't want to denigrate that in any way. But I can't help feeling that at the same time they should be saying to Sir Kevan Collins, here is the money you asked for in order to support and sustain our education system. There needs to be much more help for people **before** they get involved with crime.

****

17TH FEBRUARY

Well the good news doesn't last for long of course. **The criminal justice system, as I have implied before, is facing a complete collapse**. The fact that this is not, and never has been, main news is very disturbing. As over a quarter of junior criminal barristers along with nearly half of all silks have left criminal practice in the past five years so we hear that **194 criminal trials had to be abandoned from their start dates between July and September 2021 because there was either no prosecution or no defence advocate available**. One quarter of those trials were for serious sex and violence offenders. The year before only six trials across England and Wales were shelved because of shortages of advocates. But by last July ministers knew shortages were mounting fast as 52 trials had to be abandoned in just the previous three months. There is real concern that victims of rape and other sexual offences are having to wait up to five years from recording a crime to a concluded trial.

Jo Sidhu QC writes in *The Times* today that criminal advocates have seen **a drop of 40% in real-term earnings which is the direct result in cuts to legal aid** and a failure to pay for the dozens of extra hours worked to meet the demands of cases and courts buckling under increased pressure. And of course there has been no regard to inflation.

But a statement from the Ministry of Justice said that the reason for the abandoned trials was because lawyers had Covid, were self-isolating or were involved with other trials which had overrun.

You see? This is what we are dealing with. **Not only are they in a parallel universe, they are on another planet.** They close their eyes to the actual problem and don't even acknowledge it.

So if they don't understand the problem they can never do anything about it.

Dominic Raab has today pleaded for patience while he tries to get his brain around it all but it is now **four years since an independent**

review into criminal legal aid was first committed to by ministers. How long does his brain need?

As Jo Sidhu writes "The government's actions are causing the criminal justice system to grind to a halt before the Criminal Bar has even held a ballot on whether to take its own action. **If Raab delays his action on addressing the legal aid funding, the criminal justice system will die a needlessly painful death.**"

****

19TH FEBRUARY

We need to get more detail about what I thought was good news when writing on the 11th February. I know I was desperate to write about something positive but sadly I was too hasty. These new prisons are not going to replace the battered, disgusting and unacceptable Victorian prisons but instead there will **actually be 4,000 new prison places as the government plans for a 25% increase which could take the prison population to an all-time high.**

We already imprison more people than any other European country and it will cost the tax payer over £43,000 a year for each and every prisoner. Are you happy with that? About the same cost as a year at Eton. This is a huge admission of failure by the Ministry of Justice.

Peter Dawson, director of the Prison Reform Trust, said: "Endlessly making the same announcement about building new prison spaces is not going to solve the chronic failure of our prison system. **For 30 years overcrowding and the continued use of prisons built in the 19th century have made a mockery of promises of reform. Nothing in the government's plans changes that.**"

****

But I have just been looking at the web site of the Howard League for Penal Reform and reading some reports of prison inspections and I think they are so important that I need to quote some of them here.

Foston Hall is a women's prison and was visited last November with the report being published on the 9th February. They found that conditions had deteriorated during the pandemic and women were routinely locked in their cells for 24 hours a day at weekends. Use of force by staff had doubled and violence and self-harm incidents were high.

Andrea Coomber Chief Executive of the Howard League said,

"Such a horrifying account of extreme mental distress and self-harm makes clear why ministers should abandon their plans to build 500 more prison places and return instead to the strategy the government published in 2018, focused on keeping women out of a failing system that is designed for men.

A decade and a half on from the Corston report, these findings are a massive indictment of the failure to act to keep women safe."

Chelmsford prison is a prison for men and was visited last August with the report published on the 24th November. It was found to be holding more than 700 men in overcrowded conditions with **piled up rubbish and an infestation of rats.**

Andrew Neilson Director of Campaigns at the Howard League said, "This is one of the worst prison inspection reports that we have seen in recent years.

It is almost impossible to appreciate the sheer scale of human misery that lies within a rat-infested, violent, overcrowded prison, where hundreds of men are left to suffer in their cells for hours on end by disengaged and demoralised staff who show next to no concern for their needs.

The only answer is to reduce the number of people held behind bars and take bold action to reshape a prison system which is failing prisoners, staff, and the country at large."

And **Cookham Wood prison is a Young Offenders Institute** which was also visited last August with the report published on the 16th November.

Inspectors visited the prison in August this year while it was holding 87 boys aged 15 to 18. They found that the children were locked up for most of the day with little to do, **in conditions even worse than when the watchdog last inspected the prison in 2019.**

Andrew Neilson said, "When a child is in trouble, we should do all we can to keep them safe, guide them away from crime and give them a brighter future. This does not happen in Cookham Wood, where boys are held in their cells for hours on end and exposed to violence and abuse. Even when the prison is only half-full, the environment is so toxic as to create more crime and distress. **It is no place for a child.**

It is time for a new approach that stops children being hurt and helps them to realise their potential. It starts with keeping them out of prison and giving them the care and support they need."

Just to re-iterate: Dominic Raab wants to **increase** the prison population. I am about to write to the Ministry for Justice and include these reports because I am absolutely convinced that they cannot have read them.

****

14TH MARCH
Criminal barristers have voted overwhelmingly to take industrial action over levels of legal aid funding next month.

94% of barristers voted in favour of refusing to accept returns – which is where a barrister steps in to represent a defendant whose original barrister is unable to attend court because his previous case has over-run. This action will begin on 11th April.

The Criminal Bar Association describes the usual acceptance of returns as "a gesture of goodwill to prop up the criminal justice system." Well, all good will has disappeared because of the way they have been treated by this government and by successive Justice Secretaries.

The CBA has expressed concerns that the minimum increase recommended by the review is insufficient and that barristers may not see any real increase in their legal aid fee income until 2024.

But by then there will be very few criminal barristers left and what used to be the gold standard criminal justice system will be broken beyond repair.

****

11TH APRIL

The industrial action of criminal barristers begins today. Jo Sidhu spoke on the *Today* programme this morning and expressed his concern about the exodus of barristers. As he said, a junior barrister starting out on his career earns about £12,000 a year after he has paid all of his expenses. The pay increase offered by the Secretary of State is completely inadequate.

The backlog continues.

****

26TH APRIL

A report in *The Times* today by Matt Dathan states that a **police station is being closed once every fortnight.** 217 stations have shut since 2015 when the coalition government came to an end.

And you may remember that by 2016 over 20,000 police officers had been cut from the force. At the 2019 general election Boris Johnson said he would recruit 20,000 police officers so bringing it back to the 2016 count. Well so far he has recruited 11,000.

Ed Davy leader of the Lib-Dems said that "shuttered police stations have become a symbol of the Conservatives' failure on crime. Too many people feel unsafe on their own streets, and too many criminals are getting away with it."

****

5TH MAY

Barristers and the Law Society are criticising Mr Johnson for his remarks about "left-wing lawyers" which was the headline in *The Mail*. Legal action is being taken over the Rwanda idea for asylum seekers. As The Secret Barrister says **"Only plans which breach the law are at risk from lawyers, left wing or otherwise."**

Stephanie Boyce, President of the Law Society says that this is "misleading and dangerous." She says that, "Attacks like this from the highest politician in the land undermines the rule of law and has real life consequences."

I say be careful Mr. Johnson because you might need a lawyer sooner than you think.

****

18TH MAY

This sounds like a power grab to me.

Priti Patel announced an independent review after the ousting of Cressida Dick the Metropolitan Police Commissioner. **She wants to know whether the Mayor of London, Sadiq Khan, has too much influence in the hiring and removing of Police Commissioners.** Dick's deputy has apparently accused the Mayor of not following due process.

It is his job, however, to hold the Met to account, and any diminishing of his role would be likely to cause real anger at City Hall and would actually need legislation.

Also today Priti Patel has written a letter to the police forces lifting restrictions on stop and search powers. They will be able to stop and search even if there is no expectation of serious violence.

And yesterday she gave her annual speech to the Police Federation. Goodness it was long. But she was confronted by a detective who said, **"I have never known it to be this bad in 23 years of service. I have never felt this poor."**

Steve Hartshorn, head of the Police Federation, said, "It angers me to hear good and experienced people talking about leaving the job--- not because they want to, but because they can't afford not to."

****

And so we hear of a new three word slogan from the prime minister which he blustered out at a cabinet meeting yesterday and which would be laughable if it wasn't so serious.

Here it is: **"Crime, Crime, Crime."**

Well good luck with that one. As we have seen, the criminal bar is in melt down and barristers have left in droves. The number of criminal cases waiting for trials could reach 195,000 by 2024. The police force is under staffed and under resourced. Police stations are closing all over the UK. Prisons are bursting at the seams.

Maybe, people are saying, he should look close to home and start with the Tory party. There is plenty of crime there.

100 fines and fixed penalty notices, about to break the Northern Ireland Treaty, lying to Parliament and then this:

Yesterday we hear that a Tory MP has been arrested for alleged crimes of sexual harassment, bullying, inappropriate behaviour in a public place and rape.

Yes crime indeed and plenty of it in Westminster.

He really does not have a clue.

****

30TH MAY

A report in *The Times* today re-emphasises what we already know. The severe lack of judges, prosecutors and defence lawyers is a deliberate policy of under-funding by this government. Poor pay means that fewer young barristers are attracted to criminal work and the lack of judges is now at the highest level in eleven years.

In the last three months 280 serious offence trials were delayed at the last moment compared with the same period in 2020 when only four trials were cancelled **because there was no judge available.**

In the interests of fairness I quote a Ministry of Justice spokeswoman who said the Criminal Bar Association's interpretation of this data was inaccurate and that 'cases were postponed for a number of reasons (oh so she agrees they were postponed) including everyone having to self-isolate if ill with Covid. (But I thought the pandemic was over.) "All cases involved have since been heard or **will be in due course,"** she added.

If you are in any doubt whatsoever as to whom to believe here then I refer you to the book "**Nothing But the Truth**" just published, by The Secret Barrister.

****

7TH JUNE

We hear today from the chief inspector of prisons Charlie Taylor. He is very concerned about what he calls the post-pandemic torpor of prisoners as workshops and classrooms continue to be empty as lockdown style approaches to prison management had remained in place due largely to lack of staff. Prisoners are whiling their time away watching television and sleeping and such boredom is not conducive to rehabilitation.

He spoke to an audience in Middle Temple and told them there "will be a price to pay".

****

11TH JUNE
Criminal barristers are to vote today on whether to support full strike action.

****

15TH JUNE
Yesterday lawyers managed to stop the flight to Rwanda, with asylum seekers on board, at the very last minute. The European Court of Human Rights pronounced it illegal.

Today Mr. Johnson has suggested that lawyers representing refugees were "abetting the work of criminal gangs."

Also today the Bar Council and Law Society of England and Wales issued a joint statement condemning the "misleading and dangerous" comments from the Prime Minister.

They call on the Prime Minister to stop attacks on legal professionals who are simply doing their jobs."

If this Prime Minister is stopped by anyone from doing exactly what he wants, whenever he wants, whether it breaks the law or not, he attacks anyone in his reach and tries to change the laws. He is getting more and more dangerous and deranged.

****

20TH JUNE
Criminal barristers will strike for three days a week for four weeks.

40% of junior barristers have left the profession in one year.

Specialist criminal barristers in their first three years of practice can expect to earn a median income of £12,200. This is below the minimum age and is not sustainable.

The criminal justice system is collapsing and requires immediate and major investment to survive. For the Bar to strike just shows how desperate the situation is.

But with Dominic Raab as the Justice Secretary I can't see any help forthcoming.

****

27TH JUNE
Today criminal barristers strike. I understand that they are in fact striking for two days this week, three days next week, four days the week after that and a whole week during the fourth week.

They are protesting outside courts in London, Birmingham, Bristol, Leeds, Cardiff and Manchester.

So what is our Minister for Justice doing about it?

Well Dominic Raab calls the strikes "regrettable." He also says that only 43.5% of barristers voted for the strike and that they should be happy to accept the 15% or £7,000 pay rise they have been offered.

The trouble with this Mr Raab, is that that is all a complete lie.

As The Secret Barrister says in fact 81.5% voted to take strike action and there has been **NO** offer of a pay rise whatsoever.

I would like to ask a question Mr Raab. Why do you think these barristers are going on strike if all is well? Why would they stop doing the job they love and for which they have worked so hard unless they were extremely worried about the future?

They call it a last resort. Is it too much to hope that you could actually meet them and talk to them and above all to listen to them?

****

18TH JULY
A prison doctor has written a disturbing article for *the i* in which he describes how sending people to prison creates 'career criminals'.

Dr Shahed Yousaf says that the reason prison so often fails to rehabilitate prisoners is because prisons become "a breeding ground for crime, radicalisation, substance misuse, mental health issues, self-harm, rape, suicide and murder."

He cites cuts in prison officers, and cuts in budgets, to which I would add zero concern.

****

The future of our criminal justice system looks bleak. Strike action by criminal barristers is unprecedented. And the state of our prisons is completely ignored. Have you seen any of this in the main news?

No-one is interested. No-one cares.

****

The next two chapters emphasises the attitude this government has to some of the most vulnerable in our society. Women and children are at the bottom of the pile and are treated with disdain and indifference over and over again.

WOMEN

2021

13TH NOVEMBER

We have to talk about Priti Patel.

As part of her strategy to tackle violence against women and girls launched in July of this year, she promised a "**multimillion communications campaign with a focus on targeting perpetrators and harmful misogynistic attitudes.**" So far so good. However I see that it is being delayed and won't be launched now until next year. It is still apparently at the "concept" stage. I presume that means that no-one thinks it is sufficiently urgent to push it forward.

5TH DECEMBER

This goes back to one of my stories at the beginning of this book. A report in *The Observer* today by Nic Murray and Hannah Summers states that pregnant women in prison are five times more likely to have a still birth and twice as likely to give birth to a premature baby that needs special care.

This week the House of Lords prepares to vote on proposed changes to bail and sentencing laws that would improve the rights of pregnant women and mothers facing criminal charges. If amendments to the Police, Crime, Sentencing and Courts bill are passed judges will be required to state how the best interests of a child or unborn baby are considered, when sentencing a pregnant woman or primary carer.

I do not know how it can ever be morally correct to imprison a pregnant woman. Janey Starling, co-director of the campaign group 'Level Up,' said changes to bail and sentencing laws were long overdue. "Prison" she says, "will never be a safe place for pregnant women and new mothers, and the government must change the law to stop their imprisonment."

I will certainly keep an eye out for this amendment.

****

2022

18TH JANUARY

And I see that a new report came out yesterday called "**Why are Pregnant Women in Prison?**" and it is calling for alternatives to custodial sentencing for pregnant women. Again please remember the story at the very beginning of this book about a pregnant woman giving birth to a dead baby in prison with no help or support whatever. I ask how many pregnant women are in prison and the answer I find out is that about 600 pregnant women enter prison each year and about 50 are in prison at any one time.

The lead author of this report, Rona Epstein of Coventry University, said the imprisonment of pregnant women was ""unnecessary" and called for the use of community orders or suspended sentences instead. "The women we surveyed arrived in prison with a variety of complex needs stemming from poverty, homelessness, domestic violence and substance misuse," she said. **"The prison environment only adds another layer of trauma for these women and can be dangerous for the unborn child."**

Nearly all pregnant women sent to prison have committed non-violent crimes.

Many countries around the world already have laws to prevent pregnant women from going to prison such as Russia, Brazil, Mexico and Columbia.

Obviously the UK has not yet caught up with this humane treatment of pregnant women.

The woman whose baby died in prison is bringing a law suit for breaches of human rights and discrimination because she did not receive the same standard of care as she could expected in the community. She told *The Observer*, "I need accountability and I need to get justice for my daughter."

But of course we know that the **Ministry of Justice are building 500 new prison places for women** and they say that "Our new prison places will give them (women) greater access to education, healthcare and employment and we are introducing specialist mother and baby liaison officers across the estate."

Well doesn't that sound marvellous?

But the chief executive of the charity 'Women in Prison', Kate Paradine, said: **"There is another way – when women are supported in the community**, they have better access to care and can tackle the issues that sweep them into crime in the first place, like trauma, domestic abuse and poverty."

How much more sensible and humane to give these women help **before** they are forced to resort to minor criminal offences. It would be much cheaper for the tax payer as well.

As I have said before, and will no doubt go on saying, many, many sentences are short enough to warrant a community sentence, but if spent in prison, it is long enough to destroy a woman's life and expose her and her new born baby to the risks of the prison system.

I honestly cannot believe that this country is prepared to spend a lot of money in order to be able to send often heavily pregnant women to prison when it could be better spent in the community.

****

23RD JANUARY

Six months have passed since the Home Secretary announced a **major strategy designed to tackle the growing problem of violence against women**. This was called for after the murder of Sarah Everard and called for again after the murder of primary school teacher Ashling Murphey in Ireland just over a week ago.

Campaigners are saying a number of central pledges have disappeared without trace or have not been implemented without proper explanation.

Women's groups argue that they do not know what has happened to a £5 million **"safety of women at night fund"** or another £3 million to "better understand what works to prevent violence against women and girls".

We would also like to know what has happened to the **StreetSafeapp** which allows women to record where and when they feel unsafe. A three month pilot scheme ended in early December but there has been no sight of it as yet.

So much money is being spent on reports and discussion but absolutely no sight of any action.

****

[Russia invades Ukraine]

24TH FEBRUARY

During the pandemic women were able to purchase the two pills necessary for a home termination of an unwanted pregnancy after a phone consultation instead of, as previously, a visit to a clinic. All medics and women's groups have said that this was safe, effective and often preferred by those facing terminations. This will be extended for another six months but will then be scrapped by the government in the autumn.

This will then mean that a woman can only take the **second** pill at home provided the first is administered at a clinic following a consultation. The Church of England is worried that by doing it all at home, women's ages are not being verified and also no one knows how far along in their pregnancy they are.

Well presumably the woman concerned will know.

But of course we live in a society where women are infantilized and men make the rules. As for the Church of England, their history of the subordination of women is legendary.

So once again it is deemed acceptable for those in government to have control over women's reproductive rights.

The abortion issue goes on and on, particularly in America, and I know that my anger does not really come across on this page. This is because I have been angry for so long that I am beyond anger.

In my poetry writing days back in the 1990s I wrote the following poem with this introduction.

Dr. N.J. Berrill (my father's elder brother and my Uncle Jack) was a Professor of Zoology at McGill University in Montreal and a Fellow of the Royal Society of London and Canada. He was an author of many books.

On the cover of "The Person in the Womb" are these three statements:--

No child must be born without hope--

No woman must bear a child against her will—

And the sons of men must not overwhelm the earth.

This is my poem:

ABORTION

Please do not try to tell me what to do
How to live my life, what to believe.
By what authority, what right have you
To force your mind on mine?
Can't you perceive
The everlasting anguish it can cause
The gross invasion of my privacy
If you insist on passing laws
Affecting my body; Affecting me.

No —one has abortion without sorrows
But no-one else has any right to take
Decisions for me about all my tomorrows
Because of one unfortunate mistake.
If I get pregnant, I will then decide---
Do you not understand, can you not clearly see?
I know if it is time to have a child
Affecting my future; Affecting me.

If you so hate abortion, then you're right
To have your babe whenever you conceive.
But if you force your views on me I'll fight,
I'll break the law and do what I believe.
You'd send us all to back streets once again
Condemned to loneliness and utter misery
To dirt and blood and death and gnawing pain
Affecting my body; Affecting me.

Babies have rights too, indeed I know
They must be wanted, planned for carefully
So when they're born they too can live and grow
Surrounded by love and in security,
So pregnancy can be a time that's full
Of peace, contentment and tranquillity
And birth—life's most wondrous miracle
Affecting our future; Affecting me.

****

4TH MARCH

There is an article today in *The Guardian* by Polly Toynbee which draws our attention to the plight of single mothers and their fight to get maintenance for their children. She has been following the actions of the Child Support Agency (now called the Child Maintenance Service) since its conception in 1993.

As she states, "There is a deep political, cultural and legal bias that lets fathers get away with it. It's the same women-are-to-blame instinct that tilts the benefit system against single mothers. **90% of single parents are women and if fathers paid the due maintenance they would lift at least 60% of families out of poverty**" she writes.

But just let us see what Boris Johnson wrote about single mothers and their children shall we?

On Thursday 28th November 2019, Jon Sharman of *The Independent* unearthed **an article written by Boris Johnson for *The Spectator* in 1995.**

This is what he wrote: He said it was, "outrageous that married couples should pay for the single mothers' desire to procreate independently of men".

And he suggested it was "feeble" for a man to be unable or unwilling to "take control of his woman."

But his most famous quote on this subject, and in this article, is the one about the children of single mothers. He describes them as "ill-raised, ignorant, aggressive and illegitimate."

This, ladies and gentlemen, is our Prime Minister and is someone who actually needs to examine his own (not so very) private life.

****

8TH MARCH

International Women's Day today so what better day than to be told by the government that they have **no plans to look into the cost and availability of child care.**

A petition calling for an independent review on funding and affordability was signed by 113,713 signatures so triggering a debate in Parliament.

In September last year a survey of more than 20,000 working parents said the government was not doing enough to support them with childcare and that childcare in the UK was too expensive.

It revealed that low-income parents and those on Universal Credit had to use food banks. According to data from the 'Organisation for Economic Co-operation and Development,' the **UK has the third most expensive childcare system in the world behind only Slovakia and Switzerland. A full-time place costs on average £   2,376 a year.**

Joeli Brearley, the founder of the charity **Pregnant then Screwed** said it was "quite astounding that the news had been delivered on International Women's Day."

She went on to say that, "Affordable childcare is a critical component of gender equality." And, "We will never have gender equality whilst women cannot afford to go to work. Happy International Women's Day to you too!"

****

22ND MARCH

Jenn Selby of *The Guardian* highlights the problems of **underfunding of nurseries** in an article today.

Research by the 'National Day Nurseries Association' found that 95% of nurseries in England did not have enough funding to cover basic costs after the pandemic. 85% said they would run at a loss or just about break even this year.

So we have a government who says that everyone eligible must get a job, yet not realising that if mothers cannot afford child-care then they have to stay at home to look after their children. Is this really so difficult to understand?

In April, nursery finances will be squeezed even further by a 6.6% rise in the national living wage, a 1.25-percentage-point rise in national insurance, and a sharp rise in the cost of heating and electricity bills.

The government will say that they are giving extra funding to help cover childcare costs for eligible two- to four-year-olds in April, but this will be at less than the rate of inflation. **According to providers, it falls far below what is needed to keep nurseries running.**

Dr Mary-Ann Stephenson, the director of the 'Women's Budget Group,' said that, "single parents – the majority of whom are women – would be most affected by any further rises in childcare costs."

"A really simple thing that the government could do right now would be to start paying the childcare element of universal credit upfront instead of in arrears."

So we await the Chancellor's Spring Statement tomorrow to see exactly how much help he will give to the vitally important early years.

****

23RD MARCH

Well there is very little help for families with young children in the spring statement today. There is a doubling of free hours from 15 to 30 for working parents but there is fear that there will not be enough childcare places available, due to childcare providers opting out on offering the scheme. So many nurseries are facing difficulties with extra funding needed for heating and insurance and staff payments.

****

31ST MARCH

Well this is amazing. I have some **good news** to report. MPs voted on an amendment to the Health and Care bill yesterday and voted to continue the use of telemedicine services for abortion. 215 voted in favour and 188 voted against in a free vote.

It has been hailed as a major victory for abortion rights and women's rights.

Louise McCudden, the UK advocacy and public affairs adviser at MSI Reproductive Choices said, "Making this safe and popular service a permanent option will particularly benefit those who struggle to attend face-to-face appointments, including those in abusive relationships, those with caring responsibilities, and those without transport."

At last women have been listened to and it is a beacon of light during a dark and depressing time.

****

22ND APRIL

But the light does not shine for long.

There is a report in *The Times* today by Eleanor Hayward their Health Correspondent about a **nationwide shortage of HRT**. Demand has surged in recent years because of a high profile campaign about the menopause in general and the benefits of HRT in particular. The government have failed to keep up with this increase in demand.

Also, last October the government had said that women in England would be able to get a batch of prescriptions for up to 12 months with just one prescription charge. But we are now being **told that this will not come into effect until April next year.**

The Labour MP Carolyn Harris who is chairwoman of the government's menopause task force, claimed they had shown "total disregard" for women's health.

Apparently some women are being forced to buy their HRT on the black market.

****

26TH APRIL

Well the health secretary is appointing an HRT 'tsar' to help with the supply problems so that is good.

And Caroline Noakes in *The Guardian* today says,

"This is a welcome step – but the new appointee needs to crack on to solve the problems with supply immediately. I have no doubt they will have met manufacturers, but the issues we're now seeing are neither new nor unexpected."

It is not a new problem because as she goes on to say, "Even before the pandemic I was hearing from my constituents about inconsistencies in the supply of some forms of HRT.

"Ministers need to sort out this delay quickly. Our coalition of menopause campaigners won't go away quietly, so the new tsar had better be as determined as we are."

****

27TH APRIL

There is a very well-timed and interesting article by Alice Thomson of *The Times* today. She writes about the way in which women's issues, health or others, are always so belittled and **how on so many levels women feel disenfranchised.**

As she writes, "at every turn women seem to struggle unnecessarily with too many problems: periods, contraception, pregnancy, justice for rape, equal pay, domestic abuse and finally the menopause."

To which I would add child-care, prisons and misogyny. I expect you could add more of your own.

****

For today I also see this.

It is a copy of the report by the All Party Parliamentary Group on Women in the Penal System (APPG) and it makes dreadful reading. I just pick out a few points that they raise.

Their inquiry states that:

"Prisons are unable to address the physical and mental health needs of women and in fact make them worse.

"**The focus should be on stopping unnecessary use of custody – not prison expansion,** which would only pull more women into a system that fails to provide the care and support they require."

They have called for the repeal of legislation that gives the courts the power to remand people in prison 'for their own protection'. **When this power is used, it is often due to a lack of appropriate mental health services in the community.** (I hear today, 12th July, from the Howard League that this is in a new draft bill).

The inquiry considered Ministry of Justice data showing that more than half of women in prison have reported experiencing emotional, physical or sexual abuse in childhood. More than half have reported being victims of domestic violence as adults.

I have issues with this report. The APPG on Women in the Penal system launched an inquiry in 2019. Today in this report they pretty well say the same things as they said then and tell us what we have known for years.

But still our prisons stay in the same disgusting state and this government plans to build yet more prisons for women.

They also say that **women in prison were not always listened to or believed** when they raised health concerns or asked for help.

Well surprise, surprise. Women have trouble being heard in every walk of life and this is no different. Report after report after report from people with good intentions but no guts to actually do something.

****

And then there is this.

Misogyny is alive and well in the House of Commons.

Two days ago the *Mail on Sunday* reported that an anonymous MP had criticised shadow deputy leader Angela Rayner and said that, **"she knows she can't compete with Boris's Oxford Union debating training but she has other skills which he lacks."** He went on to say that she continually crosses and uncrosses her legs in order to distract him.

The back-lash has been huge.

Johnson has apologised to her personally and said that it was "the most appalling load of sexist, misogynist tripe" and threatened to unleash the "terrors of the earth" on to the culprit."

Yes this is how he talks. A quote from King Lear which is really not necessary or informative. We need to know exactly what he will do. (Well nothing as yet. July 15th)

The leader of the House, Sir Lindsay Hoyle, has summoned the editor of the *Mail on Sunday* in order to discuss this article.

But what is also very interesting is the response I got from a tweet I sent out on Twitter on the Sunday afternoon.

I have only been on Twitter for a couple of months, basically in order to promote my books and all has been fairly quiet. But I was very pleased to have got 60 followers.

I was so incensed at this attack however that I tweeted in her support. I have heard her speak in Parliament recently and believe me she is dynamite. She speaks eloquently, and passionately, and intelligently and knocks the spots off the blustering, shambolic, incoherent words of the PM.

Well the response was immediate. **Within 24 hours I had more than 14 thousand 'likes' and 477 followers.**

The papers, MPs, journalists, and absolutely everyone are talking and writing about the misogyny women have to put up with, especially in Parliament.

At the moment there are 56 MPs facing sexual harassment charges.

****

Also today *The Mail on Sunday* has said it will not go to a meeting with the Speaker of the House of Commons about their story on Angela Rayner.

And actually I absolutely agree with *the Mail* that they should not.

And that is a sentence I never thought I would write!

This is because I feel that it is absolutely imperative that we know exactly what our MPs of all persuasions are saying. They all need complete and open scrutiny.

Stop grumbling about the publication of the story.

We need to know the name of the MP who said it.

****

It has just been reported that the Conservative Party is investigating claims that a Tory MP watched porn on his mobile phone while sitting next to a female minister in the Commons chamber.

Another MP corroborated her account.

I hope you can keep up with all of this. This chapter and the chapter on our children are the most depressing chapters for me to write.

****

29TH APRIL

The MP watching porn has been named as Neil Parish, chairman of the environment and rural affairs committee. He had the whip removed today and is the subject of the Commons Standards Commission and the Independent Complaints and Grievance scheme. People are asking why it has taken so long to remove the whip and are saying he should resign immediately. He is saying that he thinks he must have got on to the porn channel by mistake.

Oh yes? How many times have we heard that one?

****

30TH APRIL

Women MPs on the *Today* programme are saying that the misogynist culture in the House of Commons has got worse during the last two years. They also said that respect and common courtesy should come from the top. Draw your own conclusions about that one.

They also called for the idea of the "whip" to be removed altogether. It is outdated and an abuse of power. I do so agree.

****

3RD MAY

There has been a leaked draft from the Supreme Court in the USA about a possible decision to overturn Roe and Wade. This is unlikely to happen here but it is important to know what is happening in the States.

****

16TH MAY

In *The Guardian* today there is yet another article **about pregnant women in prison** by Rhiannon Lucy Cosslet.

This government has **repeatedly rejected calls** by Harriet Harman, chair of the joint committee on human rights, and others, **to amend the policing bill to ensure that judges take into account the best interests of children and unborn babies when sentencing.**

I do not understand why they reject this.

How can they be so inhumane to vulnerable women?

****

21ST MAY

Some good news today which makes a welcome change and I must report it when I hear it. The government HR tsar has said that pharmacists **can** prescribe alternative HRT medication if there is a shortage of a specific type.

****

10TH JUNE

Sophia Sleigh of HuffPost UK has done some interesting research to find out what has happened to the **new 888 phone number** which was announced at the beginning of October last year.

This came about after the murder of Sarah Everard and was hailed by the Daily Mail as a:

"NEW PHONE LIFELINE FOR LONE WOMEN"

adding that "Priti backs plan for 888 number".

Hmm that last bit should give you a clue. She also said this, **"This new phone line is exactly the kind of innovative scheme which would be good to get going as soon as we can. I'm now looking at it with my team and liaising with BT."**

It would mean that women would be able to use a mobile app, potentially with the number 888, to summon police if they felt threatened.

BT CEO Philip Jansen said it might cost as little as £50 million and **could be up and running by Christmas 2021.**

Just check today's date.

Yesterday, HuffPost questioned both the Home Office and BT about it and no-one was able to give any answers.

Having been directed to BT from the Home Office, BT said,

"We're looking at the role we can play in enhancing personal safety. This needs to be a team effort, with the telecoms industry, police, regulator and government talking to the whole community and to those groups campaigning on the safety of women and other individuals."

When HuffPost UK repeated the question: **"Is the 888 project still going ahead? Or not?" they were simply told the telecommunications giant had nothing more they could share.**

Shadow home secretary Yvette Cooper described it as a "disappearing hotline" and an example of the Home Secretary making promises for "short term headlines".

It is the same story over and over again with this government.

They can't deliver.

****

24TH JUNE
A very, very dark day for women everywhere. The Supreme Court in the United States of America have overturned the Roe v Wade abortion law to declare that the constitutional right to abortion which has been upheld for 50 years, no longer exists.

The backlash has been enormous and the young women of today will not let this go ahead without an enormous fight.

This has of course nothing to do with the sanctity of life or the protection of life. **Banning abortion does not prevent abortions it** just prevents safe abortions and many young women will die as a result of this ban.

This is control of women's bodies and their reproduction rights. It is very chilling.

Interesting too to note that the US has refused to tighten up gun laws so whilst you are not permitted to abort a foetus it is perfectly acceptable for children to be killed by nutters with guns.

****

29TH JUNE

People are saying again that we mustn't be complacent it could happen here. I say that young people here are tough and resilient and strong. They have had to be and they won't stand for any of this nonsense.

But yes some men have stood up here and said it is important for them to take control of women's bodies. Those are not the actual words they use but it is the meaning behind their words.

But I also say let us look at the definition of life.

Life begins when you take your first breath. It ends with your last breath.

****

21ST JULY

But here we go. Be afraid, be very afraid. Just today I read that, on the 7th of July, at the International Ministerial Conference on Freedom, there has been an **amendment by the UK government** to a 'Statement on freedom of religion or belief and gender equality.' **They have quietly removed "sexual and reproductive health and rights" and "bodily autonomy" from this statement. It is there on the Gov.UK website.**

Abortion is a human right. Women and girls everywhere, you need to be aware what is being done, slowly and secretly by this government, in your name.

****

We all need to fight to make women's voices heard and everyone needs to listen to the voices of women. And together with women go our children, as women are, always have been, and always will be, their primary carers.

****

OUR CHILDREN

This is the most difficult chapter for me to write. The care, kindness and support which all our children need is totally unforthcoming from this government. It is beyond my understanding how negligent, dismissive and, yes, cruel a government can be when confronted with some of the situations I describe. I will totally understand if you can't read it. But I think you owe it to our children to do so.

2021

18TH OCTOBER

In my previous book I spoke about the dreadful conditions of Rainsbrook Secure Training Centre where they locked up boys as young as 12 for 23 hours a day.

That centre has now been closed but I hear of another one which sounds just as dreadful. Why, oh why, does this country think that it is OK to lock up our children in such a way? I am quite sure they can be extremely challenging young people as a result of coming from dysfunctional homes, but this is exactly why they need professional and dedicated adults to look after them.

This one is called **Oakhill Secure Training Centre near Milton Keyes**. After many inspections an Urgent Notification Notice was sent to the

Secretary of State for Justice which means that they have to make improvement and respond within 28 days.

The following is a part of the findings as reported by Ofsted. It is long but it is so important. Please, read it and as you do please keep saying to yourself, "this is how we treat children, in England, in the 21st century."

Key findings of the full inspection in October 2021

- Children live in a dilapidated environment, experience frequent incidents of violence and use of force and are often cared for by inexperienced staff.

- Staff are reluctant to challenge low level poor behaviour. This failure frequently leads to more serious incidents, including violence. This is exacerbated by the lack of an effective behaviour management strategy to support staff in how to deal with challenging behaviour.

- Levels of use of force are very high. There are incidents where the use of force on children is not justified and contrary to legislation. Staff are not sufficiently skilled in the use of physical restraint techniques to ensure that children are always safeguarded. Governance and quality assurance of the use of force and the physical restraint of children is ineffective. Poor practice is not identified and addressed quickly enough, leading to delays in taking action.

- Systems for safeguarding children are in disarray. Senior leaders failed to ensure that safeguarding concerns and allegations are referred to statutory agencies as required. There is a considerable backlog of safeguarding concerns awaiting action. Children therefore remain at risk of serious harm.

- Safeguarding concerns have been investigated internally contrary to statutory guidance. This could compromise any future investigations.

- Children have access to inappropriate adult content channels via their in-room televisions. Senior managers have been aware of this since March 2021 but no action has been taken.

- Most children reported a lack of confidence in the complaints system, discouraging them from raising concerns. This has serious implications for safeguarding as it could allow harmful behaviour to go undetected.

- Residential staff are not able to access key information to inform their day-today care of children. In addition, some staff stated to inspectors that they had been given the choice of whether to read relevant information. Some had chosen not to. Children are therefore being cared for by staff who are not equipped with all the information they need to keep the children safe and to meet their individual needs.

- Staffing of the centre remains fragile. The centre's records dated September 2021 show an annual staff attrition rate of 27%, resulting in unstable, transient relationships with children. This has been a primary factor in children's experiences of poor care and control.

- Frontline staff are poorly managed and supported. Many have not received any purposeful training and development beyond their mandatory programmes. No training needs analysis has been completed.

- The decision by senior leaders to lock children into their rooms for an average of approximately 19 hours per day in July and August was wholly inappropriate and risk averse. Children's experiences during this period were bleak, and barely met minimum standards of human decency. This practice ended shortly after the monitoring visit.

- The centre director has begun to exert some grip, but as she is a temporary appointee, we do not have confidence in the sustainability of progress. The provider advised that a recruitment campaign is under way to appoint a new director. We do not know whether the provider will be able to provide high quality and consistent leadership through the appointment of a director with suitable skill and experience, including specific experience in children's care and services, to make the necessary improvements rapidly.

Ofsted and partner inspectorates have shared our findings with the Ministry of Justice and the Youth Custody Service, so that they can ensure that the necessary actions are taken promptly. We will publish the inspection report in due course and will review progress at our next inspection.

Yours sincerely, Amanda Spielman Her Majesty's Chief Inspector

I am so disgusted that I write the following email to the Ministry of Justice and copy it to my MP (Oliver Dowden), Sonia Sodha of *The Guardian*, Rachel Sylvester of *The Times*, Tom Parry of *the Mirror*, The Howard League and Richard Garside at the Centre of Crime and Justice.

I am writing to the Ministry of Justice to express my horror and concern about the recent inspection of Oakhill Secure Training Centre. I understand that the Inspectorates have issued an urgent notification to the Secretary of State for Justice, Dominic Raab.

However apparently Oakhill has not been judged higher than "requires improvement to be good" for the "overall experiences and progress of children" since 2017. Can you please explain to me how this situation has been allowed to continue in this unacceptable manner for so many years?

To quote one small point from the inspection they say that they "highlighted unjustifiable -and in some cases unlawful- levels of force being used on children as young as 15. Staff lack the skill to carry out restraint safely while oversight of the use of force is inadequate."

"Systems for keeping children safe are in 'disarray', leaving children at risk of serious harm."

The report is absolutely damning. I have no doubt that some of these children are challenging which is why they need professional adults who are skilled in caring for these vulnerable children. They are only there in the first place because of lack of suitable care from adults.

Rainsbrook Secure Training Centre has been closed because of similar failings. Why is it that we think it is acceptable to treat children in such a cruel and inhumane way?

I also do not understand why it gets very little coverage from the media.

I look forward to your reply.

And I will let you know if I get one!

****

OCTOBER 19TH

A report in *The Times* today by Nicola Woolcock discloses that there is a degree of anxiety and concern about the **promised catch-up tutoring programme** for our children. Apparently it is not going as well as expected. Are we surprised?

Seamus Murphy, who is chief executive of Turner schools in Kent, says "Unusually in education, it is not the lack of finance that is holding us back but the lack of workforce. Having been promised a national tutoring programme over 12 months ago, we had to wait three months before the bureaucracy cranked into action. This year the system has simply ground to a halt and we have been advised to source tutors ourselves."

He went on to say, **"Despite the prime minister's insistence on the new sunny uplands, the reality is more like looking for a black cat in a coal cellar".**

I love his turn of phrase! They are so desperate they are thinking of sending flyers to University students and offering them Deliveroo vouchers and cash bonuses in order to persuade them to sign up as tutors.

****

25TH OCTOBER
And then I read this in a report by Oliver Wright in *The Times* today.

Rishi Sunak has decided to rule out longer school days which would have helped boost the catch up programme. Why? Because, he says, the government had already "maxed out" its capacity to spend the existing Covid catch-up money on programmes such as tutoring **and he hinted strongly that no more funds would be forthcoming.**

Plans for a longer day were one of the key demands of Sir Kevan Collins the education tsar appointed by Boris and who resigned when his original £15 billion plan over three years was rejected by the government.

"Tutoring in small groups and support and training and development for teachers are more important and makes the biggest difference to children's learning" says the Chancellor. But please what does he know? And nothing can be done without adequate funding.

And the children's commissioner, Dame Rachel de Souza, disagrees with him here. **"I'm very keen on the extended day"** she says. "We shouldn't have schools closing at half past two. I'd like to see schools able to provide that wrap around care and teatime homework and all the activities. It's doable."

Oh my goodness that is like manna from heaven to me. What an inspired woman. I make no apologies for quoting my letter to *The Times* once more which was published on the 2nd September 2020.

Sir, It is quite astonishing that secondary schools should finish the day at 3pm. I think that they should be kept open until at least 6pm with sports and clubs and supper available plus quiet area where they could do 'homework or rather 'independent' work. Before the Unions go apoplectic obviously teachers could complete their contact teaching at say 4pm but then sports coaches, music teachers, club leaders and others could be employed for the next 2 hours. This will still leave time for the school to be cleaned etc. Yes it will cost money, but it will give employment to many, allow parents to do a full day's work without worry, and it is actually about time that we put children first.

But until we get a different government that will never happen. This Chancellor doesn't have a clue and children are still, and always will be, at the bottom of the pile. **But they are our future and they will need to be tough.**

****

5TH NOVEMBER
In *Times 2*, today Richard Morrison highlights the fact **that yet another manifesto pledge from this government is being broken.**

The Tories election manifesto promised the creation of an "arts premium" for secondary schools. It was for £270 million and was supposed to start this month. It is now being put "on hold" while the government focuses on "new priorities" due to Covid.

Oh yes we've heard that one before.........and we will be hearing it again and again and again.

It is all science and technology that is important now apparently, but as Richard Morrison says, "a rounded education is one where science and the arts are recognised as mutually enhancing". In a large comprehensive school near him there is nobody who can play the piano and no-one who has the confidence and training to lead a choir or an orchestra.

He goes on to say that **"the very existence of music and the arts in some state schools is hanging by a thread."**

The hostility and non-interest in the arts by this government is staggering.

****

15TH NOVEMBER

I get a reply from Tom Parry of *The Mirror* after I sent my **email about Oakhill Secure Training Centre a second time to everyone. Thank-you Tom**.

He directed me to an article in *The Guardian* written on the 3rd November which I had missed. Again, thank-you Tom. It was a brilliant article about Oakhill, by Eric Allison, *Guardian* prisons correspondent and Simon Hattenstone a *Guardian* correspondent.

But what I don't understand is, when there are articles like this and books like mine and The Howard League for Penal Reform and the Centre for Crime and Justice all doing their best to highlight this treatment of our vulnerable children , why are people not jumping up and down in absolute horror?

It could be **your child or your grand-child** if they just get in with the wrong crowd. At the very least you should be writing to your MP. These centres should not exist.

****

And so I find the reply to the urgent notification notice that was sent to Dominic Raab and I see a response from the charity Article 39 which was written on the 11th November.

Here it is:

"The Justice Secretary Dominic Raab has responded to the urgent notification issued in respect of G4S-run Oakhill Secure Training Centre by Ofsted, Her Majesty's Inspectorate of Prisons and the Care Quality Commission last month. His letter to Ofsted's Chief Inspector describes the serious concerns raised by the inspectorates as "deeply troubling" and says the failures in safeguarding processes and procedures at the child prison are "totally unacceptable.

At the end of September, a whistle-blower contacted Article 39 with a number of very serious allegations relating to child protection and children's safety. We then wrote to the local authority responsible for investigating significant harm, copying in the inspectorates and the national Child Safeguarding Practice Review Panel. We subsequently wrote to the Justice Secretary calling for a judicial inquiry and assurances over the immediate steps taken to protect children. We also wrote to the G4S director of the prison asking her to pass on letters to children informing them of their right to seek legal help.

It is our understanding that the 4-8 October inspection, after which the urgent notification was issued, was arranged in response to Article 39 notifying the authorities of the whistle-blower's very serious concerns."

Article 39's Director, Carolyne Willow, said: *"Today's action plan continues the long history of the government giving G4S unlimited chances to fulfil basic child protection obligations. The correspondence does not answer why government monitors, and the Youth Custody Service, did not themselves notice and then deal with chronic and severe failures to keep children safe, including the unlawful use of force and breach of safeguarding rules. It is our understanding that the October inspection only happened after we alerted the local authority and the inspectorates to very serious allegations brought to us by a whistle-blower. A safeguarding review by a former Director of Children's Services will not get to the bottom of G4S's actions and inactions over many years, which is why we are pushing for a judicial inquiry.*

"We know from past experience that the prison service sending in one of their own prison governors to try and rescue a child prison is the first step to closure, though G4S will continue to receive significant public funds for every day and week Oakhill stays open. These penal institutions have the suffering of children built into the walls; they cannot be redeemed."

So I really hope that they can get a judicial inquiry. Obviously I will be looking out for what happens next.

****

23RD NOVEMBER

There are disturbing reports about the number of children in care at the moment. An article by Katie Gibbons and John Reynolds in *The Times* today says that up to 95,000 vulnerable children will be placed in council care by 2025.

Apparently there is a huge lack of foster carers and too much bureaucracy with assessing families' suitability for fostering. The government has announced £500 million in funding to get children, "the best possible start in life," but Tim Oliver chairman of the County Council Network said that councils are in a "vicious circle" caused by cuts in preventive services and a lack of alternative solutions such as foster care." He goes on to say that "with the situation becoming unsustainable we need additional funding and an unrelenting focus on preventing family breakdown and keeping families together alongside systemic reform of how councils work with their public sector partners to achieve these aims."

I really believe that far more investment of all kinds, economical, practical, emotional and social, **needs to be directed at the early years**. The cost of child care alone is prohibitive for many families.

And I still do not understand why the Conservative government cut funding to Sure Start programmes, which were introduced under a Labour government, causing so many of them to close.

Pippa Crerar of *The Daily Mirror* reported on the 16th August 2021 that

"The Institute for Fiscal Studies found that the **benefits of the (Sure Start) centres were 'substantial,' with children in poorer neighbourhoods getting most out of them.** Sure Start centres, which brought together health, parenting support and childcare for the under-5s, received £1.8 billion a year at their 2009 peak. But spending has fallen by more than two-thirds over the last decade under the Tories with many centres scaled back or closed. The IFS research, funded by **the Nuffield Foundation, found that the early years programme delivered long-lasting health benefits for children well into their teenage years.**"

'Early Years Alliance' chief executive Neil Leitch said: "The fact that the Sure Start programme is still paying dividends for children into their teenage years is yet more confirmation of what we already know - **that investing in young children is not only the right thing to do, it is also a sound financial decision.** Recent governments have shamefully let down children and families by not only cutting Sure Start services which reduce hospitalisations, and do much more good besides, but also by allowing funding for under-five education to dwindle to far less than the cost of delivering it."

And to put the government's point of view a Department for Education spokesperson said: "We recognise that the early years of a child's life are the most crucial, which is why we have put unprecedented investment into childcare over the past decade". Another spokesperson!

This statement is manifestly untrue. There has been cut, after cut, after cut in nursery provision since the Tories came to power in 2010. It was Labour who introduced the free nursery school sessions for 4 year olds followed by some for two and three years olds. **This government is child blind.**

****

30TH NOVEMBER

More and more schools are asking parents for financial help. More than half of parents said they were concerned that financial pressures at their school were harming their children's education. The charity 'Parentkind' found that 45% of parents were asked to contribute to school funds with 38% doing so in the last year. This is the highest percentage of requests and contributions the survey has found in six years. **Tight school budgets, according to parents, are having a negative impact on many school's ability to deliver a first-rate education.**

****

5TH DECEMBER

There is **a crisis in foster care** in the UK which is obviously affecting the well- fare of our disadvantaged children enormously. There is a critical shortage of carers due to, you guessed it, cuts in funding, and poor support leading to low morale. Kevin Williams, chief executive of 'Fostering Network,' says, "The saddest thing is that we've known about these issues for some time, and they don't seem to be getting any better."

He goes on to say that, **"If local authorities are not properly funded, then actually they cannot fund foster care properly.** Foster carers are not treated and valued and respected for the skills that they bring. These are really complex roles."

Apparently some 70% of foster carers do not receive any retainer payments in between fostering. So more and more children are being looked after in residential homes which can be exorbitantly expensive for local authorities to have to fund.

The care for our disadvantaged and vulnerable children in the UK is in need of a huge overhaul with their needs being put first and foremost.

****

7TH DECEMBER

Refugee children are being put in hotels on their own because the care system is stretched to breaking point, says the head of Ofsted.

Nicola Woolcock, the education reporter of *The Times*, writes that Amanda Spielman will say at the publication of the regulator's annual report that the number of vulnerable children is at a record high, leaving them at risk. Ofsted's report will also cover the impact of the pandemic on schools and colleges but it is particularly concerned with **the plight of unaccompanied migrant and refugee children.** Apparently unaccompanied children are routinely being housed in hotels, on their own which the inspectorate has described as unacceptable, because of delays in transferring them to local authority care and a lack of suitable places for them to live.

There are grave concerns about the safety of these hotels. The government has temporarily made mandatory the national transfer scheme, which means that local authorities must accept children into their care from other areas but although this is a positive step the inspectorate is calling for the wider strains on England's "creaking" care system to be addressed.

Spielman said: "Children should be treated as children, not least those arriving on our shores without friends or family, wanting safety, security and a better future. It is extremely challenging to find them a place to live but using hotels is neither acceptable nor sustainable. **No one would want that for their own children."**

Absolutely. Now I thought for a while about which chapter I should put this into....... Children or Asylum Seekers. But then I thought that children are children wherever they are and we are all responsible for their welfare. So it is here. Local Authorities are at breaking point and it all urgently needs an overhaul.

****

23RD DECEMBER

In a report today the charity Shelter estimates that roughly **200,000 children are at risk of becoming homeless this winter.**

A poll carried out by YouGov for Shelter found that 104,000 families in privately rented homes received eviction notices in the last month, or were behind on their rent and were in danger of losing their homes. Shelter estimated that 55,000 children, along with their families, have already been evicted in the last three months.

Many families said that their children worried about becoming homeless and it was the cause of a lot of anxiety issues.

Shelter's chief executive, Polly Neate, said: "No child should have to worry about losing their home this Christmas, let alone 200,000."

She goes on to say that, "Thousands of families are teetering on a cliff-edge. It's only with the public's support that we'll be able to keep answering calls and help as many of them as possible keep the bailiffs at bay."

But hopefully we will see the government stepping in to help out with this distressing situation.

****

But today I also read a powerful poem written by a teenager who lives in Tottenham. He was awarded Foyle Young Poet of the Year.

His name is Giovanni Rose and my heart goes out to him and all those others like him.

The poem is called **"Welcome to Tottenham"** and it made me so angry. Tottenham is only a few miles away from Westminster but so far as Tottenham is concerned it is in **a parallel universe.**

How any politician can say that they are looking after the young in this country is beyond me. None of them have the first idea.

Here is the poem.

WELCOME TO TOTTENHAM
BY GIOVANNI ROSE

Welcome to Tottenham.
Where we wake up to the smell of 'Chick king',
Mixed with the odour of the corpse from the night before.
Where we cover our blood stained streets with dried up gum,
Where kids have holes in their last pairs of shoes,
Where daddy left mummy and mummy's left poor.
Welcome to Tottenham.
Where if you look like me then it's harder for you,
Where everybody's equal unless they're darker than you.
Where the police see colour before they see the crime,
Where children get stopped and searched
and aren't allowed to ask why.
Welcome to Tottenham.
Where the drug addicts sit at the back of the 149.
Where education and sports are the only ways to shine.
Where we ride around on stolen scooters,
Where we can't afford tuition so the streets are our tutors.
Welcome to Tottenham.
I love but I hate my home,
I still listen to the voicemails of my dead peers in my phone,
I live in a nightmare. I had to learn how to dream,
I'm afraid to open up because you won't survive if you're weak.

Welcome to Tottenham.
The devil's playground.
We fight over streets we don't own,
Knife crime's on the rise because the beef can't be left alone.
Why does no one understand that we just
want our youth clubs back,
Why do they claim they're not racist but
label the violence here black?
Welcome to Tottenham.

I thank Giovanni Rose for giving me permission to share it with you.

****

27TH DECEMBER

Well we had a sort of Christmas, so Johnson will be pleased about that.

But many families, including ours, had at least one family member isolating due to testing positive with Covid.

And of course, as everyone says Christmas is really all about children isn't it? Well not if you have a Tory government it's not.

Today I get to see an article in the BMJ which makes horrific reading and displays the sheer incompetence, ignorance and complete disregard for the welfare of our children, once again, by this government.

These excerpts are written by Christina Pagel who is the first female director at the 'Clinical Operational Research' unit at UCL which applies operational research, data analysis and mathematical modelling to problems in health care.

On the 23rd December she wrote: "In August, one of us (CP) wrote about **schools being the gaping hole in the English Covid strategy.** This was written in the face of the highly transmissible delta Covid-19

187

variant. Three failings were identified: delayed vaccination of 12-15 year olds; lack of public health measures in schools such as masks and ventilation; and continued high community transmission leaving schools vulnerable.

So what happened? **And what needs to happen next?"**

Well she goes on to write about the main areas which urgently need to be vastly improved.

The first is **vaccinations** for children.

The government have been dragging their feet on this and the roll out for 12 to15 year olds has been very slow. And vaccines have been approved for 5 to 11 year olds but recent indications are that they will only be recommended for clinically extremely vulnerable 5-11 year olds.

The BMJ article finds this unacceptable. It goes on to say that **"Vaccines are safe and they work**. By reducing the chance of primary infection, vaccines reduce cases, transmission, long Covid, and school disruption. They also protect children from becoming severely ill. With Omicron the dominant variant for next term, we cannot rely on previous infection to prevent a new wave of infections in schools. We must offer as many teenagers as possible their second dose before term starts. The Joint Committee on Vaccinations and Immunisation are reported to have decided that only clinically vulnerable children should be offered the vaccine. With the most recent ONS infection survey reporting almost 6% prevalence in under 12s and over 3% of primary school children off with Covid at the end of December, **we urge them to reconsider."**

The second area is about **clean air in schools.**

Well ventilated schools are vitally important in the fight against Covid and at the moment the government has not delivered nearly enough help with this.

In the article Christina Pagel says: "We (therefore) recommend a CO_2 monitor for every naturally ventilated classroom, **rather than the current one to two shared across a school.**

Where ventilation is still insufficient, HEPA units can provide clean air by filtering out the infectious respiratory particles. The technology was shown to be effective against Covid in hospitals, and many low-cost home "air purifiers" have the required H13 filter standard and can deliver enough clean air with several units per classroom.

With guidance on sources and numbers required, schools can quickly take advantage of these, **rather than being limited by the two models currently recommended by the government. In the longer term, infrastructure upgrades combining clean air with energy efficiency represent a good investment for the future."**

The present help is obviously completely inadequate and is compromising the health of our children.

At the end of the article she says, **"Children are the least protected group in England and their needs are being forgotten as we race to boost adults. Another term of infection and disruption would be a dereliction of duty."**

That last paragraph is the most damning accusation of this government that I have ever read but confirms the words which I write in my introduction to this chapter.

****

29TH DECEMBER

There are two stories in the media today about the treatment of our children in this country which make disturbing reading. Can and should the government be doing something about them? Yes I think they can and they should.

Tom Ball writes in *The Times* about the prevalence of **illegal and unregistered schools in England** and the fact that due to a legal loophole Ofsted is unable to investigate in the normal way. In spite of pledges by the government to tackle this problem more schools like these are being discovered each year. The fact that Ofsted have neither the resources nor the legislative backing to inspect these schools means that they can become a **haven for physical and sexual abuse.** Indeed the individual stories from some such children make harrowing reading. There would appear to be no real political will to tackle this as some of these schools are religious schools and the authorities are scared of being called racist.

However I quote a spokeswoman for the department of education who says that: "the department remains committed to ensuring that anyone found to be running an unregistered school faces the full force of the law, and the taking forward of measures to make it easier to investigate and prosecute unregistered schools – including strengthening Ofsted's powers."

Parallel Universe indeed. So they do know about these schools and there is still a major problem.

****

The other story is equally harrowing and it concerns teenagers in care. It is also reported in *The Times* today by Neil Johnston. Anne Longfield who leads the 'Commission on Young Lives' said that the care system to support vulnerable teenagers was "infuriatingly inadequate" and had been designed with younger children in mind. A recent report by her states that, "**Children are being handed over to ruthless criminal gangs and abusers by a social care system that is not fit for purpose."**

In some cases **county lines gangs take over a care home and use it to facilitate exploitation and drug dealing.**

The commission called on the government to set up a ministerial task force for vulnerable teenagers at risk and introduce a support package to fund new children's homes as more and more older teenagers are going into care.

The Department for Education said: "while the independent review of children's social care continues we are urgently reforming the system to address growing pressures." **Parallel Universe** again.

****

30TH DECEMBER
Some good news; but not from the government.

On BBC Breakfast this morning we hear about a **heart-warming charity called Zarach.** I mentioned this charity in '**Beneath the Bluster'** and today its founder, a primary school deputy- head teacher, Bex Wilson, spoke about the work they are doing.

Four years ago she was teaching Year Six and preparing them for Sats tests when one of the boys in the class seemed very tired and irritable. When she asked how he was he said, **'I'm always tired Miss, I don't have a bed'.**

On inquiring further she discovered many children in poverty-stricken households were sleeping on cushions or floors and she decided to start this charity. She spoke with such passion and clarity, as we saw people delivering beds, mattresses and bed linen to houses in need, that many viewers said, please can we have her as Prime Minister. If only. She is an absolute hero.

Bex and the Zarach team were busy this Christmas supplying families with beds and much-needed furniture but, as someone said, a bed should not be seen as a gift, it is a basic need.

If you want to have your faith in human nature restored look up the Zarach website. It is inspirational.

****

But these stories too are equally inspirational.

They are about two young boys who have been awarded the **British Empire Medal for charity in the New Year's Honours lists at the beginning of this year. They are amazing.**

One is 12 year old Max Woosey who has been camping outside in a small tent in his garden for almost 640 nights to raise money for the North Devon Hospice. Max, from Braunton, in Devon, was 10 years old when he was inspired to raise money for the hospice after they cared for his neighbour Rick Abbott before he died from cancer. Rick had given him the tent and told him to have adventures with it.

In November, the hospice said it had **received nearly £680,000** from Max›s fundraising and the **money equated to almost 20 nurses working for 12 months**.

Max said he hoped the award would help him to raise more money. The 12-year-old said he would "definitely hit the two-year mark" and "would love to raise £1m." He suggested his mother should rent out his bedroom as he has no plans for sleeping inside just yet but I don't think his Mum is quite ready to do that!

****

The other is about an even younger boy **Tobias Weller who is 11-years-old and also received this award.** Tobias, who has cerebral palsy and autism, was nicknamed "Captain" after he was inspired by his hero Captain Sir Tom Moore to start raising money during the coronavirus lockdowns.

He said he was "chuffed to bits" to have been recognised by the Queen after raising £157,000 for the special educational needs Paces School, where he is a student, and The Children's Hospital Charity, in his home town of Sheffield, South Yorkshire. Tobias, who raised the money by completing sponsored walks and marathons, said **he now cannot wait for a chance to meet the Queen at a royal garden party.**

****

So I can end this year with hope that so-called 'ordinary' men, women and especially children will carry us forward with kindness, compassion, determination, courage and hard work, whilst those in positions of power and authority continue to be found wanting.

****

2022

3RD JANUARY

A really devastating statistic to come to terms with at the beginning of this New Year is the fact that the number of murders of teenagers in London in 2021 is the highest since records began. **Knife crime in the capital is at an all-time high.**

And so because of an excellent letter in *The Times* today which draws attention to this I learn of yet another brilliant charity which puts the welfare of our children at its heart unlike this present government. **It is called the Foyer Foundation.** This is what they stand for.

At The Foyer Federation, we believe that every young person has a talent to share and a unique set of strengths that make them who they are. We work with our national network of member Foyers to draw out and build on those strengths through our exciting programmes, inspiring training workshops and meaningful partnerships.

They have existed for nearly 30 years and I have only just become aware of them.

The letter in *The Times* is written by Don Macdonald who was founding Chief Executive of this charity in London and who **accuses the government of not caring enough about our children, especially throughout the pandemic.**

"They did all they could to help the hospitality venues but youth services spending has been cut by three quarters in a decade with about half of London youth clubs closed."

He writes that, "London borough council funding for sport has fallen by more than a quarter in the past year with facilities closed or taken over for other uses." He is scathing about those in government and those in power who just **speak platitudes but take no significant action.**

This, I am afraid, is the mantra of this government.

Why, oh why, do they just not care enough to give our children what they need?

****

5TH JANUARY

Well today I get a sort of reply to the email I sent to the Ministry of Justice about the **Oakhill Secure Training Centre on the 18th October.** I actually signed up to receive the Ofsted reports and they have just sent me the most recent report which was in response to an urgent notification process being invoked due to the serious and widespread failures found in an earlier inspection..

The inspection was unannounced and the purpose of the visit was to ensure that children are safe and that adequate steps have been taken by G4S to safeguard and protect the welfare of the children. There are some improvements.

I will just pick out the most relevant findings, as I see it, of the report.

There are now far fewer children here than previously and that has enabled staff to engage more meaningfully with the children, and to use the spaces available for positive activities and engagement with children. The lower numbers mean that living units were seen to be far less cramped.

The children's living environment has notably improved, and a programme of refurbishment has started. However although the house units are much cleaner, staff have not always ensured that all living areas are kept to a good standard. Some kitchens had ingrained dirt on cabinets and inside cookers.

The quality of safeguarding outcome records is improving. The head of safeguarding identifies areas of learning and development. However, there remains some delay in the completion of staff practice supervision where this is a required outcome of a safeguarding concern.

Oversight of the incentives scheme has improved. There is a new focus on being 'open and honest' when communicating with children about their behaviour and incentives levels. Inspectors found that most children could only access the incentives they were entitled to.

While there was a reduction in incidents of violence in November, levels over the previous six months remained high when taking into account the reduced population of the centre. Previous delays in incidents being reviewed at the weekly restraint minimisation meeting have been addressed. However, records of this meeting were poor. This hinders the ability of managers to track actions. Some restraints reviewed by inspectors could have been avoided. There are examples of poor communication and staff not turning on their body-worn cameras.

Residential staff are now able to access key information that informs them about the day-to-day care needs of the children. The information is up to date and relevant in identifying any risks to children. Staff understand this information, which enables them to help keep children safe. The immediate serious and widespread concerns identified in the key recommendations from the last inspection have been addressed, meaning children are safer.

However, it is very early days, and the changes have not yet been embedded. In conclusion they are told that they must ensure that the recommendations from the October 2021 inspection are fully addressed, embedded and sustained.

So some improvements have been made and would appear to be on-going although I think there are too many 'howevers'. It just appals me that something like this is necessary. I look forward to the next report.

****

23RD JANUARY

There is a **reading crisis in secondary schools** where some children at the age of eleven have a reading age of six. Obviously some of this is blamed on the pandemic but other factors do come into play.

Many primary schools do not have a decent library, even now, in 2022.

Promised computers were not delivered to every child who needed one during the pandemic.

The President of the 'Association of School and College Leaders,' who is also head of a school in Yorkshire says, **"This is a nationwide issue.... The habits of reading are becoming a dying art."**

Parallel Universe. The Department for Education said it was committed to raising literacy standards, with an "ambitious recovery plan" being rolled out.

Amazed that the phrase 'world beating' was not in there somewhere.

****

26TH JANUARY

The Times Education Commission, which is chaired by Rachel Sylvester of *The Times*, is half way through its year and has just published an interim report. It makes really interesting reading. Its members are drawn from various fields encompassing education, politics, commerce, science, technology and the arts They are all convinced that **education needs to be reformed for a generation rather than be subordinated to the short term cycle of electoral politics and Treasury spending rounds.**

Oh my goodness how many years have we been saying this?

The existing curriculum neither adequately incorporates advances in knowledge nor teaches skills in sufficient depth to prepare our children for productive working lives. The 'Commercial Education Trust' wants much greater focus on commercial skills such as time keeping, resilience and self-motivation. They estimate **that this could generate an extra £124.6 billion in profits, equivalent to £1,860 for everyone in the UK.**

Sir James Dyson said that the country was ill equipped to train engineers, partly blaming the downgrading of design technology lessons by Michal Gove when he was Education Secretary. He said that Gove, "put it on the same level as cookery which is a wonderful thing…. but it doesn't create exports, technology or manufacturing businesses." As he says, "Children are creative, they love building and making things but as they get closer to GCSEs and A levels all that is squashed out of them."

Robert Halfon, Tory chairman of the Commons Education Committee says that **A levels should be replaced with an international baccalaureate and we should stop the narrowing of education at 16.**

The present system of exams is bureaucratic and unwieldy. It has become even more narrow, limited and box-ticking.

They say that they have much work still to do but it is obvious to me reading the conclusions so far that **our education is stuck in a time warp and is not equipping our young people for the modern work force**.

The editorial in *The Times* ends by saying "**One conclusion we can firmly state is that teaching is not only a vital task but a noble vocation**. Those who embark on it deserve respect and admiration for their efforts. They need support in the work of conveying enthusiasm for learning. Helping them to accomplish this would put students and the nation still more in their debt."

As a retired Primary School teacher this is of course music to my ears! I can tell you that the most successful teachers are those who spill over with enthusiasm for their subject and really enjoy the company of young people.

But yes education must move with the times and *The Times* must be congratulated for initiating this report.

****

27TH JANUARY
A cross party alliance of regional mayors are urging the PM to devolve more power over education or risk undermining the government's levelling up agenda. Andy Burnham, mayor of Manchester, said: **"The Department for Education is "the most devolution-resistant government department"** and **"it's holding English cities back."**

Andy Street, mayor of the west Midlands said, "The economy is different in different parts of the country" and he said **that mayors should have more power over education so that they could make the skills taught in schools and colleges more relevant to the local economy market.**

Sadiq Khan, Mayor of London said there was wide support for further devolution of education across the party lines. "We know the employers, we know the further education providers, we know the training providers. We also are planning ahead in relations to our economy for the next three years".

It sounds very good sense to me.

****

31ST JANUARY

And Rachel Sylvester writes another brilliant article in *The Times* today.

Last year she visited **Estonia, which she says, has the best education system in Europe. Children do not start school until seven but almost all go to high quality affordable kindergartens before that from the age of 18 months.** They are heavily subsidised so that parents never pay more than 20 percent of the minimum wage. There is a pre-school curriculum to encourage learning through play and nursery teachers must have a degree.

Britain, by contrast, treats early years' provision as a baby-sitting service and it is hugely expensive.

Indeed, as we all know.

The important point here is that the third of all pupils who fail their GCSEs and are therefore written off as failures, **can be spotted before they even get to school at the age of 5.**

She points out that Rishi Sunak in his budget speech said that the earliest years are the most important and announced 75 "family hubs" and yet over 1,000 Sure Start centres have been closed.

The Duchess of Cambridge's 'Royal Foundation Centre for Early Childhood' found that the social cost of failing to intervene early enough is more than *£16 billion a year in* **England because of higher**

rates of crime, unemployment and mental illness that could have been avoided.

"The failure to prioritise preschool education is a false economy," says Rachel Sylvester. "Levelling up should be about giving everyone a fair chance in life right from the start."

Why do successive governments not understand this? The Conservatives have been in power for 12 years and they still don't get it.

****

1ST FEBRUARY
A new report has highlighted **"extensive failures" in the way child sexual exploitation by criminal gangs is tackled.**

The Independent Inquiry into Child Sexual Abuse (IICSA) said police and authorities are **potentially downplaying the scale of abuse over concerns about negative publicity.**

We have been waiting for this report to come out ever since we heard of the appalling cases in Rotherham and Rochdale. It is not yet complete but will be laid before Parliament later this year.

Professor Alexis Jay, who chaired the inquiry, said: "The sexual exploitation of children by networks is not a rare phenomenon confined to a small number of areas with high-profile criminal cases.

"We found extensive failures by local authorities and police forces in the ways in which they tackled this sexual abuse.

"There appeared to be a flawed assumption that child sexual exploitation was on the wane, **however it has become even more of a hidden problem and increasingly underestimated."**

What I find most incredible, and frankly disgusting, is the way in which the police and other authorities so often **blamed the children for the abuse they suffered** some of whom reported being raped, abused, and in one case forced to perform sex acts on a group of 23 men while held at gunpoint.

Some were labelled "promiscuous" and some had criminal records slapped on to them in connection with their sexual offences, whilst the perpetrators of child sexual exploitation were often not investigated or prosecuted.

****

And then I hear Boris Johnson speaking on LBC a couple of years ago, when he said **that money spent on historic child abuse cases and that "malarkey" is just money being "spaffed up the wall".** He goes on to ask, "what on earth is that going to do to protect the public now?"

I apologise for this language, but, ladies and gentlemen, I say to you.................. **this is your Prime Minister.**

****

4TH FEBRUARY
In a letter to *The Times* this morning the government is criticised **for not giving this report the political attention it deserves.**

****

We also hear, that two days ago on the 2nd of February, the Supreme Court threw out a legal challenge against the government's **child citizenship fee of £1,000.** Obviously many families cannot afford this. Many, many children who are eligible for British citizenship because of their birth never actually become British citizens.

The reason this challenge was over-ruled was because this level of payment proposed by the Home Office **was agreed in Parliament and therefore cannot be changed by the courts.**

The Home Office will now continue to profit from the fee of £1,012 for a process that costs £372, unless it changes its policy or if Parliament acts. So lawyers and campaigners are now calling for Parliament to intervene and limit the fee to administrative costs, or scrapping it altogether for children in care and for those who cannot afford it.

Steve Valdez-Symonds, Amnesty International UK's refugee and migrant rights director, said: "**This fee deprives thousands of children of their citizenship rights, yet the Home Office has chosen to keep overcharging, despite the alienation and exclusion this is causing.**"

They are now also calling for changes to the fee to be made through the Nationality and Borders Bill.

The Office of Priti Patel never fails to disgust me.

****

10TH FEBRUARY

A damning report has been published today by the 'Education Policy Institute' think-tank. It talks about **the educational gap between pupils in long-term poverty and their richer classmates.**

Eleanor Hunt, co-author of the report said, "Our research shows that despite government policy interventions, there has been a **decade of failure** to improve the relative outcomes for students in long-term poverty – with these students still trailing their better-off peers by over a full grade and a half at GCSE". She also says that, "the proportion of poorer students falling into long-term poverty is now on the rise.

"The government must do more to address the fundamental drivers of deep- rooted educational inequalities, including poverty."

We are also hearing that there has been a **decline in teacher recruitment**. Jack Worth, an economist and the school workforce lead at the 'National Foundation for Educational Research' said: "The latest initial teacher training application figures show a clear deterioration in the recruitment situation compared to a year ago. The government needs to give teachers supply a shot in the arm if it wants to prevent the teacher supply challenges of the last decade rapidly re-emerging."

More and more under investment, not just from this government but from the past 12 years of Conservative governments. A devastating lack of commitment, understanding and adequate funding.

****

13TH FEBRUARY

We see time and time again that our children and young people are at the bottom of the pile with this government. They announce "world beating" programmes and then try to get them on the cheap.

A "flagship" **National Tutoring Programme** was set up to help pupils across England whose learning had been most disrupted by the pandemic. This was initially run by the 'Education Endowment Foundation' at the beginning of 2020. **In its first three months they had enrolled 125,000 pupils which was half of their target for the whole year.** It was brilliant and having met these targets it was widely assumed that this charity would be tasked with running the whole programme.

However, the government decided to award the contract to a Dutch company called **Randstad**. Why was this do you think? Yes you are absolutely correct: **because it was considerably cheaper.** The government had proposed a maximum of £62 million and Randstad severely undercut other charities including the EEF by submitting a bid of £25 million.

However it is now reported, in an excellent article by Anna Fazackerley of *The Guardian,* that the government is thinking about terminating this contract because they do acknowledge that the results have been "disastrous".

As one Head Teacher said **"they promised the earth and delivered very little."** (When have we heard that before?) Pupil enrolment is 90% below target, tutors cancel lessons 10 minutes before they are due to start and tutorials are being run by people with no knowledge of the subject they are teaching. One tutor asked whether the school had anything on the four times table! **Saturday mornings were also important for these children but three times out of four the tutors would not turn up.**

Their main web-site is too difficult to use and many schools are now turning their backs on the main route and organising tuition through a schools-led route instead.

This has all happened because this government tries to get things on the cheap especially when it involves our children. No sense of urgency whatsoever to sort this out. **Meanwhile our children continue to suffer.**

****

18TH FEBRUARY
The 7,000 air purifiers that were promised to schools to help with ventilation in classrooms have still not arrived as the second half of term begins.

****

Also today Jamie Oliver accuses Boris Johnson of **playing politics with children's health.** When Johnson got Covid and was in hospital he attributed his ill health partly to his obesity. He decided that it made sense to put a tax on salt and sugar. However it is looking as though he might renege on this idea and dump it in order to keep the right wing section of his party on side. Nothing, but nothing, must stand in the way of him staying in power.

But Jamie Oliver says, **"Children's health and access to nutritious food should be a non-negotiable priority.** It should be the first thing every Prime Minister and Minister thinks about. It should be above party politics. **It's a human right. And a child's right."**

****

[Russia invades Ukraine]

24TH FEBRUARY.
It is announced today that students entering higher education next year who take out a £45,000 loan will start repayments when their salaries reach £25,000 a reduction from £27,200.

They will also have 40 years in which to pay it back rather than the present 30 years. This means that some will still be repaying as they approach retirement. Some will face paying back £100,000. **Rather than reducing the tuition fees as requested they will be frozen at the present £9,250.**

Martin Lewis who runs the 'Money Saving Expert' web-site said: "The plans will see most university leavers pay far more for their degrees over their lifetime than they do now. **It effectively completes the transformation of student 'loans' into a working-life-long graduate tax."**

****

27TH FEBRUARY
Will Hutton writes in *The Observer* that: "Far more worrying is the impending squeeze on the incomes of our 140 universities: fees are

to be frozen until 2025 as inflation surges, implying a **real cut of close to 20% in their incomes."**

Spending on further education has halved in real terms over the last 11 years and nearly 22% of all our 18 year olds are neither in further education nor in a job which involves training. As he goes on to say: **"It is a rank injustice, fatally undermining our economy and the cohesion of our society."**

****

And another edict from this government concerns GCSEs. They have just announced that **students who fail maths and English will be barred from securing higher education loans in England.** The DoE did say that consultations were still in place and there could be exemptions for certain types of students, as those with dyslexia feel they are being discriminated against.

Why do they announce these blanket so-called reforms without thinking it through properly and so causing a lot of worry and distress? This is obviously a rhetorical question because we all know the answer.

As the poet Zephanaih puts it so succinctly and sensibly, **"Not everybody should go to University, but not everybody who fails their GCSEs shouldn't not go to university"**

He also says that in school he was a failure but now school children study his books to pass exams. In many things, he says, "you can't have a one-size-fits all approach".

Absolutely, and when educating and inspiring our young people, the approach musty be creative and exciting and open–minded and yes, individual when necessary.

But every good teacher knows that. It is just the admin people who haven't got a clue.

****

2ND MARCH

As the draconian **Nationality and Borders bill** passes through Parliament we hear about more and more amendments being defeated in the House of Lords.

And today we hear about a defeat for the government by Lord Dubs who argued that unaccompanied refugee children who are stranded on the continent should be allowed safe passage to the UK to be re-united with their families here. Who on earth would vote against this? Well 130 peers did apparently

We just hope that MPs will listen to this and accept it when the bill returns to the Commons. How can they not?

****

3RD MARCH

And talking about the House of Lords we all get a shock of enormous magnitude today when it is announced that **Gavin Williamson is to be knighted.**

We all went into meltdown. This is the biggest insult to children and their teachers since the resignation of education tsar Sir Kevan Collins.

If you were not aware before you certainly will be now: this government does not have any regard, interest or concern about the nation's children whatsoever.

Gavin Williamson is the man who, throughout the pandemic and the lockdowns, was incompetent to the point of dangerous neglect. He opened schools and then closed them a few days later. He denied free school meals and food vouchers to disadvantaged children leaving it for footballer Marcus Rashford to shame him into a U-turn. He then confused Marcus Rashford with the rugby player Maro Itoje who also happens to be black. He failed to get laptops to children who needed them and his attempted organisation of the A level results was so appalling that there had to be a U-turn there as well.

He was the worst education secretary in living memory and **was sacked from the Cabinet** last September returning to the back benches.

Funnily enough he was **also sacked by Theresa May** when he was Defence Secretary when there was an inquiry into a leak from the National Security Council.

So this knighthood is seen as a reward for failure.

But prior to this he was chief whip under Theresa May so he obviously knows all the dirt on everybody including the PM and **so it is also seen as a price for silence.**

But as Laura Kuenssberg pointed out on Twitter, what could he possibly know that would make the British public think any worse of the PM than they already do?

Well I leave that one with you.

****

9TH MARCH

Apparently there are no statistics which show how many children there are in England let alone how many children are receiving education. Can you believe that? **How can a government plan for the future of education or of children's health if they have no idea of the numbers involved?**

Rachel de Souza is the children's commissioner and has just concluded a report which surveyed all 151 local authorities and discovered that many did not have figures for those in home-schooling or attending independent schools in their areas. As she states, "It is crucial that we know where all children are, and that we develop the necessary infrastructure to maintain this understanding."

She goes on to say that, "There are hundreds of children that have never interacted with the education system that we know nothing about, including children who may have gone missing from care or been trafficked into the UK".

The Local Government Association said, "The safety net that schools and councils provide to ensure that children do not miss out on their entitlement to education is stretched to capacity, exacerbated by a lack of resources and powers available to councils to fulfil their statutory duties – which worsened as a result of the pandemic.

"We would like the government to work to raise the profile of children missing formal full-time education, and to resource councils adequately to fulfil their responsibilities in ensuring all children receive a suitable education."

I find it difficult to believe that this government cares so little for our children and young people that they haven't a clue as to where many of them are.

People who are concerned have been pushing the government to introduce a national register for all those who are being home schooled but the government's response last week to a 2019 public consultation on the issue said the rollout was still "subject to securing the necessary resources", and "details of what penalties parents may face have yet to be determined."

2019! Not a lot of urgency there then.

Some are opposed to a register apparently (there are always some) but as the Commissioner says: **"The register of children not in school is vital in making sure that we are able to keep children safe and engaged, wherever they are learning."**

****

27TH MARCH

On June 17th 2021 In **'Beneath the Bluster'** I write about children's care homes and the provision of private providers which are an exorbitant expense to local authorities. Today we hear that **the ten largest providers of children's social care placements made more than £300 million in profits last year.** The largest four are called Outcomes First, CareTech, Polaris, and Priory now called Aspris.

Local councils have reported that spending on residential placements has increased by 84% since 2015 and that they are now having to divert funds from other areas, such as early help for families, in order to meet spiralling costs.

The government has commissioned an official review of children's social care which, as I have said earlier, will report later this spring. So once more the lack of urgency is desperate.

To quote just one case at a care home in Bolton: A young boy there had not bathed, changed his clothes, or been provided with a home-cooked meal for four months. Ofsted suspended their licence....... but it should have been shut down.

I said it in Volume 1 and I say it again here: **They are not Children's 'Care' Homes, they are Children's 'We Don't Care' Homes.**

****

28TH MARCH

The schools white paper was published today. Hopes were high because it was no longer the premise of Gavin Williamson but sadly the immediate reaction was not encouraging.

"Inoffensive," said one commentator. "I'd give it a C-minus, or a GCSE grade 4," said another. "It's a pass, but not a good one." Not much to object to, little to inspire, and **inadequate funding to achieve any of its stated ambitions.**

It actually drew a lot of ridicule from teachers and parents as it focused on maths, literacy and tutoring, all of which it was felt that, after 12 years of Tory government, they should not be needing further focus.

There are so many schools without a library even, and we know about the lack of tutors and teaching assistants. We also know about the burn-out of teachers themselves who are under-supported, under-valued and under paid.

There is no new money available. So this is another paper which will be proved to be ineffective.

44% of teachers are saying they will leave the profession within the next two years.

But the single most important announcement was the proposal **that all schools in England would either be in a multi-academy trust or in the process of joining one by 2030.** In other words they would be moved away from the local authorities. This will affect many primary schools because many secondary schools are already academies.

But there is some disquiet about this and how it actually works in practice.

Angela Rayner, Shadow Chancellor, said that the Tories had wasted money on academy conversions, while school budgets were squeezed year on year, leaving head-teachers with little choice but to beg parents for donations.

We also see a **rise in exclusions and off-rolling in academies which is completely unacceptable.** Money is spent on executives and head teachers and last year *The Guardian* reported that the Department for Education wrote to 94 trusts asking them to justify these high pay awards.

Kevin Courtney, the joint general secretary of the National Education Union said that: "Some schools have had to endure multiple re-brokerings and a number of different sponsors, each bringing a change of ethos and approach, new school uniforms, a turnover of staff and a rise in exclusions and off-rolling. **There is no stability in such a system and it is pupils, parents and staff who lose out."**

Angela Rayner says, "Labour will end the Tories' programme of forced conversion, re-empower local communities and properly invest in all our schools."

****

1ST APRIL

You might remember that in 2014 a report was published, the Jay report, which described how more than **1,400 children were groomed, trafficked and sexually abused in Rotherham, South Yorkshire between 1997 and 2013.** Some of the earliest findings told how several managers of local children's homes set up the "taxi driver group" and they investigated reports that taxis driven by Pakistani men were arriving at care homes to take children away. This report accused the South Yorkshire Police of failing to prioritise the issue and declining to act.

The report found that eight officers had a case to answer for misconduct and six for gross misconduct five of whom have faced sanctions but none of whom have lost their jobs or faced criminal charges. Indeed an ex-Detective was accused of having sex with a young girl and passing on drugs.

Ms Jayne Senior, who worked for council-run youth project 'Risky Business', which supported young people a risk of abuse said the victims at the time had been treated in an "absolutely abhorrent" manner.

"They were seen as consenting to their own abuse, they were seen as children who wouldn't come forward, that wouldn't make good witnesses."

"Children don't consent to abuse, they don't consent to rape."

I am writing about this today because David Walker, a former detective, was cleared yesterday of all allegations against him marking the end of the planned actions against the South Yorkshire police officers. He was one of the 47 serving and former officers who were investigated by the Independent Office for Police Conduct. **Apparently every officer investigated over the Rotherham sex abuse scandal went on to keep their job.**

The solicitor who was representing some of the women involved was appalled at this outcome. "It's extremely disappointing that despite the best efforts of the brave women I represent, **the police discipline system has delivered zero accountability" he said.**

I too am appalled. Young, disadvantaged women continue to be invisible and of no importance to the system at large. Ignored, discounted and of no interest whatsoever. Let us brush them all under the carpet.

****

3RD APRIL

Ministers are being warned against **loosening the rules around the number of children nursery staff can care for** after it was revealed that they are looking at ways in which they can cut costs for parents.

Neil Leitch, chief executive of the 'Early Years Alliance' said: "Relaxing ratios will do little to reduce childcare costs and will **simply place increasing and unnecessary pressure on an exhausted workforce.** Education ministers are well aware we have a recruitment and retention crisis never witnessed before, so it beggars belief that they would wish to consider such a short sighted approach."

Well I am sorry to disagree with you Mr. Leitch but I can absolutely believe that this government is prepared to take the easiest, cheapest, most ineffectual and dangerous approach possible.

****

6TH APRIL

There is an excellent and very revealing article in *The Times* today by James Kirkup, director of the 'Social Market Foundation,' about the detrimental effects of closing schools during the pandemic, the lasting harm this has caused to our children and the lack of concern displayed by the government.

He was concerned that schools remained shut even when we were all being told to "eat out to help out" as pubs and restaurants opened up again. He paraphrases a response he got from a senior figure in the Department of Education which he had almost exactly a year ago. It went like this: **"Yes, we know it's bad for kids and really bad for poor kids. But no-one at No 10 will listen so the schools will stay closed."**

The Education select committee, a cross-party group, called it a **'national disaster for children and young people'**. It continues to this day. But as he says, "the issue never makes it to the top of the priority."

He ends by asking: **"What does it say about us as a country when we decide there are more important things than helping the children we failed to care for?"**

I leave you to answer that question.

****

21ST APRIL

It really is so disheartening to hear that **Primary schools in particular are struggling due to a devastating lack of funds**. Teaching assistants, school trips and equipment are all having to be cut back.

The Sutton Trust has been told by two-thirds of all primary school head teachers that **they have not received sufficient catch-up funding this year**.

Sir Peter Lampl, co-founder and chairman of the Sutton Trust has said that, **"The government must make an enormous investment in education recovery so that all pupils are given a chance to succeed."**

Well yes absolutely. No-one would argue with that.

Oh wait a minute. This government already has. It refused to give the money asked for by Sir Kevan Collins.

****

23RD APRIL

We have so many wise people who know about education and who are giving advice to anyone who will listen. **Sir Michael Wilshaw who is a former head-teacher and Ofsted boss,** writes in *The Times* today about the possible future of education. He writes about the exam structure which he says needs total reform and then is scathing about the lack of sufficient funding and the low value the government puts on education. **Other countries are spending seven times as much as we do he says.**

It is a long, wise and informative article but unfortunately we know that no-one in the present government will hear him or take any appropriate action whatsoever.

****

26TH APRIL

The PM had a Cabinet meeting this morning to ask for ideas as to how they can help with the soaring increase in the cost of living as the rising prices of food and energy push up inflation. As someone has pointed out, 12 years of Tory government and they still haven't a clue.

So what idea has Johnson come up with? Guess. Well the title of this chapter gives you a very strong clue.

Yes, child care.

This was being discussed on the 3rd April but is now back on the government's agenda because they have run out of ideas as to how they can tackle the rising cost of living. No, sorry I am mistaken. There has never been a plan.

According to sources at the BBC he has told his ministers he wants to reduce childcare costs by easing health and safety rules.

At the moment it is a legal requirement that there must be at least one member of staff for every three children aged two and under. For over twos there must be one member of staff for every four children.

But the PM wants to lower these limits and allow more children per members of staff in order to reduce costs.

I cannot begin to tell you how angry this makes me. Early learning years, as everyone says over and over again, are the most important years of a young life.

A move like this would be nothing short of criminal.

****

27TH APRIL
I think you should be made aware that one of the other ideas for saving money promoted at the cabinet meeting yesterday was that cars need only have an MoT every two years instead of annually.

In the paper today there was an outcry over this saying that actually in the long run it could be more expensive, as mechanical failures would get worse and cost more to repair.

Also of course it would be more dangerous on the road. The article in *The Times* was reasonably long and right at the end, in the very last two sentences, they mentioned the proposed cuts in childcare safety measures.

No surprise there then.

We are much more concerned about our cars than we are about our children.

****

And today I hear the story of a young child who saves his school dinner to take home to share with his parents.

****

28TH APRIL
An article in *The Guardian* today by Polly Toynbee picks up the idea of cutting more staff in nurseries put forward by this government as a way to reduce the costs of child care. **She calls it an act of brutalism and actually says that years of brutalism have stunted early years care.**

As we have seen, many nurseries are on their knees and Ofsted reports that more than 5,000 child care providers have closed down in the past two years.

On the *Today* programme yesterday we heard Amanda Spielman, head of Ofsted, reminding us that under-twos have lived all their lives under Covid rules and urgently need extra help with delayed speech vocabulary and social skills. More help is needed not less.

Neil Leitch of the 'Early Years Alliance' says that more than 16,000 nursery places have been lost in the last five years. He believes that any more cuts in the staff-to-child ratio would result in more nursery teachers leaving the profession.

As Polly Toynbee goes on to say, the destruction of Labour's 3,600 wonderful Sure Start Schemes, by the Tory party in 2010, was a **"monstrous act of vandalism."**

These schemes had become community hubs which gave all round support to parents and young children. Absolutely what all parents starting out on parenthood are crying out for. **They had midwives, health visitors, speech and language therapists, open-door play schemes, psychiatric help for depressed parents, help with job seeking and adult education and training.**

A child's first 1,000 days matter the most and every family should get the earliest support possible.

But I hear the Shadow Secretary of Education, Bridget Philipson and it is music to my ears. She has pledged to increase the early years' pupil premium more than fourfold and improve the quality and provision of nursery support.

She has also said that **she is set to reprise the great value of Sure Start.**

I have only just discovered her but she is already my political hero.

****

8TH MAY

The Institute for Social and Economic Research at the University of Essex has found that teacher's wages have fallen by 9% in real terms over the past decade. This has caused a fall in experienced male teachers in secondary schools especially.

Many teachers feel they would be better off financially if they leave the profession and fewer and fewer can afford to live and teach in London.

Of course recruitment and retention is difficult too. 30,000 teachers leave every year while fewer people are signing up for teacher training programmes.

It is indicative of the value the government puts on teachers. The pressures are unsustainable and one in seven teachers give up after a year.

****

14TH MAY

Today the government has been accused of more **dither and delay. They are being heavily criticised for failing to tackle childhood obesity.** The Department of Health has just announced that its plans to ban multi-buy deals for junk food and pre-watershed TV advertising will be delayed for a year.

Apparently this is so that officials can assess the impact on household finances as families struggle with the increasing cost of living.

I cannot even begin to try to understand this.

Health campaigners have accused the PM of "playing politics" with children's health.

Professor Graham MacGregor, a cardiologist at Queen Mary University said "Boris Johnson could have left a legacy of being the first prime minister to address obesity in a meaningful way. Instead he has given in to his own MPs who, in an ironic way, were starting to comply with these new policies."

Labour's shadow health minister Andrew Gwynne said: "Instead of cutting childhood obesity, preventing ill-health and easing pressure on the NHS, this chaotic government is performing **another U-turn."**

Meanwhile, Barbara Crowther, of the' Children's Food Campaign', said ministers should be urgently curbing multi-buy offers instead of "delaying and dithering".

"Obesity is spiking and millions of families can't afford to put proper food on the table. **Multi-buy offers make people spend more on junk, and less on healthy food,"** she said.

"This delay threatens the UK target to halve childhood obesity by 2030. **Boris is playing politics with our children's health."**

Over and over again we see the same story. A government and prime minister who are ignorant, incompetent and uncaring. No plans, no details, no vision, no intelligence. Our young people will suffer the most.

****

15TH MAY,

Bridget Phillipson, the Shadow Education Secretary addressed the Annual 'Progressive Britain' conference yesterday. It was a long speech in which she set out Labour's plans for children and young people. Every word touched my heart.

She said: "The word 'children' does not appear as much as once in the Spring Statement itself. **Children don't even register in the Chancellor's thinking**. And this isn't just about short-term announcements.

"We have seen it for 12 long years of their government, as real terms funding for children dropped year after year. We've seen it in our schools, as a focus on seeing children as the employees of the future, not the society of the future, has narrowed the curriculum time and again. We saw it in the pandemic, when at every turn children were an afterthought for this government, when the support they needed to learn at home was delayed, when exams were thrown into chaos for not one year but two, and **when pubs were reopened before schools**. Our whole country is failed when we let our children down."

So what would Labour do?

"We would introduce breakfast clubs, so every child starts their day with a proper meal. Afterschool activities, so every child gets to learn and experience art, music, drama, and sport. Mental health support, because every report we see tells us children's development has fallen behind in the pandemic."

There would be, "Continued professional development for teachers, because every child deserves teachers second to none to support their learning. Targeted extra investment, right from early years through to further education, to support the children at risk of falling behind, because attainment gaps open up early, and need tackling early. And it's child-centred, future-centred thinking that lies behind so many of our announcements last autumn. A National Excellence Programme, to drive up standards in schools because every child deserves to go to a school with high expectations, and high achievements. Thousands upon thousands of new teachers, in subjects with shortages right now, because every child deserves to be a taught maths and physics by people who love their subjects."

If you are concerned about the future of our children and our grand-children **you just need to be worried about the fact that children do not feature in the thinking of this government.**

****

Ofsted reports today that after inspecting 32 children's homes, 17 are judged "requires improvement to be good." In other words they are not delivering good care to the vulnerable children and young people who live there.

****

17TH MAY

William Hague, former leader of the Tory party, says the U- turn on the prospective bans on advertising and two- for- one offers to tackle obesity is **weak, shallow and immoral.** He says **the PM is just giving way to the right wing of his party who threaten to send in letters of no-confidence if he does not do their bidding.**

He writes a long article in *The Times* today deploring the fact that it is seen as curtailing people's freedom. As he writes so eloquently, people want the freedom to live healthier and longer lives, children need to be able to skip and jump, adults to run down a country lane and older people to keep their quality of life to the end.

Breaking news: 2pm

I have just watched Jamie Oliver speaking to camera outside 10 Downing Street. He is furious with the PM for turning his back on the obesity plans.

He is brilliant, angry and very articulate. He is asking the PM to admit he has made a mistake and do another U-turn to restore these bans. He is giving him 36 hours to do so. **If he doesn't then he has invited everyone who possibly can to get hold of an Eton Mess desert and go to Downing Street at 12.30 on Friday.** Mums, dads, chefs, teachers, campaigners just for 15 minutes. No shouting or noise. Just hold it high. You went to Eton Prime Minister he says, and this is a mess. Stop playing politics with children's lives.

I became quite emotional and my admiration for Jamie Oliver knows no bounds. We need more like him.

****

18TH MAY

The unprecedented rise in food prices effects our children obviously. And today on the radio we hear a discussion about school meals and whether children will be allowed one potato or two.

****

23RD MAY

'The Independent Review of Children's Social Care' is published today. It started its findings 14 months ago and it was chaired by Josh MacAlister, a former teacher. It is the one we have been waiting for, for so long.

The review reports that the whole child care programmes have been getting worse over the years and there are 80,000 children in care at the moment. Without major reform there could be 100,000 children in care by 2032.

There needs to be far more help with struggling families in the **very early years** rather than suddenly descending on them at the peak of the crisis.

The review berates the government for a "lack of national direction" over social care and urges ministers to commit to a **five-year, £2.6 billion programme to reform a system which is under "extreme stress"**

It criticises children's services as too often rigid, remote, stuck in crisis mode and disconnected from the needs of families they support and the wider interests of the children they care for, "especially when it comes to considering children's need for connection and love".

"What we need to do," Josh MacAlister says, "is to tilt the system firmly back to supporting the adults, the carers, the parents, the families who love their children."

It has been noticed that the words **'love' and 'loving'** are mentioned time and again in this review which is of course what children need above all else.

And they also mention the older children who are so often completely ignored. They call for legislation to create new care standards aimed at ending the scandal of unregulated care in which thousands **of 16- and 17-year-olds** are placed in potentially unsafe accommodation without supervision.

A proposed new **"family help" service** would be based in schools and children's centres and made up of social workers, mental health practitioners and domestic abuse workers, who would provide intensive support to about 500,000 children in need. It would lead to thousands fewer children entering care, the report says.

It recommended giving **financial help to extended family members who can step in and look after children such as grand-parents, aunts and uncles**. At present they have to go through the bureaucratic process of becoming an official foster parent before they can access funding.

And the other thing this report is saying, which is music to my ears, is that **Young O:ffender Institutes should be scrapped as part of this radical reset.**

'Wholly unsuitable' young offender institutes should be phased out over the next decade, it says. "Instead, troubled youngsters would be placed in 'secure children's homes' or 'secure schools', which would be less institutionalised and prison-like and 'more caring'."

The big five children's charities – NSPC, Barnardo's, National Children's Bureau, The Children's Society and Action for Children – welcomed the review, saying in a joint statement: **"It provides a once-in--generation opportunity to fix a struggling system and create a step change in the way children and families are supported."**

Everyone is saying this, including our Education Secretary, and it is so good to be able to write something like this. I just emphasise that it was first mooted in 2019 and it is now 2022.

What we all need to have now is a firm commitment from the government for the money required, and the man-power and mind-set to step up to the task.

I will try to remain positive.

****

25TH MAY
But not for long. A headline on the front page of *The Times* today reads "**Drugs gang boss is running home for vulnerable children.**"

A report by Billy Kenber, who is the senior investigations reporter for *The Times*, just serves to emphasise the **complete lack of concern about our most vulnerable children by successive Conservative governments**.

He reports that despite Ofsted's obligation to vet company directors the ringleader of a drugs gang who spent 14 years in prison in the late 1990s co-owns an Essex children's home which receives £70,000 a month of tax payer's money.

*A shortage of places has pushed the average fee to more than £4,000 a week per child.

*Failing homes have continued to have children in their care despite concerns from Ofsted.

*Inspection reports state that a failure to recruit qualified staff meant that homes are not keeping children safe.

*There is a complete lack of adequate regulation of the ownership of care companies and of the market itself.

An Ofsted spokesperson said that, "For several years now we have consistently said that the Care Standards Act is not fit for purpose."

The consequence of all this is, of course, that the children who need quality care the most are the ones being pushed more and more into deprivation, criminality and neglect. These are the children who will end up in our failing Youth Offender Institutes.

But the basic question is should local councils be outsourcing something as fundamental as the care of its most vulnerable children to the profit making sector in the first place?

The review says children's social care should stay under local government control, and while it considered and rejected nationalising private children's, homes, it says in principle profit should play no part in children's care provision.

The Independent Review is the chance that the government has to rectify all of this and I will be keeping an eye on it long after this book is published.

****

28TH MAY

An article in *The Guardian* today by Anna Fazackerley makes my blood run cold. **It is one of the most horrifying things I have read and that is from a very low bar.**

She is saying that all initial teacher training providers in England must be re-accredited by the Department for Education to continue educating teachers from 2024. However, two-thirds of providers, including some top universities, were told this month that they had failed the first round of the new accreditation process.

The University of Nottingham, a member of the prestigious Russell Group, has failed in spite of being rated outstanding by Ofsted just two months ago. Inspectors praised the "exceptional curriculum taught by experts".

The University of Birmingham also failed the first round and they had been chosen by the Department for Education as one of their specialist partners for its new school based National Institute of Teaching.

The head of one university that failed, who asked not to be named for fear of deterring applicants, said: "Our staff involved in teacher education, who are excellent, were devastated by not being successful. They find it hard to believe, because of our track record."

So what is going on?

Well I can tell you what is going on. **This right-wing government thinks that the teaching curriculum in many Colleges and universities is too left-wing.**

Mary Bousted, the general secretary of the National Education Union, said: "This was the brainchild of [former schools minister] Nick Gibb, who was obsessed with the idea that university departments of teacher education were hotbeds of left-wing intellectualism. I told him I didn't know how to convey my frustration that he was coming out with this rubbish."

Prof David Spendlove, Associate Dean of Manchester University's faculty of humanities and former head of initial teacher education, said: "People who have been doing this for a very long time are being told they aren't fit for purpose, despite all the positive inspections they've been through. That's a farce," he said.

They are being told they can re-apply but some big universities are so outraged they could walk away from teacher training altogether.

Cambridge University did not apply for the accreditation due to fears its curriculum would be compromised.

This is at a time when we are desperately short of teachers.

We already know that teacher training applications are down by about 24% from last year and that recruitment is proving extremely difficult.

Prof David Green, vice-chancellor of Worcester University, which has a strong focus on teacher education, says that, "This new DfE system risks destroying much existing high quality teacher training. That would be a disaster for children who will be recovering from the educational devastation wrought by the pandemic for years."

A report by the National Foundation for Educational Research in March said that a large range of secondary subjects would not meet teacher recruitment targets in 2022. These include shortage subjects such as physics, maths, chemistry and computing, but also those that typically recruit well such as English, biology and geography.

This is really serious. **We have a government interfering with the teaching curriculum of educational places of excellence.** To me this looks like the thought police. What does it look like to you?

****

31ST MAY
I hear this on the radio this morning: a mother says her young son got two bowls out for breakfast. She said, oh that's a bit greedy you can't have two bowls of cereal. He said, no, one is for you because I haven't seen you eat for days.

****

1ST JUNE
The free school meals for young children issue has raised its ugly head again.

This week 12 school leaders from teaching unions and trusts have written to the Chancellor and to the Education Secretary calling for the **free school meals scheme to be expanded to all families on Universal Credit.**

The 'Child Poverty Action Group' says that about 1 million children in poverty miss out on free school meals because of "restrictive, arbitrary and complicated welfare systems." Why does it have to be so difficult?

In **Scotland** free school meals are now universal for all primary school children.

Wales is doing the same from September.

England?

Free school meals are only given to children whose family income falls below £7.400 after tax.

In **Northern Ireland** the cap is set at £14,000 a year.

Once again children in England are ignored and especially now with the huge rise in the cost-of-living, can go to school with an empty stomach and not eat all day and no-one cares.

You cannot learn, or indeed function at all, if you are hungry.

****

10TH JUNE

The NSPCC reports today that the **number of child cruelty offences** in England jumped by a quarter last year, according to police data which they have collected.

Obviously this has a lot to do with the stress people suffered during the pandemic but the chief executive of the NSPCC, Sir Peter Wanless, is calling on the government.to treat this as a priority and to do much more to help struggling families.

They also say that more help should be available to families before they reach crisis point.

How many times do we need to say this?

How many times do we need to say this?

How many times do we need to say this?

Just asking.

****

14TH JUNE

Defending his decision to make a U-turn over the tax on salt and sugar Boris Johnson comes up with a plan for all those struggling to feed their families.

Are you ready for this?

Here it is:-

"Eat Less"

****

15TH JUNE

The final report of the **Times Education Commission** is published today. I will give a much edited version of it here. You can read the full report at thetimes.co.uk/tac

They highlight 12 points:

1. **A British Baccalaureate** instead of the narrow A level system.
2. **Electives Premium** to be granted to all schools to be spent on drama, music, dance, sport and a National Citizen Service

consisting of volunteering and outdoor expeditions for every pupil.

3. **A new cadre of career academies** with links to industry and a focus on creativity and entrepreneurialism.

4. **Help for early years** with a boost for funding and when every child would have a unique pupil number from birth and every primary school would have a library. (Oh at last)

5. **A tutorial boost** when undergraduates could act as tutors and earn credits towards their degrees.

6. **Digital skills** which would give every child a laptop or tablet.

7. **Welcome Wellbeing** which should be at the heart of education with a counsellor in every school to encourage pupils to actively build resilience.

8. **Restore the status of teachers** with better career development and a new category of consultant teachers.

9. **A reformed Ofsted** with a wider range of metrics including wellbeing, and school culture.

10. **Special needs focus** to give a greater focus on inclusion and training for teachers to be able to identify needs.

11. **50 new university campuses** and a transferable credit system between universities and colleges.

12. **A 15 year strategy** putting education above short term party politics.

And just to remind you why we need this as if you didn't know.

Between 2010 and 2025 spending on the health service will have increased by 42% whist the education budget will have gone up by 3% over the same period.

I ask the government to implement the review on children's social care and this education review with a degree of urgency and I ask them to give the early years' top priority.

****

18TH JUNE

But I am in cloud cuckoo land if I think even for a moment that they will, for today we hear that **school building projects, swimming pools and libraries have been earmarked for huge emergency cuts**. Patrick Butler of *The Guardian brings* this to our attention and says that town halls have been hit by an unexplained £1.7 billion hole in their budgets.

Unexplained? For goodness sake how can you be £1.7 billion short without knowing how it happened?

****

We also hear this week that the government will increase the funding rate for infant free school meals from £2.34 to £2.41 a meal. This is for just years one and two. **And that, as we can all work out, is an increase of 7p.**

This is the second increase since the policy was first introduced in 2014 and exceeds the first increase which was 4p.

It has been called inadequate, which of course it is.

The Shadow Schools Minister, Stephen Morgan, said, "This government is once again asking schools and providers to do more with less. As costs soar, funding of just 7p extra a meal will do little to ensure children are getting a healthy, balanced meal,"

It will mean children getting smaller portions with fewer ingredients.

****

27TH JUNE

It has just been announced **that Sheffield Hallam University is to cut its English Literature degree course.** Like the University of Cumbria it will be incorporated into a general English degree.

A number of universities have made cuts to arts and humanities courses after a government crackdown on what ministers regard as "low value" courses.

We are all outraged about this but Philip Pullman, the award winning author, is one of a number of writers to raise concerns and he puts it very eloquently as you would expect.

He told *The Guardian*: "Without literature, without music and art and dance and drama, people young and old alike will perish of mental and emotional and imaginative starvation. We really do have a government of barbarians."

We see this happening in schools as well where music is all but disappearing.

****

5TH JULY

A joint letter from 250 business leaders which has been shown to *The Times* says that schools are failing students by not adequately equipping them with the skills they need for work. They say that "too many young people are leaving school without the entrepreneurial skills necessary to succeed. They call for entrepreneurship to be included in maths, English and design which would bring these subjects to life and make them more relevant.

The Times Education Committee praised Estonia schools for focussing on 21st century competencies including comprehension, collaboration, entrepreneurship and critical thinking, "the qualities that employers say they want."

****

9TH JULY

And there is a shocking report in *The Times* about sex education in our schools. You will find this difficult to read.

Sex education has been outsourced and many schools have contracted out the teaching. Sex education is now compulsory in all schools. However those who teach it from outside sources are not required to have any education or child development qualifications and there is no professional register or regulation of their curriculum.

When I read what is being taught I understand it to be a severe case of child abuse.

A nine year old child came home "shaking" and "white as a sheet because they had been taught about rape in detail."

Young children had fluffy toy animals and were told how to pretend they were masturbating with each other.

Some organisations taught them about "kinks" such as being locked in a cage, flogged, caned, beaten and slapped in the face.

When a 14 year old girl asked a question about her sexual relationship with a 16 year old boy she was not told that this was illegal.

When another girl said she felt "dirty" after being persuaded to have sex for money she was told that actually sex work can be rewarding and maybe she should find better clients.

There is so much more. Rachel de Souza the children's commissioner is going to review sex education being taught in schools but this is only after an MP got in touch with her after being contacted by the mother of the nine year old child.

So just to be clear, under this Conservative government we cannot get qualified teachers of physics and maths but we can get unqualified adults to teach kinky sex practices to young children.

****

10TH JULY

This government is paying £310 per annum for every school child. Before we get too carried away we need to know that in the States they pay £1,600 per child and in the Netherlands they pay £2,500 per child.

****

So I say to this government: stop trying to get education on the cheap and then wasting money on ridiculous reforms, after reforms, after reforms. It is our children who suffer. We need action not words and we need action NOW.

But I know that this is a pipe dream and that so long as the present government remains in power nothing will change.

Are you happy with this? Are you aware of all of this?

All I ask is that next time you hear a politician say, "Of course children are our top priority," as you no doubt will, just shout out at the top of your voice,

"LIAR."

****

And so we go on to look at another issue which has had similar disastrous consequences for so many because of the same level of ignorance, incompetence and sheer stupidity.

We take a deep breath as we talk about ....

BREXIT

2021

I finished the chapter on Brexit in my last book by saying Brexit will go on........ .and on......and on. And so it has, and so it does, and so it will.

The **Northern Ireland Protocol** continues to cause unrest, uncertainty and anger. As the EU chief negotiator says, the UK is seeking a 'path of confrontation' over Northern Ireland. Certainly there seems to be a 'war of words'. Lord Frost said earlier this month that the European Union would be making a 'historic misjudgement' if it wasn't prepared to make changes to the Northern Ireland Protocol.

And not only words, as only this morning at 6.30am two masked and armed men boarded a bus and poured fuel over it before setting it alight in Newtownards, County Down.

Always blame the EU seems to be the motto of the day. But this treaty was drawn up and signed by the PM.

****

As Ian Dunt writes in a brilliant article in *the i* on the **29th October**, "But then, that's the game we're in now. This is the culture the UK has helped create. Since Brexit, any dispute has been jumped on by No 10 as an opportunity to stoke the anti-European culture war.

Brexit minister Lord Frost is engaged in a seemingly endless quasi-religious battle, in which he trashes the agreements he himself only just signed."

He finishes his article by **saying, "This is the real face of Brexit and the future it promises: inconsequential technicalities exploding into angry tit-for-tat hostilities, severing the moral and political authority of the West.**

And we had better get used to it, because there'll be plenty more to come."

****

But I jump back a bit to **October 24th** and an article in *The Times* by David Aaronovitch. **He thinks that there is a pro-EU lobby stirring.**

He begins his article by encouraging everyone to book early this Christmas to take your family to **Frostworld**. He says it is a place "where everything is going swimmingly as we bask in the freedoms that Brexit has given us." In other words, as I would call it, **a parallel universe!**

He does admit that any discussion about Brexit and re-joining the EU will not happen in the foreseeable future because as he says **Get Brexit Done means Stop Talking About It**.

The wonders of Brexit were not mentioned in the PM's conference speech and all that Sir Keir said was, "A botched Brexit has left a big hole. The government is learning that it isn't enough to Get Brexit Done. You need a plan to Make Brexit Work."

And that was all. Brexit is the elephant in the room. Nobody will talk about it.

But I will!

Mr. Aaronovitch thinks it will be a generational matter and that amongst younger people it will be open for discussion, especially when they start to feel, very strongly, the thousands of vexations being out of Europe will cause. "The argument," he says, "will be there to be had."

I actually think, and hope, he could be right.

****

31ST OCTOBER

And William Keegan in *The Observer* will. Apparently he was asked by a top academic whether he was absolutely certain that **we could re-join the EU. The answer, he said, was that he was not. But he went on to say that, "as the evidence of the damage of the foolish referendum decision accrues, it is becoming more and more certain that we should try."**

And of course at the very least we should be attempting to **have as good a relationship as possible with the EU and he admires the Shadow Chancellor Rachel Reeves who is all for this approach.**

The Europeans can see the disaster that is Brexit for what it is. A Brussels commissioner Thierry Breton said, "Look at what is happening on the supermarket shelves. Look at what is happening at the petrol pumps. Look at what is happening with the shortage of nurses and doctors. Look at what is happening in the construction sector."

And Peter Schmeichel, former Manchester United player, when asked his view of Brexit by a member of the audience during an interview that was meant to be all about football he replied, **"What on earth were you thinking of?"**

The government tries to say every difficulty is Covid related and the problems are world-wide. **"Funny" says William Keegan "how**

Germany, which admitted a million immigrants instead of repelling them, is not suffering the shortages of labour that we are."

****

10TH NOVEMBER

And an example of the UK ramping up the problems with the EU can be seen in the way the **Northern Ireland Protocol** situation is being negotiated by Lord Frost and Boris Johnson. They are threatening to trigger Article 16 of the treaty drawn up and signed off by Boris Jonson.

And just a couple of hours ago we hear this:

Lord Frost has said that **triggering Article 16 will be the "only option"** if talks between the UK and EU fail to resolve Northern Ireland Protocol problem. He is trying to put all the blame for lack of progress on to the EU which is the usual approach he takes.

However European Commission (EC) Vice-President Maros Sefcovic has warned that there will be **"serious consequences"** if the UK triggers Article 16. He said that despite a "big move" by the EU on its proposals, "until today we have seen no move at all from the UK side". Mr Sefcovic said the move would be "serious for Northern Ireland as it would lead to instability and unpredictability".

And in the United States, several senior members of the House of Foreign Affairs Committee published a joint statement criticising the UK's position on the protocol standoff as **'dangerous'.**

"The Good Friday Agreement and broader peace process took patience and time to build, with good faith and contributions from the communities in Northern Ireland, the United States, the United Kingdom, Ireland, and others," the statement said. "In threatening to invoke Article 16 of the Northern Ireland Protocol, the United Kingdom threatens to not only destabilize trade relations, but also that hard earned peace. **We call on the UK to abandon this dangerous** path, and to commit to implementing the Northern Ireland Protocol in full."

And two days ago another bus was hijacked and set alight in Newtownabbey, Country Antrim. This is such a dangerous time and very, very worrying.

****

12TH NOVEMBER

And I read that the government is considering dropping out of the EU science and research programmes worth £77 billion because of **deteriorating relations with Brussels**.

This entire situation is absolutely appalling. They are threatening to pull out of Horizon Europe, the EU's funding scheme; Copernicus, its satellite system; and Euratom, its atomic energy treaty. This appears to be because Lord Frost and his cohorts are concerned that the EU will eject them from these schemes anyway as a lever, if Article 16 is invoked.

****

13TH NOVEMBER

And a little snippet from our friend Dominic Cummings. Arj Singh of the *Huffington Post* reports Cummings as saying, **"Boris Johnson did not understand the most intensely contested issue of the entire Brexit saga until after the UK left the EU.** It was not until October 2020 that the PM finally understood what leaving the customs union meant".

The dreadful thing is that I can absolutely believe that.

****

16TH NOVEMBER

Addressing the Lord Mayor's Banquet last night in London, the Prime Minister said, in his usual diplomatic fashion, that suspending parts of Northern Ireland's post Brexit arrangements unilaterally could be "the only way left" to protect its place in the Union.

I think this is so damaging and I completely despair at the way in which he and Lord Frost are speaking to our European friends.

****

4TH DECEMBER

Today I get an email from an old school friend who now lives in Sweden. She had just finished reading my chapter on Brexit in '**Beneath the Bluster'**. Well, she said it was worse than she thought.

She goes on to say that she has **actual experience of Brexit in Sweden** and tells me of an incident when she was sent a box of chocolates from a friend in Wales. This is what she says:

"I didn't think of your European market when I told you about the paperwork of the chocolates - but now I'll come clean so that you know the situation. You can forget the European exports! The chocolates were the most exclusive you can imagine: import VAT 28 kr. Declaration fee 75 kr including VAT 15 kr. Total to pay 103kr. To say nothing of the bureaucratic delay! As I remarked before, the whole Brexitisation process is stupid. And more than stupid - it's economic suicide!"

She then goes on to write about another difficult and expensive experience.

*I ordered a book from a small publishing company in the spring. They specialise in local Midlands' history, and I wanted this in connection with my Bubbenhall history. (A village in the Midlands.) Again, import VAT and a Declaration fee, putting a disproportionate extra cost on the price of the book. **Makes one think twice before importing anything from England.***

****

10TH DECEMBER

Many, many years ago when I worked for Coventry Cathedral as its Director of Public Relations, as part of my job I had to travel to Yugoslavia (as it was then) to represent the Cathedral in the planning of its cultural Yugoslav week. This was a huge venture as I was organising visits to Coventry for orchestras, soloists, national dancers, exhibitions and of course events at the Belgrade Theatre, all of which would take place in the summer as a positive, friendly cultural and good will gesture to Yugoslavia. **We were delighted to receive some sponsorship from the British Council and I was also really grateful for their help and support whilst I was in Belgrade.**

What I read in the paper today fills me with horror.

When we were in the EU the British Council administered the Erasmus scheme. After Brexit this was replaced by the Turing scheme which they devised, set up and administered. They have been running student exchange schemes with Europe since the Second World War and in its first year the Turing scheme helped 41,000 students to study abroad, 48% of them from disadvantaged backgrounds.

But now we hear that this government has stripped the British Council of its role running this scheme. Instead, the outsourcing firm Capita has won the contract in a government tender. Why? **Because it can run it for less money they say.** Always, always get things on the cheap.

But as Kirsty Lang asks in *The Times* today where is their quality and expertise? Where is its track record on student exchanges? Where is its legitimacy in the world of higher education? "It cannot," she writes "have international tentacles stretching across the world and going back almost 100 years as the British Council has."

She concludes her article with these words: "Pulling the rug from under its feet with the Turing decision makes no financial sense and inflicts another wound on one of the key instruments of UK soft power around the world. **If this government is serious about Global Britain it should be backing quality. Going for a cut-price Capita deal is a false economy."**

****

And also today we hear that **Britain's trade performance is lagging increasingly behind that of the G7 goods trade rankings**. A report by *Reuters* says that, according to official data published by each country, including British data yesterday, Britain is the only G7 advanced economy to have failed to regain the level of goods exports seen in late 2018.

Supporters of Brexit say Britain will, in the long run, be better able to tap into faster-growing markets than when it was in the EU. But many economists are sceptical and say that this will not make up for lost trade with the EU bloc. **Other indicators of trade have also pointed to a level of weakness that is unique to Britain.**

****

We are still hearing that there is a crisis in our care homes due to an extreme shortage of staff. The government is being urged by the Migration Advisory Committee to make it easier for foreign care workers to come to the UK.

****

18TH DECEMBER

There has just been an **agreement by the UK on the Northern Ireland Protocol**. I think our government has seen sense which is not a phrase I use often in this book. The UK has made a key Brexit concession to accept a role for European judges in Northern Ireland in a bid to unblock negotiations with the EU. This was always a sticking point with the UK who were repeatedly threatening to trigger Article 16 which would scupper the whole agreement.

But there it is in black and white that **Lord Frost, the Brexit minister**, says that Britain now accepts that the European Court of Justice (ECJ) must be allowed to interpret the protocol of the Brexit agreement.

Well that is a huge relief all round. Lord Frost has been a very combative negotiator so this is good news.

****

19TH DECEMBER

Why, why, why do I tempt fate and say the words 'good sense' and 'government' in the same sentence? Late last night we hear that Lord Frost has resigned from the Cabinet. He does not like the direction of Boris Johnson's government and in his letter of resignation he says he hopes, "we will move as fast as possible to where we need to get to: a lightly regulated, low-tax, entrepreneurial economy, at the cutting edge of modern science and economic change." He also does not wish for any more restrictions because of the pandemic.

Hmm the phrase '**parallel universe**' keeps coming into my mind. Some are saying that this is a smoke screen and actually he is finding it too difficult to negotiate a treaty that he signed and now finds that it is not working out the way he anticipated.

The columnist Ian Birrell puts it very colourfully when he says that: **"He highlights also the breath-taking hypocrisy of those chancers who pushed a hard-line form of Brexit, then ran away like infants suffering a tantrum over an untidy bedroom when confronted by the mess they created."**

And more and more people are realising that Brexit is indeed one almighty mess.

****

One of the reasons for Brexit was that the Europeans over here were supposedly taking away jobs from the British.

Today I read that our daffodil industry is in crisis. Why? Because since Brexit there has been no-one to pick them. About 80% of the world's daffodils are grown in the mild climate of Cornwall. Harvesting begins in the first week of January and a workforce of about 2,500 people are required to pick them. It is back-breaking work in all weathers and Eastern Europeans used to do it all. So what is the response of Brits to this?

The owners of Varfell Farms in Penzance, one of the largest growers in the country, had a recruitment drive for local people and had an open day at the farm which was widely publicised on local social media groups and newspapers. **Only four people turned up.**

Many smaller daffodil farms are expected to give up growing daffodils altogether.

Apparently the government has promised to extend a visa scheme allowing famers to bring in seasonal workers from overseas to harvest fruit and vegetables but at the moment non-edible crops are excluded.

They have been told that non-edible crops **will** be added but with only two weeks to go they are really worried and as they say they have heard promises from the government before and are still waiting.

Why does that not surprise me?

****

23RD DECEMBER

Today we see a report by Joe Mayes, the financial journalist for Bloomberg, and it makes disturbing although not surprising reading. He states that the pandemic has masked the damage that has been done to the economy by Brexit but that it is beginning to become more and more obvious.

"Brexit has been a drag on growth" he says. He goes on to say that, "it brought new red tape on commerce between Britain and its largest and closest market, and removed a large pool of EU labour from the country on which many businesses had come to rely. The combination has exacerbated supply chain shortages, stoked inflation, and hampered trade."

Well I think we know all of that but as he says people are beginning to notice and the result of a poll in November by Savanta Comres, states that a majority of the British population would now vote to re-join the EU.

Of course they would. They were fed a pack of lies.

****

24TH DECEMBER

A report by Adam Forrest of *The Independent* warns of a disaster waiting to happen as new Brexit controls come into force on the 1st January. Some businesses are still struggling with the red tape needed for imports and exports and there will be a whole new raft of paper work which could well cause many smaller businesses to collapse completely.

David Thomas, co-founder of organic gin company Jinn Talog says, **"The government told us Brexit was done but it's barely even started. I know a lot of small businesses struggling to survive with all the red tape since Brexit."**

****

26TH DECEMBER

So many articles today about the state of the Conservative Party and none of them make happy reading if you are a Tory.

Nick Cohen in *The Observer* writes a long article about the fact that this government is no longer fit to govern and are just concerned about all their ideology divisions. He says that, "they still cannot admit that Brexit was an attack on wealth creation. 'The Office of Responsibility' forecasts that it will cause twice the long term economic damage of Covid, leave trade 15% lower, bring £100bn annual hit to national income and cost £40bn in lost tax revenue." He goes on to say that, **"When you pull your country out of the largest free-trade area in the world, you have no right to protest about economic decline."**

He says that, **"they have dissolved into an extremist rabble contorted by magical thinking, heresy hunts, fits of temper and doctrinal spasms**."

Gosh I couldn't put it better myself!

And if you think that is bad enough then just see what Alastair Campbell wrote in *The Independent*. He begins a hugely long article with the following paragraph:

"There is a very clear reason for the mess the country is in right now. It is called the Conservative Party. It has been in power for over a decade. **A lost decade**. A wasted decade, in which the big choices and challenges faced have been decided, not with the national interest in mind, but on the basis of the internal divisions and difficulties of the wretched Tory party."

And he ends his article with the following paragraph:

"Johnson is in a mess politically because of lies told about wallpaper and Christmas parties. But the effects of the far bigger lies told about Brexit – before, during and since the referendum – will sadly be with us long after he is gone, when the Christmas parties are forgotten. Cameron came to power in part by pushing the myth of "broken Britain". Brexit is in danger of making that myth a reality, and those who brought it about have to pay a far bigger price than merely seeing Johnson forced out of No 10, with another opportunist Tory installed in his place. **If Britain is breaking, it is because the Tory Party, and Brexit, have broken it."**

Brexit is a huge disaster for this country and it came about with lies and false promises.

****

2022

3RD JANUARY

So many small businesses are still unprepared for the new regulations which came into force on the first day of this year. Indeed it is reported that some could abandon trade with the European Union altogether unless they get more government support.

The antiquated IT systems are not helping matters either and food supplies face further disruption because government software is plagued with technical bugs. Importers are facing reams of additional red tape and Michael Szydlo, founder of 'Quick Declare,' a company that helps dozens of businesses who import and export goods says that it is, "like **we have gone back to medieval times and we are copying books by hand instead of using a printing press."**

'The Federation of Small Businesses' warned last month that only a quarter of small businesses were ready for the new border controls.

****

Not surprisingly, having read all of this, public attitudes towards Brexit have changed. A clear majority have said that it is going worse than they expected including 40% of Leave voters.

****

5TH JANUARY

As well as cost of living rises which are predicted to be very significant, energy prices are spiralling upwards and could rise by about 50% in April this year. The Prime Minister is being urged to cut VAT on energy bills to help those who are the most vulnerable.

20 Conservative MPs have written to the PM asking him to remove this tax because it is the cause of Britain "increasing prices faster than any other competitive country." VAT is levied at 5% on energy bills. And of course we remember what Boris said about this very subject during the referendum campaign.

"In 1993", he wrote, "VAT on household energy bills was imposed. This makes gas and electricity much more expensive. EU rules mean we cannot take VAT off these bills. **When we vote Leave we will be able to scrap this unfair tax.** It isn't right that unelected bureaucrats in Brussels impose taxes on the poorest, and elected British politicians can do nothing."

Well Mr. Johnson you are not only an elected British politician, you are the Prime Minister. So please can you explain the answer you gave to a question asked at your press conference yesterday? You said that you would not be scrapping this tax at the moment because it would be such a blunt instrument that it would probably help a lot of people who don't actually need the help.

Yes that is what he said. At the moment he is rejecting this request.

Well he should be very careful. Many of the 20 Conservatives who signed the letter in 1993 were his fellow Brexiteers.

****

6TH JANUARY

One of the main problems with Brexit which is affecting the economy is the shortage of labour in the UK today.

Under immense pressure the government has offered temporary 12 month visas for 4,700 foreign HGV drivers, 800 pork butchers and 5,500 poultry workers. But would it surprise you to learn that nowhere near these numbers have taken up the offer? **Well why would anyone want to uproot their family for just 12 months to come to a country which has treated them so appallingly?** Anyway the 'Road Haulage Association' needs at least 100,000 drivers, and the 'British Meat Processors Association' needs at least 15,000 meat workers so it is all just a drop in the ocean even if the fully allowed number came here.

There is an article in *The Times* today by Simon Nixon which makes very interesting reading. His headline reads **"The global outlook is optimistic but Britain could fall further behind."** He writes that this is because, unlike most other countries who are short of materials and equipment, **the most pressing shortage in the UK is indeed labour.** In fact he says that the most recent CBI quarterly trend survey shows that labour shortages are at levels not seen since the 1970s. The biggest shortages are in unskilled labour. He compares us with the Eurozone where things are looking better. He ends his article by saying, "For the first time in a decade political risks in the EU appear to be receding. It is too soon to say that of Britain."

Please someone explain to me the benefits of Brexit.

****

13TH JANUARY

Today Liz Truss, who has replaced Lord Frost as Northern Ireland's Brexit negotiator, had her first face to face meeting with Maros Sefcovic who is the European Commission vice-president. It will be very interesting to see how this goes. She is playing the tough guy at the moment. She has said that the European Union had a 'clear responsibility' to solve the problems caused by Northern Ireland's post Brexit deal. They must show a 'pragmatic approach' she says.

Excuse me? Whose Brexit deal is this? Who constructed and voted for this deal? It certainly was not the EU. They are already distinctly unimpressed with her threats to trigger Article 16 if they don't do as she wants. Not a good way to enter negotiation talks.

So it will be interesting to see how these talks go. She is entertaining them at Chevening, her country retreat in Kent. We know how much she likes to wine and dine so what are they having? A dinner of Scottish smoked salmon, Welsh lamb, and apple pie made with fruit from Kent. Hmmm lovely!

****

14TH JANUARY

Trade deals are really not going at all well just now. We are led to believe that Liz Truss adopted a slightly more conciliatory tone in her meeting yesterday but there has been **a warning from Washington that London can forget about a trade deal with the US if its actions in Northern Ireland threaten the still-fragile peace.**

The Trade Minister **Penny Mordaunt** gave a speech in the US last month in which she urged Washington to side with the UK in what she called **"a global battle between two competing versions of capitalism."**

A free-trading UK is on one side, she argued, and the EU - "a trading bloc that is pushing its regulatory system on the rest of the world" - is on the other. **"Brexit,"** Ms Mordaunt went on, **"is a major geo-political event and it calls for a US response that recognises the moment, and the opportunity that comes with it."**

I don't even know what this is supposed to mean.

Many critics were not impressed, describing the speech as begging for American support in matters of trade. Anton Spisak, head of policy at the Tony Blair Institute, called it, **"a solid candidate for the most embarrassing speech delivered by a government minister in 2021."**

Oh goodness how has it come to this? Such thick headed ministers speaking for Britain. Where have these people come from?

So with US trade looking hopeless, formal talks about a trade deal with India were being announced in New Delhi yesterday. It is the biggest negotiation the UK government will launch this year. It is also the most ambitious. The UK would like to conclude a deal by the end of the year but the EU has been trying for years to reach a meaningful deal with India, and Australia too has been working on a deal for a decade.

Why we think that we should be any better I do not know. But then I am not on their planet. But the uncomfortable fact is that the UK is trying to rebuild its trade policy almost from scratch at a time when many governments are concentrating on domestic economies. They are just not interested.

And we have just walked away from the largest trading bloc in the world which is on our doorstep. Yes I know I have said this before and I will most likely say it again and again and again because maybe then I will begin to understand it. Except actually I know I won't.

It is just such complete madness and it is this government which is responsible.

****

22ND JANUARY

There **are long, long, lorry queues at Dover due to new customs regulations. Hauliers are frustrated and furious. "It's insane," they say. "It's all due to Brexit, Brexit, Brexit!" And if you think it is bad now it is only going to get a lot worse.** There are new checks coming in in September.

There is a 17km lorry queue on the M20 and National Highways were being accused of switching off the traffic cameras deliberately so that people would not be able to see them. Don't worry. I have just seen this queue on the news and it looks dreadful.

****

23RD JANUARY

William Keegan writes in *The Observer* today about the tragedy that is Brexit.

"Brexit", he says, "is an unmitigated disaster and the damage is getting worse."

He does admire Sir Keir's "forensic demolition" of the Prime Minister during PMQs, but he objects strongly to him saying that we cannot re-join the EU.

****

25TH JANUARY

For reasons best known to her Liz Truss is in Australia. But she is not covering herself in glory.

The former Prime Minister, Paul Keating, has accused her of making "demented" comments about Chinese military aggression and urged her to hurry **back to her collapsing, disreputable government."**

He also said **Britain "suffers from delusions of grandeur and relevance deprivation"** and its tilt to the Indo-Pacific lacks credibility. **"She is not simply irrational, demented",** is what he said.

It really is not a good look for the UK.

****

31ST JANUARY

It is two years since we left the EU and the government is set to bring forward a new "Brexit Freedoms" bill. This, apparently, will make it easier to shed EU regulations post Brexit.

So what is this all about? Well he says it is about cutting red tape.

The Prime Minister listed ending VAT on sanitary products, simplifying complex EU alcohol duty rates, forging ahead to remove the ban on selling in pounds and ounces as well as restoring **the crown stamp on to the side of pint glasses as successes during the year.** Well we have all been waiting for that one!

However there are two facts of clarity needed here. Apparently EU law **does not** prevent markings from being placed on products, so long as it does not overlap or be confused with the CE mark. So the crown sign was not prevented by the EU from being stamped on pint glasses.

And whilst it is true that EU laws have required member states to tax tampons and sanitary towels at a minimum rate of 5%. the EU is now in the process of abolishing the tax.

So not anything very amazing there then.

And the PM made no mention of **Northern Ireland** in his New Year's message about Brexit, where there are still huge trade problems with the operation of the agreement and ongoing talks with the EU about how to proceed.

****

2ND FEBRUARY

We hear today that DUP minister Edwin Poots, whose officials are responsible for carrying out Northern Ireland Protocol checks, said he had ordered his permanent secretary to stop them at midnight tonight. **This would be a breach of international law and the EU officials have responded with shock and anger.**

The UK government have said that it's nothing to do with them which I don't understand because this is the agreement which they signed.

This is an appalling lack of accountability and responsibility to a serious and escalating situation and a possible breach of international law.

****

3RD FEBRUARY
However in spite of all this, lorries were still being checked at Belfast Port earlier today.

****

This evening we hear that Paul Givan has resigned as Northern Ireland's First Minister with effect from midnight tonight.

This means that the leader of Sinn Fein is automatically removed from office.

Apparently the Assembly can continue to function until the next election but with little effect. **The move is part of the DUP's escalating protest against the Brexit's Northern Ireland Protocol.**

The DUP leader Jeffrey Donaldson had apparently been warning for months that Paul Gavin should resign if the protocol agreement was not resolved.

He also said that he had **received an apology from Boris Johnson for not recognising "the harm" caused by the protocol.**

What? An apology from the PM for Brexit? Is that what I am hearing?

Well not exactly. There has been no apology to England, Scotland or Wales as yet.

But no, he doesn't listen to anyone but himself. Everything he touches turns to dust.

Everyone else was aware of the damage this would do and he was warned by Sir John Major and Tony Blair the very people who had been involved in the Good Friday Agreement.

As the editorial in *The Times* states today, **"For the people of Northern Ireland the benefits of Brexit have never looked more unattainable."**

****

4TH FEBRUARY

A High Court Judge has ruled that the checks of goods into Northern Ireland have to continue until there is a judicial review which can be heard in full.

Shaun Woodward, a former Secretary of State for Northern Ireland, was strongly critical of the Prime Minister in an interview on the BBC today.

He compares him unfavourably with three former Prime Ministers, Gordon Brown, Tony Blair and Sir John Major. They all spent an inordinate amount of time in Northern Ireland, negotiating, talking, listening, and bringing deep thought and wisdom to try to solve the enormous problems there.

The only person who can sort it out now is the Prime Minister, he says. **He** should be over there not anyone else. **But he is too busy shoring up support at home to concentrate on critical problems elsewhere**.

He goes on to say that the PM cobbled together the border down the Irish Sea and told one thing to one group and another thing to another. **He just told everyone what they wanted to hear with no regard for the truth.** He is not in control of any of the big issues. He has put the Union under threat.

It was a damning and shocking interview and I was appalled, listening to it.

****

6TH FEBRUARY

Well I have a problem here. I need to write about the effect that Brexit is having on our economy, the levelling up programme and Boris Johnson. They are all intertwined and I have separate chapters on each of them but I **will** write about it in this chapter!

In an article by William Keegan in today's *Observer* he writes about the levelling up programme and the package by the Chancellor to alleviate energy costs. He say that there is a slight problem with all of this and it is called money. He writes "**The hit to this economy for, wait for it, "getting Brexit done" is enormous.**"

He goes on to mention all the tragic outcomes that I have already written about and then says, "After years of economic decline vis-à-vis our European neighbours, we entered what was then the European Economic Union in 1973 for good economic reasons".

Mr Keegan goes on to say that, "With Brexit, this benighted country has in effect voted to go back to the path of relative economic decline."

He then asks, **"Why is Gove's budget for levelling up so pitifully limited? The answer is that the Brexit those charlatan's sold to a gullible public has lopped tens of billions of pounds off the Treasury's potential tax revenues."**

****

And in the editorial of *The Observer* today **they re-enforce the damages of Brexit.** Whilst some are hoping that there will be better economic times around the corner they say that, "**Brexit, the great unacknowledged economic dampener, will continue to depress economic growth in the coming years**. Worse still, Brexit is very likely to widen the gap in economic performance between London and the south-east and the rest of the country."

In 2021 the equivalent of £32 per person was awarded from the Levelling Up Fund for the north of England which means nothing if you compare it with the drop in council spending per person of £413 since 2011.

"This" they say "is the parlous situation in which the country now finds itself just over five years after a referendum that paved the way for Boris Johnson to become Prime Minister and irrevocably damage standards in public life."

Indeed so. He needs to go as soon as possible. They finish their article by saying, **"It is not what Britain deserves."**

****

9TH FEBRUARY

It is reported today by the Commons Public Accounts Committee **that "costs, paperwork and delays are the only detectable impact of the EU exit for businesses so far".** Apparently leaving the EU was supposed to give firms "headroom to maximise their productivity and contribution to the economy" but instead has landed them with border hold-ups and red tape.

Well the **lorry queues are still winding their way round the M20 at Dover so perhaps our new Brexit opportunities minister should go and speak to the lorry drivers there. "It's Brexit" they say "It's all Brexit."**

The report added that a plan to deliver by 2025 the **"most effective border in the world"** looked "optimistic, given where things stand today" and the committee were not convinced by it.

That sounds like our Prime Minister.

And another problem is the delay in building infrastructure at Dover which will not be ready until 2023.

Forward thinking and forward planning is not exactly in the DNA of this government.

****

At PMQs today the PM was asked about the Northern Ireland Protocol.

Yes, he said if our friends (the EU) don't show common sense **we might well have to trigger Article 16.** The words diplomacy, negotiation, commitment and understanding are never in his vocabulary.

****

10TH FEBRUARY

Today the PM is in Brussels which just happens to coincide with a speech being given at the Whitehall think-tank the Institute for Government by **Sir John Major.**

It is entitled "**In democracy we trust?**" which is of course very apposite for today's political scenario.

He doesn't pull his punches and in a scathing speech he says: "At Number 10, the Prime Minister and officials broke lockdown laws. Brazen excuses were dreamed up."

He went on to say that, "Day after day the public was asked to believe the unbelievable. Ministers were sent out to defend the indefensible – making themselves look gullible or foolish.

"And so far as Brexit is concerned" he said, "It now seems that on January 1st next year, Brexit may be even more brutal than anyone expected. Because of our bombast, our blustering, our threats and our inflexibility **– our trade will be less profitable, our Treasury poorer, our jobs fewer, and our future less prosperous.**"

Now Sir John has been a long- time critic of Johnson and so the right wing papers will say well what do you expect? However, I can tell you that most thinking people will agree wholeheartedly with everything he says. The facts are there.

****

20TH FEBRUARY

A survey last week of 1,000 firms by the British Chamber of Commerce showed that **71% said that Brexit had meant that their businesses are failing**.

The Brexit deal they say has put the UK at a competitive disadvantage. David Smith writing for *The Sunday Times* says: "You do not need to be a Hercule Poirot to work out that Brexit, and a trade deal put together by the negotiating equivalent of Inspector Clouseau, has damaged Britain's overseas trade, in both directions, whatever the new minister for Brexit opportunities says. **I admire what successful exporters do but they are operating with a ball and chain attached to their ankles.**"

Well I think that is put very succinctly and I just do not know how much longer certain elements of this government can possibly go on pretending that all is well.

****

Well the exact same sentiments are echoed in *The Observer* by William Keegan! His headline is "**How much longer must we pretend that Brexit might work?**"

In a long article he criticises Labour for thinking that they can rebuild a relationship with the EU and could actually 'make Brexit work.' He writes that "the truth that dare not speak its name is **that Brexit doesn't work, and never will.** The experiment has been tried – and has failed. All this stuff about the 'opportunities of Brexit'? There are none.

Johnson may have packed his sordid cabinet with Brexiteers and time-servers, but the all-party public accounts committee is beyond his soiled hands. They point out that the **only detectable impact of Brexit is 'increased cost, paperwork and border delays'."**

The damage goes on, businesses fail, the UK loses its standing in the world and everyone appears to be accepting it all.

Our eyes are shut, our ears are blocked and our minds are closed. When oh when will we wake up from this nightmare?

****

24TH FEBRUARY
As Russia invades Ukraine the 27 EU countries meet together to discuss sanctions and other plans.

Members of our Cabinet meet, on their own, in splendid isolation, in Downing Street.

****

27TH FEBRUARY
Scientists are very concerned about the possibility of a **brain drain because of ongoing rows over Brexit.** A deal had been agreed which would have allowed Britain to continue to play a major role in Europe's vast scientific research programme. But the subsequent failure of talks with Northern Ireland has led to a major delay with this arrangement. Dozens of scientists given grants earlier this month as part of this year's round of EU funding awards had these offers revoked only a few days later.

A malaria project at the London School of Hygiene and Tropical Medicine was given a grant of £6.7 million from the EU's Horizon programme and they were thrilled with this. As they said, "it had been very hard work putting together the project and setting up partnerships in Africa. Then, a couple of days later, we got a new letter saying the UK was now ineligible to take part."

No wonder then Martin Smith, head of policy at the Wellcome Trust says, "**There is a real prospect that bright young scientists will decide it will be better for their careers if they leave the UK.**"

The government has said it is trying to find ways to make up lost funds but scientists point out that the European Research Council grants are so prestigious that cash substitutes are unlikely to be enough to keep young scientists in the UK.

The government has said that it will guarantee funding for the first wave of eligible, successful applicants to Horizon Europe who have been unable to sign agreements with the EU, but for goodness sake why do we have to go through all this uncertainty just because we have a government incapable of pursuing sensible negotiations with our friends in mainland Europe?

****

2ND MARCH

In yesterday's *Guardian* there is a very disturbing article by Rafael Behr about politics in the UK today. I just quote a tiny part:

"The age of levity is over. Putin's bombs should shake British politics into sobriety. When that happens, **it will be clear that the past six years, the detour into Brexit fantasy land, have been squandered**; that we need to restart relations with our neighbours from scratch.

That will be hard for a Prime Minister who has sunk so much political capital into Eurosceptic frivolity, and appointed a cabinet in his image. But the shift is inevitable.

"If Britain is to be an ally to Ukraine, it must learn to speak the language of European solidarity that Brexit despises and denies."

******

3RD MARCH

Then I see an article by Michael Heseltine which is a letter to Jacob Rees-Mogg about his new role as minister for Brexit opportunities and government efficiency. (Yes really!) He talks about the reality of the Brexit situation which seems to by-pass the present minister and ends his 'letter' with these words:

"Nothing so reveals the reality of Brexit as the meeting of European leaders in Brussels, in the aftermath of Vladimir Putin's assault on Ukraine. Our continent faces a threat as severe as anything since the end of the cold war. **I am ashamed that the country that in my lifetime saved European democracy has now absented itself as others determine Europe's response.**

There will, Mr Rees-Mogg, be more councils covering the climate crisis, our environment, international crime, control of the internet.

In every case we will be absent. That is what Brexit means."

****

8TH MARCH

Vans and lorries which are carrying aid to Ukraine are stuck at customs in Dover. Over 13 lorries have been there for over four days now. This is of course a direct result of Brexit with so many rules and documentation. But as the charities involved say, the goods are not for sale they are "aid".

It beggars belief that this is not being speeded up and fast tracked.

****

More news about the benefits of Brexit. Apparently the government is thinking about using its new Brexit regulatory freedom **to allow**

certain pesticides, which are currently banned in the EU, on food imported to the UK.

Brussels announced it was **banning 10 pesticides on imported fruit and vegetables** in February last year and the UK was at the time widely expected to follow suit. But over a year later the Department for Environment, Food, and Rural Affairs (Defra) says **no decision has yet been made** on whether Britain will follow the EU or continue to permit the chemicals on food.

For goodness sake what do they think they are doing? It is a no brainer. Or is this their way of culling the population?

****

16TH MARCH

Well this is just what we need. **A Brexit Festival!** Did you know about this? Well by the time this book is published maybe you will have been attending some of the planned "10 awe-inspiring new ideas, shaped across science, technology, engineering, the arts and mathematics by brilliant minds working in unexpected collaborations."

Because as the event planners say, **"Unmissable events and unforgettable experiences are coming to places and spaces right across the UK**: from coastal towns and city centres to breath-taking areas of natural beauty."

The event is now officially known as "Unboxed: Creativity in the UK". But Jacob Rees-Mogg the Brexit opportunities minister just calls it "Festival of Brexit." Are you still feeling OK?

Well you probably won't be after this. **It is costing tax-payers £120 million.**

A cross-party-culture media and sport select committee has been scathing about the government's handling of this. They are concerned that very few people even know about it and it is due to start in March this year and run till October. Wait a minute. What is the date today?

Apparently it opened in Paisley on March 1st. But the whole thing has been vague and lacking in strategy and vision from the start. Well we know that those words 'strategy' and 'vision' are not related to those in government in any way shape or form whatsoever. The committee say that for something that the government, **"by their own admission, 'did not know what it was' is an irresponsible use of public money."**

Julian Knight, the Conservative MP who chairs the culture select committee, said the festival's "muddled approach" was a "sure-fire recipe for failure".

He says that, **"Unless the government urgently addresses this lack of strategy and vision, it will continue to risk squandering the benefits such occasions can bring, while wasting the hard-earned money of taxpayers."**

Are we surprised? Not in the slightest.

****

18TH MARCH

Today we hear the dreadful news **that P & O have sacked 800 of their seafaring workers by video link and with absolutely no notice**. They have hired cheaper foreign agency workers with no training. This is a form of fire and rehire and it must be illegal. Some workers are refusing to leave the boat and the Unions and the government are jumping up and down in anguish. All sailings will be suspended for a week to 10 days.

This comes on the same day as we hear from the Public Accounts Committee which says that **it is uncertain whether Brexit free trade agreements negotiated by Boris Johnson's government will provide any "actual economic benefits".**

Oh my goodness how has it taken them so long? Have they not read my book '**Beneath the Bluster**'? We said this would be the case months before the referendum. Brexit is the biggest disaster this country has faced since the Second World War. Who is going to save us and when?

****

22ND MARCH
In the wake of the firing of the 800 workers by the P&O Company, which was roundly condemned by all MPs, Labour called for an emergency debate yesterday in the Commons. They wanted to make 'fire and rehire' illegal.

Every single Conservative MP abstained.

****

But what is this I hear? A name has just cropped up in relation to all of this which is extremely concerning.

Whilst certain senior government officials claim that this sacking is illegal it would appear that there was a change in the law in 2018 when it was amended to say that the Secretary of State does not have to be notified of mass redundancies on ships registered overseas which is the case with P&O. So who was the person who signed this amendment off? None other than **Mr Chris Grayling.** I need say no more.

****

27TH MARCH
Brexit has been blamed as the reason why the UK's post pandemic global trade has not recovered as quickly or as far as other countries. **The global average was a rise of 8.2% in the three months to January whilst our exports fell by 14% during the same period.**

This was reported in a new world trade monitor published earlier this week by the 'Netherlands Bureau for Economic Policy Analysis.

On it goes. Who is going to lead the march back to the EU? I want to be there.

****

30TH MARCH

Brexit checks on EU imports, which should have been implemented in June 2020 and have already been delayed three times, are due to be delayed yet again at the beginning of July. **The trouble is that if put into force it could add around £1 billion to the costs of trade and thereby to the cost of living.**

At the moment any delay gives EU firms a competitive advantage as they can send goods here without the costly bureaucracy confronting UK exporters. But if the checks are put in place everyone is worried that EU suppliers will choose to shun the UK as the dreadful Brexit red tape continues to grow **which will mean some foods disappearing from the supermarket shelves.**

Jacob Rees-Mogg would like to dispense with the checks for ever but any further deferral will result in people accusing the government of running away from the consequences of the hard Brexit that they chose in order to 'take back control' of its borders.

And many large traders have spent a lot of time and money in order to get ready for the extra paper-work and will be furious if there is more delay because the firms who are not ready will appear to be being rewarded for their inaction.

****

8TH APRIL

There are still **queues of lorries on the M20 approaching Dover**. It is now 23 miles long and the M20 was closed between junction

8 and junction 11 to all non-freight traffic yesterday. It is estimated that there are more than 2,000 lorries in the queue. Some have been there for over 50 hours and there are no facilities and nowhere to buy food or water.

The government is saying that it is all down to shortage of ferries, bad weather and holiday traffic. But anyone with a grain of sense points out that people do not tend to go on holiday in lorries, there are no queues in Calais and these queues have been there since last year.

It would be really good if a government minister, perhaps the Transport Secretary Grant Shapps for example, could go and speak to some of these lorry drivers. He would then understand that **Brexit** is the first and foremost cause of this debacle. But no this is the word that can never be spoken here.

Local traffic is also snarled up and the leader of the Dover district council is thinking of declaring it a **'major incident'**. Probably not before time. Food going rotten, supply chains stalled, drivers losing their jobs, verges being used as toilets, emergency services not getting through, yes probably a major incident I would think.

****

22ND APRIL

The PM is on a two day visit to **India to try to secure a trade deal**. He hopes to secure this by the autumn and he is trying to play down the differences between the attitudes of our two countries to Russia.

That's right Prime Minister whatever you do don't let your conscience get in the way.

He is also saying that he will **relax the visa rules for Indians** to enter the UK for work as we have a labour shortage crisis at the moment.

I wonder why that is exactly?

****

23RD APRIL

Government sources say today that a final decision had yet to be made and there **were no settled plans for a Northern Ireland bill in next month's Queen's Speech**. That could be because European diplomats are flexing their muscles and saying that Johnson will destroy any international leadership capital that Britain has built up since the invasion of Ukraine if he overrides the post-Brexit trade arrangements with Northern Ireland.

It seems obvious to me that Johnson and Truss are completely out of their depth and have no idea what to do.

****

28TH APRIL

We now hear that all import controls on goods coming in from the EU will be delayed for a fourth time. They are saying they won't be introduced until the end of 2023 when they hope to move to smarter technology.

What exactly does this mean?

Well many businesses have been working hard and spending a lot of money to try to get ready for the 1st July and are now beset with chaos and uncertainty.

Labour's Shadow International Trade Secretary Nick Thomas-Symonds accused the government of delaying the implementation of post-Brexit border checks of **"leaving businesses stuck in limbo"**.

It also means that there will continue to be numerous forms to fill in in order for goods to be exported but goods coming in especially chilled meats, and plant and animal products will be imported without any checks whatsoever.

Vets are particularly worried about this as they say the lack of checks on goods coming into the UK will **remove the UK's "first line of defence against disease coming into the country."**

Leaders at the British Veterinary Association are so alarmed by this move that they have called for an urgent meeting with Jacob Rees-Mogg.

To do this at any time is irresponsible but to do it a time when we are just beginning to recover from a deathly pandemic is the height of negligence and, to my mind, criminality.

Hilary Benn chair of the UK trade and business commission said: "Today's announcement is an admission by ministers that introducing **their new customs controls would hamstring our economy and worsen the cost of living crisis by artificially making trade more expensive for business and consumers**. Meanwhile British businesses trying to export to the EU will continue to face costs, delays and red tape which the same minsters have imposed on them."

And our Brexit minister Jacob Rees-Mogg says that if we had gone ahead with the post Brexit border checks, "**It would have been an act of self- harm and would have increased costs for people.**"

Well yes. That is why Brexit was such a bad idea Minister.

'An act of self-harm' sums it up perfectly.

****

13TH MAY
The Democratic Unionist Party has refused to elect a Speaker in protest over the Northern Ireland Protocol. This means that the Northern Ireland Assembly cannot function.

Boris Johnson is visiting Northern Ireland on Monday (16th) presumably to use his somewhat limited negotiating skills to work something out.

We really are in a very dangerous situation. Boris Johnson signed this deal and knew at the time that it probably wouldn't work. He always does whatever it takes to get him out of a pickle, usually of his own making, and never mind the consequences.

For Suella Braverman, the attorney- general, to say, as she did today, that it is all the fault of the EU and it would be perfectly legal to rip up part of the agreement is an absolute travesty of the truth.

They are playing politics with the peace process. Jonathon Powell, chief British negotiator for Northern Ireland from 1997-2007, says **"Surely reason will prevail and even now the government will do the responsible thing for peace."**

I am afraid there is no certainty that common sense will prevail. We see the lack of any wisdom over and over again.

****

15TH MAY
Nick Cohen says in *The Observer* today that, "Johnson chose well when he chose Braverman. **If he thought she would take a stand on principle he would never have given her the job**. Equally, if he doubted for a moment that she was not committed to attacking the EU, judicial review and the Human Rights Act she would have remained an obscure backbencher."

I cannot begin to tell you how frightened I am of the ongoing threat to the democracy of our country.

****

16TH MAY

Johnson arrives in Belfast to a chorus of boos from the crowd. He blusters his way through in his normal fashion and then we see an interview by Channel 4 when the interviewer says to Johnson, **"you must be fuming with whoever signed that deal."**

Nadine Dorries wants to get rid of Channel 4 and it doesn't take a genius to work out why.

And part of the reply was, "Yes I agreed it. (NI protocol). **I hoped and believed our friends (the EU) would not necessarily want to apply it."**

So this is the intellectual level of the person who was voted in to the highest office in the land in order to run our country.

****

17TH MAY

Justin King, the ex- Sainsbury's chief executive, says that food prices will rise by 5% **due to Brexit**.

He also forecasts the collapse of one of the food retailers as a result of pressures upon margins.

****

20TH MAY

The US House Speaker, Nancy Pelosi, has said that if the UK breaks the Northern Ireland Protocol treaty there would be no free trade deal between the UK and the US.

She also said that, "The children of Northern Ireland, who have never known the bloody conflict and do not want to go back, deserve a future free of the violence where all may reach their fulfilment."

And tomorrow a nine strong delegation from the US which will include Democrats and Republicans will travel to London to meet Liz Truss, Keir Starmer and others to try to diffuse tensions and to help broker a UK- EU deal.

Richard Neal is chairing the meeting and he has said that he hopes to have a meeting with the PM but so far nothing has been arranged.

He said it was important to pull back from the brink of unilateral action to breach the Brexit treaty.

Good luck with that one.

As João Vale de Almeida the UN Ambassador to the UK says, "We can't renegotiate the protocol: the ink on the signatures is hardly dry."

****

Liz Truss? Yes we do have to mention her yet again in this chapter. Read and despair.

Alexandra Hall-Hall, is a former British ambassador to Georgia and she was the lead Brexit envoy for the UK Government in Washington for several years.

However she resigned this diplomatic role in 2019 saying **that she no longer wished to "peddle half-truths" on behalf of leaders she did not "trust".**

She said that, "A low point for me was when I heard a senior British minister openly and offensively, in front of a US audience, dismiss the impact of a 'no-deal' Brexit on Irish businesses as just affecting **'a few farmers with turnips in the back of their trucks',".**

This comment was made in 2019 and it was Liz Truss who made it.

****

21ST MAY

There is appalling news today for the scientists and researchers of this country. The EU has held up the UK's application to take part in the latest round of their $95billion **Horizon** programme because of the threats to the Northern Ireland Protocol.

Tim Bradshaw chief executive of the Russel Group of leading universities said, "This is the biggest collaborative research project on the planet and we should be part of that. Now, more than ever, we need to be able to talk to our friends, collaborate with our friends, and use the networks that we have to solve some of the big problems facing our society and the world economy."

So once again all those unable to deliver on Brexit are turning the UK into a pariah state. It will inevitably mean that there will be a brain drain of talent from UK universities and we will be excluded from major scientific research.

In fact it is already starting. Nicholas Walton, a research fellow at the Institute of Astronomy, **reluctantly passed his leadership role in the €2.8m pan-European Marie Curie Network research project to a colleague in the Netherlands on Friday.**

The European Commission had written notifying him that UK scientists cannot hold leadership roles because the UK's membership of the flagship £80bn Horizon Europe funding network has not yet been ratified.

He is one just one of a handful of British physicists approved for a Horizon Europe grant but must now take a passenger seat in his own project.

And Carsten Welsch, a physicist at Liverpool University, who has won €2.6 million in funding, also from the Marie Curie network, for long term research on a novel plasma generator, is also facing the same dilemma – **move to the EU or hand over leadership to an EU institution to secure the research role.**

"This is really heart-breaking," he said, "given the long and extremely successful track record in scientific collaboration between the UK and EU."

The government is stepping in to give alternative funding but Carsten Welsch says, "While the UK Research and Innovation guarantee fund provides vital financial support and allows UK institutions to contribute as Associated Partners (without EU funding**), it means that UK institutions can no longer lead projects, can no longer be in charge of project milestones, and overall it feels as if the UK is losing important leadership."**

And he says that, "The damage is already being done ... our influence is eroding."

We seem to be shrinking everywhere you look and we will soon be completely isolated, irrelevant and ignored.

Be in no doubt. Absolutely everything this government touches collapses around our ears.

****

22ND MAY

Sir Howard Davies, chairman of NatWest bank, has just written a book called "**The Chancellors**" and in a recent interview he says he is pessimistic about the future of the UK. "**Brexit,**" **he says, "was a significant mistake**. You don't solve the problem of the left-behind by damaging the one area of the country that's been writing the cheques. **London is paying large amounts of tax and will be damaged by Brexit over time.**"

Actually I think we can already see that happening now.

****

Also today I hope you have not forgotten **those desperate lorry drivers stuck on the M20 in their bid to cross the Channel.** The queues are still miles long and so Kent County Council has just agreed a six-month contract with RE-ACT Disaster response charity at a cost of £180,000. **This charity usually respond to earthquakes, major disasters and refugees but hopefully they can now provide these drivers with loos, food and drink.**

The council said that the pandemic had masked the true severity of the hold-ups caused **by Brexit and they expect up to 50 days of gridlock every year on the motorways leading to Dover.**

****

1ST JUNE

Our Brexit minister, Jacob Rees-Mogg has come up with a Brexit benefit which is to "abolish the EU regulations that restrict vacuum cleaner power to 1400W". Oh that is amazing and just what we were all waiting for. **Stronger sucking powers from our vacuum cleaners.**

****

7TH JUNE

It is the end of half term. So many people had booked holidays abroad many for the first time in two years after the lockdowns during the pandemic but the travel chaos at airports has been catastrophic. More than 85,000 people were affected by cancelled flights both to and from the UK. More than 90 flights were cancelled last Sunday alone leaving many stranded abroad and unable to get home.

Unions have said that the disruption is unlikely to be sorted out before the summer holidays.

It is all due to staff shortages mainly because of Brexit. Grant Shapps the Transport Secretary has ruled out calls from the airlines to relax immigration rules allowing them to fill vacancies by recruiting applicants from mainland Europe.

The travel industry accused ministers of "passing the buck" and blamed government policy for the disruption.

****

10TH JUNE

Mehreen Khan of *The Times* highlights today an analysis by the Centre for European Reform think tank which says that although it is difficult to separate the impacts of Brexit and Covid **they do blame Britain's exit from the EU as being largely responsible for the UK's "stunted growth."**

John Springford, the author of this research, says that, "Brexit is the main reason why Rishi Sunak is raising taxes to their highest share of GDP since the 1960s. **While the chancellor says increased national insurance contributions will fund the health service and social care, these tax rises would not have been needed if the UK had stayed in the EU."**

****

13TH JUNE

Liz Truss and Boris Johnson are saying that they have been told that it will be perfectly legal to produce a bill which will tear up the **Northern Ireland Protocol** and it has been unveiled today with **Liz Truss describing it as "a reasonable, practical solution to the problems facing Northern Ireland".**

Well that is very interesting because she, together with Boris and some MPs who belong to the right wing group of the party, the ERG, are the only ones who think this.

Thomas Byrne who is Ireland's Europe affairs minister has said this decision will be "astonishing to many people around the world."

Exactly. We have been saying for ages that if we break international law how can we expect others to honour their agreements with us?

As the Irish Prime Minister Micheal Martin said, it was a "fundamental breach of trust" and Labour accused the government of pressing the "nuclear button" over the protocol.

And so we hear today that the European Union will restart legal action against Britain over breaches of the Brexit Withdrawal Agreement, with a looming threat of a trade war if the government refuses to comply.

Apparently these legal proceedings can take up to 35 months, meaning that the case against Britain could last into 2024.

Under the terms of the withdrawal treaty, the European Court of Justice or an independent and binding arbitration process can hit Britain with fines, with further sanctions to follow, if the government refuses to pay penalties or comply with rulings to overturn the legislation.

This could lead to the suspension of all or parts of the post-Brexit trade deal brokered with the EU.

The bloc could also move to end financial equivalence for the City of London to European markets, or officially end Britain's accession to the Horizon research programme.

I think the Horizon programme is already finished.

This whole debacle is extremely risky as well as being illegal. A trade war with the EU would be catastrophic. And we need to remember that the US will refuse to trade with us as well.

****

16TH JUNE
Today the leaders of France, Germany, Italy, and Romania all visited Ukraine and vowed to **back Kyiv in becoming an official candidate**

of the EU. "Ukrainians are ready to die for the European perspective," commission President Ursula von der Leyen said.

"We want them to live with us, the European dream."

I watched them all arrive with enormous sadness that our country was not there too.

My dream is to have a dignified, compassionate and intelligent Prime Minister who could lead us back into the EU.

23RD JUNE
It is six years ago today since the country voted to leave the EU. We are still waiting to see the benefits. Anyone?

****

24TH JUNE
Even Harrods are in trouble. They have delayed their summer discount sale because their supply chain is running two or three weeks behind where it should be according to their managing director, Michael Ward.

He also say that, "it's almost impossible to find the right staff. We've lost significant amounts of people as a result of Brexit. And it's not the skilled or qualified, it's the people we need to do jobs that unfortunately the British will not do."

How often have we heard that?

****

28TH JUNE
There is trouble regarding the trade deal with Australia. MPs are urging the government to **block the Australian trade deal as they say that it has been rushed through and not been properly scrutinised.**

They are saying that farmers are going to suffer and the climate crisis will be sacrificed. **In fact the government's own assessment revealed that the deal will cost farmers and food production a loss of almost £300 million.**

Canberra has paused on ratifying the agreement.

****

Also today the TUC accuses ministers of disregarding worker's rights in trade deals. They have said that ministers have been in talks with nations which have a worrying track record of employment rights such as Brazil, Burundi, Qatar and Saudi Arabia.

18 months ago the government promised that union representatives would sit in on post Brexit trade advisory groups but has so far failed to confirm any appointments.

Now why does that not surprise me?

And more and more people are saying please don't let them convince you our troubles have anything to do with the pandemic or the war in Ukraine.

There is a story about just one small family business who are desperate to keep going and who have cut back to the bare bone. They have sold their warehouse and cut back on their rented accommodation and laid off all staff bar one. The four family members are working night and day but they now earn in a year what they used to earn in a month. Leaving the EU in such a chaotic and unplanned way has caused serious hardship. Businesses thrive on stability and certainty and they say that the people we elect to look after us are lying to us. Brexit has ruined family businesses and when questions are asked in the House of Commons, Rees-Mogg the Brexit minister, gets up and says don't worry the sun is shining and all will be well.

And it has just been announced (very quietly) that the Brexit divorce bill has risen by nearly £10 billion from the original estimate.

We ALL need to speak up about the calamity that is BREXIT.

****

30TH JUNE

Air terminals are in a dreadful mess and air travel looks absolutely chaotic. Michael O'Leary of Ryanair has slammed the British government and what he branded 'the disaster' of Brexit that had stopped airlines easily hiring European staff members, with the industry being hit hard with staff shortages in recent months.

'This is without doubt one of the inevitable consequences of the disaster that has been Brexit,' he told the business publication, 'Withdrawing from the single market, just so that they can say "We got Brexit done" was the height of idiocy'.

But then they are all idiots."

****

23RD JULY

Schools break up for the holidays. At last people can get away for a foreign break. Oh wait a minute.

There are six hour queues at Dover. Ferry bookings are being missed and cars are stretching back for miles causing disruption on several major motorways. Since Brexit everyone has to have their passports stamped by the French customs. Liz Truss is blaming the French for their inefficiency. Brexit problems are always the fault of the EU of course if you are a Tory MP.

But it is interesting to note that the government turned down a £33million bid from the Port of Dover executives to help upgrade the port to cope with the additional pressures of Brexit. This request was made in 2020 and in December of that year they were given just £33,000. The Port of Dover will not be able to cope with the volume of traffic unless major investment takes place.

Lord Ricketts, a former ambassador to France says, **"This will be the new normal."**

****

But now just read this. At the beginning of the year, Edwina Currie was asked by Matt Frei on LBC, "What are the tangible benefits of Brexit so far?" After being pushed for an answer she replied "Freedom". "Freedom to do what?" she was asked. To which she replied, **"Two fingers to Brussels. It's fabulous."**

Now I have just finished reading **"My Secret Brexit Diary" by Michel Barnier**. If you want to know what really went on in these four long years of negotiations then this is the book for you. And this is exactly the sort of attitude that was displayed by the UK team and it makes cringing reading. If the UK team had had a quarter of the integrity, wisdom, intelligence, politeness, work ethic or patience of the EU team then we would possibly not be in the mess we are in today.

Michel Barnier starts his diaries by describing his preliminary visits to all 27 member states of the EU and his meetings with the presidents and prime ministers and heads of states. He knows them all so well and has worked with many of them. As I read his descriptions of welcomes and talks in so many different countries I feel a strong sense of envy and I desperately want to be a part of this community. I am European and I want to belong. It sounds amazing. It sounds and is unique. What have we just thrown away?

When talking about the European Union Agency for Fundamental Rights and the creation of Europol and the Schengen Information System he asks, **"Is there any other region in the world where sovereign states trust one another enough to establish such high-level cooperation on internal security? Is there any other region** in which sovereign states have created a common space together without internal border controls? A region in which citizens can protect their fundamental rights? This degree of cooperation is both unique and unprecedented. It is made possible by the trust that member states have for each other."

I write this in full because we need to know exactly what we have lost through the myriad of lies and false promises from our government.

But all the time throughout these diaries we see the intransigence of the UK team and their threats and accusations whilst Monsieur Barnier has to concentrate hard on keeping his cool.

In the summer of 2018 the new Foreign Secretary Jeremy Hunt went on a tour of all the European capitals to blame the consequences of a possible no deal on the EU. "Help us, otherwise Brexit will be a tragedy," he said. The UK were asking the EU to sacrifice the integrity of the Single Market and agree to take on a new customs system with a double charge at the external borders that the British themselves could not explain. "In short" says Michel Barnier, "the Europeans are meant to pay for some of the economic consequences of a Brexit they did not want and which they regret."

So often he remarks on the fact that the British struggle to come to terms with the direct consequences of their decision to leave the EU.

And the Northern Ireland backstop comes up time and time again.

An entry in October 2018 says that his team worked for two hours with the economic and social representatives of Northern Ireland to try to explain what the backstop actually meant. They then had another two hour meeting with the DUP leader Arlene Foster and the party's MP Dianne Dodds. He gets exasperated with them and finds it hard to keep his composure, though he does. He says that they are opposed to everything and don't want to hear any of the concrete proposals they make. As he says it is not a question of rebuilding a border either on land or sea. "Over and over again I repeat the point:

'It is your vote for Brexit that has created the problem. We expect you to come up with ideas and proposals. You are not coming up with any. **So when will you take responsibility for the consequences of your own actions?'** "

"Every day" he writes, "I see evidence that Brexit is a step backwards, and **it is in Ireland that this step backwards is the most serious and is felt the most strongly."**

And then we have this in November 2018. Dominic Raab was addressing an audience of worried business leaders presumably trying to reassure them. Barnier is not sure he succeeded because he suddenly heard Raab saying: "I hadn't quite understood the full extent of this, but if you look at the UK and look at how we trade in goods, **we are probably particularly reliant on the Dover- Calais crossing."** Yes well we did all hear about this one and we couldn't believe our ears.

Michel Barnier obviously couldn't either. "I don't even want to crack a smile at this" he says, but there is definitely something wrong with the British system. It is now almost two and a half years since a majority of British people voted for Brexit under the leadership of politicians like Dominic Raab, and every passing day shows that **they have not realised the consequences or what is truly at stake here."**

And time and time again the UK accuses the EU of not being prepared to negotiate at all times and say they are being threatened by them and every stand-off is the EU's fault. Even towards the end in October 2020 David Frost is threatening and rude to Michel Barnier and his team.

He says, "We agreed to seek a deal by mid-October. You did not play the game. The EU was unfair to us at the European Council. The conclusions call upon the UK to change its positions. You are trying to teach us a lesson with the threat of a no-deal. This is unacceptable. Especially as it is a request on behalf of only a few member states."

Michel Barnier and his team stare at each other in disbelief. He says in his diary, "It is almost childish. I answer calmly, 'David, the European Union has always expressed its positions clearly and will continue to do so. You know what they are. They are not going to change. If that shocks you then there is not much else to say'." At the end of the discussion he remarks that the whole episode seemed quite ridiculous. He also said that it was the UK who elected to leave the EU, the EU did not elect to leave the UK. He comments that, "Over the past weeks and months, we have had more than enough reasons to lose patience and to introduce drama into the negotiations in reaction to this or that British statement or attitude. **But once again- and to the end- we will control ourselves and keep our nerve."**

This is just a tiny flavour of the writings in this important diary. The maturity and patience and courtesy of Michel Barnier is displayed time and time again in the face of the incompetence and inadequacies and rudeness of the British contingent. One photograph says it all. On the 17th July 2017 Michel Barnier and his two deputies, Sabine Weyand and Stephanie Riso received David Davis, Tim Barrow and Olly Robins for a meeting. There they are sitting opposite each other with the three EU members holding loads of documents and papers and the three Brits with nothing. **They had left their papers behind!** Can you believe it? The most important negotiations since the Second World War. They sit there with sheepish smiles on their faces staring into the camera and looking like the complete and absolute idiots that they undoubtedly are.

And yet in the very last paragraph in this book Monsieur Barnier can write, **"At the end of this Diary, I simply wish the best to the British people."** He sees a future in which the challenges and risks will be so great with pandemics, terrorism, climate change, and financial instability that we will have new reasons to cooperate. What a dignified, wise and polite politician. They don't make them like that anymore in our country.

Hopefully our future generations will grow up with more vision and more maturity and more honesty than the present generation, in order to make this happen.

****

FARMING AND FISHING

I have decided to do a separate chapter on the above although a lot of their problems are due in no small part to Brexit. But Covid has played a part too as, of course, has the complete lack of support and total lack of care from this government, in particular the Department of the Environment and Rural Affairs.

Farming and fishing are central to the well-being, health and prosperity of this country and I feel it is important to highlight the catastrophic times they are experiencing now.

2021

26TH NOVEMBER

French fishermen are threatening to block ports and the Channel tunnel for several hours today to raise pressure on the UK to grant them their licenses for boats to fish in inner British waters.

"We don't want handouts we just want our licences back," Gerard Romiti, head of the national fisheries committee, said.

"**The UK must abide by the post-Brexit deal**. Too many fishermen are still in the dark. We have been waiting with bated breath for 11 months. The patience of professionals has limits. We hope this warning shot will be heard."

This should be able to be sorted out calmly and pragmatically but no............we call in the French Ambassador. George Eustice, our Environment secretary, says, **"Two can play at that game"** and our Foreign Secretary, Liz Truss says, **"We won't roll over."** This is the standard of British diplomacy today.

Under pressure from France, the European Commission has given the British government until December 10th to resolve the conflict with France before considering measures to force compliance.

****

27TH NOVEMBER

A report on Sky news by Helen-Ann Smith today highlights the ongoing crisis in **pig farming**. It makes appalling reading. Since Brexit there have not been enough butchers in abattoirs to get them off the farms. This is a sector that relied heavily on migrant labour.

Thousands of healthy pigs are being killed every week but not for the food chain, simply to make space on the farms. **It amounts to the largest culling of healthy pigs in the history of farming.**

Duncan Berkshire has 17 years of being a pig specialist vet and he says, "Here we are on the point of food poverty and there are people starving around the world and yet we have animals that have been killed, stuck in a skip, or burnt."

He goes on to say that, **"What's happening amounts to farmer's worst nightmares, and it's totally out of control. And it's happening because of human error. It's unforgivable".**

****

And this is the week when all farmers will start to feel the financial pain of Brexit.

When Britain was a member of the EU, 85,000 farmers received an allowance from a basic payment scheme (BPS) from the British share of the single market's Common Agricultural Policy. This week Defra will make the first payments of a new post Brexit regime. These will obviously be funded by the British rather than the EU. But they will be phased out until finally axed in 2028. In their place will be a new Environmental Land Management Scheme ELMS for short.

In a report in *The Sunday Times* by Robert Watts, he says that, "there are concerns that ministers are creating a new regime too focused on cutting carbon emissions and helping nature –and less interested in food production. **After all, importing more food by air and truck to compensate for leaner yields from British agriculture makes scant environmental sense**".

In the past, payment was determined by the size of the farm. In the future it will depend on whether farms can deliver on at least one of six "public goods". **Would it surprise you to know that food production is not one of them?**

No I thought not.

I think we all need to go and live on this **parallel universe**.

****

11TH DECEMBER
French and UK relations continue to deteriorate.

Yesterday was a deadline set by the French for the dispute over fishing licences to be settled. The UK government has said that it doesn't recognise that deadline and of course have not settled anything. The French have said that they will begin a blockade of our ports. They are still waiting for 104 new licences mainly for trawlers that were replaced since 2016. Apparently discussions are taking place over their size. But as the French say these are fishermen and for every job at sea there are four jobs on land. The French are also saying that if the UK can promise to give out a few licences today with the others coming later as a gesture of goodwill then they can accept that. But if Britain refuses to budge, the French will ask the European Commission this weekend to announce the start of legal proceedings. The whole history of this dispute is recorded in '**Beneath the Bluster**'.

My message to our French friends is don't hold your breath. There is not a lot of good will, common sense or wisdom floating around the UK government at the moment.

****

22ND DECEMBER

Those of you who have read '**Beneath the Bluster**' will have been shocked by the treatment of the **fishing trawler the Kirkella**. It is a huge trawler, based in Hull, and it fished in Norwegian waters providing the UK with 8-12% of all fish sold in the UKs fish and chip shops. Most of the 30 strong crew have been fishing since they left school. But ever since the UK lost the right to fish in Norwegian waters a year ago the Kirkella has been mothballed in Hull while post Brexit negotiations have been ongoing, and the men have been out of work. But, a few days ago I heard that fishing rights had been re-installed with Norway and I was absolutely delighted.

However (and there is always a 'however' with this government I have found) I hear today from the BBC that the owners of the UK's biggest trawler have described a new government deal to win back fishing rights following Brexit as **"too little, too late"**.

How often do we hear this?

Fisheries said they were "absolutely devastated for the crew" as the new quotas **offered just one week's work**. This is pure madness. I can't believe it.

First mate Charlie Waddy said, "The self-employed, 30-strong crew of the 81m (266ft) freezer trawler were paid per trip and have been "sold down the road". I feel for the men," he said. **"Their lives have been fishing since they left school. All they wanted to do was come fishing. They loved the job".**

He went on to say that he felt the government had encouraged fishermen to back Brexit, but he was now worried for the future of the industry.

Jane Sandell from UK Fisheries, said the latest deal had left the company "more than disappointed. **We're absolutely devastated for the crew**. The government was fully aware of what we need to operate a viable business."

Fisheries Minister Victoria Prentis said the arrangements ensured a strong balance, that would benefit the fishing industry and "the protection of the marine environment".

I say to her go up to Hull and speak to the people of the Kirkella

Look them in the eye. Meet their families. Stand up straight and start talking sense. Is that too much to hope for?

****

2022

9TH JANUARY

Farmers are still very concerned that they have had no real detail about the environmental land management schemes (ELMS) that are designed to replace the previous EU payments.

In a public accounts committee report of cross party MPs released today they said **that Defra's plan for post-EU land and farming subsidies was based on 'blind optimism'**. NFU vice president Tom

Bradshaw said: "This lack of information, at the exact time direct payments from current support schemes are being phased out, leaves farmers in an untenable position."

It would appear that many farmers will not be eligible for these payments. He goes on to say that, "There are incredibly limited options for upland farmers, who stand to lose far more support than they will gain from new measures announced so far. And it's not clear how accessible it will be for tenant farmers **who are responsible for managing over a third of the land.** These farmers play a vital role in rural communities and maintaining the farmed landscape we all value."

The NFU and other industry bodies have always maintained that enhanced environmental delivery must go hand-in-hand with sustainable food production. **But they have concerns over the government's lack of detail on how food production fits in with its proposed new schemes.**

But I thought farming was all about sustainable food production. It would be madness of the highest order if it became necessary to import food from the other side of the world and accept lower standards than ours just because DEFRA has failed in their planning and hasn't listened to the concerns of farmers. Surely this isn't going to happen is it?

****

Well already I read **that Asda is backtracking on its pledge to stock only British beef.** A 20% cost increase for British beef has been registered and whilst the premium 'Extra Special' range will stay completely British it will now import Irish beef which is about 20% cheaper . Looks to me as though the rot is already setting in.

******

30TH JANUARY

Minette Batters the President of the National Farmers' Union has accused the government of using British food producers as a "pawn" in post Brexit trade deals.

In an interview with Joanne Partridge of *The Observer* she said that, **"the most prized food market in the world had been handed over for nothing** by ministers in their rush to sign wide–ranging free-trade agreements in Australia and New Zealand."

"These are really bad trade deals for the UK as there are no checks and balances."

She goes onto say that the Tories manifesto in 2019 promised, "they would never undermine farmers in their trade deals". **She believes that this promise has been broken.**

Post Brexit and post pandemic labour shortage has resulted in rotten unpicked fruit lying in fields, and a cull of healthy pigs and all this is before the trade deals from the other side of the world have kicked in.

We heard a pig farmer talking the other day about the lack of interest from George Eustace the Environment Secretary. This farmer has to go into the pig sties and shoot young healthy pigs which is a horrible thing to have to do. He pleads with the minister to come out of his office and visit his farm but **he never even has a reply.**

And Minette Batters says, "I feel now that politicians are very, very removed from food production. Agriculture underpins the entire rural economy. In some very fragile parts of the country **if you didn't have agriculture, the village schools, the community, the allied trades, the local veterinary practice, the auction market are all put at risk**."

****

1ST MARCH

Yesterday the UK signed a free trade agreement with New Zealand similar with the one signed with Australia last year.

Responding to this news the, NFU President Minette Batters said:

"As expected, this deal takes the same approach as the UK-Australia deal in eliminating tariffs for agricultural products, meaning that even for sensitive sectors like beef and lamb, dairy and horticulture, in time there will be no limit to the amount of goods New Zealand can export to the UK."

She goes on to point out that it is not so much each individual deal that is a problem but it is the cumulative impact of each deal when added together. She says she was right to be concerned.

"There remains an urgent need for government to have a **coherent approach across all of its departments to focus on UK farming's productivity**, as well as recognise and remedy the contradictions within current domestic policy, which is still woefully sparse on the detail of how farmers will be supported to become competitive food producers at a time when food security is an increasingly important concern."

She is concerned that ministers seem far removed from food systems and food produce.

"My greatest fear was that we would be used as a pawn in trade deals, and effectively that has been what's happened," she says.

****

And then I discover her speech to the NFU conference a week ago.

This is a long and passionate speech from someone who is a farmer and who has come from a generation of farmers. As she say says we have a lot that we can be proud of:

- Our high standards of food production.
- Our net zero ambitions.
- And our education programme which reached a third of a million children last year.

But she goes on to say that,

"We have completely contradictory government policies:

- Raising the bar for environmental standards at home but pursuing trade deals which support lower standards overseas.
- Claiming to value domestic food production but making it difficult to find workers to harvest or process it.
- Stating there are many export opportunities for British food but failing to prioritise the resources to open up those new markets."

We really do need reasoned and educated debate as, "Polarised debates are getting us nowhere... and they're not allowing us to focus on the very real challenges around food supply in the future."

She says, "There is an angry mob which likes to shout loudly that 'cows are a problem' without understanding the science behind the carbon cycle, the environmental benefits of grazed pasture-land and, of course, nutrition.

By the way, the demonisation of cows is often promoted and supported by companies who have a big profit at stake in shifting ultra-processed plant-based proteins."

And as she so rightly says, all over the country farmers are regenerating the soil in a way that is needed for modern agriculture and nature to thrive together. **Farmers are the custodians of the countryside and they are the experts who know what is needed.**

"Are we turning a blind eye to the impact of global food production while we pursue a domestic vision of a chocolate box countryside?" she asks.

She goes on to talk about the difference in approach for funding from the Welsh and Scottish governments compared with England.

"The Welsh and Scottish governments have committed to continue with the current levels of BPS until 2024. This means we have a two-tier approach to farm support in the UK. How is it right that farmers in England are being treated differently to the rest of the UK?

There needs to be a PLAN. A plan which enables Britain to keep on farming and to continue to be world leaders in high quality, safe and sustainable food. Food from your farms."

I hope the government are listening to her.

Why do I keep saying this? We know that they don't listen to anyone and it is extremely concerning.

****

3RD MARCH
Then today I hear from a **very prolific pig farmer** Kate Morgan and it is so distressing.

Because of the disaster in Ukraine, the seed price has increased and so it's more expensive to keep feeding the pigs. On her farm 1,000 pigs are born every week but because of the rise in the cost of food it ultimately has a negative impact on the health of the pigs as they can't be processed and will feel the effect of this in years to come.

Pig farmers used to get £30 per pig which was very lucrative. Not anymore. Farmers are **losing in the region of £40 per pig.** The pigs are in this system and there is no way out.

Most pig farmers are relying on their banks to help keep their heads above water, but the effect on their mental health is catastrophic. The supply chain is broken. The current Tory government are not helping farmers when, as she points out, governments all over the EU and

Wales, Northern Ireland, and Scotland are all receiving help. England is not.

The fact that there are not enough butchers is due to the lack of planning due to both Brexit and Covid. Eastern Europeans don't need to come here anymore. We also used to export the 5th quarter to China. (The 5th quarter of the pig is what we generally don't eat, but China does). Different plants surrendered their licences and China is now producing more pigs of their own.

As Kate Morgan says this is a crisis which desperately needs solving.

There needs to be more transparency in the supply chain. People need to look carefully at the labels when they buy to make sure that the food they are buying is not just packaged in Britain but produced in Britain.

But we also need George Eustace, the Environment Secretary, to actually visit a few farms, to reply to farmers who contact him, and to give the farmers support. **40,000 healthy pigs have been culled and no-one seems to care.**

****

17TH MARCH

Environment Secretary George Eustace says today that, "The terms of reductions that we're making to the subsidy payments, farmers have more than recouped that through the increased income they've been getting for the produce they've been growing."

Minette Batters tweets, "It's official, one of us is clearly living in a **Parallel Universe."**

Welcome to my book!

****

6TH APRIL

Kate Morgan, the pig farmer, was on the *Today* programme this morning talking about the food supply chain and saying that the government just do not understand agriculture and begging someone, anyone from the government, to visit her farm and see for themselves the drastic problems they are having due to the lack of labour.

****

30TH APRIL

In the chapter on Brexit you will have read about the lack of checks on border controls. **British farmers** are appalled at this decision as they now face onerous and costly checks when they ship their goods across the Channel.

****

11TH JUNE

The government is about to issue a **white paper of its food strategy** following a major review published in 2021 by Henry Dimbleby, co-founder of Leon restaurant.

The entire document has been leaked and it is being criticised as **"bordering on the preposterous"**. Apparently ministers are set to reject certain key recommendations.

Calls for a sugar and salt reformation tax appear to be ignored as I think we already know but it is also ignoring calls to make sure that the budget for payments for farmers to deliver environmental benefits, such as restoring nature, preventing floods and improving soils, is guaranteed until at least 2029.

In his report, Mr Dimbleby had also said some money raised by the tax should be spent on addressing the inequalities around food, by expanding free school meals, funding holiday activity and food clubs, and providing healthy food to low-income families.

But the government instead ignores all of that too and repeats a pledge to preserve the budget in the current Parliament.

Labour criticised the leaked document as "nothing more than a statement of vague intentions". Now when have we ever heard that before?

Jim McMahon, the Shadow Secretary of State for Environment Food and Rural Affairs, said: "The UK is in a cost-of-living crisis with food prices spiralling, real-wages falling, growth plummeting and taxes up. It is clear now that the Government has absolutely no ambition to fix the mess they have created.

A food strategy is of vital importance, but the Government has dithered, delayed and now failed to deliver."

That sums it all up perfectly.

****

21ST JULY

Last night at midnight the Australian Free Trade Deal was ratified without any scrutiny by MPs in The House of Commons. This is a direct breach of the Constitutional Reform and Governance Act 2010 which states that all treaties should only be ratified after debate and scrutiny by MPs in the House of Commons. This has had no debate and no vote.

The result will mean that the UK could be flooded with cheap cuts of beef and lamb that have been subjected to lower welfare standards than we have in the UK and it means that many farmers will go out of business. But presumably this is what those who voted for Brexit wanted.

****

30TH JULY

Minette Batters has written a long article in *The Mail* today asking which of our future would-be PMs will stop a food shortage from being the next big crisis? She warns of a global famine that should be taken as seriously as the sending of tanks to Ukraine. She ends the article by saying that, "the next Prime Minister needs to be clear they will not let our levels of self-sufficiency fall."

It is a hugely chilling article.

****

Do we have politicians of sufficient calibre to address these concerns?

I think we need to look at what is happening in the House of Commons and at the actions, words and decisions taken by those who represent us and who are causing so much stress to so many people.

****

STANDARDS, TRANSPARENCY AND JUDICIAL REVIEWS

2021

We start with a story which I think will run and run.

3RD NOVEMBER

There has just been a vote in the Commons today which to my mind will prove to be the beginning of the downfall of this corrupt government. If this is not the case then the future of this country, which already looks bleak, will be put at considerable peril.

The Standards Committee is a cross party group of MPs, which aims to uphold standards in our Parliament. In October 2019 an inquiry began on the **Conservative MP Owen Paterson** following a media report which alleged that Mr Paterson had lobbied government officials and ministers on behalf of two companies which retained him as a consultant: Randox Laboratories Ltd (Randox) and Lynn's Country Foods (Lynn's). **Together they pay him more than £100,000 a year.**

Now this committee states very clearly that the House provides Members with accommodation, and supporting services, to enable them to carry out their parliamentary responsibilities and paragraph 15 of the Code states "**Members shall ensure that their use of public** resources is always in support of their parliamentary duties. It should not confer any undue personal or financial benefit on themselves ...."

The House of Commons rules also require a Member to declare their interests, such as outside employment, on any occasion when others might reasonably consider those interests to influence them. The unanimous view of the cross-party committee found that **Paterson is guilty of an 'egregious case of paid advocacy' and a 'clear pattern of confusion between the private and public interest.'**

The report goes on to say that, 'Mr Paterson has been informed of the nature of the case against him. He has had an opportunity to respond to the evidence and produce his own evidence. The Commissioner is independent with no personal interest in the outcome and she has set out the evidence she relies on in her Memorandum. In these circumstances the inquiry does not breach the principles of natural justice.'

He was therefore due to be suspended from the House for 30 days.

However, although sanctions imposed by this committee are usually approved as a formality, Mr Paterson has a lot of long-standing friends in Parliament and these supporters tabled an amendment today **seeking to change this process because they believe he has not had natural justice.**

One such amendment would pause this case and **convene a new select committee** to consider if this verdict should be overturned. This committee would be chaired by Sir John Whittingdale who has shared the Conservative bench with Owen Paterson for the last 25 years.

It is interesting to note that the Standards Committee has only ever been challenged twice before and each time the challenge failed.

The Speaker granted a vote on this amendment and it was passed by 250 votes to 232, a majority of 18, after Tory MPs were ordered to back it on a three-line whip. Not only were they ordered to back it but apparently they were threatened that if they didn't, **then their constituencies would be starved of funds.** "That is government as an extortion racket" writes Andrew Rawnsley in The *Observer.* There were cries of "shame" and "what have you done to this place" as the result was announced.

Labour said **"it was a grubby stitch-up"** and that "**Standards in public life in this country are under attack. This is very dangerous indeed."**

And so this government continues to do what it does best..........change the rules to suit its own incompetent, and corrupt shabby agenda.

****

But I have to go back to **Tuesday 2nd November.** This was the second day of the Cop 26 conference and it was the day that Boris would return to London. And return he did and in some style. **He flew back on a private jet** which you would think would not be a good look at the end of a climate change visit and of course you would be right.

So what was the hurry? Well he went to a dinner with some old mates at the (men only) Garrick Club. One of those mates was his old friend from his time on *The Daily Telegraph,* its owner Charlie Moore. **The Paterson affair was discussed because *The Telegraph* had written a piece at the weekend saying Paterson had been shabbily treated by the investigation and by the Commissioner, Kathryn Stone.** So Boris knew he could rely on *The Telegraph* to support him in his attempts to undermine this committee. It has also been noted that Kathryn Stone is proceeding with further investigations into the refurbishment of the Downing Street flat.

However............... it is now **November 4th** and not only has there been the **fastest U-turn ever** but we can actually hear the screeching of tyres and the burning of rubber.

303

The opposition parties **refused to agree to sit on a new committee** and so there was no way it could go ahead. So we see Rees-Mogg, the Commons leader, return to the Commons to say that the motion passed on Wednesday night had "created a certain amount of controversy" and "conflated the individual case with the general concern," that **there was not an appeals process for MPs who felt the punishment they faced was unfair.** Therefore because the other parties had boycotted the idea of a new committee the plans could not now go ahead.

Well the Tory back benchers who voted for it yesterday, many of them very reluctantly, are now furious. **They feel their loyalty has been betrayed.** Owen Paterson, who was told of this decision by a phone call when he was out shopping in a supermarket, immediately resigned.

So everyone is a loser. If Owen Paterson had taken his punishment on the chin he would have been suspended for 30 days and could then have continued as an MP.

The Chief Whip would not be facing censure for his strong arm tactics.

The MPs would not be exploring their consciences and be feeling disgusted with their own behaviour.

Andrea Leadsome and Jacob Rees-Mogg who brought forward this amendment, would not be being called **"the most lethal comedy duo since Arsenic and Old Lace"** (Andrew Rawnsley) and Business Secretary Kwasi Kwarteng would not be being accused of bullying when he spoke on the radio and said that the parliamentary commissioner Kathryn Stone should review her position.

And after all this **Owen Paterson still maintains he is innocent of any wrong doing,** that he was not allowed to put forward any witnesses and that he was not able to launch an appeal.

But we read Chris Bryant in *The Observer* today the **7th November**. He is the chair of the committee. He talks about the bullying and determination of the government machine which spent months trying to lobby anyone they could find. He writes, "**They spread noxious rumours about members of the committee. They tried to get the Speaker to block the publication of our report. They endlessly misrepresented the process, claiming that witness statements were ignored (they weren't), that Paterson was denied a fair hearing (he wasn't), that the commissioner decides the sanctions (she doesn't) and that there was no appeal (there was)."**

No wonder I call this book a **parallel universe**. This government are all there.

But if you think that all sounds terrible there was more to come. **Sir John Major** gave an interview to the *Today* programme two days ago. In this interview Sir John suggested the **Johnson administration was "politically corrupt"** over its treatment of the House of Commons and said its attempt to overhaul the standards system was "rather a bad mistake" but "it isn't a mistake on its own. There's a general whiff of 'we are the masters now' about their behaviour," he said. "It has to stop, it has to stop soon."

He went on to say, "I have been a Conservative all my life. And if I am concerned at how the government is behaving, I suspect lots of other people are as well. It seems to me, as a lifelong Conservative, **that much of what they are doing is un-Conservative in its behaviour.** This government has done a number of things that have concerned me deeply: they have broken the law, the prorogation of Parliament. They have broken treaties, I have in mind the Northern Ireland Protocol. They have broken their word on many occasions."

Well Sir John is a Remainer and proud of it and has often criticised Boris Johnson but I heard the whole interview and coming from a former Conservative Prime Minister I thought it was shocking.

And what does Boris say about all of this? Well, in his customary statesman- like way he says **"I am pissed off"** and **"who got me into this mess?"**

Well I have news for you Boris because everyone is saying all this mess has come right from the top. **I think, unfortunately, that that is you**.

****

7TH NOVEMBER

The polls are not looking good if you are a Tory. Boris Johnson's personal approval rating has dropped to its lowest level on record and the Tory lead has fallen to a single point in the past week.

And there is more to come. **Randox**, one of the firms paying Owen Paterson, was awarded two Covid testing contracts last year worth £480 **million without going out to tender**. They were then awarded a further £347 million after failing to deliver on the previous contract **as 750,000 testing kits had to be recalled due to concerns about their safety.**

The Sunday Times editorial sums it all up perfectly. "The fish rots from the head and many of these problems begin and end at the top with the culture Mr. Johnson presides over. Either there is nobody brave enough to tell the Prime Minister when he or his ministers are doing something sleazy that can only end badly, or when they do he ignores them.

Voters will not ignore it, or the 'one rule for them, one rule for everyone else charge' against the government, which is hitting home. It does indeed have to stop. And very soon."

But George Eustice Environmental Secretary says, "It is just a Westminster storm in a tea cup."

Well I will let you all know exactly when this storm blows over.

****

8TH NOVEMBER

This afternoon the Lib Dems have won an emergency debate on the events of last week and I will be watching with interest. **Sir Keir Starmer has demanded an apology from the PM.** But people are saying he won't even be there. Marie Anne Trevelyan said this morning words to the effect that oh no he is the Prime Minister he has far too many really important things to do that can only be done by the PM. They really do take us for fools.

****

9TH NOVEMBER
Where's Boris?

We all watched the debate yesterday with interest. **And no, Boris was not there.** He was honouring a 'long standing' visit to a hospital in Northumberland. Indeed we saw him there. He was not wearing a mask. Hospital guidance states that visitors should wear masks "at all times." He was interviewed and refused to apologise or to express any regret for the way he handled the Paterson case last week. He arrived back in London by 5pm so could have gone to the Commons for the next 2 hours of the debate but......he didn't.

We have to presume that Boris just does not care. He doesn't care for the well-being of patients and staff in hospitals, he does not care for his fellow MPs and he does not care for Parliament.

So we have to ask ourselves, why is he there?

The debate was calm and measured but MP after MP criticised the Prime Minister for his appalling judgement during the whole of this debacle. It was interesting to note however that although the opposition benches were full to bursting the Tory benches were half empty. Again they were following their non-leader to snub the debate. But of those that were there Mark Harper, a former chief whip, said that, **"If the team leader gets it wrong he should come and apologise** to the public and to this House." Many, many so called Red Wall Conservatives were very angry.

Johnson was also strongly attacked by Sir Keir Starmer who accused Boris Johnson of **"damaging our democracy" over the Owen Paterson sleaze row.** He urged MPs to resist the Government's "politics of cynicism". And he went on to say that: **"His concern as always is self-preservation, not the national interest.** We will not stand by while he trashes our democracy. The Prime Minister should have told Mr Paterson that the right thing to do was accept his punishment. His duty of care and basic decency demanded that. Instead the British people were let down, and Mr Paterson was let down - used in an extraordinary attack on our commissioner for standards."

Sir Keir also said that the row formed part of a **"pattern of behaviour"** by Mr Johnson. "This is the Prime Minister's way of doing business," he added. "He knows that the rules apply to him, but his strategy is to devalue those rules so that they don't matter to anyone. That way politics becomes contaminated, and cynicism replaces confidence and trust. **The prime minister hopes to drag us all into the gutter with him."**

And the headlines in the papers today will make extremely worrying reading for Mr. Johnson.

Daily Express: Just say sorry for the mess Prime Minister

The Mirror: No apology no shame, no respect & no mask

Metro: I'm a Prime Minister get me out of here

Independent: Johnson 'running scared' over Tory sleaze storm

Times: Anger as PM skips sleaze showdown in Commons

The i: PM refuses to apologise for trying to tear up sleaze rules

The Guardian: Johnson is leading the Tory party 'through the sewers' says Starmer

And then we get to the **Mail** and the headline there is:

Top MP earns fortune for working in tax haven

Well this is another interesting story. Apparently **Sir Geoffrey Cox MP** is in the Caribbean at the moment so he voted remotely in the debate yesterday. **Whilst in the British Virgin Islands he has been paid more than £1million for legal work on top of his £82,000 salary as an MP.**

Well nice work if you can get it but people aren't happy.

****

So on to yet another story which is not looking good if you are a Tory. The Conservative Party has been accused of **guaranteeing peerages to a group of multi-millionaires who have donated more than £3 million to the party.** Wealthy backers who take on the temporary role of party treasurer appear to be offered a seat in the House of Lords once they have donated the set figure. All 16 of the Conservative's main treasurers, excluding the most recent, were offered a seat in the Lords in the past two decades including Peter Cruddas, Lord Spencer, Lord Fraser, Lord Lupton and Lord Farmer.

****

And this was also mentioned in the debate yesterday. Peter Wishart, the SNP spokesman on House of Commons matters, told MPs that he has asked the **Metropolitan police to investigate whether the Conservative party has broken the 1925 law banning the sale of honours.** He says he was prompted by these revelations at the weekend.

I actually could not believe what I was hearing yesterday when the Met was mentioned. For one brief minute I thought they were getting the police in to investigate Boris. But no.

So just to be clear. If you have £3 million to spare and there is a Tory government and you donate that amount of money to them you can become a member of the House of Lords.

****

And a footnote to the Owen Paterson affair. Apparently he will be allowed to have a security pass which will enable him to return to the House of Commons whenever he likes to roam the corridor unescorted and unchecked. Any MP who has served for more than six years in Parliament is entitled to apply for such a pass. Just saying.

****

11TH NOVEMBER
Did I really think that that was the footnote???!!!

Today we all hear about the rent expenses loophole. MPs, including the Right Honourable MP Geoffrey Cox, (spot the inappropriate words there) are apparently allowed to, and so therefore certainly do, use taxpayers money to rent a flat in London whilst renting out their own homes which are also in London, for about £10,000 a year. Sir Geoffrey Cox QC owns a property in Battersea but he rents out his own property in London for £1,900 a month which is being paid for by us. They claim up to £22,920 a year in expenses.

About 14 other MPs are doing this.

****

13TH NOVEMBER
Some polls are saying today that Labour is now 6 points ahead of the Tories. Matthew Parris in *The Times* writes the headline:

"Flight Bojo 2019 has begun its final descent".

The Independent today says that,

"Boris Johnson will be looking over his shoulder."

And it is also interesting to note that there is a **judicial review** being brought against the Prime Minister by the senior civil servants union, the FDU, over his decision to support Priti Patel when she had been found guilty of bullying the permanent secretary of her department Sir Phillip Rutman. **He** resigned instead of her and received £340,000 in settlement with a further £30,000 in costs.

Alex Allan, Johnson's Independent Advisor on the ministerial code, also resigned last year after the PM ignored his advice to ask for Patel's resignation as she had been accused of breaking the ministerial code. Johnson said she hadn't.

The full story is on page 218 in my first book when the judicial review was first announced in November 2020. And it comes to the High Court next week on the 17th and 18th. I think Boris wants to get rid of the Electoral Commission if he can for some reason. And yes, I truly think that Johnson's days are numbered at last.

****

15TH NOVEMBER
Priti Patel has pulled funding from a counter extremism programme despite a government report finding it had prevented hundreds of thousands of people from being radicalised.

The 'Building a Stronger Britain Together' scheme has given £60 million to community projects and workshops teaching British values since 2015, including a body in Southend that the MP Sir David Amess was involved with. If you remember Sir David Amess was fatally stabbed when at his surgery seeing constituents at his office in Southend West.

The strategy was shut down this year, forcing the closure of activities and events that ministers praised for turning youngsters away from extremism.

A source involved with the unit said that the two previous Home Secretaries had understood the importance of its work but Patel and Boris Johnson "had failed to understand how counter extremism works." How can they? The source went on to say that "Stronger Britain was a brilliant bit of work and so much has been lost now they have junked it."

It really does beggar belief.

****

14TH NOVEMBER

Well, well, well diaries are the popular format at the moment! After David Davis, Michel Barnier and, of course, mine, we now have those of **Jennifer Arcuri!** She is about to hand over these diaries to the police for further investigation. You may remember that she was Johnson's mistress when he was Mayor of London.

These are pretty explosive and display Boris Johnson as the immoral, sleazy, self-obsessed character that we know him to be. If you are in any doubt just read John Ware in today's *Observer* and you will be disgusted as I certainly am. Sexual principles, the Nolan principles, business principles, family principles or in fact any degree of morality just does not exist in the person who is Boris Johnson. And he is still our Prime Minister.

****

2ND DECEMBER.

There was a debate in the House of Lords last week on **transparency**. This is really excellent to hear because the lack of transparency is something I, and many others, have been worried about for many years with this government.

Lord Callaghan, Minister for Business, Energy and Corporate responsibility was speaking in the debate.

Hang on a minute what is he saying? He attacked Britain's **freedom on information law as a "truly malign piece of legislation".**

Apparently there is a relatively new science agency which cost the government £800 million and is called the **Advanced Research and Invention Agency**. It was brought in by Dominic Cummings when he was in No 10 and Lord Callaghan spoke **against** a move to place this agency under the scope of the Freedom of Information Act.

I can't believe it. He goes on to say that "People just modify their behaviour and communication to take account of the fact that private conversation may be released in the future. I genuinely do not think that it achieves anything at all."

So he is saying that the Freedom of Information act just encourages people to clam up and say very little because they think it could all be too easily exposed.

Well yes this is what the word transparency means Lord Callaghan. .

He also called for those making freedom of information requests **to be charged which would be in direct breach of a key principle of the act that information be provided free.** The Department for Business, Energy and Industrial Strategy has for the past nine months blocked a *Times* request for information about this decision to exempt the agency.

There are already concerns about lack of transparency over the sleaze allegations. Maurice Frankel director of the' Campaign for Freedom of Information' said: **"No minister has ever referred to FoI with such undisguised contempt. This refusal to see any value at all in FoI suggests attacks on it are more likely."**

Parallel Universe: As well as being a business minister Lord Callaghan serves as the government's UK champion for the 'Extractive Industries Transparency Initiative,' promoting transparency and anti-corruption measures in the oil and gas sector. And a government spokesman (what him again?) declined to comment on Callaghan's remarks but said that they remained fully committed to its transparency agenda. Not that we know what that is exactly.

I am indebted to George Greenwood of *The Times* for bringing all of this to our attention.

****

4TH DECEMBER

Boris defends the freedom of the press today after Meghan Markle won her legal fight with the *Mail on Sunday*. A government spokesman said that **"a free press is one of the cornerstones of any democracy."** He went on to say that **"This government recognises the vital role that newspapers and the media play in holding people to account and shining a light on the issues which matter to communities."**

I think that means that he supports transparency.

****

2022

12TH JANUARY

All has been a bit quiet on this front for a while as we have been concentrating on the shenanigans of Boris Johnson and his parties at No 10, which is all detailed in the chapter with his name at the top.

However, in a ruling today by the High Court it has found that the government's use of a so-called **'VIP lane' that gave preferential** treatment to a pest control firm and a hedge fund and awarded them nearly £600 million worth of PPE contracts was unlawful. The 'Good Law Project' and 'EveryDoctor' 'took legal action over £340 million in contracts given to 'PestFix' and £252 million handed to 'Ayanda Capital' by the Department of Health and Social Care.

In her ruling today, Mrs Justice O'Farrell ruled that while she accepted that there was 'evidence that opportunities were treated as high priority even where there were no objectively justifiable grounds for expediting the offer' she also concluded that a large number of masks and other equipment supplied by 'PestFix' and 'Ayanda' were not suitable for NHS use - **leading to tens of millions of pounds of taxpayers' money being wasted.**

'Good Law Project' director Jo Maugham said: 'There's nothing that can change the past - but **Ministers will now know that if they ever put something like this in place again they will be breaking the law** - and very arguably committing misconduct in public office.'

Responding to the High Court's ruling, Liberal Democrat health spokesperson Daisy Cooper MP said: "This damning judgment confirms what the public already suspected. Not only did the Conservatives give their mates privileged access to lucrative Covid contracts, **they did it unlawfully."**

Are we surprised? No but we are disgusted.

****

15TH FEBRUARY

In an article today by Polly Toynbee of *The Guardian* she reveals the stark problems of the **way in which our political parties are funded**. It really does make disturbing reading. I think we know that the Tory party relies on donors from millionaires as we keep hearing that some of them are fed up with the present lot and so are withdrawing funds.

But it is interesting to read how the Tories **are directing their biggest donors to apply for public posts.** Indeed in my first book, '**Beneath the Bluster**' I mention this fact in the chapter on the Arts on page 213 where I say that **"with the backing of Downing Street, Oliver Dowden is believed to have blocked many re-appointments at the top institutions in favour of candidates more in tune with the government's thinking."**

Just ten people donated a quarter of all Tory funds (more than £10m) since Johnson became prime minister.

But look carefully at the new Election Bill. It will abolish the Electoral Commission's power to prosecute illegal donations. Why? This is yet another pernicious bill by this government that will destroy any transparency, any decency or any honesty in our governing body.

Ms Toynbee then looks at Labour who are of course reliant on the Unions. At least with them we all know exactly what they are saying as they shout it out loud and clear. They were in threatening mood last week but Sir Keir Starmer said, **"The Labour party I lead is not going to be influenced by threats from anybody, whoever they are, and that is just an absolute matter of principle."** Direct and to the point and no equivocation and to which I say 'three cheers for Sir Keir.'

But the point of all this is that somehow we have to see that the funding of our political parties is open and transparent and free from pressure.

In his speech last week Sir John Major said: "The system needs cleansing, to stop politics being the plaything of the rich or of pressure groups. Limit donations by individuals and unions so donors no longer sway policy through an open cheque book".

There are other ideas but it is vital that discussion takes place and a solution is found as soon as possible.

****

16TH FEBRUARY

In my first book on page 223, March 29th, I write about the appointment by Matt Hancock of Baroness Dido Harding to be chair of the NHS Test and Trace task force. I mentioned the fact that she was married to a Conservative MP and that also a colleague of hers, Mike Coupe, was appointed director of the Test and Trace system. I mention also that campaigners had launched a judicial review into the claims that both Hancock and Johnson had acted unlawfully by appointing their "chums" to these posts in their fight against Covid.

Well today we get the result of that judicial review.

It was brought about by the 'Runnymede Trust' which is an independent race equality think tank and two judges in the High Court have ruled that Matt Hancock **did not** comply with a public sector equality duty when he appointed the Conservative peer Baroness Dido Harding and Mike Coupe her former colleague.

The say that, **"Compliance with the law does not allow members of the executive to simply appoint their friends to senior public sector jobs without giving, at a bare minimum, due consideration to the Equality Act."**

In a joint statement, Dr Halima Begum, the chief executive of the 'Runnymede Trust', and Sir Clive Jones, the chair of Runnymede's board of trustees, said: "Neither Baroness Harding nor Mr Coupe is medically trained. Neither has a lifetime of public administration under their belt. It should not be acceptable to drop our standards during complex health emergencies when countless lives are at stake, in particular the lives of some of our country's most vulnerable citizens."

It added: "This judgment sends a strong message to the government that it needs to take its obligations to reduce inequality far more seriously. **It also serves as an unequivocal reminder that all future public appointments must give due consideration to equalities legislation."**

Jason Coppel QC, who led the two organisations' legal teams, told the court the challenge was based on equality legislation and public law.

He said the government had a "policy or practice" **of "making appointments to posts critical to the pandemic response" without adopting any, or any sufficient, "fair or open competitive processes".**

He also said that people "less likely to be known or connected to decision-makers" were put at a disadvantage. The government was failing to offer "remuneration for high-level full-time roles" and **"excluding all candidates who were not already wealthy"** or held other posts for which they would continue to be paid.

This, I would like to remind everyone, is the test and trace system which Boris promised would be world beating and **which turned out to be a complete disaster and a waste of £37 billion pounds.**

****

And with the Russian troops lining up on the borders of the Ukraine there is mounting pressure everywhere you look, on the Foreign Secretary, Liz Truss, on Boris Johnson our PM and on the **amount of Russian influence in UK politics and the amount of Russian money in London.** None of it makes reassuring reading. It is beyond the scope of this book to give a detailed analysis of all of this but I can just give some indication from others who can and who do.

I certainly remember rumours abounding at the time of the Brexit referendum that the Russians had been influential in the outcome.

There is renewed interest in the **Russia report** which was published in July 2020 and is the report of the British Intelligence and Security Committee of Parliament. Its publication was initially blocked by Johnson so that it would not see the light of day until after the 2019 election.

It was looking into allegations of Russian interference in British politics including alleged Russian interference in the 2016 Brexit referendum and the 2014 Scottish Independence referendum.

Their findings from last year suggest that the government failed to tackle Russian interference in our democracy and, would it surprise you to learn that **none of the 21 recommendations have been implemented**?

The report says that around £2 **million in Russia-related money has been given to the Tories since Boris Johnson became Prime Minister**. Also the Tories have accepted 280k in Russian related donations in the year since the publication of the Russia report. In fact I have just heard Chris Mason of the BBC read out an item about the wife of a former Russian finance minister paying £200,000 for a tennis match with Boris. Her name, just for your interest, is Lubov Chernukhin.

Actually on further delving into this **I find out that she actually paid £45,000 for the tennis match, £30,000 for a private meal with Gavin Williamson (WHAT?) in the Churchill rooms off Westminster and £135,000 for a night out with Theresa May.** What is it with these people? On every level you can think of it is positively obscene.

The report also revealed that there was an influx of Russian cash to the UK which went to "PR firms, charities, political interests, academia and cultural institutions".

It went on to say that **"Russian influence in the UK is 'the new normal', and there are a lot of Russians with very close links to Putin who are well integrated in the UK business and social scene, and accepted because of their wealth".**

But, listen to this, last month, a cross-party group of MPs and peers have decided to ask the High court to give the go-ahead for a legal challenge against the government over its alleged failure to investigate Russian interference in UK elections. **Wow that is apparently the first** time that sitting MPs or peers have taken legal action against the government of the day on the grounds of national security.

And of course it is going to be quite difficult for the PM to threaten Russia with sanctions etc. and to support the Ukraine with all this going on. As Tom Tugendhat, the Tory MP who chairs the House of Commons' Foreign Affairs Committee, recently said, the U.K.'s efforts to support Ukraine risk being "undermined" if the government doesn't act to stop "dirty Russian money flowing through our system."

****

Is Liz Truss the correct person to be negotiating with Russia at the moment?

That is a rhetorical question because it is as plain as a pikestaff that she isn't. Her geography, as we have seen is non-existent, and when William Hague draws attention to a lengthy article written by Putin about the historic unity of Russia and the Ukrainians, it is obvious she has not read it. If she had, a letter to *The Times* today points out, she might have noticed some areas of common ground which could have been the start of some solid negotiations for building a lasting peace.

But no. She is too busy with **her photo opportunities** and finding a large furry hat to wear to Moscow that would go with her fur coat. A review of the government's official account on the photo-sharing platform 'Flickr' reveals that since the day she took up post, **more than 700 pictures have been uploaded featuring her** --- an average of more than four and a half a day or about one in every five hours in the job. These are photographers paid for by the tax payer.

The Foreign, Commonwealth and Development Office said that "our photographers play a leading role in supporting the government's digital communications activity."

Oh for goodness sake.

****

18TH FEBRUARY

And today we hear that an **RAF P-8A Poseidon flew 330 miles** from its base in Lossiemouth, Moray, Scotland, to RAF Waddington in Lincolnshire just so that Boris Johnson could have his photograph taken standing beside it.

He also had a photo taken of him sitting in the cockpit of an RAF fast jet which had flown from its home base of RAF Coningsby which was only 15 miles away. And this was the image plastered all over the front pages of the newspapers.

So what was he trying to tell us with this photo exactly? That he is ready to pilot a plane any time anywhere? It is appalling on so many levels, including of course, carbon footprints and tax-payers money, but also the narcissist character of the PM.

Both aircraft flew back to their respective bases after the PM had left.

****

20TH FEBRUARY

More and more disclosures about millionaires funding the Conservative Party and allegedly being offered access to Ministers including the PM and also top culture posts as I have already reported.

But it is worse than we thought. Apparently there is something called an **'advisory board'** which is a secret group of ultra-wealthy Conservative party donors. Last July Labour was calling on the government to explain the existence of this board. There has been a leak of several thousand documents (I don't know where from) which explain in detail what exactly this board is about. Its existence has never been formally admitted by the party. The fact that it is a Conservative rather than a government body means it **is not subject to transparency laws**.

Are you beginning to get the picture?

These millionaires were getting very worried about the effect that the pandemic was having on their businesses and at a meeting on the 15th May 2020 they requested the relaxation of restrictions designed to stop transmissions of Covid. They were told that their concerns would be relayed directly to the PM. Lord Udney-Lister, the PM's longest-standing adviser and confidant was all ears according to one source. "It was a two-way street" he says. "They gave us information on what was going on. We gave our advice." **Their investments happen to be property, construction, and big tobacco.**

The combined wealth of the board members, their companies, and their families exceeds £30 billion. They have donated £22 million to the Conservative party including £9.9 million since Johnson became PM.

None of the meetings appear to have been minuted or attended by civil servants, so there is unlikely to be any record of the advice or lobbying which took place.

When donors where asked to join the board the chairman's pitch was simple. "**You are going to give us the money and the advice we need to stay in power.**"

I would like to know what they have done with that money.

I am indebted to Gabriel Pogrund and Henry Zeffman of *The Sunday Times.*

****

And we also hear that Johnson has appointed **six Tory donors to help run the country's leading cultural institutions since entering Downing Street**. The donors, who between them have contributed more than £3 million to the Tory coffers, were appointed to the boards of the National Gallery, the National Portrait Gallery, the British Museum, and the Tate.

David Ross is the chairman of the National Portrait Gallery and had to stand down from his chairmanship of the Royal Opera House last year as the Tories wanted him at the gallery and he couldn't do both. So he is with Chris Grayling (what??) who is also on the board. Had you forgotten about Chris Grayling? I knew he would be lurking somewhere. And here he is. Lurking at the National Portrait Gallery. Lost and now found. What on earth has this poor gallery done to deserve this?

****

23RD FEBRUARY

And so, as Russia continues to make preparations to invade Ukraine and in actual fact has already crossed the border in two areas, we watch our Prime Minister and Foreign Secretary in dismay and disbelief.

Liz Truss did the media rounds this morning and the PM took PMQs as usual and both **tried to distance themselves from Russian money in the Conservative Party, in elections, and in London generally**. They did not convince anyone.

Sanctions have been put in place but are thought to be far too little and ineffective. We have a corrupt government and everyone with eyes to see, knows this, and yet on they all go.

****

24TH FEBRUARY....... RUSSIAN INVADES UKRAINE.

Everyone's worst fears have come true.

It is beyond the scope of this book to comment on the details of this war because there will be plenty of well qualified people who can and who will. I will just comment, in appropriate chapters, on those aspects which seem to me to be an inadequate response from individual members of the government.

****

27TH FEBRUARY

There is a report in *The Observer* today by Jon Ungoed-Thomas who writes that the names of many companies which benefitted from billions of pounds of Covid-19 loans schemes are to be kept confidential and they will not be named.

How can this possibly be you might ask? Come on you must know the answer by now. There is yet another new bill going through Parliament which is called the **Subsidy Control Bill**.

Under the EU rules all pandemic business loans above 100,000 Euros had to be publically declared. But the new government rules say that nothing needs to be declared if it is under £500,000. This applies from January 2021 and these schemes have been called a "bonanza for fraudsters."

So **that** is why the government are not going after the £4.9 billion lost in fraud. We now understand.

The **government now faces a legal challenge under freedom of information laws** from the campaign group 'Spotlight on Corruption.'

As their campaigner George Havenhand says, "Publishing those names would support the government's efforts to recoup the money lost to fraud and increase accountability for this national scandal." The Lords has already approved an amendment to reduce the amount threshold for public disclosure.

A definite lack of transparency here so no surprise there then. When the existing laws do not help your levels of honesty then change them.

****

18TH MARCH

They've changed their minds! **Yet again another U-turn.** After the Owen Paterson lobbying affair the government decided that it would be a good idea to put a limit on the amount of money MPs could earn from second jobs. There was also going to be a limit on the number of hours spent on second jobs. This, if you remember, was partly because it was discovered that Conservative MP Geoffrey Cox made almost £1million from legal work in the past year and was doing a lot of this work from his office in the Commons. Obviously not spending nearly enough time with the problems of his constituents. But apparently there are over 30 MPs who earn tens of thousands of pounds from consultancy jobs, including one who picks up £15,000 for two and a half days' work.

But now we are hearing that they have decided that may be it **is not necessary to impose these restrictions after all and so they are planning to ditch them.** No 10 chief of staff Steve Barclay and Commons leader Mark Spencer said: "It is the government's initial view that the imposition of fixed constraints such as time limits on the amount of time that members can spend on outside work would be impractical."

They also go on to say that, "In respect of a cap on earnings from outside work to impose such a limit could serve to prohibit activities which do not bring undue influence to bear on the political system."

Well it is a sharp contrast to remarks made by ministers in the wake of the Paterson lobbying scandal and I think what they really mean is, **"oops, goodness, how on earth are we going to be able to pay for school fees, foreign holidays, second homes and a new yacht, if we have to survive on an MP's salary only?"**

****

29TH APRIL

The Tory MP who was found watching pornography on his phone in the House of Commons, has been named as Neil Parish MP for

Tiverton and Honiton in Devon. He is being referred to the Standards Committee and he said that he will resign if he is found to be guilty.

Excuse me? Does he not know whether he was watching porn or not? I really do find it difficult to understand these people who don't know whether they have broken any rules or not. They are supposed to be the leaders of our country.

****

30TH APRIL

He has resigned. Not only that but he was interviewed on television when he made a full apology and explained exactly what he had been doing. He used to be a farmer apparently and was looking at tractors on his phone when he switched on to another site with a similar name which turned out to be a pornography site. He continued to look at it which he should not have done and he also owned up to looking at a site on a second occasion.

Well I deplore this behaviour but at least the man acknowledged his guilt and resigned.

Come on Mr. Johnson, when oh when will you follow his example?

****

2ND MAY

This is just so awful that I find it difficult to believe. Except I have seen it for myself.

In just three days' time there are local elections. These should be about how your local council is benefitting your local community but in actual fact they are being seen as an opportunity to say what people think of the government.

The Tories are getting desperate and are slinging as much mud as they can possibly make up at the Labour party.

I use the words "make up" advisedly. In trying to forget about the parties at Number 10 they keep trying to accuse Sir Keir of something similar. The worst thing they could find was a photo of him drinking a beer at lunch time at a work event in Durham. The police were not interested.

But oh my goodness gracious me what is this that they have found? Nadine Dorries has just tweeted a photograph of **Sir Keir eating a curry with others and accused him of breaking lock down rules.** This does look dreadful.

Oh but wait a moment. This photo is cropped but in the uncropped picture you can see that Sir Keir is sitting next to Frank Dobson a Labour MP. **The only trouble is, that Frank Dobson died in 2019 and people are remembering going to his lovely funeral.**

I am disgusted by this and I thought that deliberately spreading misinformation was a crime. A lowering of standards? They are all down in the troughs.

****

24TH MAY

Liz Truss has just announced that there will be a **major shake-up in foreign aid which will link overseas aid to expanding trade.** She also says that Britain will direct aid to bilateral projects rather than through international bodies.

This could mean that aid could be slower to arrive after emergencies.

You must know of course by now, that whenever the name Liz Truss crops up, as with the name Priti Patel, it is not good news.

So we hear from Sarah Champion who is the chair of the Commons International Development Committee, and she says, "Aid for trade is dangerous. It can distort the core, legally stipulated purpose of our assistance – which is to support the poorest and most vulnerable, whether in the countries of sub-Saharan Africa or in Ukraine. **Supporting the poorest in the world should not be conditional on a trade deal or agreeing to investment partnerships."**

Stephanie Draper, chief executive of the Bond organisation of aid groups, said: "The UK has missed a golden opportunity to properly rethink its role on the world stage – **and risks abandoning those most in need."**

Lowering of standards, lack of commitment, lack of concern, can we do it on the cheap? That is the way this government thinks all the time.

****

I have to move away from these corrupt politicians for a while and talk about some decent, principled people who are fighting for their lives.

****

NAZANIN ZAGHARI-RATCLIFFE

2021

12TH NOVEMBER

I have been following the plight of Nazanin Zaghari-Ratcliffe for many years.

Last week I went up to the Foreign and Commonwealth office to meet Richard Ratcliffe who is on a hunger strike outside its doors. I gave him a copy of my book '**Beneath the Bluster'** which has a chapter about Nazanin in it.

I sat with him and we talked and it was a very humbling experience. His family, his friends and his supporters were all with him. Today is his 20th day on hunger strike and he feels that he cannot go on for much longer. He had been waiting to hear what happened when ministers spoke to the Iranian Deputy Prime Minister who visited London on Thursday. But having spoken to James Cleverly MP he is very disheartened as he feels they are making no progress whatsoever. Talking about the debt that is owned by us to Iran he said they just clammed up and would not say a word. As his MP Tulip Siddiq said it was so hard to see him so deflated as he came out of the meeting.

Here is part of her reply to an email I wrote earlier.

I have read the chapter on Nazanin, which is a strong reminder of the many failures of consecutive Conservative Government's in this case.

I know he (Richard) takes great strength from these visits and good wishes. I am doing all I can to press the Government for resolutions on this issue, and I have managed to secure a debate on Nazanin's situation in Parliament on Tuesday.

So I will obviously be listening out for that debate and will report it here. And just to note that I wrote to my MP, Oliver Dowden, about Nazanin on the 25th October and am still awaiting a reply from him.

****

13TH NOVEMBER
Richard Ratcliffe finishes his hunger strike today. We are hoping that the huge publicity he has had will have some effect on this government and galvanise them to get their act together and pay this legally owed debt. But I have never known a less galvanised looking government than this lot.

Spineless, corrupt, incompetent, immoral, and unintelligent describes them more accurately to my mind.

****

16TH NOVEMBER
The debate on Nazanin was held in Westminster Hall this afternoon.

The hall was packed with MPs who were all urged to keep their questions short as so many wanted to speak.

Tulip Siddiq opened the debate by talking about the hunger strike that Richard Ratcliffe was on directly outside the foreign office and said how disappointed she was that during that time **the Prime Minister never came to visit him.** In answer to a question, she said that although the PM did meet them shortly after he became Prime Minister he had not been properly involved since then.

The debate went on to discuss the debt of course, the lack of a fully resourced consular support, and the ongoing inaction and uncertainty.

Speaker after speaker praised the dignity and determination and courage of Richard Ratcliffe.

****

17TH DECEMBER

Today I get a long reply from Oliver Dowden my MP. This is his penultimate sentence.

With regard to the IMS Ltd debt you mentioned, as the Government has been clear, this is a wholly separate issue which relates to contracts signed in the 1970s with the pre-revolution Iranian government regarding the sale of tanks. The Government continues to look into how the dispute can be resolved but it is entirely separate from the arbitrary detention of our British nationals.

As I keep saying I think that if we paid the debt I believe she would be released pretty quickly. Surely it is worth a try.

****

I email Richard's publicity person to ask how things are going. They have heard nothing at all from Liz Truss, our new foreign secretary.

They are singing carols outside No.10 at 5.30 pm on Monday the 20th. This will be their sixth Christmas apart.

****

22ND DECEMBER

Liz Truss has just been given the job of Brexit negotiator to replace Lord Frost who has just resigned. This is in addition to Foreign Secretary and Minister for Women and Equalities. So yesterday I wrote a letter to *The Times* and today **it is published**!! Here it is:

Sir, I hope that, with her new responsibilities, Liz Truss will still have plenty of time to concentrate on the plight of Nazanin Zaghari-Ratcliffe who is about to face her sixth Christmas away from her husband and young daughter.

Short but to the point and I know it won't make a scrap of difference. The quality of all recent Foreign Secretaries, including the present one, has been abysmal. It is important to keep Nazanin's name in the public eye but will it elicit any response? I doubt it.

****

2022

13TH JANUARY

There is a tiny, tiny flicker of hope today as we hear that a British Council worker has been freed from Iran and is back in the UK. Aras Amiri was arrested in March 2018 and was sentenced to 10 years in prison. We have to cling on to news like this with both hands.

****

9TH FEBRUARY

Two questions are asked at PMQs today about Nazanin Zaghari-Ratcliffe. One about the debt we owe and the careless words of the Prime Minister when he was Foreign Secretary and one from her MP asking for a meeting with the Prime Minister. The PM did promise a meeting but blamed Iran and only Iran for the imprisonment of Nazanin. Never, ever any responsibility or accountability from him.

You may remember Johnson's careless words when he was Foreign Secretary as he commented that Nazanin was in Iran to **teach journalists**. She was actually there to see her parents but this remark encouraged the Iranian regime to accuse her of being a spy.

****

10TH FEBRUARY

We hear today that Britain reached an agreement with Iran last summer to repay the £400 million debt to secure the release of Nazanin Zaghari- Ratcliffe but that the deal collapsed. Her MP is urging the Prime Minster to revive it but we have no idea why it fell through. Nazanin has voiced her anger and fury at Boris Johnson's refusal to disclose the reason for the collapse.

****

13TH FEBRUARY

Richard Ratcliffe says that, "We're essentially being held in a waiting room. It's a game of cat and mouse being played."

And Nazanin says, "Why am I still here? They have ruined my life, day by day, for six years. Where is Johnson's urgency?"

****

19TH FEBRUARY

I say this very, very quietly. **There are reports in the media today that the final stages of a nuclear deal with Iran are being thrashed out**. It is now apparently up to the leadership of Iran as to whether they will approve it in the next few days. Diplomats on all sides are saying that a **deal is closer than it has been at any time** since the long pause in talks during the Iranian presidential elections last June.

It still all hangs in the balance and Richard Ratcliffe says, "Nazanin is quite hopeful in a way that she wasn't at Christmas. Who knows what will happen but it feels that we will either get good news or we won't. Before it was 'we will either get bad news or no news.'"

We all keep Nazanin close in our hearts and minds and hope that good times will be ahead.

****

15TH MARCH
Good news, good news, amazingly, wonderful, good news.

Today we hear that Nazanin has been given her passport back. Also there is a British negotiating team in Tehran. We all hold our breath. Some are saying she could be released very soon. My heart is thumping as we think of her and of Richard and Gabriella.

****

16TH MARCH
10.43am.Oh, Oh I am in tears. I cannot believe this but 9 minutes ago we hear that Nazanin is on her way to the airport.

11. 22am. Nazanin is at the airport and has been handed over to the British team.

12.15 The Iranian judiciary have officially said that she has been released.

Reuters says she has left Tehran together with another British National. It has also reported that the £400 million debt was paid by the UK government before they were released. We wait to hear that the plane is actually in the air.

12.44 Just read on Twitter from Ben Clatworthy, transport correspondent of *The Times* that Nazanin is in Muscat and will

travel home on a private government chartered aeroplane to RAF Brize Norton landing just after 10.30 pm.

13.36 I have just seen a photo of Nazanin on the plane to Muscat. All over the news and everyone so emotional. She looks terrific.

18.30 She is on the plane home. She will be arriving a bit later than we thought at about 20 minutes after midnight. Richard and Gabriella are on the news looking so unbelievably happy. Richard a completely different man from the one I met during his hunger strike.

I have had goose pimples all day. The BBC female newsreader was very emotional.

******

17TH MARCH

The plane touched down at Brize Norton at 8 minutes after 1 this morning.

As Nazanin walked down the steps of the aircraft we heard Gabriella say "Is that Mummy?" When told that it was we heard her call "Mummy" as she ran to hug her and we were completely undone all over again.

There will be much talk and discussion about the payment of the debt and the timing of it and why it could not have been paid sooner. There will be questions about how it was linked to her release and the American involvement with it all.

But we leave all of that for now and just rejoice in the present, and a day we thought might never come.

In my previous book I finished my chapter on Nazanin with the words,

"This is a woman who just needs to get home."

Today I can say, "She is home."

****

13TH MAY

Today Nazanin Zaghari-Ratcliiffe went to a meeting with the Prime Minister together with her husband, daughter and MP Tulip Siddiq.

Apparently she didn't hold back when speaking to the PM about her dreadful ordeal. She sat beside him for an hour and told him in no uncertain terms how his words had influenced her situation and questioned why it took so long to pay the debt which was legally owed.

Speaking after the hour-long meeting Tulip Siddiq said: "She was sitting next to the Prime Minister and she told him very clearly and categorically that his words have had a big impact on her and that she had lived in the shadow of his words for the best part of four and a half years. And I have to say the Prime Minister looked quite shocked when she said that."

He honestly seemed to have no idea that his words had been so ignorant and so damaging. But then that is the story of his life.

She was asked if he had apologised. "Not specifically, no" she said.

****

24th May Nazanin gave an interview to the BBC last night as she wanted to tell her story. She was calm, dignified and articulate but the enormity of her experience was very obvious to see.

I will just pick up one important point. When speaking to the Prime Minister a few weeks ago he told her that as soon as the huge debt we owed to Iran had been paid she was released. **So yes there was a**

direct link between her continued captivity and the money. The main reason for her capture was to try to force us to pay up.

So all the replies I have received from the Foreign Office and from my MP saying that the debt we owed Iran was in no way connected to the imprisonment of Nazanin were not correct.

Was this misinformation from the Foreign office, incompetence, ignorance, prevarication, or fudge? Or all of those?

****

This has been a dreadful stain on the Foreign Office and on the Prime Minister.

But we can now let Nazanin and her family build a new life together and we wish them well for the future.

****

But after a story with a happy ending I turn to those who do not have a happy ending so long as this government is in power.

****

ASYLUM SEEKERS

There is a chapter on asylum seekers in my book 'Beneath the Bluster' and I just quote the last paragraph when I say:

"I think that the treatment by this government, and by the present Home Secretary, of many of those seeking asylum, is inhumane, neglectful and cruel. I feel ashamed to live in a country which treats any vulnerable people in this way."

As you will see nothing has changed.

****

2021

19TH NOVEMBER
The number of refugees seeking asylum in the UK continues to be an enormous problem as, although the overall number is going down, the numbers of small boats arriving on our shores seem to be increasing. It would be really good to think that this problem was being treated with compassion, understanding, co-operation, diplomacy, intelligence and practicality but as the name **Priti Patel** crops up here it won't surprise you to know that this is not actually the case.

The new legislation which authorised a **"push back" of boats out of British waters has already been deemed "unworkable" inside government**. This, you may remember involved people on jet skis, two or three to a boat, pushing the bow of the small dinghies round and then shoving the stern off in the direction of France. The legal bar for Border Force vessels to reach before they can carry out a push back is seen as so high that it would never happen in practice.

And there is an **increasingly ill-tempered stand-off with France from our Home Office officials** which has also dogged efforts to stop the migrants. Priti Patel likes to blame others for the difficulties here, and France and Paris are usually first on the list.

And now there is a scheme being talked about whereby **migrants are to be sent to Albania, within seven days of their arrival in small boats, for off-shore processing**. It is thought that the prospect of a long wait there whilst their claims for asylum were being processed would be a deterrent. Discussions with Albania are in early stages the Home Office states, but Ministers say that chances of a deal with Albania are looking good. The possible cost has been calculated by officials as £100,000 per migrant. This is after the costs of flights of 1,500 miles, and accommodation have been taken into account.

And this is more than twice what it costs in England and Wales to keep an inmate locked up in prison for a year. We have no precise details as to how this is going to work as Britain cannot detain the migrants at the centres against their will as that **would breach international law**.

Well this is not usually a problem with our present government. So primary legislation is needed in order to authorise the removal of asylum seekers and it is being included in the **Nationality and Borders Bill** which is at the committee stage in the Commons and is due to receive royal assent by the spring.

I hope you have kept up with all of this.

****

20TH NOVEMBER

Well, the good news is that you don't have to keep up with all of that. The Albanian Prime Minister is absolutely furious about this and says that there have been no talks with the UK at all. **"Zero" he adds just to be perfectly clear.** Well the UK did say that this plan was in the early stages which actually I suppose could mean it was still just a thought in Priti Patel's head.

Boris is apparently so fed up with the look of it all that he has drafted in another minister, Stephen Barclay, to help out. There have been, and still are, so many different ideas and possible plans to try to sort this out, some completely fantastical and others just so unworkable, that, to me, it really does need a completely different mind-set and preferably one that does not always blame everyone else all the time.

I just quote Matt Chorley in *The Times* today when he says that, "Priti Patel is living proof that good things don't always come in small packages" (She is very short in stature).

****

And new laws in the forthcoming Nationality and Borders Bill **will make it, for the first time, a criminal offence to pick up migrants in the channel.**

In a letter in *The Times* today it says:

"If the government is serious about workable solutions it should focus instead on providing more safe routes to people fleeing war and persecution who are at present forced to take evermore dangerous journeys to find safety. This should include a commitment to resettle at least 10,000 refugees a year from around the world. The **government's Nationality and Borders bill** will be debated over the coming weeks and **we urge MPs to reject these cold hearted policies and instead work together to create a fair, compassionate and effective system of which Britain can be proud."**

This was signed by Mike Adamson, **CEO British Red Cross**, Tim Nair Hilton, **CEO Refugee Action**, Andrea Vukovic and Paul Hook, **co-directors Asylum Matters,** Sonya Sceats, **CEO Freedom from Torture**, Enver Solomon, **CEO Refugee Council** and Sabir Zazai, **CEO Scottish Refugee Council.**

****

21ST NOVEMBER

The editorial in *The Observer* today is scathing about the refugee crisis. As it rightly points out, although there has been an increase in asylum seekers arriving across the channel in small boats, there has been an over-all decrease in asylums seeking a refuge in the UK. It is less than half of what it was in the early 2000s. The editorial writes about the way in which Priti Patel has repeatedly sought ways in which to deter people from seeking asylum here, **many of them illegal within maritime law.**

The editorial ends by saying, "The world urgently needs renewed moral leadership on asylum and refuge of the sort that led to the 1951 convention. But we cannot expect it from Priti Patel who is more interested in using asylum seekers as pawns in the government's culture war and is thus leading us in the charge to the bottom."

And so we will look forward to hearing the results of the forthcoming bill and we will see if this government has taken any notice of eminent people who are very concerned at the way in which the government is treating these vulnerable refugees.

****

23RD NOVEMBER

Yesterday, Priti Patel gave a statement to the House about asylum seekers and her response to the crisis. And I am very pleased to be able to report that she and the Prime Minister between them are doing one thing **spectacularly well**.

She said that they have to make this country as unattractive as possible in order to stop refugees from wanting to come here.

But, Home Secretary, do you have any idea about the state of the countries they are fleeing from? Iran, Iraq, Afghanistan? And she is still talking about setting up processing centres in Albania.

Every time she opens her mouth to talk about this crisis I despair.

****

24TH NOVEMBER
A report has just come out today from the Home Affairs Committee which makes really worrying reading. It is all there on the parliamentary website.

It states that four years after the **Windrush scandal** first emerged, the Home Affairs Committee found that **the vast majority of people who applied for compensation have yet to receive a penny.**

As of the end of September, only 20% of the initially estimated 15,000 eligible claimants had applied to the scheme and only 5% had received compensation. Twenty three individuals have died before they received any compensation for the hardship they endured at the hands of the Home Office. The report states that instead of providing a remedy, for many people the Windrush Compensation Scheme has actually compounded the injustices faced as a result of the Windrush Scandal.

The documentary evidence they need, the long delays in processing applications and then making payments, the inadequate staffing, and the fact that there is no provision for urgent payments for those in desperate need all **adds up to a completely inadequate process.**

They go on to say that they can only conclude that four years on from the Windrush scandal **vital lessons have not been learned.** The treatment of the Windrush generation by successive governments has been truly shameful.

They say that in order to increase trust and encourage more applications the **scheme should be transferred to an independent organisation and away from the Home Office.**

****

25TH NOVEMBER

Yesterday saw the most appalling tragedy regarding refugees **when 27 people were drowned in the Channel** having been put into seriously overcrowded and flimsy un-sea-worthy inflatable dinghies by criminal smuggling gangs who make an enormous amount of money by putting these people at risk.

Obviously there is no easy answer to this problem although I think that building proper processing centres in the north of France (please not Albania!) where people could be processed by British authorities and then brought across the channel legally, in safe boats, could be a solution.

However in order to achieve this there would have to be an enormous well of good will and co-operation between the two countries. Were we still in the EU this would have been easier but as Johnson appears to be deliberately stoking up animosity with France in order to make it look as if Brexit was a good idea, that really does not look as though it is going to happen any time soon. At the moment both France and the UK are involved in the blame game and using these poor people as political pawns.

Having said that, however, I think the PM does think that this is an election loser which does mean he might concentrate his mind on it a bit. So I will see what transpires over the next few weeks.

****

Priti Patel will travel to France on Sunday (28th) for a meeting with Gerald Darmanin the French Interior minister and other European ministers from Belgium, Germany and the Netherlands. Home Office officials will be in Paris for advanced talks tomorrow.

****

26TH NOVEMBER

Oh no she won't. Priti Patel has been **un-invited by the French Interior minister** to these talks.

Last night our Prime Minister tweeted a letter to President Macron stating five actions that he thinks could be taken, involving the French, to solve the asylum crisis. Macron said the letter was very disappointing **and the fact that this was sent out on twitter and not as a private letter made it all even worse**.

The PM is being accused of rushing something out in time for the media headlines and hoping to gain some political accolades rather than thinking through what is the best and most humane way forward.

As the editorial in *The Times* today says, **"It is perhaps too much to hope that the deaths of 27 people in the Channel yesterday, among them a small girl and a pregnant woman, might bring a change of tone to the debate over migration."**

I'm afraid it is. It is so unbelievably cruel.

But here are Mr. Johnson's five ideas:

- Joint patrols on the French coastline to stop boats from leaving.
- Deploying more advanced technology such as sensors and drones.
- Reciprocal maritime patrols in each other's territorial waters and airborne surveillance.
- Deepening the work of the countries joint intelligence cell.
- An agreement to sending refugees back to France.

And here are mine!!

- Establish safe routes for refugees in order for them to travel safely to the UK.
- Bring back the Dubs amendment which required the UK Secretary of State to make arrangements to relocate to the UK, and support, a specific number of unaccompanied refugee children from Europe.
- Speed up the processing procedures and arrange to do them in France before they make the crossing to the UK. **(This has been offered by the French apparently but been turned down).**
- Allow refugees to work and so replace all those lovely Europeans who went home after Brexit.
- Provide decent accommodation for all refugees, possibly purpose built, until they are able to make a life of their own.

I expect many people will be able to pick holes in my suggestions! After all I am no politician and no expert in these matters. But what really disgusts me is the way in which Boris and Patel treat refugees as though they are criminals.

But I just quote *The Times* editorial once more. They too are concerned about the lack of safe routes to the UK. And they say, "it is not the case that all those crossing the Channel are economic migrants: almost 70 percent end up being granted refugee status. Nor is it the case that migrants are refusing to claim asylum in other safe countries. Germany has received more than 13,000 asylum applications this year and France 70,000."

And you might be interested in this: "A programme to accept 20,000 Afghan refugees, promised after the fall of Kabul, (on the 15th August) is not yet operational, while one set up in 2019 to accept 5,000 refugees a year from around the world has taken just 1,171.

Let no-one dare say we are doing well until they read these facts. This government makes my blood boil.

****

28TH NOVEMBER

Well of course this topic is all over the Sunday papers and many I see advocate some of my ideas!

But there is a really wonderful letter in *The Sunday Times* from a doctor in Hastings. As she says, **there is no refugee crisis** as the overall numbers are down from last year. And she goes on to say that the **kindness and outpouring of support from the people of Hastings** for these refugees has been overwhelming. They meet them and talk to them and see them as real but vulnerable people who need help. She says that, "if we do have a crisis, it is a crisis of the attempted and wilful destruction of our empathy - which nevertheless burns brightly in our town."

I say a heartfelt thank you to the people in Hastings and to Dr. Felicity Laurence. We need a panacea to combat the continual messages of hate, unkindness, bullying and blame that emanates from this government. I am heartily sickened and disgusted by it.

****

1ST DECEMBER

A report by Amnesty International talks in detail about the Nationality and Borders bill going through Parliament at the moment. They say that, "Despite Ministers asserting the measures included are aimed at cutting costs, breaking people smuggling gangs and protecting people seeking asylum, the Bill fails to deliver in all these and other areas." I will just pick out a few sentences but it will give you the general idea.

"The Bill will do the exact opposite of what Ministers' claim, allowing smugglers to thrive".

"Criminalising people for making these journeys doesn't take away people's need to seek asylum in the UK."

"Nothing in the Bill creates or supports the creation of safe routes for people seeking asylum."

"In truth, the UK is far behind many European neighbours, such as France and Germany, in terms of numbers of asylum applications received and people provided protection."

"While Ministers claim the Bill will save money, it will instead increase costs to the taxpayer. As is recognised expressly in the Bill, some of its provisions will require additional spending on legal aid, financial support for asylum applicants and their accommodation."

Priti Patel wants to deter refugees from seeking asylum in the UK.

I find it strange that she doesn't understand that if the distinct possibility of death by drowning doesn't deter people then nothing will.

She is also persevering with the push back scheme which has already been explained to her is against all maritime law and will cause more deaths.

****

And then our new Justice Minister pipes up. Dominic Raab is going to **overhaul the Human Rights Act.** Is he allowed to do this? Article 8 protects the right to family life and he wants to tighten the scenarios in which it can be used by refugees to avoid deportation. However you will be relieved to hear that Articles 2 and 3 which relate to torture and inhumane treatment will not be changed. Phew that's a relief. Wait a minute though. Surely treating refugees as criminals and allowing them to drown is inhumane treatment?

I am permanently angry with this government as you can probably tell! **But their treatment of refugees is the worst treatment of innocent people that I have ever encountered by a government in the UK, in my lifetime.**

****

I now read that the Public and Commercial Services (PCS) union representing the Border Force staff has announced it is taking part in a legal challenge against the plan by Priti Patel to push back small boats in the Channel. They say it is an **"unlawful, unworkable and above all morally reprehensible" policy**.

Other organisations, including 'Channel Rescue' and the charity 'Freedom from Torture', have launched separate legal challenges against the pushback plans.

And Border Force staff in Dover have told of suffering "night terrors" and mounting emotional distress after witnessing overturned boats in the middle of the English Channel. Many of them are suffering from post-traumatic stress - the most severe mental health stress response - and it is a real concern for the PCS. At present, those on the front line of the refugee crisis are not offered treatment for it.

Asked if Border Force will enforce the policy, one employee said he'd rather lose his job.

It would appear that no-one involved in this on-going procedure is being treated, by this government, as a human–being.

****

2ND DECEMBER
I think you need to sit down in a quiet place and, if you are over 18, to pour yourself a large gin and tonic before you read these next few sentences. If you have not read the entirety of the new bill going through Parliament, and if you are already appalled at the inhumanity of Priti Patel when it comes to the treatment of refugees, I think that you will be shocked into disbelief.

Priti Patel has just bowed to pressure and tabled an amendment to the bill **which will protect the RNLI and other charities from being** prosecuted for rescuing asylum seekers from drowning in the Channel.

Yes you read that correctly.

The law, as it is at the moment, would make it a **criminal offence to "facilitate the entry of asylum seekers" by taking them ashore if they are in trouble**. Can you believe that? I have to ask it again.

Can you believe that? Please read it carefully. Is this what this country has come to?

Our Home Secretary is asking one of our favourite charities to stop maritime rescue.

****

And I read today that the "push back" plans are still approved and will go ahead when we had all thought they were being scrapped. There have been wide-spread protests over the prospect of this manoeuvre as it **is so dangerous and is bound to be the cause of more tragedies at sea.**

I re-iterate my solutions. Process refugees in Calais (already agreed by the French); send those who qualify across the Channel in ferries; allow them to work, especially in those jobs vacated by our lovely European neighbours who returned home after Brexit; and tell them they are welcome. Why is that so difficult?

****

4TH DECEMBER

There is a special report in *The Independent* today by Bel Trew and May Bulman about refugees in Syria. Hundreds of vulnerable people caught up in the violence and war were told they could have sanctuary in the UK as long ago as 2018 and were told their applications would take a few months. **But three years later they are still waiting with no apparent progress.**

They are asking the question: Why has the UK abandoned us?

There are in fact refugees in Lebanon, Egypt, Turkey, Jordan and Iraq who have been approved for resettlement by the British government but are stuck in limbo as their living conditions drastically deteriorate and they get more and more desperate. What is going on? Ministers condemn those crossing the Channel by boat and say that refugees should use safe legal routes instead. I don't think there are any safe routes, and negligence and incompetence at the Home Office continues.

The **UK Resettlement Scheme**, formed in February of this year, originally promised to resettle 5,000 refugees from Syria and Afghanistan. But the Home Office scrapped this target and said the numbers will instead be "kept under review." This has caused considerable concern among charities, lawmakers and the United Nations refugee agency.

Parallel Universe. The Home Office declined to speak about specific cases which were highlighted in the report but told the Independent that the UK "has a long history of supporting refugees in need of protection."

I can't bear it.

****

8TH DECEMBER
A whistle blower has described the Foreign Office at the time of the evacuation of the people of Afghanistan as shambolic and dysfunctional. As he says, less than 5 percent had received any help and it is **"clear that some of those left behind have since been murdered by the Taliban."**

There was no sense of urgency even when Raab eventually returned from holiday. He was on a beach in Crete at the time and was in no hurry to get home. It took hours for him to engage with any notes about cases and he then demanded that all cases be resubmitted on a spread sheet.

Sir Philip Barton, permanent secretary to the Foreign office was also away at the time and he did not return until 10 days after Dominic Raab.

And then we hear this. There have been rumours that a special plane was sent to Afghanistan to rescue the charity worker Penn Farthing and his dogs. But of course that would be completely unacceptable **and the Prime minister said that neither he nor his wife Carrie, an animal rights activist, had told officials to evacuate Farthing his staff or his animals.** Denials all the way.

But today we see a letter. Trudy Harrison who, at the time, was one of Johnson's Parliamentary Private Secretary personnel, wrote to Farthing to say that she had received confirmation from the Foreign Office, the Home Office and the Ministry of Defence that "you, your staff and their dependents could travel to Kabul airport." She also wrote that the Secretary of State has also confirmed that **animals under the care of Nowzad can be evacuated on a separate chartered flight**. "The Ministry of Defence," she wrote, "will ensure that a flight slot is available."

This letter was read out at a Foreign Affairs Committee hearing on the evacuation yesterday by Chris Bryant a Labour MP. The letter was signed off from her using her title of Parliamentary Private Secretary to the Prime Minister.

The sub-title of my first book sums up this debacle so accurately when it says "Incompetence, Ignorance, Confusion and Lies." But the sub-title of this book is accurate too. "Arrogance, Corruption, Dither and Delay."

When, oh when, will we get a government of Honesty, Compassion, Transparency and Wisdom?

****

17TH DECEMBER

And we still hear that Channel migrants continue to be held in "very poor" conditions after arriving on the Kent coast despite the Home Office promising that "significant improvements" had been made.

What upsets me most is the fact that **still lone children are being held with unrelated adults and are being housed in yet another totally unsuitable military site in Kent.**

Sir Roger Gale, is the MP for North Thanet, where the facility is located, and he told the House of Commons on Wednesday the 15th that there had been "no consultation" with him as MP, or the local authority or the local health services about the plan.

As reported in *The Independent* he says, "All we were told by the civil servant leading the project, who was I understand working from home and has not visited the site, is that the Home Office is establishing a processing centre before Christmas," he said.

He accused ministers of a "lack of foresight and preparation", and he added: "Trying to railroad a bad idea through the shelter of Christmas recess can only have unfortunate and undesirable consequences for the communities, and the people affected and the government."

On it goes and we continue to see vulnerable people, including lone children, being treated without any kindness or compassion.

****

22ND DECEMBER

A report by Lizzie Dearden in *The Independent* yesterday states that Priti Patel has been over-ruled by the Court of Appeal as **judges**

quashed the convictions of three asylum seekers who had been wrongly jailed for "assisting unlawful immigration" by steering dinghies across the channel. This ruling is expected to cause other verdicts to be over turned.

Judges were so incensed by what they called a "legal heresy" they demanded that the CPS explain "how it came about that the law was misunderstood when investigating, charging and prosecuting these cases." **The judges found that men who had been labelled "people smugglers" had not committed a crime.** They said that, "Even though an asylum seeker has no valid passport or identity document or prior permission to enter the United Kingdom this does not make his arrival at the port a breach of immigration law." Those steering the dinghies are asylum seekers too.

****

24TH DECEMBER
It is reported today that the Home Office is considering fitting all adult migrants who cross the channel with **electronic tags.** This is in an attempt to stop them from absconding whilst their asylum claims are processed.

Enver Solomon, chief executive of the 'Refugee Council' said that these plans "smacks of desperation from a government that doesn't know how to manage our asylum system in an orderly, effective and humane way. **Treating innocent adults who have fled war and persecution like criminals is cruel, draconian and punitive."** He goes on to say that it won't act as a deterrent and that more safe routes should be created and everyone who reaches our shores should be treated with humanity.

****

2022

6TH JANUARY

The Border Force Officers are threatening to strike over Priti Patel's "pushback" tactics in the Channel. The 'Public and Commercial Services Union' and 'Care4Calais' a refugee charity said they would take the Home Office to court over the policy.

The judicial review will challenge the lawfulness of the policy which according to the PCS "contravenes international law". The Immigration Act 1971 does not give the Home Office power to compel vessels to travel from UK waters to France. It will also be argued that it breaches Article 2, the right to life and Article 3 the right not to be subjected to torture or cruel, inhuman or degrading treatment of the European Convention on Human rights.

Priti Patel has been criticised by two former Home Secretaries Lord Blunkett and Lord Reid of Cardowan.

But listen to this. A Home Office source played down the threat of legal action saying, "I'm totally shocked that a Corbyn-supporting Mark Serwotka (general secretary of the PCS) doesn't want to defend the nation's borders."

Yes there are people who think this way.

And just to add to the list of criticisms, 100 civil society leaders including charity chief executives wrote a joint letter condemning the Nationality and Borders Bill as "overtly racist".

How does this country allow Priti Patel to continue as Home Secretary?

****

17TH JANUARY

As part of the Prime Minister's Operation Red Meat programme (see chapter on Johnson) he is going to put the **Royal Navy in charge of the Channel refugee crossings.**

Plans are also being drawn up to send refugees to countries such as **Ghana and Rwanda for processing and resettlement at enormous cost to the tax payer.** The government is willing to pay hundreds of millions of pounds to any country willing to take up this offer but, surprise, surprise, so far none have offered to do so. What are they thinking?

****

Apparently the Home Office had thought of using **sonic booms** in the channel to deter refugees. Their innovative ideas of torture never cease to amaze me.

****

We also hear yesterday in *The Independent* in a report by May Bulman, that hundreds of unaccompanied children are being placed in hotels meant for adults and they are **being forced to share rooms and sometimes even beds with adults they do not know** . She writes that, "ministers have been accused of **'washing their hands' of child asylum seekers** by operating an age assessment process that often wrongly labels them adults, leaving local authorities to pick up the pieces and take them into children's services when the decisions are found to be incorrect."

****

18TH JANUARY

And we hear today that this practice has just been ruled unlawful by the High Court. A judge said the policy of detaining young people for an age assessment immediately upon arrival, without an appropriate adult to support them, **breaches the law**. It seems to me that nearly everything that this Home Office does is legally highly suspect.

****

Well, would you believe it, there is a bit of a backlash over the plans for the Navy to step in and put a stop to crossings in the Channel. They have said that they will certainly not be any part of any "push back" plan but would focus on escorting migrants to shore for processing in new migrant hubs.

This is in spite of the fact that Priti Patel insists that the push back method is still "absolutely the policy of this government." She says that "means are being tested, technology is being used, but also the way in which boats can be pushed back has also been well tested." She is nothing if not thorough.

But the military say that this policy will not be pursued. "This isn't about bumping small boats and turning them around—that will never work," they say. "You can't do that in the Channel it's too narrow."

It strikes me that maybe there hasn't been enough communication between the Home Office and the Navy.

But I was lucky enough to drop in to a debate on all of this on the *Parliament channel* this afternoon. So we hear inevitably I'm afraid of people saying that this will encourage asylum seekers to come over and they will use the naval ships as a ferry. Someone did ask whether we had any spare ships......... and then an elderly red faced Tory MP stands up and says, " **these people should be arrested and put in prison and then returned home."**

I had to switch it off but I think he needs to get a dictionary and look up the meaning of the words 'refugee' and 'asylum'.

****

20TH JANUARY

Another plan being drawn up by the PM and Priti Patel is that every single male migrant who crosses the Channel in small boats will be detained and held in immigration removal centres. **The Nationality and Borders Bill** now going through Parliament will make it a criminal offence to be found in a vessel in the Channel without pre-authorisation to enter the UK. **Individuals will face a maximum prison sentence of four years under the new law**. However, as asylum seekers, **individuals will be able to claim other rights** that they are entitled to under the Human Rights Act and the UN Refugee Convention that restricts the state's power to detain refugees.

Well I hope there are enough lawyers around to sort this one out.

****

25TH JANUARY

I have just discovered another piece of proposed legislation in **the Nationalities and Borders Bill** dreamt up by Priti Patel and it really is extremely upsetting. **She is closing off the safest routes for families left behind in war-torn countries who wish to be re-united with their families in the UK**. This will, of course, mainly affect women and children .The 'Refugee Council' says that this "flies in the face" of commitments by this government to ensure that there are safe routes.

So to be clear about this. If you enter the UK by an illegal route you will be classed as a criminal and imprisoned for four years, but all safe and legal routes have been scrapped.

****

27TH JANUARY

The Navy is saying that there are no spare vessels to tackle the Channel migrant crisis and employing more ships might encourage more people to make the crossing.

Tom Sharpe who has served in the Royal Navy for 27 years told the Commons defence committee that, **"We have to acknowledge right at the start, in terms of context, about where the solution to this lies, and it's not at sea."**

And Mark Serwotka, general secretary of the Public and Commercial Services Union, which represents some border and immigration officials said, "We cannot have a situation where our members could be open to potential civil and criminal action for implementing a policy that they do not agree with and know is not safe."

****

And yet more evidence of the story on the 8th December about the evacuation of dogs and cats from Afghanistan and which sets out to prove that it was authorised by the Prime Minister. A whistle blower in the Foreign office has released a trail of emails which looks pretty damning.

But Boris Johnson who is today in North Wales wearing his hard hat and high-vis jacket says, "**It is totally rhubarb**" to suggest that he had anything to do with it. Yes he really does talk like that.

****

The *Byline Times* is run by a small, dedicated team of journalists providing a platform for freelance reporters and writers to produce fearless journalism not found in the mainstream media. And in a special investigation, Katie Tarrant reveals yet more appalling treatment of asylum seekers by the Home Office.

Apparently they have been taking the phones off migrants as soon as they step ashore and threatening them with legal action if they did not give them up. They have taken the phones of more than 7,000 migrants and the Home Office is now facing a **judicial review** which could conclude that it acted unlawfully by seizing the phones for data extraction without an official policy in place authorising this.

"Kiosk data extractions" as they are called, allow officers access to all immediately available data on a device – including messages, calls, GPs, photos, and contacts. Some of the phones have still not been returned since they were confiscated last year.

Sarah Champion MP told *Byline Times* "Imagine being trafficked into the country, abused on the way in, and then having your mobile phone seized leaving you completely cut-off from your loved ones or vital documents without knowing when – if ever – it will be returned. It is inhumane and it is vital a high threshold is met before it can occur."

Solicitor Clare Jennings said that one of her clients lost contact with his wife and daughter for months – they "didn't know if he was safe, he didn't know what had happened to them".

****

14TH FEBRUARY

If you look back to my entry on the 22nd December you will see that I refer to the overturning by the Court of Appeal of a ruling made by the Home Office who accused three asylum seekers of acting illegally as people smugglers by steering the dinghies across the Channel.

Today there is another report, again by Lizzie Dearden, whereby judges have thrown out 12 more cases of asylum seekers being jailed for crimes they did not commit.

There is, apparently, a fundamental "error of law" that originated in the Home Office, then spread to prosecutors and the courts. This has been used by prosecutors to criminalise innocent people. **Having now identified this fundamental "error of law", the Court of Appeal is expected to overturn more wrongful convictions.**

The Home Office and the CPS have refused to apologise to these asylum seekers which does not surprise me in the least. In fact they have not even publicised these findings and have not acknowledged the quashing of their convictions.

As I have said before, the Home Secretary is avowed to make all asylum seekers criminals with the new Nationality and Borders Bill which is going through Parliament at the moment. But the judges said that they were ruling under the present law rather than the one being proposed in this bill which will say that asylum seekers can be prosecuted for "arrival" – rather than "entry" – to Britain.

Asked whether it would apologise to the 12 asylum seekers who were wrongly jailed and falsely smeared as "people smugglers", the Home Office said: "We must do all we can to prevent the further tragic loss of life on the Channel and put an end to dangerous people smuggling across our borders."

Absolutely and completely on a parallel universe. A universe of cold, uncaring, unseeing, uninterested and inhumane individuals.

****

17TH FEBRUARY

Priti Patel has appointed Alexander Downer to review the Border Force system in the UK. You might remember that he was the former Australian minister who backed his country's 'inhumane' programme of offshore asylum processing. His role will include looking at the response to small boat crossings in the English Channel.

Of course we have heard the Home Office repeatedly talk about offshoring refugees but so far every country approached has refused to be involved in any way whatsoever.

****

24th February.................Russia invades Ukraine

This war is, of course going to mean many, many people fleeing their homes with their families in order to search for safe havens. It is very early days and of course there is hope that many Ukrainians can find safety in west Ukraine and ministers are expecting refugees to stay in Eastern Europe.

Nevertheless, there is concern that **Britain has not yet set up a route for Ukrainian refugees to reach UK shores.**

The UK has stopped accepting visa applications from Ukrainians stuck in the country, meaning there is no safe and legal route for them to seek asylum in Britain unless they have British relatives.

The Nationality and Borders Bill, allows a change to immigration rules meaning that asylum applications from people who have temporarily resided in safe third countries can be declared "inadmissible". This will mean that Ukrainians forced to travel to countries such as Poland, in order to obtain UK visas, may later be refused asylum.

****

26TH FEBRUARY

So many countries are saying that they will welcome Ukrainian refugees. Ireland is waiving all visa applications from Ukrainian refugees and saying that **they are all welcome including their pets of cats and dogs.**

Meanwhile a Tory immigration MP tweeted that there were safe and legal routes for refugees, and Ukrainians could apply to come to the UK in order to be fruit pickers or abattoir butchers. The tweet was deleted fairly quickly but Priti Patel is under increasing pressure to rip up the existing bureaucracy and tell all Ukrainian refugees they are welcome.

Let us wait and see if there is a grain of humanity inside the person who goes by the name of Priti Patel.

****

28TH FEBRUARY

Yesterday the Home office published updated guidance on the refugee status saying that Ukrainians could come if they have relations here. But when examined properly that meant it would allow 'immediate family members' only. In other words it did not apply to brothers, sisters, grandparents or adult children.

Most of these refugees are women and young children. All men over the age of 18 are staying in Ukraine to bravely fight for their country.

****

1ST MARCH

Well Priti Patel has been dragged kicking and screaming into the Commons this afternoon to give a statement to the House. There is still a lot of clarity needed here but there is some easing of immigration rules. But why can't they get it right first time?

She is only here because the Speaker threatened an urgent question if she didn't attend.

****

5TH MARCH.

David Miliband, the head of the International Rescue Committee, criticises western governments for being slow in their response to the refugee crisis in Ukraine. **But he singles out the UK for its restrictive visa policy which he called unjustifiable and "quite wrong".**

"There's no justification for saying that unless you have a link to the UK you can't come in," he said. "We know that the vast bulk of refugees always end up in countries neighbouring those they flee, so what is Britain afraid of? The British people aren't afraid of Ukrainians claiming refugee status, and the British government shouldn't be afraid either."

The government indeed absolves itself by saying that most refugees will want to stay near their country so the visa system is fine and many won't come this far.

In that case, do as the EU have done and waive the visas for goodness sake **Why are we always so out of step with everyone else?**

****

8TH MARCH
I listen to James O' Brien of LBC this morning and, as he says, Priti Patel's immigration programme is working perfectly. **He calls us all out (well all Brexiteers listening) for getting what they voted for.**

So Ukrainians, who manage to get all the way to Calais, in fear for their lives, are met with a notice which says, "No visas here. Go to Brussels or Paris." They are also told that there are pop-in centres there open Wednesday to Friday. There have been 8,900 requests for visas and so far the Home Office has granted 300. Priti Patel says there is an **army of officials at Calais** ready to help and she is about to open another safe route for Ukrainian refugees.

An army?

BBC cameras at Calais yesterday showed an empty centre with just three officials from the Home Office with a trestle table on which was a box of crisps, some water and some kit-kats. A family who turned up there after being told to go from building to building, were then told to make an appointment on the 15th March about 200 miles away in Paris.

Another personal story, just one of many, is the experience of Misha, his wife and children, which is typical. A British citizen, with a home in north-east London, he drove 2,000 miles to Poland to rescue his Ukrainian wife Maria and two children, 17-year-old Gabrielle and six-year-old Misha Jr. They had walked 45 miles to escape the war and reach the border.

He drove them to Calais where they have been now for six days, having been turned back by Border Force officers at the ferry terminal because they did not all have visas.

Even Conservative MPs are turning against the Home Office as they call on Priti Patel to resign for telling MPs that a visa centre had been set up in Lille when there was no such centre as yet in place.

****

15TH MARCH

Well Michael Gove has stepped in and has, in the words of Quentin Letts of *The Times,* "parked his tanks on Patel's lawn."

He has announced the launch of Britain's refugee scheme called **Homes for Ukraine** which will allow individuals, businesses, charities and community groups to bring people escaping the war to safety even if they have no ties to the UK.

Sounds good but it is not up and running quite yet and we are actually in the third week of the war. And of course the web site crashed pretty much straight away.

It is not straight forward and it would appear that there are still requirements for them to have visas. This is impossible for many, fleeing from war, but out of the question for unaccompanied children.

In fact last week in Romania's airport, flights to Austria, Poland and Ireland were jammed **full whilst flights to London Luton were the only flights that were half empty.**

In contrast a refugee in Warsaw airport asked to go to the UK and was told she needed a visa before she could get on a plane. But then someone from Ireland said "who is from Ukraine?"

"And" she said "they gathered up my group and took us to the plane."

Once they arrived in Ireland they were ushered to a bright and airy building which was full of toys, sim cards, cots, changing rooms, free food and soft drinks. Mothers could leave their children in a supervised soft play area next door to pick up toiletries and care packages from a series of rooms converted into free shops stacked with everything from toothpaste and tampons to shampoo and baby clothes.

The airport authority had even brought down its collection of lost buggies.

This, Ms Patel, is what compassion looks like.

****

22ND MARCH

Well praise be, the Church of England has just woken up to the fact that the new Nationality and Borders bill will turn all asylum seekers into criminals. So many people and charities have been saying this for months. But today we hear that the **Most Rev Justin Welby, Archbishop of Canterbury, has become the latest figure to criticise this bill which returns to the Commons tomorrow.** He has given a 'rare' interview to *The Times*.

I have written about this at length so I will just say that I am delighted that he has become involved. But why are these interviews so rare and why has he not been outspoken sooner? **In fact why is the whole church not voicing their concerns about this or about any of the issues in this book?**

That is what I would like to know.

****

The Nationality and Borders Bill

The Lords' amendments were voted on today. This afternoon I watched this government march into the lobbies to vote down pretty well every amendment that had come back from the House of Lords. I was shocked and appalled but sadly not surprised.

Some went through on the nod and I didn't get all of them but basically they have in essence voted to:

Strip citizenship without notice.

Ignore the Refugee Convention. We were the big players in formulating it in 1951

Transfer asylum seekers to offshore detention centres for processing. Well this is unlikely to happen because all requests have been turned down and it would be prohibitively expensive. David Davis said it would be cheaper to put them up at the Ritz and send the children to Eton.

Imprison all refugees who arrive here with the incorrect papers for a maximum of 4 years. This, of course would include the Ukrainian refugees.

During the debate Damian Green pointed out quite reasonably that if the government didn't provide any safe routes for refugees – these were done for those fleeing Iran, Iraq, Syria and Yemen – then refugees would be forced to take unsafe ones. **And he said that a civilised country was duty-bound to provide safe routes.**

But, Mr Green, the Home Office, as we have seen, is determined to make it as difficult as possible for all refugees to enter the UK and has just chosen to make itself a nastier, more unfriendly country.

The most impassioned speech of the day was made by Liberal Democrat Tim Farron, who called the bill a "traffickers' charter" and said that voting for it was voting for more deaths in the Channel.

It was the worst piece of legislation he had seen in 17 years, he said.

****

6TH APRIL

There are still disturbing reports about the **inefficiency of the Home Office in dealing with Ukrainian refugees.** Priti Patel is said to be clashing with Liz Truss as she demands more staff to help deal with the refugee problem. However the Foreign Office says it was already stretched trying to deal with the invasion of Ukraine by Russia.

Rafael Behr, a columnist for *The Guardian*, writes today about the difficulties his family has had when they offered to host a Ukrainian family. Just to get to the visa application stage was a complete nightmare he says. His case is now in some sort of limbo and we are talking, now, 6 weeks into this war.

Criticism of Boris Johnson reaches an epic high. As we all know he loves a three word slogan which turns out to be completely meaningless. "Homes for Ukraine" is up there on a par with "Get Brexit Done."

Well 'sources' have told *The Times* that actually **the PM is getting fed up with the Home Office and has privately branded it "a basket case"**. In that case for goodness sake do something about it Prime Minister. While you dither and delay lives are being destroyed.

****

14TH APRIL

Well it would appear that actually the PM is also a 'basket case'. As we continue to witness nearly every day, the law of the land obviously makes not a scrap of difference to this government. The PM flew by helicopter to a military base in Kent this morning so avoiding the traffic chaos on the M20.

Whilst there he declared that asylum seekers crossing the channel will from now on be 'offshored' more than 6.000 miles away to Rwanda.

Do I need to write anything else? I keep thinking I have no words but words are all I have got.

He also said the **military will be in charge of stopping the Channel crossings.**

But I have serious concerns apart from the obvious ones of cruelty and inhumanity.

1. I honestly thought that something like this should be announced in Parliament first.

2. I honestly thought that there had to be a debate and a vote.

3. I honestly thought that this was in the Nationality and Borders bill which has not yet received royal assent.

4. And I honestly thought that the Navy had already said that it would be far too dangerous in the Channel because it is so narrow and so busy and they had declined the offer.

This is what I wrote on the 27th January:

The Navy says there are no spare vessels to tackle the Channel migrant crisis.

But the PM said the Royal Navy would, from today, take over "operational command" from Border Force in the Channel to ensure "no boat makes it to the UK undetected".

There is a huge backlash about this disgusting Rwanda announcement and of course it has been fired out now to take our minds off the

Partygate fines and the fact that we have people endeavouring to run the country who are law-breakers.

The PM has actually acknowledged there could be legal problems and he took aim at any lawyers who might want to challenge it. So he says this:

"If this country is seen as a soft touch for illegal migration by some of our partners, it is precisely because we have such a formidable army of politically motivated lawyers who for years have made it their business to thwart removals and frustrate the government."

This man continually takes my breath away. I really hope for his sake that he does not need a lawyer anytime soon. **Lawyers interpret the law**.

He defended the cost which will include an **initial payment of £120 million** plus eye watering expenses for each refugee every day.

Timothy Kirkhope, a Tory peer who was Immigration Minister under John Major said that as Immigration Minister he had examined the issue of offshore processing and rejected it. **"It's impractical, it's extremely expensive, and it's subject to legal challenge, including under international law, because I think it is absolutely against the principles of the refugee convention."**

The UK was a founding signatory to the UN refugee convention and these refugees are exercising their rights to seek asylum in a country of their choosing.

****

Then I read May Bulman, social affairs correspondent of *The Independent*.

She writes that just 10 months before Priti Patel signed this agreement **the UK had raised alarms about a failure by authorities in Rwanda** to properly investigate alleged human rights abuses and to protect and support victims of trafficking. Apparently Rwanda already has more than 127,000 refugees

And most of them are in camps and not allowed to work.

May Bulman goes on to say that, "The UK's international ambassador for human rights Rita French in July 2021 expressed 'regret' that Rwanda was not conducting 'transparent, credible and independent investigations into allegations of human rights violations including deaths in custody and torture.' "

She added, "We were disappointed that Rwanda did not support the UK recommendation to screen, identify and provide support to trafficking victims, including those held in government transit centres."

So it is really interesting to hear Mr Johnson, as he announced the plans today, praising Rwanda as "one of the safest countries in the world", adding that it is "globally recognised for its record of welcoming and integrating migrants."

As I say, he takes my breath away.

****

16TH APRIL

It has emerged that the only way that Priti Patel was able to get this agreement with Rwanda was to issue a ministerial direction. This means that her civil servants in the Home Office were unhappy with this plan and felt it was not value for money nor legal and so would not process it.

There is apparently a lot of discontent amongst her staff with resignations and transfer requests on the cards.

Let us be absolutely clear about this. **This is a one-way ticket to Rwanda. They are not being assessed for refuge in the UK.** And per capita Rwanda already hosts five times as many refugees as the UK.

But, she says that this will be **'world leading'** and other countries will follow suit.

Mark my words it won't happen. Lord Dubs, who was himself a refugee, says it will be fought in the Lords. "I think it's a breach of the 1951 Geneva conventions on refugees. You can't just shunt them around like unwanted people," he says.

****

17TH APRIL. EASTER DAY

Three cheers for the Church of England. And that is a sentence I don't write very often.

First we hear the Archbishop of York on the radio this morning saying that the plans to send **migrants to Rwanda were 'depressing and distressing' and 'there is no such thing as an illegal asylum seeker'.**

Then we hear the sermon by the Archbishop of Canterbury when he says:

"This season is also why there are such serious ethical questions about sending asylum seekers overseas. The details are for politics. **The principle must stand the judgement of God and it cannot.** It cannot carry the weight of resurrection, justice, of life conquering death. It cannot carry the weight of the resurrection that was first to the least valued, for it privileges the rich and strong. And it cannot carry the weight of our national responsibility as a country formed by Christian values, because **sub-contracting out our responsibilities, even to a country that seeks to do well like Rwanda, is the opposite of the nature of God who himself took responsibility for our failures."**

It was so refreshing to hear people of morality speaking out and highlighting what is true and good against what is inhumane and cruel. Just wonderful not to hear MPs trying to defend the indefensible once again.

****

18TH APRIL
Well, well I spoke too soon.

Today we have **Jacob Rees-Mogg** saying that the Archbishop of Canterbury actually "misunderstands" the policy.

We really are so lucky to have someone with the brain power of Rees-Mogg ready to correct the most senior clergyman in the Church of England.

And he goes on to say that this policy of the forcible deportation of vulnerable people to Rwanda is in fact "almost an Easter story of redemption" for Rwanda.

No, I do not have a clue what he is talking about either.

Then we have **Priti Patel** writing in *The Times* basically saying 'well can you think of anything better' so actually agreeing that she is not up to the job.

And an editorial leader in *The Times* accuses the Archbishop of interfering in politics.

So I write the following letter to *The Times*:

Sir, As Priti Patel is devoid of any humane ideas for asylum seekers I offer her this. There needs to be an assessment centre in Calais and then those who qualify for refuge in the UK can come across the Channel safely on the ferries. This idea was first suggested in 2015 by the United Nations when Peter Sutherland their special representative on migration said, "You could set up an immediate system for assessing how many of these people are refugees. You could do it in a very short time and you could do it as a joint responsibility." Or is any co-operation with the French impossible since Brexit? And to talk about the inhumanity of a scheme which will forcibly deport vulnerable and traumatised people to a country to which they do not want to go is not talking politics, it is talking morality.

****

19TH APRIL

Well it is published this morning! They do edit it and take out the first and last sentences but the essence was there.

****

It is PMQs today and I describe that circus in the chapter on Johnson. However, beforehand, **we had to listen to Priti Patel defending her immigration policy** and responding to questions for over an hour.

It was exhausting and traumatising. I watched her closely and noticed her techniques when trying to shut people down and I realised exactly how she could bully and destroy all those who are unfortunate enough to work for her.

There were many scathing remarks including one from Theresa May who said, '**I do not support the removal to Rwanda policy on the grounds of legality, practicality and efficacy."**

Shadow home secretary Yvette Cooper called the scheme **"unethical and unworkable"**.

SNP home affairs spokesperson Stuart McDonald said, **"This is a cruel and a catastrophic policy. It will not hurt smugglers but will further seriously harm people who have fled persecution."**

Priti Patel calls it "**bold and innovative**".

I want to know how exactly you get people on to an aeroplane when they don't want to go.

****

We also heard that the PM had criticised the Church of England. He said that it had been more critical of him and the Rwanda decision than of President Putin. **This is of course an absolute lie.**

I will quote exactly what the clerics of the Church of England have said about Putin and this dreadful war and you can then judge for yourselves.

At the outset of the war, Archbishop of Canterbury Justin Welby and Archbishop of York Stephen Cottrell released a joint statement condemning Putin, calling his attack **"an act of great evil."**

Then a sermon by Fr Marcus Walker on 27th February at St Bartholomew the Great, the oldest parish church in London said, "A Christian Orthodox leader has unleashed unimaginable death and destruction upon a Christian Orthodox nation. He has seen the Gospel of peace and heard the words of love given to us and given to him by our God, and he has kissed the icons of the mother holding her child, **and he has decided to trample untold numbers of children into the frost and mud of Ukraine and see how many mothers weep at the sight of their dead children."**

This present PM and his cabinet do not like criticism of any sort. **You cannot speak truth to power.** Everything is someone else's fault.

****

17.20PM
I just hear, 2 hours, ago that the government has **vowed to jail asylum seekers** for steering their own dinghies across the English Channel, claiming they could face life sentences.

It is pressing ahead with the "cruel" plans despite a warning from the UN Refugee Agency that such prosecutions could violate the Refugee Convention and should not happen.

****

24TH APRIL

An anonymous whistle blower who is working in the Home Office on the Homes for Ukraine scheme has said that **the whole refugee plan has been "designed to fail".** This is, apparently, because they want to limit the number of people who can come into the UK.

Apparently they only had three hours of training and any complaints or suggestions to improve it all were met with silence. There was no follow-up help at all.

But the worst thing of all is that they are **issuing visas for all family members except for one young child.** This means, of course, that the entire family is held up. This is just so disgusting. The whistle blower said that he came across four or five cases each day in which a single child from a family had not received permission to travel, and he believed this was "too much of a coincidence" for it not to have been encouraged.

****

25TH APRIL

But this is amazing news. It has just been reported by *The Independent* **that Priti Patel has abandoned all plans to use the push-back method for deterring refugees in the Channel.**

Oh my word that is wonderful. Has she at last realised just how dangerous and inhumane this would be?

Well no. Basically the PCS Union, 'Care4Calais', 'Freedom from Torture' and 'Channel Rescue,' were all due to challenge this practice in the High Court at a three day hearing on the 3rd May.

Jeremy Bloom, lead solicitor representing PCS and 'Care4Calais' said: "We are convinced that the Home Secretary has withdrawn the policy because she knew that she would lose in Court if she went to trial.

"The Court would have found that she does not have a power under existing legislation to do this, and that she would have been authorising her officials to use force unlawfully, and in breach of the rights to life and to be free from inhumane treatment, which are rights protected by the Human Rights Act."

As we know, the Ministry of Defence are taking over operations in the Channel and a letter to the Home Secretary says that the MoD did not have permission to deploy the pushback tactic.

The judicial review claims have now been withdrawn, and the Home Office have agreed to pay the claimants costs.

That is a win for law and human rights and we wait to see what else might yet go the same way.

****

3RD MAY

The utter shambles of the Home Office in its dealings with visas for Ukrainian refugees is being highlighted in the news today. **Would-be sponsors under the Homes for Ukraine visa scheme are threatening Priti Patel with legal action**. A law suit is being prepared over "inordinate and unreasonable delays" in processing hundreds of visa applications that were made in March.

The groups bringing this action are due to launch an online Crowdfunder this morning to raise up to £15,000 to help pay the legal costs.

Charities including 'Save the Children' and the 'Refugee Council' said the Homes for Ukraine programme needs to be overhauled urgently as it was endangering vulnerable children and adding "trauma on top of existing trauma" since Russia's invasion. Lone children are especially at risk.

****

7TH MAY

Last night there was an annual spring dinner for the Conservative party in Bassetlaw, Nottinghamshire. The main speaker was Priti Patel. As she started her speech a young protester stood up and started heckling her. The protester was booed and a steward hustled her out at which point another heckler stood up and was also then ushered out. This happened about five times in a very well organised protest. Their main chant was:

SAY IT LOUD, SAY IT CLEAR

REFUGEES ARE WELCOME HERE

This morning they said that, "Last night we disrupted Priti Patel because her Rwanda plan is cruel and morally bankrupt and it will cost lives. We demand the Government drops this widely condemned policy and provides support for people seeking safety. **No matter where we come from, we all deserve dignity and respect.**"

****

8TH MAY

I am convinced that this scheme will not happen. And today we hear that the **first legal challenge has been launched** against it. It says that these proposals run contrary to international law and the UN Refugee Convention as well as breaching British data protection laws. Priti Patel is refusing to disclose key documents explaining which migrants may be eligible to be removed. The law firm 'InstaLaw' has issued the challenge and Patel has three weeks to respond. It could result in her being challenged in the High Court.

It is also interesting to note that this plan was never debated in Parliament.

It will never see the light of day.

****

24TH MAY
Hmm well apparently 50 refugees have been told that they **will** be sent to Rwanda. However they cannot go before the 6th June because of legal challenges.

A pre-action letter has been sent to the Home Office on behalf of the pressure group 'Freedom from Torture' and it questions government claims that the east African state is "generally a safe country" for refugees.

They are also worried about LGBT individuals and how they would be treated in Rwanda.

The Home Office has to respond within seven days.

Sonya Sceats, the chief executive of 'Freedom from Torture,' said: "The government's wilful blindness to the risks facing people expelled under this scheme are frankly horrifying, including attempts to minimise the threat posed to LGBT people in Rwanda."

Because let us look again at the advice for travellers to Rwanda from the Foreign Office. They state that: "Individuals can experience discrimination and abuse, including from local authorities. There are no specific anti-discrimination laws that protect LGBT individuals."

****

The report about the evacuation of people in **Afghanistan** is out today. It concludes that, as I say in my entry on the 8th December, it was a complete 'disaster'.

Tom Tugendhat who chaired the committee said, **"The timeline of misery exposed by this report reveals serious systemic failures at the heart of the UK's foreign policy."**

****

1ST JUNE
We are now hearing that the 50 refugees due to go to Rwanda will now go on the 14th June not the 6th.

****

5TH JUNE
Yet more inhumane treatment of refugees. Unaccompanied children aged as young as 14 are being incorrectly classed as adults and are said to be in the first wave of those being forcibly sent to Rwanda.

'Care4Calais' is an amazing charity which does fantastic work with refugees. They are saying that over 70% of those with Rwanda notices have suffered torture or trafficking either in their home countries or on the incredibly dangerous journeys they have made. As a result, many have serious physical and mental scars and are finding the intense stress of detention, coupled with the threat of being sent Rwanda, intolerable.

They say that, "Every single one of the people we have spoken to is shocked and traumatised at the thought of being forcibly sent. We've had a five day hunger strike and numerous late night conversations with people who feel suicidal. One said 'They can send my dead body to Rwanda, but I would rather die than go there'"

'Care4Calais' says, "There is a more humane and civilised solution right in front of us now. **If we gave all refugees visas to cross the Channel, in the same way we do with Ukrainians, no one would need to risk their lives in small boats, and people smugglers would be put out of business overnight**. This must be possible – we are taking seven years' worth of Channel refugees in our 200,000 Ukrainians this year."

There really are humane ways to help refugees.

****

8TH JUNE

The most recent chief inspector of borders and immigration was appointed last March, 15 months ago. Hs name is David Neal and he has yet to meet the Home Secretary. He said he was 'disappointed' to have had five or six meetings with her cancelled.

Well yes it is very disappointing but not in the least bit surprising.

****

9TH JUNE

We hear that there has been an application for **an emergency High Court injunction to stop the flight planned to take 130 refugees to Rwanda next week.**

And all over Twitter I am seeing that actually the government has known all along that this would be illegal and would be stopped by the courts. Well if I have known that then I would presume they would know as well wouldn't you?

But they put this enormous plan out there to placate the right wing who would be so happy to say, 'Aha, we are solving the asylum problem Hooray.'

Then when the courts prevent it from happening they can say, 'of course it is the lefty lawyers who are preventing this' and so absolve themselves of all responsibility.

And here we are right on cue with the headline in the *Daily Mail* today:

"LAWYERS SET TO GROUND FIRST RWANDA FLIGHT"

We have already heard Mr. Johnson say that "we always knew that liberal lawyers would try to make the plan difficult," and that "left-wing legal eagles are attempting to put a spanner in the works".

Actually it has been pointed out that this headline should read:

"LAWS SET TO GROUND FIRST FLIGHT TO RWANDA"

How many times do we have to say to the prejudiced and the not- so-bright that there is no such thing as a left or right-wing lawyer, they are all bound by the law.

****

10TH JUNE (FRIDAY)

Well how wrong can we be? All day today we have been watching and waiting for the High Court judgement on the application for an interim injunction to stop the flight to Rwanda on Tuesday. This was brought to the court by the charities 'Care4Calais' and 'Detention Action' and the PSU which is the Union for the border forces.

It was at 6.30pm this evening that we heard that that the judge has ruled that the deportation flight can go ahead.

What? I am in shock. Surely this is a mistake.

About **130** asylum seekers, currently being held in immigration detention centres, are due to be flown to Rwanda from a secret location in the UK by an undisclosed airline this Tuesday. All very hush hush because the government knows that it is wrong.

The judge apparently said there was a "material public interest" in allowing the Secretary of State to be able to implement immigration control decisions. He also said that some of the risks of sending asylum seekers to Rwanda outlined by the claimants were very small and "in the realms of speculation".

He also said that, "I accept that the fact of removal to Rwanda will be onerous."

Onerous? To force innocent people on to a plane to be transported to a country with dubious human rights must be against their human rights and to me seems reminiscent of Nazi Germany. Onerous? It is cruel and inhumane.

There is to be a judicial review in July and I would have thought it would be sensible for the Home Office to wait for the outcome of that.

Indeed a spokesman for the Border Forces Union spoke on the radio this morning to say that his members were extremely unhappy about this decision. Mark Sewotka, head of the Public and Commercial Services told Sky's *Sophie Ridge on Sunday* that, "**Priti Patel would not ask civil servants to carry out the policy before its legality has been tested in court if she had any respect, not just for the desperate people who come to this country, but for the workers she employs.**"

But we are hearing this evening that the number of refugees on this proposed flight has been **reduced to 37.**

And 'Asylum Aid' and 'Freedom from Torture' have been granted leave to appeal on Monday so my fingers are still crossed.

****

13TH JUNE
Today is the day of the appeal.

13.30: We are hearing that out of the 37 refugees, lawyers, by working on individual cases, have managed to get 27 more released. So at the moment the number of refugees on this proposed flight is **down to 10.**

This is amazing. The flight is not due to leave until tomorrow evening so just maybe, maybe, maybe it will not happen?

Some of these refugees are children under 18 and the Home Office in their customary brutality uses some sort of dental technique in order to assess their ages. It then manages to class them as adults.

But the British Dental Association has said that it does not recognise the Home Office's technique of using dental checks to work out a migrant's age.

There were two protests against the Rwanda scheme yesterday that I am aware of. One was in Manchester and the other was at Brook House, the immigration removal centre near Gatwick.

14.30: NUMBERS DOWN TO 8!

16.30: APPEAL REJECTED.
This is such disappointing news and I am really horrified that this cruel and inhumane scheme can go ahead.

However it is understood that Home Office sources are saying there is a "real prospect" of the number of refugees falling to zero.

But then we hear that the Home Office says that the flight would take place even if there is just one person on it.

I can't begin to get my head round all of this. All I know is that I used to be proud of being British.

Not anymore.

20.15: NUMBERS DOWN TO 7!
And actually I've changed my mind. I **am** disgusted by this government and this Prime Minister but I **am** proud to be British. I have just seen on Twitter pictures of hundreds of people gathering outside the Home Office with posters saying **"Refugees Welcome here".**

The so-called 'ordinary' members of the public are absolute heroes. Ignore them at your peril.

****

Anonymous voices speak out about some of the realities of Rwanda. One person says that, "As a British citizen of Rwandan origin, I know better than most, the country's challenges, failings and regional instabilities."

Rwanda is a small country of just 12 million people. Over half of its people live in poverty, according to the World Bank, and families everywhere struggle with totally inadequate health services. Human rights abuses of Rwandans by their own leaders have been documented by various bodies over the past 28 years.

As Rwanda's opposition leader warned recently, and with great bravery, in *The Times*: "Everybody knows that we have a dictatorship in Rwanda. That is not a secret. **It is unacceptable that a democratic country sends refugees to a non-democratic country**."

Indeed there are other ways to address English Channel crossings, such as **creating a transit centre in Calais, where people on the move could be assessed and those in need of protection, welcomed**.

How many times do we have to say this?

We see what tomorrow brings.

****

14TH JUNE
We know at least three refugees are having their cases heard today.

Liz Truss is saying on the morning media round that even if there are only a couple on the flight it will be worth the money. That is £500,000 for the flight alone. It will set the precedence she says. It will stop the people smugglers, and asylum seekers in Rwanda will be well looked after and taken good care of.

In that case I would like to know, if it is going to be so lovely, how will that be a deterrent?

****

And in *The Times* today there is a letter from the two Archbishops and all the Bishops in the Church of England. This is a part of what they write:-

"The shame is our own, because our Christian heritage should inspire us to treat asylum seekers with compassion, fairness and justice, as we have for centuries. Those to be deported to Rwanda have had no chance to appeal, or reunite with family in Britain. They have had no consideration of their asylum claim, recognition of their medical or other needs, or any attempt to understand their predicament."

And the letter ends:-

"Deportations — and the potential forced return of asylum seekers to their home countries — are not the way. This immoral policy shames Britain".

Once again I have to say three cheers for the Church of England.

****

17.30 But we are now hearing that the three refugees who had their cases heard today have lost their appeals. One of them has a 21 year old son who will stay in the UK. He will never be able to visit the UK to see his son. Many of them have suffered torture in countries on their way here. Many of them do have family connections here.

The Boeing 767 has flown from Madrid this morning and is due to take off from Boscombe Down at **22.30.** It looks as though there will be 7 refugees on board. It has 235 seats.

19.50 Oh my goodness what is this I am seeing on Twitter? First I see it is 6 people. Then someone said that injunction can happen as late as when people are in their seats just before take-off. And then someone is saying 24 minutes ago that an injunction has already been granted against the flight taking off.

Well it is all touch and go. There are apparently 6 now on board and work is going on with those that remain.

21.30 There are 3 remaining.

22.00 Zero, and flight will definitely not take place.

NO-ONE IS GOING TO RWANDA

Congratulations to Care4Calais for all their legal work.

This final ruling is from the European Court of Human Rights.

And tomorrow, mark my words, we will hear from our law abiding PM that he will endeavour to change the rules.

****

15TH JUNE

Yes, true to form, he is saying that we should probably come out of the European Court of Human Rights.

He is doing his old trick of attacking lawyers and generally sounding more and more deranged at PMQs.

This is a very dangerous man.

****

386

16TH JUNE

An asylum seeker who was due to be deported to Rwanda has spoken to *Sky's* home editor Jason Farrell and he described how four security officers, working for the private firm Mitoie, had entered his holding room and grabbed him by his hands, feet and head.

He told them, when he was down on the floor, that they didn't need to use force as he would go with them. But they continued to hit him and kick him and push him through doors.

When he got to the airport he saw his friends who had been tied up. They had all had their phones taken off them and one was dragged to the plane by his hair.

Many of these refugees have family in the UK and all have suffered severe trauma.

****

17TH JUNE

Another of my letters is published in *The Times* today! Here it is:-

Sir, DN Reed, in a letter to The Times this morning challenges people to come up with their own suggestions to accommodate asylum seekers. It has been suggested many times that there should be an assessment centre in Calais where applications could be processed and those successful could then cross the Channel on a ferry. This would be a safe and legal route where there are none at the moment. Be in no doubt. This government treats all asylum seekers as criminals and does not wish to help any of them.

****

And more disheartening news about Ukrainian refugees. Data published yesterday by the Department for Levelling up, Communities and Housing **reveals that 660 households from Ukraine are being forced to register as homeless.**

Many have been left without a place to live after the relationship or accommodation arrangement with their UK hosts broke down, or the British home was judged unsuitable.

Two-thirds of those made homeless were on **the Government's family scheme** where they had a relative in the UK. The remainder were on the **Home for Ukraine** programme, where they were due to have been hosted by British families.

David Renard, housing spokesman for the Local Government Association, said councils were concerned because they received **no data on, or funding for, people made homeless under the family visa scheme.**

And in other cases, refugees coming under the Homes for Ukraine scheme have been placed with un-vetted hosts and in unsuitable homes **because the government has yet to give councils any funding for vital safety checks.**

This is an appalling indictment of the working of the Home Office although no more nor less than we have come to expect. But they could make it a bit easier for everyone if the government would allow people to switch between the Homes for Ukraine scheme and the family scheme.

Currently, if a placement under the family scheme breaks down, the household is not permitted to move over to the Homes for Ukraine scheme – despite many individuals offering to host still not having been matched with refugees.

Clive Betts, Labour MP and chair of the levelling up committee said the fact that Ukrainian families were falling homeless was "entirely avoidable" and demanded that ministers allow people who become homeless on the family scheme to rematch under the Homes for Ukraine scheme. "It would save money and human cost. It would save trauma to refugees. The schemes are broken. The government's approach is wrong and blinkered."

Complete incompetence actually. Not fit for purpose.

****

18TH JUNE

Priti Patel is exploding with anger today as she calls the European judges who stopped the Rwanda flight "racists." She accused human rights lawyers of "jumping on the bandwagon" and using "politically motivated" tactics. She told MPs that she would not wait for the judicial review in July and it is understood that the preparations for the next flight have already begun.

****

9TH JULY

Mutiny. The Royal Navy is threatening to walk away from Johnson's and Patel's plan for them to control the small boats crossing the Channel. They are saying that it is a complete waste of naval time and the navy is already overstretched.

I actually thought that they had decided not to do it ages ago but yes, it always was a ridiculous idea.

****

The judicial review has been adjourned until September to give Care4Calais more time to prepare their case.

****

19TH JULY

The documents have been presented to the High Court at a hearing today calling into question the legality of the government's Rwanda plan. They say that Rwanda was "initially excluded from the shortlist of potential partner countries for Priti Patel's proposed immigration policy **on human rights grounds".**

The reasons given included that it "has been accused of recruiting refugees to conduct armed operations in neighbouring countries", has a "poor human rights record regardless of the conventions it has signed up to" and has been criticised by the UK for extrajudicial killings, deaths in custody, enforced disappearances, torture and crackdowns on anyone critical of the regime."

So how is it that whenever questioned about the human rights record of Rwanda the PM always said it was a perfectly safe country?

And as I have already reported, when I looked up the Foreign Office's travel advice they said it was a dangerous place and you would need to exercise extreme caution.

The High Court have said that the full judicial review of the Rwanda policy should still be held on 5th September.

But I cannot see how this policy can possibly go ahead.

****

So, far from "taking back control" of our borders, whatever that was supposed to mean, we have absolutely no working plan, no future policy, no safe and legal routes, no consistency, no debates in Parliament, no meetings with the chief of the Border Force and a complete absence of trust, and respect for the Home Office. Control? It is a gruesome farce which is the cause of the death of many innocent people.

****

So now we need to look at all of the new laws being introduced by this government in more detail as they will affect every single one of us at some point in our lives.

****

DRACONIAN LAWS

2021

These laws are being rushed through Parliament, very often without significant debate. I think that our democratic freedoms are in peril.

14TH DECEMBER

Dominic Raab is to outline a sweeping overhaul of the **Human Rights Act** that he claims will counter "wokery and political correctness" and expedite the deportation of foreign criminals. I have written about this before but these highly controversial reforms, are to be announced today and many people are voicing their concerns. These reforms, it is being said by Dominic Raab, will create a new bill of rights and will introduce a permission stage to "deter spurious human rights claims" and change the balance between freedom of expression and privacy.

But lawyers have described the proposed changes to the **Human Rights Act** as dangerous and fuelled by political rhetoric rather than necessity. The following people have expressed their concerns in strong terms.

Stephanie Boyce, president of the Law Society, said any changes to the **Human Rights Act** should be led by evidence and not driven by political rhetoric.

Martha Spurrier, director at Liberty described the plans as "a blatant, unashamed power grab," adding: "Today's announcement is being cast as strengthening our rights when in fact, if this plan goes through, they will be fatally weakened. This government is systematically shutting down all avenues of accountability through a succession of rushed and oppressive bills. We must ensure the government changes course as a matter of urgency, before we very quickly find ourselves wondering where our fundamental human rights have gone."

Sacha Deshmukh, the chief executive of Amnesty International said: "If ministers move ahead with plans to water down the Human Rights Act and override judgments with which they disagree, they risk aligning themselves with authoritarian regimes around the world."

Prof Philippe Sands QC, who sat on the 2013 commission on a Bill of Rights, said: "The concern is that this will mark a further step in the government's eager embrace of lawlessness, undermining the rights of all individuals, the effective role of British judges and the European court, and the devolution settlement into which the Human Rights Act is embedded."

Adam Wagner, a leading human rights barrister with Doughty Street Chambers, said: "If this is to be a true bill of rights, instead of a party political rights wish list, as this appears to be, the government should obtain cross-party support."

This is horrifying and chilling and we should all be very afraid

****

As I read criticisms of this government by so many eminent people I truly believe that unless they are got rid of very, very soon we might never recover.

****

19TH DECEMBER

And the **Elections Bill** which was introduced in the House of Commons on the 5th July and was mentioned in my previous book is yet another controversial and deeply worrying bill that this government is trying to push through Parliament.

The most controversial measure in the bill is that **voters must show photo ID before getting a ballot paper in a polling station.** This would affect UK parliamentary elections and local elections in England.

But why is this deemed to be necessary? **There is no record of any significant fraud in English elections.** There was only one conviction for impersonation after the 2019 election, and the Commons committee described the government's pretence that there was a hidden epidemic of voter fraud as "simply not good enough".

It is thought that older people would be more likely to have driving licenses or passports or other ID than younger people and the older ones are more likely to vote Tory! Do you believe that?

It is yet another gambit to try to get more Conservative votes and the whole process will come at a **great cost to the tax payer**. There has been very little debate or any opposition.

I finish by quoting Nick Cohen of *The Observer* when he writes today that, "After the revival of Labour and Liberal Democrat fortunes, you might find it ludicrous for Conservatives to think they can be in power for ever. If so, I urge you to look at how they are playing with electoral law to give themselves the best possible chance of doing just that."

****

Also today there was a protest outside No 10 about the **Nationality and Borders Bill** which is currently going through Parliament

Tens of thousands of people have called for this bill to be scrapped. Organisations including 'Media Diversified,' 'Stand up to Racism,' the 'Association of Muslim Lawyers,' 'Bail for Immigration Detainees' and 'Windrush Lives' came together in this a mass protest in Downing Street.

Anger is focused on Clause 9 of the bill, covering "notice of decision to deprive a person of citizenship". It exempts the government from having to give notice of removing a person's citizenship if is not "reasonably practicable".

In effect, **individuals could be stripped of their British citizenship without warning,** which is set to disproportionately affect millions of black, Asian and minority ethnic citizens. MPs approved the bill on its third reading earlier this month despite criticism from all sides of the Commons. It will now go to the House of Lords where it will be debated at its second reading stage on 5th January.

Patricia Williams, 58, from London, told *The Independent:* "This law will mean that every black and brown person residing in Britain, born to migrant parents, like me, are effectively second-class citizens in our own country. How is that right? **It's the most racist piece of legislation that I've seen in my lifetime."**

****

2022

18TH JANUARY
This **Election Bill** has just had its third reading in the Commons and is now going back to the Lords.

Also yesterday the Lords voted against a range of measures in the **Police, Crime, Sentencing and Courts Bill.** This is another very controversial bill and there are loads of protests around the country about it.

Both bills appear to threaten our democracy. I know we don't want people glued to roads, or ambulances blocked, but I am sure there are already laws to prevent that sort of thing. They are talking of banning noise. Baroness Jones described the government's plans as "oppressive" and "plain nasty".

"How do you seriously think a protest is going to happen without noise?" she asked.

Labour's Lord Hain called the move **"the biggest threat to the right to dissent and the right to protest in my lifetime"** adding that it would have "throttled" protests by the suffragettes.

The bill now faces going back and forth between the Commons and Lords.

****

19TH JANUARY
What is also worrying is the way in which so many of the most contentious bills are introduced. Eighteen pages were added to this bill in the Lords in November **without having been previously considered by the Commons**. This is outrageous. Little by little they are chipping away at our democracy.

****

23RD JANUARY
There is a long article in *The Observer* today by William Hutton who is saying that despite the defeats in the Lords over the **Police, Crime Sentencing and Courts Bill** Priti Patel will not give up.

He writes that **democracy is in retreat worldwide**. "A basic precondition for democracy – respect for different opinions – is vanishing in fractious times; adversaries are seen not as part of the same polity but rather abhorrent "others" to be quashed."

This is so true. Even in some universities, reasoned debate seems lost to a cancel culture, whereby those who hold alternative views are not welcome.

He goes on to say that **"for all the democracies' weaknesses they remain the best protector of liberties and the rule of law."**

He is damning about this horrible bill. He says that if over a million people can be bothered to march like the ones we have had about the Iraq War or the Brexit Referendum then may be "the policy in question has serious, perhaps fatal, flaws. The wise democratic government takes note."

The word to notice there is 'wise'. Sadly, as we have seen so often, there is no wisdom in the vicinity of our leaders today.

As he points out, there is really no need for further restrictions in a new bill as

"Mrs Thatcher's Public Order Act already makes peaceful protest harder than in almost every other democracy, according to the police and government exceptional powers".

"Priti Patel belongs in today's Hong Kong, Beijing or Singapore – not Britain, a former beacon of democracy."

Oh my word Mr. Hutton **you are the best!** I have been implying this for ages but you have put it into such perfect words. Thank you.

****

13TH FEBRUARY
Today we hear about some very worrying actions taken by the police against **"kill the bill" protesters** in Bristol on March 21st last year.

38 protesters have been charged with riot which is the most serious public order offence and can result in custodial sentences of up to 10 years. **Only 22 people have been convicted of riot since 2011.**

Apparently demonstrators took part in a sit down protest outside a Bristol police station. They were pepper sprayed and beaten by the police who had claimed that they, the police, had been attacked and that the police station and police vans had been vandalized. There seems to have been a high level of violence on both sides and the report just out says it is not clear who started it. There were injuries on both sides, but the police eventually withdrew widely reported claims that officers suffered broken bones and a punctured lung.

These charges come amid growing concern from civil liberties groups that the **law is becoming more and more draconian.**

Matt Foot, a criminal defence solicitor is co-writing a book on the policing of protest and he said, **"This is by far and away the biggest use of riot charges since the mid-1980s."**

Priti Patel is apparently taking an active interest in these policing decisions. I knew her name would not be very far away in a story such as this.

****

22ND FEBRUARY
The Electoral Commission has written to the government accusing them of making an **unprecedented attack on our democracy.** The letter, which was signed by the commission's independent board, urges ministers to think again about proposals in the new **Elections Bill,** now going through the House of Lords. They are concerned that the watchdog would have to "have regard to the government's strategic and policy priorities" set by ministers. Critics fear this could be used to prevent politically sensitive investigations. Although ministers have insisted they will not use the powers to interfere in an independent oversight all the commissioners except one warned that

this was no guarantee that a future government would not misuse the powers.

Actually it is no guarantee that this present corrupt government will behave honourably either in my opinion.

This is a bill which is not necessary, claiming to put right criminal issues which do not exist, and in so doing it will make it harder for certain people to be able to vote.

****

28TH FEBRUARY

The **Policing, Crime Sentencing and Courts Bill** is heading towards its final stages in the Lords as amendments are now being considered and a royal assent is imminent.

We should be, and indeed are, all worried about this draconian bill but last week a 'FairChecks' campaign was set up by the 'Transform Justice and Unlock' charities and they are highlighting the facts that there are changes to the cautions system which will result in possibly about 16,000 more people having to declare some very old or very minor convictions to potential or current employers.

In other words when trawling through your DBS checks, a student brawl or a stupid bit of vandalism can follow you for life. This could compromise your insurance, and rule out many jobs involving healthcare, or even taxi-driving. The devil is in the detail and it all needs looking at extremely carefully. I am indebted to Libby Purves for highlighting all of this in *The Times* today.

I actually think that with all these bills it would save time if we all just acknowledged we are criminals and go from there.

****

24TH MARCH
The Fixed-term Parliament Act has been repealed. This means that the PM can call an election whenever he likes rather than every five years.

****

26TH MARCH
We hear that Priti Patel is privately worried that the **Nationality and Borders bill could be timed out.** It is going back and forth between the Lords and the Commons so often that if it is not able to receive the Royal Assent by the end of May it will fall.

We are all crossing our fingers.

****

4TH APRIL
The Lords delivered a massive defeat for the government this evening as they voted to remove some of the worst elements of the **Nationality and Borders bill. A Bishop described this bill as "inhumane" and an ex-Supreme Court Justice said that it "flagrantly breaches" our human rights requirements.** Over ten amendments were sent back to the Commons. As they are on holiday for two weeks it is touch and go whether it will get through.

I just cannot believe the inhumanity of this terrible bill. One of the worst clauses was the one which would prevent unaccompanied child asylum seekers in Europe to be allowed to join a family member in the UK. This was one which was overturned by the Lords. But all of them are dreadful.

****

20TH APRIL
I watched MPs in the Commons today vote down all eleven Lord's amendments to the **Nationality and Borders bill.** The debate before

the vote was rushed through due to lack of time. There is so much time being taken up trying to defend the PM that time for important debate on bills is being compromised. Very few MPs were there listening to the debate. Not interested, not bothered, minds closed and the vast majority voting for the cruellest and most inhumane bill ever brought before Parliament, in my opinion.

****

25TH APRIL
There is an almighty dash in the Commons this week as the Tories try to get ten controversial bills through Parliament before Thursday when Parliament is prorogued before the Queen's Speech.

We really have to hope they run out of time or the Queen runs out of ink.

****

28TH APRIL
Parliament is being prorogued today until the Queen's Speech on the 10th May.

And we see that yesterday they did indeed managed to rush through six controversial bills. The first five are all bills that will erode our democracy step by step and the tragedy is that I cannot see any of this being reported in the media apart from *the i*. Debate on these bills was insufficient and indeed I heard one MP state that he would "canter" through his points because they were so short of time.

The House of Lords repeatedly put in various amendments to all of these bills but their battle ended on Tuesday night after Baroness Stroud withdrew her name from a key amendment on giving asylum seekers the right to vote, reportedly after a threat that she would be stripped of the Tory whip.

These are the bills now awaiting Royal Assent:

The Police, Crime, Sentencing and Courts bill............no longer able to protest freely and noisily.

The Nationality and Borders bill...........all asylum seekers will be criminalised as there are no safe and legal routes to the UK.

Elections bill and the Electoral Commission...... you will now have to have a photo ID to be able to vote but also it will give government ministers, rather than Parliament, greater say in the commission's work as the Electoral Commission is now under government control and no longer independent.

Health and Care Bill................... passed despite attempts to cap the cost of social care.

The Judicial Review and Courts bill .... there will be no more legal aid support for families at public inquests and the bill risks undermining individuals' ability to hold the government to account.

The Building Safety Bill............... although set to become law today, the bulk of the provisions will not come into effect for another year to 18 months.

Its aim is to eradicate the catalogue of errors that led to the tragic fire at Grenfell Tower in west London in June 2017. This is the only bill which does not impact on our democracy.

****

10TH MAY. THE QUEEN'S SPEECH

The speech today was read by Prince Charles because the Queen was suffering from episodic mobility problems.

I used to love all the pomp and ceremony but I feel it is a bit incongruous just now with everyone struggling with rising bills. However he read it perfectly in a rather flat monotone as we suspect there was a lot there that he would rather have left out. It was 10 minutes long and contained 38 bills.

The most controversial bills I think are the **bill of rights, public order, Brexit 'freedoms', Planning reform, levelling up and regeneration, the animal welfare bill and the bill that wasn't there. Plus one more.**

Bill of Rights:
Shami Chakrobarti writes in *The Guardian* that the **bill of rights is "constitutional butchery that will make us all less free."** She says that the 1998 Human Rights Act was an "outstanding legal achievement". Basically **changing this bill is a power grab by the state**.

We all remember Boris Johnson illegally proroguing Parliament and he will always try to change the laws to suit his personal agenda.

The Human Rights bill constrains people in power like Johnson. It doesn't undermine our own legal system, it works with it and in support of it.

This new bill will, for example, stop foreigner offenders from relying on the right to a family life to overturn deportations. Lawyers are saying that it risks the UK's international reputation for upholding human rights.

That has been going downhill ever since Boris Johnson became prime minister.

Public Order:
Draconian new powers will be handed to the police so that they can have more reasons to stop and search protesters and can seize protest gear. Protesting generally will be further criminalised.

Brexit 'freedoms':
This is yet more power to ministers without the need for parliamentary scrutiny. Ministers will be able to revoke EU laws on the UK statute book without having a vote in Parliament.

Planning Reform:
Well this does seem to be a hot potato for the government. All planning reforms are fraught with danger and ministers are apparently acutely sensitive to the political peril of any new proposals. They were elected on a manifesto which promised to build 300,000 new homes a year but a Tory backbench revolt and the defeat in the Chesham and Amersham by-election has sent them into headlong retreat. So goodness knows what is going to happen with this.

Levelling up and regeneration:
Yes, well, a very commendable goal. Trouble is they have been talking about this for a very long time and nothing has happened. Why? Because the Treasury does not want to fork out any money.

The animal welfare (animals abroad) bill:
This bill will impose a ban on the import of hunting trophies and ban the sale and advertising of holidays that involve cruelty to animals. But plans for the bill to include a ban on the import and sale of foie gras and fur have reportedly been dropped. This is directly giving way to the right wing.

The bill that wasn't there:
This is the **employment bill** which was first promised in the 2019 manifesto. Nothing has happened since then and it is left out of the Queens' speech today.

TUC general secretary Frances O'Grady said this morning "bad bosses" will be celebrating the absence of an Employment Bill, adding: **"The Prime Minister promised to make Britain the best place in the world to work, but he has turned his back on working people."**

He added that "no Employment Bill means vital rights that ministers had promised – like default flexible working, fair tips and protection from pregnancy discrimination – risk being ditched for good."

Statutory sick pay is also hit by the absence of this bill. Early in the pandemic the government began to pay sick pay from day one of sickness. However in February it switched back to being paid from day four. So those who cannot afford to take unpaid days off because they are ill will continue to struggle into work. There are also gaping holes in the system as neither the 4 million British self-employed workers, nor employees earning less than £123 a week, are entitled to sick pay. And of course 70% of the latter category are women.

Angela Rayner said, "This Prime Minister promised enhanced rights and protections at work, but instead he is dragging Britain's workers into a race to the bottom."

So women are once again discriminated against by this government. Do they wake up each morning and say, "I wonder how we can make everything worse for everyone this morning?"

I say again are we surprised? No but we continue to be disgusted.

Plus one more:
All schools will be supported in order to **convert to academies.**

This bill concerns me greatly. They sell it by saying that by 2030, 90% of primary school children will achieve the expected standard in reading writing and maths and the percentage of children meeting the expected standards in the worst performing areas will have increased by a third.

NO THEY WON'T. This will cost a huge amount of money which they refused to spend on the education of children when it was requested by Sir Kevan Collins. They think that it is more important to spend money on a change of system when what is needed are more teachers, more teaching assistants, more books and libraries, more equipment and technology, more music and drama, more sporting activities and equipment, more repairs to infrastructure, more special needs facilities and more much, much more of other things which I am too het up to be able to think about just now but which should also include decent catch-up programmes after the pandemic lockdowns.

But Geoff Barton , general secretary of the Association of School and College leaders puts it a bit more eloquently when he says that the idea of further academisation meaning the 90% target would be met was a "non-sequitur."

He says that, **"What is needed to achieve that target is a massive injection of funding and resources to provide more individualised and specialist support for children with special educational needs and those from disadvantaged backgrounds. It is totally unrealistic to think this will happen within the current financial constraints."**

Will it happen? This government's record of manifesto promises being broken means that maybe it won't.

In fact let us just hope that Johnson is deposed before the summer recess on July 21st. My birthday is on the 20th. What a great present that would be.

****

4TH JUNE

I missed this one. But it was mentioned in the Queen's Speech and it's about to have its second reading this coming week. It is the **National Security Bill** and there are some serious concerns about proposed changes to the **Serious Crime Act of 2007**. This act made it a criminal offence to encourage or assist crimes committed overseas, such as aiding an unlawful assassination or sending information to be used in a torture interrogation.

However under a new clause in this bill all of this would be "disapplied" where "necessary for the proper exercise of any function" of MI5, MI6, GCHQ or the armed forces.

'Reprieve', an international human rights charity, said it would effectively grant immunity to ministers or officials who provide information to foreign partners that leads to someone being tortured or unlawfully killed in a drone strike.

I cannot believe that this is even being considered. Aubrey Allegetti in *The Guardian* is to be congratulated for bringing this to our attention.

Maya Foa, joint executive director of 'Reprieve' said that enacting clause 23 of the National Security Bill would **"destroy the UK's moral legitimacy to condemn similar atrocities by autocratic states"** after the murder of Khashoggi, a journalist whom US intelligence agencies believe was killed on the orders of the Saudi ruler, Mohammed bin Salaman.

The campaign against the move was also supported by the former cabinet minister and civil liberties campaigner David Davis.

He added: "This bill is drafted so loosely that it could let ministers off the hook if they authorised crimes like murder and torture from the safety of their desks in Whitehall.

"I urge colleagues to constrain it to actions appropriate to our aims and civilised standards."

This is presented to Parliament by Priti Patel. I need say no more.

****

16TH JUNE
I think it is important to remind ourselves what the European Court of Human Rights stands for as the Justice Secretary plans to adapt it into a British Bill of Rights.

There are 30 Articles altogether but I will just record the first 16.

1. All are born free and equal.
2. Freedom from discrimination.
3. Right to life.
4. Freedom from slavery.
5. Freedom from torture.
6. Right to recognition before the law.
7. Right to equality before the law.
8. Access to justice.
9. Freedom from arbitrary detention.
10. Right to a fair trial.
11. Presumption of innocence.
12. Right to privacy.
13. Freedom of movement.
14. Right to asylum.
15. Right to nationality.
16. Right to marriage and to found a family.

This was drawn up after the war by Winston Churchill. The barrister Sir James Fawcett DSC QC was president of the ECHR from 1972 to 1981. He was the grandfather of Boris Johnson.

So the question is: which of these rights would you remove?

But since it was the ECHR who, amongst others, stopped the flight of asylum seekers to Rwanda, the race is on to change it. Not sure how this is done but we listened to Dominic Raab this morning saying that the right to family life is much too lax and that, for one, needs re- writing.

In fact he is also saying that last-minute injunctions could be ignored in future and that the new Bill of Rights will be published within weeks.

He did, however, play down the prospect of leaving the ECHR by saying this bill would be within the ECHR.

But there is to be a judicial review in three weeks' time and if that is successful they could launch an appeal to the European Court and it could take a year or more to resolve the case. This could mean that the Rwanda scheme will effectively be finished.

****

22ND JUNE
The new Bill of Rights is published today. I will just quote a passage from the book by the Secret Barrister called "Fake Law". It is from chapter 5.

He writes "A system of human rights which pleases those who rule over us is not a system of human rights at all: it is a system we are encouraged nearly every day to embrace. 'You don't need human rights. They're not for people like you.' Like Kaa whispering 'trust me' as he wraps himself tighter and tighter around your chest, the state promises you that it has your best interests at heart. They just happen, funnily enough, to coincide with the interests of the state."

Of course, first, it has to get through Parliament. A lot of words will happen before that.

****

27TH JUNE
Today the Conservative party votes to break international law. The second reading of the Northern Ireland Protocol Bill was passed with 295 for and 221 against.

Theresa May said in the House of Commons debate today that "that this bill will break the law and diminish the UK in the eyes of the world and it will not work."

She said that she would not be supporting it as "it is not legal in international law."

So does she vote against it? No, she abstains.

****

28TH JUNE
Two of the bills discussed in this chapter become law today.

The Police, Crime, Sentencing and Courts bill is one and we have already seen it in action.

Brexit protestor Steve Bray has been surrounded by about 20 police officers today who have threatened him, told him he can't protest near Westminster and Parliament and have confiscated his loud speaker, amplifiers and microphone.

The maximum sentence for peaceful protest is now twice the maximum sentence for grievous bodily harm.

Steve Bray has been peacefully protesting, walking up and down outside the House of Commons and talking about the appalling consequences of Brexit ever since the referendum. Today we all see on Twitter dreadful pictures of the police who are man–handling him and telling him that this is no longer permissible.

****

The second bill is **the Nationality and Borders Bill.**

From today all pilots of small boats crossing the Channel will face four year prison sentences with some facing life imprisonment.

It will also enable the government to deport foreign national offenders up to 12 months before the end of their prison sentences.

And if you overstay your visa your prison sentence will increase from 6 months to 4 years.

Well good luck with all of that I say. Criminal barristers are on strike and the prisons are full.

But be afraid, be very afraid. We are now officially a police state.

****

29TH JUNE

Well the police action against Steve Bray has really backfired. Crowdfunding was set up for him to help with legal fees and has now reached over £13K. However he is back on the streets near Parliament and the police, having followed him around yesterday, seem to be leaving him alone today. There is a wonderful clip on Twitter showing them all singing "Bye Bye Boris, Bye Bye."

But Andrea Leadsom, Tory MP tweeted yesterday that, "This action by the police to stop his violent protest is very welcome." Everyone has been up in arms because he was never ever violent.

As someone else said he used to yell through his loud hailer outside his office every day and was a pain in the neck but he defends absolutely his right to protest in this way.

So people are saying that if you are in trouble and need the police quickly get hold of a loud hailer and criticise the government. 20 police vans will be there like a shot.

By this evening Steve Bray has raised £170K and has more support than ever before.

****

1ST JULY
Ministers have announced a massive U-turn on key elements of the government's school bill.

This bill planned to give Nadhim Zahawi greater control over virtually every aspect of academy trusts in England and was seen as a huge power grab for the Department of Education.

Many of the clauses have been scrapped and critics said they were vague and open to abuse, whilst the Lords said it was a poorly drafted bill.

Geoff Barton, general secretary of School and College Leaders said, **"It was a ridiculous attempt to centralise power in Whitehall over matters which are obviously much better decided by professional educators who know the needs of their schools and their pupils."**

As Bridget Phillipson Shadow Education Secretary said, "Zahawi has ripped up his own plans and is back to the drawing board with his very first piece of legislation."

Oh goodness when will they ever get anything right?

****

20TH JULY

A law has just been passed which will allow businesses to hire skilled temporary agency workers to be employed in order to limit disruption due to strike action. **This used to be a criminal offence but not anymore.** In fact I seem to remember the outrage from the government when P & O did something similar.

Well, well, we wait with interest for all those spare train drivers, spare railway workers, spare criminal barristers, spare post-men, spare teachers and spare doctors and nurses to appear from no-where. Yes, all these people are either on strike or voting for strike action.

****

Now I wonder...............what, or who, should I write about next?

BORIS JOHNSON

Well, I have come to the conclusion that there needs to be a chapter with the above title. Yes, Boris Johnson has to have a chapter all to himself. **Even if there is nothing else to write about him after these next couple of items (which is doubtful) this needs a space of its own.**

(July 2022. A space???? It could fill the whole book. Hold on to your hats.)

2021

23RD NOVEMBER
Yesterday Johnson gave a speech to the Annual Conference of the CBI. This is a collection of top business people in the UK and was held in South Shields near Newcastle.

I listened to the whole speech and I was absolutely appalled. Johnson rattled off the speech at top speed with his eyes on his notes the whole time. It seemed to me that he never really engaged with the audience.

But it was the contents of the speech that were really weird. At one point I think he compared himself to Moses! He said something about when he came down from Sinai he said to his officials, here are the new Ten Commandments and he then rattled off ten aims for a greener economy.

Then later he was talking about electric cars and he described how he used to drive fast cars when he was a motoring correspondent and he made 'vroom, vroom' car noises to describe him taking off at traffic lights.

But then the most embarrassing bit was when he lost his place in his notes. These were all on loose pieces of large white paper which he shuffled about and waved around and could not organise at all or find his place.

"Forgive me" he said at least three times and then he launched into a speech about Peppa Pig World where he had been the day before with his son Wilfred. "Anyone been to Peppa Pig?" he asked. I think one hand went up. Well remember, they were all in the far north of England and Peppa Pig is in Southampton.

"Peppa Pig World is very much my kind of place," he said – "it had very safe streets, discipline in schools, heavy emphasis on new mass-transit systems".

I honestly did not have a clue what he was talking about and neither, I think, did his audience.

But he also said in this speech that, "it is an astonishing fact that the 16- to 18-year-olds in this country are getting 40% less time and instruction than our competitors in the OECD, and so we're turning that round."

But why is this Mr. Johnson after 12 years of Conservative government? And he goes on to say that: "We are focusing on skills, skills, skills; investing in our FE colleges, our apprentices, in the know-how and confidence of young people. We want to see the dispersal of this growth and development across the UK. That's why this government has doubled investment in scientific research – and, again, we want to see the benefits of that research across the whole of the country."

But I have just read an interesting report from the library of the House of Commons written by Sue Hubble, Paul Bolton and Joe Lewis. Although I believe it is the case that more funding is going into FE colleges now it would appear there is a long way go. This is part of what they say:

Further education colleges and sixth forms have seen the largest falls in funding of any sector of the education system since 2010–11. Funding per student in further education and sixth-form colleges fell by 12% in real terms between 2010-11 and 2019–20, while funding per student in school sixth forms fell by 23%. A report by the Institute for Fiscal Studies in 2020, Annual report on education spending in England, found that spending on classroom-based adult education in 2019-20 was nearly two-thirds lower in real terms than in 2003–04 and about 50% lower than in 2009–10. **It stood at £4.3 billion in 2003-04 (2020-21 prices) and fell to £2.9 billion in 2009-10 and to just under £1.5 billion in 2019-2020.**

The Conservative Party manifesto for the 2019 General Election did include a plan for a National Skills Fund (NSF). It was to be worth £2.5 billion over the next Parliament in England and provide matching funding for individuals and SMEs for high-quality education and training.

****

He lies all the time. Or is it that he has no idea because he can never be bothered to look at any detail?

And there is a really worrying article in the *'Thunderer'* in today's *Times* written by **Dame Kate Bingham** which makes very disturbing reading.

She starts by saying that the vaccine programme that she was head of was very successful. Scientists and manufacturers, plus 500,000 volunteers, worked round the clock in order to make it so.

But she goes on to say that **had** they relied on the existing machinery of government, the outcome could have been so different. She writes that there is a **devastating lack of skills and experience across the whole of government in science, industry and manufacturing. She writes that we need to build a peacetime capability for dealing with serious healthcare threats and she warns that other pandemics will appear.**

These threats are just as real and as serious as national security and defence yet they receive a fraction of the level of government investment and attention. The life sciences industry turns over £80 billion every year and it is vital for our safety and prosperity that it can flourish, but the government treats it with hostility and suspicion causing many companies to move to more science friendly environments such as Belgium and Ireland.

The government lacks the knowledge and interest to detect the difference between money-grabbing opportunity and valuable corporate behaviour. This leads to damaging decisions. Recently they cancelled a contract with Valnever before its Covid 19 vaccine had completed final clinical testing. **This meant that millions of potential vaccines were destroyed which could have been used as boosters and for selling to other less well-off countries.**

Kate Bingham also said all of this in a speech today at Oxford University. This is a damning indictment on the workings of this government and the civil service. She called for a pandemic security adviser or minister to ensure that the UK is properly prepared for a future pandemic.

Education and skills and sciences are vitally important and I do worry that with the gross underfunding of our schools it is all going to be compromised in a totally unacceptable way.

****

24TH NOVEMBER

Well, well the big guns were out in full this morning defending the Prime Minister and his speech to the CBI. **Dominic Raab** was on the *Today* programme saying how brilliant the PM is and listing all the fantastic things he has achieved. Brexit, social care, levelling up, transport schemes etc.

And **Dame Andrea Leadsome** was on LBC saying what a brilliant communicator Boris is.

And in *The Times* today Daniel Finkelstein made an interesting point when he said, well what do you expect? "This shambolic behaviour is Boris. This is what you voted for and this is what you are getting. Do not be surprised."

****

25TH NOVEMBER

Just a few hours ago in *The Independent*, Rob Merrick highlights an interview given to *The New European*, last week by **Ken Clarke** who used to be the Father of the House, and Home Secretary and Chancellor before having the whip removed by Boris Johnson. He was a very experienced politician who was highly regarded by everyone for his wisdom and balanced views. In this interview he warns that the UK **is "dangerously close" to becoming an "elected dictatorship" under Boris Johnson** – as he branded the Prime Minister's handling of Brexit clashes "laughable".

He lashed out at Mr Johnson's disregard for "constitutional constraints," calling his party "more nationalist than at any time in my lifetime". He went on to say that, "He gets angry if the courts or Parliament try to interfere. As the elected Prime Minister, he thinks he should not be impeded in these ways. I considered myself to be in the mainstream of the party and am not pleased that people who think like me – internationalist, outward-looking, progressive – have been marginalised.

"The party is now more right wing and nationalist than at any time in my lifetime." He ridiculed the "global Britain promise as "a slogan, an excuse for spending money on a royal yacht and flying the flag in odd places. We have to get used to our reduced role in the world," he said.

Lord Clarke, who had the whip withdrawn in 2019, said Mr Johnson was trying to "tear up" his Brexit agreement, but "find a way of doing so in a way that they can blame the French. I only hope that they have got experts working behind the scenes on an alternative plan."

On the threat to the constitution, he said: "We have relied for too long on a Victorian ideal of what we used to call decent chaps doing the right thing. We have got to the point where **we need a serious written constitution**. We need to restore the strengths of the Commons and the Lords by putting their powers into statutory reforms. **We are at the absurd point where it is up to the government whether extremely contentious pieces of legislation get to be debated at all."**

I think very many people would agree with every word he says. I just do not know how much longer this Prime Minister can be allowed to continue in his role, as the incompetence and danger to our once great nation threatens to destroy everything we hold dear.

****

1ST DECEMBER

One rule for them and another for everyone else. How often do we hear that? Well that is a rhetorical question because as we all know we hear it all the time.

And now we are hearing that last November and December, just after tier 3 restrictions came into force in London and social gatherings were banned, **there were a couple of parties in No. 10 hosted by the PM**. Allegedly there were 40 or so people, cheek by jowl, having a raucous time. Well it has not been denied by the PM on PMQs today or the Health Secretary on the *Today* programme this morning. They both just said all Covid rules have been followed to the letter.

Do you think that is good enough? No neither do I. As Sir Keir Starmer said he is **"taking the British public for fools."**

****

3RD DECEMBER
Well the Christmas party story is certainly not going away. When questioned about it Boris just talks about this Christmas and keeps saying it will all go ahead as planned and everything in the garden is rosy.

But a very interesting little story has just come out from our friend **Matt Hancock** on *Times Radio*. Referring to his resignation over breaking Covid rules last June he said: "I resigned ultimately. I resigned because of **that failure of leadership."** Well at the time we all thought it was purely because he broke the rules by getting too close to his female aide when we were all forbidden to get close to anyone. Leadership was never mentioned then. Could it be, could it possibly be that **he is having a swipe at Boris?** What do you think?

****

And yesterday there was a **by-election in Old Bexley and Sidcup.** It has been Conservative for years. No chance of a Labour win but the majority was slashed from 19,000 votes to 4,478. This is a **10.3 percent swing to Labour** which if it was replicated at a general election Labour would be in with a chance of forming a government. There is another by- election in two weeks' time in a slightly more marginal seat so it will be interesting to see how that goes.

****

4TH DECEMBER
Boris Johnson has been reported to the police by a Labour MP over the allegations about Christmas parties last year.

Neil Coyle, Labour MP for Bermondsey and Old Southwark, wrote to the Metropolitan head of police asking her to investigate. He said: "I believe they broke the law. Most of my constituents followed the rules; those that didn't faced penalties. **Johnson is not above the law, despite his bloated self-entitlement."**

Lucy Allan, Conservative MP for Telford, replied to Coyle's tweet writing: "Is this what you were sent to Parliament to do? Is this what you want the police to spend time doing? Or would standing up for your constituents and letting police fight crime be best use of public money?"

To which he replied: "221 fines were issued in the Telford region for breaking lockdown rules last Christmas. But their MP thinks her boss should get away without even being investigated. I shouldn't really be surprised that another Tory thinks they are above the rules."

I said this story would run and run and so it will. If only they said there was no party or yes we did have a party and we know we should not have done so and we apologise profusely and we all resign! For goodness sake where is the Tory MP with some moral fibre?

****

And on *Question Time*, on the BBC, our vaccine minister was asked about this party. This is of course **Maggie Throup** who no-one has ever heard of. I have never heard her on the radio or seen her on the television or read about her in the papers and when she did appear on *Question Time* she did not exactly cover herself in glory.

The questions were all about the alleged Downing Street Christmas parties last year and her answers were so inadequate that the audience heckled and then laughed at her. When the chairwoman Fiona Bruce asked the audience if they felt that the question had been answered they all shouted "NO". **"They are laughing at you" she said!**

And then on the *Andrew Marr show*, again on the BBC, our Justice Minister Dominic Raab was asked if the Met were investigating the parties. His reply was astonishing. He said that he didn't think so because they tend not to investigate anything over a year old! I beg your pardon?

Now, I remember reading somewhere a while ago that a good writer should not need to use exclamation marks. I'm very sorry but they did not expect to be writing about our government ministers!!!!!!

That remark from Raab is so extraordinary I don't know where start. But I will remind everyone that the courts have a backlog of about six years at the moment. What is happening to all of them?

****

7TH DECEMBER
Well I have seen it all now!

Boris attended a drugs dawn raid yesterday morning, with loads of policemen who were smashing down someone's front door. He was all dressed up in police gear which I actually thought was illegal according to the 1996 police act. He had a beanie hat on, with the word 'police' on it, and a large police waterproof jacket with the word 'police' on it back and front. I am led to believe that if the police actually gave it all to him then that is probably OK but it was such a shock to see him like that.

He is on a mission to shut down 2,000 county lines by 2024. We obviously wish him well with that but he perhaps needs to look very close to home as cocaine has been spotted in the Westminster lavatories.

Boris loves dressing up of course and we are used to seeing him in high-vis jackets all the time but he really did look a bit out of his depth in this one. And Jed Mecurio, writer of my favourite programme *"Line of Duty"*, agrees as he posted a tweet which I now give you in full. He wrote:

Thank you for submitting your audition for the next series of "Line of Duty" but we're looking for a character with at least one redeeming moral principle and a performance that places even just a scintilla of doubt in the audience's mind that he might not be totally bent.

I love it.

****

8TH DECEMBER
Did I say that I had seen it all? Not by a long chalk!

This morning we wake up to the news that ITV news had obtained a video of a fake press conference being held in the new multi-million pound press briefing room with Allegra Stratton, a senior government spokesperson, supposedly rehearsing some answers to questions being put to her by some colleagues about the alleged Christmas party on 18th December 2020. There she was behind the lectern laughing and giggling and saying things like **"it was only cheese and wine ..... .is cheese and wine OK? And it certainly wasn't socially distanced"** before bursting into nervous laughter.

The whole video looked appalling. People are disgusted by it, especially those who were not allowed to visit their loved ones even when they were dying. So today (Wednesday) we all waited eagerly for PMQs to see what Johnson would say.

Well he started by issuing a statement saying that yes he too was disgusted by the video and he would set up an investigation and if rules had been broken there would be consequences for the people involved.

But I just cannot understand why he can't just ask people involved about it. Apparently he was in a room not far away deciding on the way in which he would put everyone into tier 3 the next day. So surely he must have heard it. Did I say this story would run and run?

Well it has grown wings and taken off and is flying the PM and his cabinet even further into a **parallel universe.**

And this afternoon a **tearful Allegra Stratton resigns.** Who will be the next to go?

****

Then this evening we hear that at least three people who held or went to unlawful gatherings on the same day as the Downing Street party have been fined by the courts this month. The incidents, first reported by *The Evening Standard*, took place on 18 December 2020, when No 10 staff had drinks, food and played party games.

Each of the three cases that ended in fines this month would have required evidence from the Metropolitan Police and a decision by the Crown Prosecution Service to proceed.

And due to delays in the courts system, more could be coming down the track from the same period last year.

So I think the idea that criminal investigations cannot be retrospective is false, so long as a there is sufficient evidence.

****

The Electoral Commission has fined the Conservative party £17,800 after it was found to have inaccurately filed a donation used to help pay for the refurbishment of the Downing Street flat. Boris Johnson has been accused of lying to his own ethics adviser in this investigation over who funded this renovation. I wrote about this in

'**Beneath the Bluster**' and it is interesting to hear now how this has developed. The Conservative Party are considering whether to appeal.

****

9TH DECEMBER

One minister has told *The Times* that the talk in the Commons tea room was of more letters of no confidence in the Prime Minister going into Sir Graham Brady, the leader of the 1922 Committee of back-bench Conservative MPs. They say that **the party looks "divided, hypocritical, out-of-control, out-of-touch and all the other thing that the voters despise."**

And apparently there were at least six other events which took place in Downing Street when we were all in tight restrictions.

They are called 'gatherings' by the way, not parties, but the party on the 18th had been organised days in advance on Whatsapp with a follow-up email.

And it has also just come to light that Jack Doyle, the Prime Minister's director of communications, had attended the 'gathering' on the 18th and given out awards. So what I find very difficult to understand is why it is so difficult to get to the truth. **He is the director of communications for goodness sake.** Why do we need an official investigation? Just ask.

****

11TH DECEMBER

There is a petition by Change. Org headed "Boris Johnson Resign Now!"

******

An article written by Max Hastings, former editor of *The Daily Telegraph* and so Boris Johnson's former boss, has just been unearthed.

423

This was written two years ago shortly before Johnson became leader of the Conservative party.

He has known Johnson since the 1980s when he was the Brussels correspondent.

This is the most damning article I have ever read about a figure in public life. He writes about his complete unsuitability for high office.

He writes that "his premiership will almost certainly reveal a contempt for rules, precedent, order and stability." Well absolutely it has.

He goes on to say that, "Dignity still matters in public office, and Johnson will never have it. Yet his graver vice is cowardice, reflected in a willingness to tell any audience whatever he thinks most likely to please, heedless of the inevitability of its contradiction an hour later."

We are seeing that all the time.

"He has long been considered a bully, prone to making cheap threats."

That is horrible to hear. Then he says, "Almost the only people who think Johnson a nice guy are those who do not know him."

****

12TH DECEMBER

It is Sunday today and as you can imagine Johnson is all over the papers and not in a good way. They are saying he is unfit to govern. The vultures (backbenchers) are circling and new would-be replacement leaders for him are flexing their muscles. Some are giving him six months (!) but we wait for **the vote on the new Covid restrictions on Tuesday** and the Shropshire by-election on Thursday. The last few weeks have been bad for Johnson but this week could be a lot worse.

****

15TH DECEMBER

Then this evening there was a press conference. This is just a few days after his pre-recorded address to the nation about the importance of getting the booster jab. So what on earth was this about?

Well it was about the importance of getting your booster jab. I could not understand why it was thought necessary to say this again except that it was possibly important to hear from Chris Whitty who said that although we don't know everything yet about the Omicron variant everything is probably bad.

But Boris Johnson won't actually say we have to cancel Christmas parties. We must just be sensible. So what does that mean exactly? The poor hospitality sector is in bits because nevertheless parties are being cancelled left, right and centre and they are getting no help from the government. They are saying that some smaller pubs will completely disappear after Christmas. They are asking for VAT discounts and business rates relief to be extended.

But apparently the Chancellor is in the USA at the moment (why is that?) when leaders of business and hospitality say they should be round a table thrashing this out.

But there is absolutely no forward thinking with this government. Plan B should have been implemented weeks ago as everyone was trying to say, and plans could then have been put in place in an organised and helpful manner.

But no...........all done at the last possible minute, in a rush, on the hoof. Everyone let down by those who are supposed to be our leaders.

****

And as I type these words I hear that the Queen has just cancelled her large Christmas Party at Windsor.

****

17TH DECEMBER

The result of the by-election vote in north Shropshire is a huge swing to the Lib-Dems who win with a majority of 6,000. It is the 7th highest swing in history!! They have had a Tory MP for over 100 years and the previous incumbent Owen Patterson had a majority of 2,000!

How can Boris survive this? Well he is trying hard. He is blaming the media for focussing on the wrong things like illegal parties at Downing Street and sleaze and flat expenses etc. instead of all the wonderful things he is doing like jabbing arms with boosters. But watch this space and believe me when I say his days are numbered.

****

18TH DECEMBER
I think we have all just gone down the rabbit hole.

Read this bit very carefully and try to keep up because I know that, although I can promise you it is factually correct, you will find it impossible to believe.

Over a week ago Johnson ruled that there would be an investigation into the alleged Christmas parties held in Downing Street last year when we were all in lockdown. He was encouraged to appoint an independent outsider to lead this inquiry but no, he decided to appoint Simon Case who is the Cabinet Secretary and the head of the Civil Service. We all thought he would be a sensible and thorough person. In fact **he said he would get the results before Christmas so we were expecting them any day.**

Then today we hear that he has 'recused' himself from the investigation as he discovered that his department had a Christmas party as well!

How could he not know? To me it as though the entire Westminster Village was engaged in one almighty Christmas fest.

****

We have just heard about **another party** at Downing Street! My word what a fun place it is in which to work. This one was in May just after a press conference given by Matt Hancock who at that time was the Health Secretary. He was telling us to always socially distance and only meet up with one other person outdoors.

And then they all went into the Downing Street garden, about 14 of them, and sat around with drinks and food and indeed sat at tables close to each other. How do we all know this? Because **there is a photo**. And who should also be there but our PM and his wife.

Dominic Raab said on the media outlets this morning that actually no rules were broken because it was a continuation of their work meeting and they often went into the garden when the weather was nice. Really? With wine and cheese and the PM's wife? **On a parallel universe maybe.**

****

And Boris who was talking this evening about not introducing more restrictions before Christmas, when asked about this photo said very firmly it was a work meeting....they were working. They really do think we are fools.

****

21ST DECEMBER

For the moment Johnson has stopped giving press conferences. He just leaps into the library at No 10 and speaks straight to camera. So no awkward questions from the press and no more appearances in that press office. The one which cost the tax-payer £2.6 million. (I know you remember!)

He is not bringing in any more restrictions before Christmas. Probably very unwise but he knows he will be trashed by his rebellious backbenchers if he does. **It is probably true to say that he is compromising the nation's health in order to appease the right wing on the backbenches.**

****

22ND DECEMBER

Well yes I think it is true to say that, and the media think it is true to say that, but my word they are saying a great deal more this morning. I hope they keep the papers away from Boris because if he reads even half of what they are saying he will realise he is a dead man walking.

I will just quote a few extracts.

In yesterday's *Guardian* Marina Hyde wrote a long article about the arrogance of the cabinet with their cheese and wine 'gatherings'.

"Why-WHY- were these people not even professionally self-interested enough to realise that as the setters of the rules in a deadly pandemic, it was mission-critical that they adhered at all times to both the letter and spirit of them?" she writes. "**What a stunning failure of the imagination".**

And today Rafael Behr writes again in *The Guardian* that, "The Prime Minister might not have issued an explicit licence to flout lockdown rules in government, but none was needed. He radiates the entitlement to self-gratification and the pomposity that justifies it as fair recompense for a hard day's service to the nation. **It is a particular type of corruption, common to revolutionary regimes that have lost ideological momentum."**

Sam Hancock reports in *The Independent* that, "The Tories have dipped to their lowest approval rating since Boris Johnson prorogued Parliament in 2019 – a move ultimately deemed unlawful by the Supreme Court."

And so it goes on.

****

2022

4TH JANUARY

Well Boris got his Christmas and although new cases are rising every day there are no further restrictions in place. Plan B continues but in order to protect the economy we carry on as before. However because there are so many people isolating due to Covid, the economy is already suffering and schools and the NHS especially are increasingly short staffed. The government is refusing to shorten the isolation time at the moment.

There are so many articles already this week predicting the demise of the Prime Minister that this gives me the opportunity to discuss a possible successor. I am so sorry but **we have to talk about Liz Truss**. She is blatant about her wish to be the next PM and actually the next Margaret Thatcher! She has so many photos of her in so many different guises she is in the media every day. Apparently she has an enormous Union Flag at home so that whenever she goes on zoom she pulls it out behind her. We actually think she wants to be Queen or maybe Emperor of Great Britain.

However she has not covered herself in glory recently as she spent rather a lot of taxpayers' money on entertaining Joe Biden's trade representative. Her officials suggested she went to Quo Vadis in Soho which as Giles Coren points out in *The Times* today is a genuinely great British restaurant where you get value for money for top quality food.

However she explicitly asked that **5 Hertford Street** was booked for the event. Now this is a private members' club which just so happens to be owned by Robin Birley who gave £20,000 to Boris Johnson's leadership campaign, is a UKIP donor and is half-brother of the Environment Minister Zac Goldsmith.

Emails by a civil servant described the club as **"obviously incredibly expensive and more than I understand we'd expect to pay for such a venue."**

The total was said to be in the region of £3,000.

The trouble with getting rid of Johnson is that there are people like this waiting in the wings.

****

6TH JANUARY

Lies, lies and more lies. I thought that lying in Parliament was a criminal offence. But obviously not any more.

Yesterday was PMQs and because Sir Keir was isolating, having tested positive for Covid, Angela Rayner stood in for him. **My word what a fire-cracker!** I thought she was wonderful. She questioned the PM about his words in October when he dismissed fears that prices were on the rise.

When interviewed on Sky News he was asked, "Are you worried about inflation?" He replied that he was focused instead on "robust economic growth". He went on to say that **"people have been worried about inflation for a very long time and those fears have been unfounded".**

As inflation is forecast to hit 6% which will be the highest figure since 1992, when Angela Rayner asked how he could have got it so wrong he said **"Of course I said no such thing** because inflation is always something we have to be careful about."

He went on to falsely accuse the Labour party for wanting new restrictions to combat Covid when the party had not in fact argued for them, and **he said that poverty was down when that is blatantly untrue and it is a fact that numbers living in poverty have risen sharply in recent years.** He also claimed, twice, that the warm homes discount to help with energy bills is worth £140 a week when it is actually £140 a year.

I was listening to all of this and couldn't believe my ears but he blusters on so quickly that his words disappear in the fog and he is on to the next astonishing remark before you can really take it all in. It really is bluster, bluster, bluster and untruths, untruths, untruths. At the end of PMQs Ms Rayner rose again to ask if he "would like to correct the record" but he declined to do so.

So how and when will he be tackled about lying in Parliament?

****

9TH JANUARY

More parties. There are now reports that Johnson and Carrie attended a party at No 10 on the 15th May and the 20th May 2020. This was at a time when we could only meet one other person out doors and we had to stick to social distancing rules.

This is just getting ridiculous. Apparently the one on the 20th May was attended by 40 people in the garden, and the email invitation said BYOB. This, as most of you will know, means bring your own bottle. And also, just after a press conference on the 15th, about 20 met up for cheese and wine and goodness knows what else. We await the inquiry with baited breath.

****

11TH JANUARY

We have all just seen the email invitation! ITV news got hold of it and this is what it says:

"Hi all,

After what has been an incredibly busy period we thought it would be nice to make the most of the lovely weather and have some socially distanced drinks in the No 10 garden this evening. Please join us from 6pm and bring your own booze."

This was sent by Mr. Martin Reynolds the Prime Minister's Private Secretary to over **one hundred employees in Number 10 including the PM's advisors, speech writers and door staff.** Yes you did read that correctly .... Over 100 people were in invited. Over 100!

"But does it really matter as it's a year ago now?" asks my American cousin.

Well yes actually it does and this is why.

The entire UK was in a severe and complete lockdown. At 5pm on the 20th May, Oliver Dowden MP and Minister for Culture gave a press conference in which he said, *"You can meet one person outside of your household in an outdoor, public place provided that you stay two metres apart."*

This party took place **one hour later** and between 30 and 40 people turned up including the PM and his wife.

We are hearing stories of people who, on that very same day, could not visit their dying relatives. Children could not see their dying mothers, grand-children had to wave to grand-parents through windows; weddings and funerals were severely curtailed. **363 people died on that day from Covid 19.**

Schools were closed, retailers were closed, the hospitality sector was closed, hair-dressers were closed. The 'Covid 19 Bereaved for Justice Group' are appalled.

But we now just hear that Martin Reynolds has the full confidence of the Prime Minister and will remain in his role. There were thoughts that he would be the scapegoat for all of this.

12.30 pm. There has just been an urgent question to the Prime Minister in the House of Commons by the opposition party about it all. The opposition benches were absolutely full but the Conservative benches were pretty empty. Not only that but there were no Cabinet members and even worse than that there was no Prime Minister.

As Angela Rayner, still standing in for Sir Kier said, "Where is Boris? He has no official engagements this morning. He can run but he can't hide."

It looked disgraceful. The Paymaster General had been put up to answer the questions. And as the Speaker urged the opposition to be quiet he said he had a difficult job already please don't make it more difficult for him!

Their only answer is always, "we will wait for the results of the official inquiry".

As I mentioned earlier the email was sent to the door staff at Number10. Surely a simple question to them would give us all the answers we need. And who exactly are the "we" in the invitation?

Well it is being said that the Metropolitan Police **are** becoming involved so this is not going away any time soon. It does look as though Boris Johnson broke the lockdown rules probably more than once. In fact as Angela Eagle said perhaps it would be faster if there was an inquiry on the days in Westminster when there **wasn't** a party!

****

12TH JANUARY
So as we await PMQs we reflect on some of the stories we heard last night. One woman told of how she could not go in the ambulance with her mother when her mother was taken into hospital and then died in there alone and that this was at about the time this party was taking place. She was a very gentle and quietly spoken woman and she said,

referring to **Boris** "I hate him. **I know I shouldn't say that and my mother would not want me to say that but I hate him.**"

Another woman from the Covid 19 Justice for the Bereaved Group told us how her fit 54 year old father died without her being able to visit him and how when she and others met Boris Johnson in the garden at No 10 he looked her in the eye and said **he had done everything he possibly could to save him**. These are just two stories and there are of course a legion of others.

We also hear of other stories in a different vane, of students fined thousands of pounds for attending parties and who now think they should all be refunded, and of a publican who had people in his pub, sitting down all socially distanced and masked, watching a football match. Some police had just walked in to do a check when someone scored a goal and everyone jumped up, some on to the tables, and **the publican was fined £1,000**. He paid straight away which brought it down to £500 and everyone chipped in to make £300. But as he said something like this could push him out of business. But so many people were fined exorbitant amounts.

12 MID-DAY PMQS: HOW IS HE GOING TO WRIGGLE OUT OF THIS ONE?

Well the PM starts the procedure with an abject apology. He completely understands and feels everyone's upset and angry and he is deeply sorry for anything at all that he might have done wrong. Obviously the garden at No 10 is his own garden (well for the moment) and he went to the garden at 6pm and stayed for 25 minutes and then returned to his office to work. But yes it was definitely a work event.

Really Prime Minister?

Do you usually issue out invitation by email to over 100 people to bring your own booze and to enjoy the lovely weather to a work event?

Did it not seem a bit excessive that there were long tables laid out with drink and sausage rolls and crisps?

And how was it that witnesses said they saw you with Carrie and that she was drinking gin?

And why did it take so long for you to tell us all this when time and time again when asked, "Were you at this event?" you always just said wait until the result of the investigation?

So you were there, you did break the rules and as nearly everyone who spoke in the Commons today asked **when are you going to resign?**

His answer was to keep saying, "We will wait until the results of the investigation."

****

Aah, and I should have said that Rishi Sunak had a really important appointment in Ilfracombe in Cornwall today so he couldn't be at PMQs. Socially distancing from the Prime Minister Mr Sunak?

****

13TH JANUARY

This is not going to be a good day for our Prime Minister. A bit difficult to know where to start but let's first of all go to *The Times* where they say that **they have had hundreds of letters from their readers telling them their stories of lockdown.**

The headline is **"My husband met his new baby in a car park".** This was about a woman who gave birth completely alone and then saw her husband with her baby in the car park. Another woman had to say good bye to her father, who was in a care home, by video and at the very small funeral could not even hug her bereft mother who had to sit alone. How grand-children had to watch their grandmother dying on zoom and how an elderly man sat in his garden on his birthday and was fined £100 because he had two socially distanced friends rather than the legally allowed one. This was his second birthday in a lockdown and being alone all that time had taken its toll on his mental health. And there are so many stories such as these.

Then we hear from *Times* political writers giving their verdicts on the PM's performance yesterday. Each wrote about 200 words but I just quote a sentence or two.

Matthew Parris talking about the back benchers says, "Here sat his potential executioners. They were largely silent, frozen."

Daniel Finkelstein says, "The questions were devastating and the answers were ridiculous".

Rachel Sylvester says, "All the contrition in the world does not change the reality that he broke the rules."

Iain Martin says, "Putting on his best apology face which will be familiar to assorted women across the capital he said 'I wish things had been done differently that evening'. Indeed there's a phrase for the ages."

Alice Thomson says, "Only his own bully boys or the prefects in the Cabinet could have done for Johnson yesterday and none has stood to rat on him yet. But they will turn on him in the end."

So no-one is impressed with this apology. They feel it is more an apology for being found out rather than doing anything wrong. Indeed we hear that within minutes of giving this apology he was in the Commons tea rooms saying "Sometimes we take credits for things we don't deserve and this time we are taking hits for something we don't deserve." When he spoke to Douglass Ross leader of the Scottish Conservatives he told him that he **"believes he didn't do anything wrong."**

Conservative support is now at a nine-year low. But many are saying that Sir Keir Starmer would much rather keep Johnson in office in order to fight him at the next election than another new leader who might be better.

Don't worry Sir Keir there isn't exactly a stand-out contender that I can see at the moment.

Then there is an article in *The Guardian* by John Crace. He says that the best excuse Johnson has got is to say that **he is even dimmer than we all feared.**

****

14TH JANUARY
I promise you it gets worse.

This morning we hear that there were **two** parties at No 10 Downing Street on 16th April 2021 which was the day before the funeral of the Duke of Edinburgh. Covid restrictions at the time meant that the Queen had to sit on her own without any support from family or friends in St George's Chapel, Westminster and instead of 800 mourners there were just 30. The choir was also limited to just four singers, while the few guests were banned from singing and remained masked throughout the service.

But my word at Downing Street it was party time. There were apparently two leaving parties, one in the basement and one in the regular party venue, the garden. We know all this because we have had a fulsome apology. This has come from James Slack who was the one who was leaving. He is the former director of communications and this what he said:

"This event should not have happened at the time that it did. I am deeply sorry, and take full responsibility,"

Well he is now deputy editor-in-chief at *The Sun* newspaper. So a few stories there Mr. Slack. Who was with you at the party for a start?

More and more details emerge. At the basement party someone turned up the music and acted as DJ. Someone else was sent out with a suitcase and came back with it full of booze. But then they realised there was even more fun to be had in the garden so they went and joined that party and it is said that music and dancing went on late into the night. Apparently one partygoer went on the child's swing that belonged to Wilfred the Johnson's young son and he broke it.

Just to be absolutely clear the government guidance at the time said: "You must not socialise indoors except with your household or support bubble. You can meet outdoors, including in gardens, **in groups of six people or two households."**

These events are a disgrace on so many levels.

The law is being broken again and again as there is such a blatant disregard for the lockdown rules.

The ongoing drinking culture at No 10 would be completely banned in any other business.

There is a complete disrespect for the British public who kept stringently to these rules at great cost to themselves emotionally, mentally and economically, and now disrespect for the Queen personally.

The absence of any action by the police. What were they doing when these parties were blaring away?

Where is the CTV footage for all of this? This is the very centre of our government in the middle of an unprecedented pandemic. Where is the security?

But as both Polly Toynbee and Max Hastings point out in their papers today why are we surprised?

The real culprits are those who voted for Boris Johnson to be their leader knowing that he is only loyal to himself and he would bring the office of Prime Minister into complete and absolute disrepute. A man with a moral vacuum at his centre. A man incapable of changing the way he acts. As Polly Toynbee writes in her last paragraph:

"Tory MPs and members are destined by their UKIP DNA to select one of their own kind. They are no wiser than they were when they made the disgracefully unpatriotic decision to foist a lying, cheating, self-obsessed scoundrel on the country, knowing his every fault and his full unfitness for office. They are most to blame."

Indeed it is not the Conservative party anymore. **It is the UKIP party in all but name.**

And let us remember that Boris Johnson fought the last general election against Jeremy Corbyn. It wasn't that difficult was it?

****

12 midday. Downing Street has just apologised to the Queen for holding two parties the night before her husband's funeral. So they **were** parties then.

My other favourite columnists Matthew Parris and Andrew Rawnsley must be writing and re-writing their weekend articles over and over again. What more can possibly be unearthed about this corrupt and morally bankrupt government?

****

15TH JANUARY
Well we soon found out the answer to that question.

First of all it has transpired that throughout the pandemic there have been regular wine parties every Friday at No 10, known as '**wine-time Fridays'** and encouraged by our PM in order for everyone, after working so hard, to 'let off steam'. There are photos of a wine cooler being delivered to No 10 which will hold 34 bottles of wine and was installed in the press office in early December 2020

A Downing Street insider said '**it was a culture of 3am sessions.**' Apparently people used to sleep off their hangovers on the sofas and would leave a mess for the cleaners to clear up in the morning. It was very obviously a **culture of boozing** and it is also very obvious that it was endorsed at the very top.

It is also very obvious that they take us all for fools. But at the last poll before we knew about the parties on the eve of the Duke's funeral, over 70% polled said that Johnson has not told the truth about the scandal. In other words he lied. Every time a Cabinet minister is asked about it, all they say we must wait for the report from Sue Gray to come out.

The name Sue Gray is being said so often that we are all at screaming pitch every time we hear it. It was due to come out next week but apparently she is so 'blindsided' by all the extra parties she is hearing about that it will probably be the week after next. She also thinks that people are not telling her everything. (Really?)

****

The thing is that we do not need an investigation. We know what went on. They know what went on. We know they know what went on. They know we know they know what went on. They are arrogant, stupid, corrupt and blind. They are all walking like zombies towards the edge of a very steep cliff and there will be no turning back. The bookies have Johnson out by the summer. I have him out by Monday. (Today is Saturday).

But then if you re-read the first few sentences of this chapter you will realise that maybe I am not a brilliant forecaster! But basically if Johnson cannot tell the difference between a party and work then he is not fit to be in charge of anything let alone the country.

****

And then we hear this. Don't hold your breath over the Sue Gray report. In the wonderful *Independent* they have unearthed a story called **'Operation Save Big Dog'**. This is a plan which will endeavour to limit any fallout over Sue Gray's investigation. This is being run by the PM himself as he is drawing up a list of names whose heads could roll in order to save himself. Certain names have been put forward. They are saying that at least one senior political appointee and a senior official must be seen to leave Downing Street, as both groups share the blame.

So there we have it in a nutshell. **A lying prime minister who blames everyone else but never himself.**

There is also a plan for supportive ministers (who?) to take on press interviews emphasising a contrite Prime Minister and listing his achievements (what?) and the difficult choices posed by the pandemic. This is being called **'Operation Red Meat'**. Who on earth dreams up these titles?

So Johnson will announce a booze free work place (in line with most other work places), a two year freeze on the BBC license fee to help the cost of living (but not obviously the BBC), and the military to take over control of illegal immigrants crossing the channel. But most of them are legal immigrants. Covid restrictions will be lifted on 26th January, there will be new plans to tackle the backlog of NHS operations (how?) and there will be extra money for skills and job training for the 1.5 million people out of work or on Universal Credit. (when?) The levelling up white paper will be published at the end of the month. Goodness me he **is** worried.

****

Just a bit of light relief which we are all in need of: David Clark, a former aide to Robin Cook, says that one of the benefits of Brexit is that at least we have got away from the metric tyranny and are finally able to start serving wine by the suitcase again!

****

16TH JANUARY

The editorial in *The Observer* today will make uncomfortable reading for this Prime Minister who thinks he can wriggle his way out of everything. It is damning. As they say, *The Observer* has long believed Johnson to be a man of little integrity, but **even they are shocked at the level of contempt he obviously holds Parliament and the public.** They accuse the Conservative MPs of knowingly imposing on to the country an incompetent, corrupt and rotten prime minister entirely because it suited their narrow interests with no regard for the consequences. *The Observer* calls for Johnson's resignation but say that that alone will not be enough. **"The Conservative party itself must be held accountable for his disastrous premiership"** they write.

****

18TH JANUARY

The headlines today are all about Dominic Cummings saying that he would be prepared to "swear under oath" that he directly warned the Prime Minister not to go ahead with the party on the 20th May 2020. Apparently Cummings told him, **"You've got to get a grip of this madhouse."** But Boris just waved it aside.

Sir Keir is accusing Boris of misleading Parliament and Dominic Raab was asked on the *Today* programme this morning what the consequences would be if the PM was found to have lied to Parliament. Did he answer the question? I really don't know, I had to get on with my life.

The Prime Minister's spokesman issued a blanket denial yesterday that the PM knew anything about any event which breached the lockdown rules. That is completely bonkers. I'm sorry I just do not know of any other suitable word that I can print.

But the net is closing round him.

****

In the editorial of *The Times* today they say **"This is a sorry spectacle.** In a parliamentary system, the Prime Minister needs to show consistency of purpose and adhere to exemplary standards of conduct. Mr. Johnson is failing on both criteria. He is wounded, the cabinet is floundering, and voters have good reason to look on aghast."

William Hague writes, "For a Prime Minister even to come close to ejection from Downing Street by their own party over standards of probity and behaviour is unique. **If he is pushed out he will be an outlier in British political history, sitting in a lonely category of his own."**

These are just two quotes in one newspaper but this is the over- riding tone everywhere. It is being said that Sue Gray's report will be another two weeks before it is published. Frankly I don't think he has that amount of time left.

****

12MID-DAY AND PMQS.
Christian Wakeford the Tory MP for Bury South has just crossed the floor and joined the Labour Party. David Davis has said "You have sat there too long for all the good you have done, in the name of God go." Johnson replies "I don't know what he is talking about". No that is part of the trouble Prime Minister, you don't have a clue.

But we must be aware of the following words from the Third Citizen in *Julius Caesar which are*: '**I fear there will a worse come in his place'.**

Chilling words.

But I find it interesting, Prime Minister, that you don't recognise this quote from Leo Amery to Neville Chamberlain at the beginning of the war. **You wrote a book about Churchill and you mention Leo Amery on page 19.** Surely you must have seen this famous quote somewhere?

He goes on to say "I take full responsibility for everything done throughout the pandemic."

Just as well because you are going to be held to account Mr. Johnson.

****

Camilla Cavendish, who used to work at No 10, has just said in an interview, that she believes there is no way that the PM's Private Secretary could have sent out that email invitation to the party at No 10 without the PM knowing about it. Or if he really didn't know then why on earth not? He obviously is not in charge.

****

20TH JANUARY
The police have said they will not investigate these parties unless they have sufficient evidence.

Now you need to know that 'Led by Donkeys' is an activist group formed by four people initially to protest against Brexit. Today they have parked a van outside Scotland Yard and there is a huge television screen on the side of the van. Showing on the screen is a spoof scene from *'Line of Duty'*. It is about a 5 minute read so I will just give you the general gist of it.

"Who exactly does the Met Police work for ma'am? (Cressida Dick head of the Met police). **Our citizens, or Boris Johnson?"**

They say that the police say they won't investigate because there is an "absence of evidence".

But 'Led by Donkeys' say that surely it is the job of the police to gather the evidence. They then give all the evidence that it is there for all to see.

It finishes by quoting from the 'Line of Duty' and says **"When did we stop caring about truth and responsibility?"**

It is all up there in large subtitles for passers-by to see!

****

And this afternoon there are more appalling allegations at Westminster. William Wragg, a senior Conservative MP and the Chairman of the Commons Public Administration Committee, and one of the rebels, has claimed that whips have threatened to withdraw government funding from the constituencies of rebellious MPs.

In fact Christian Wakeford the MP who deflected to Labour yesterday was told **that plans for a new high school in his constituency could be scrapped unless he voted a certain way.** And it is being said that this threat came from.......drum roll.......Gavin Williamson. Oh goodness do we really have to mention him again?

Others have backed up these claims and so they have been told that they must report this to the police as it would seem to **constitute blackmail.** Mr. Wragg also claims that some in Government have **considered leaking harmful stories to the press about rebellious MPs and their families.**

Speaker Sir Lindsay Hoyle has warned government whips and special advisers that they are "not above the criminal law".

In a statement in the Commons, he said: "There are allegations about the conduct of whips and special advisers working for ministers.

"While the whipping system is long-established, it is of course a contempt to obstruct members in a discharge of their duty or to attempt to intimidate a member in their Parliamentary conduct by threats."

Just as you think it can't get any worse.

Another senior Tory MP told a BBC commentator that they are all just waiting for the Sue Gray report and that is a very, very dangerous place to be.

They all thought yesterday that there was a slight lull in the proceedings. I don't think so.

****

21ST JANUARY
We are hearing that Sue Gray has seen an email warning Johnson that inviting 100 people to drinks in his back garden would be against the lockdown rules.

It would appear that she is investigating 10 illegal parties!

We see Johnson visiting hospitals in North London and then in Taunton in Somerset. This was a round trip of 300 miles or so. In fact our PM seems to prefer to be out of No 10 and out and about. He has averaged more than 1,000 miles a month on public trips around the country visiting hospitals, schools and Hindu Temples! Anywhere but in his place of work. All good photo opportunities though of course.

Rebel MPs say they have text messages and a recorded message from threatening chief Whips.

Tony Blair says that he fears that Britain is heading for a 1970's style decline.

Meanwhile Russian troops are amassing on the borders of Ukraine.

****

And I read today that Downing Street spoke to the Queen shortly before the funeral of the Duke of Edinburgh offering her a temporary easing of the current lockdown restrictions in order for there to be more than the 30 mourners attending. These restrictions were due to be lifted in a few weeks anyway so it would just mean the Queen would be a few weeks ahead of anyone else.

However the Queen turned down the offer, saying it would be unfair to those grieving for loved ones in lockdown. **The palace said she wanted to set an example rather than be the exception to the rules.** This story first emerged in the Private Eye magazine.

****

It was just seven days later when a suitcase was packed with booze and not one but two parties were held at No 10.

****

22ST JANUARY
William Wragg has contacted the **Metropolitan Police** in order to ask them to investigate the allegations of bullying, threats and blackmail by MPs of those who are thinking of writing letters of no confidence in the Prime Minister.

****

.

So Boris will spend this **weekend holed up at Chequers trying to find ways to shore up support for his troubled premiership.** He is calling on MPs who seem to be wavering and will try to persuade them to give him their support.

Other cabinet members are also expected to make public interventions on his behalf to defend his record as Prime Minister.

I would have thought any serious Prime Minister would be spending this weekend thinking about the NHS, refugees, Ukraine, customs regulations, the criminal justice system, energy prices, school funding, Nazanin Zaghari-Ratcliffe and a myriad other vital problems facing the UK just now.

But no it is now, and always has been, all just about him.

******

23RD JANUARY

The Sue Gray investigation has been given **security data and a detailed log of staff movements in and out of No 10** at the time of the parties. There is also talk of a party or parties being held in Boris and Carrie's flat involving some of her close friends.

The Sunday papers are all over the futility and incompetence and deceit of our Prime Minister.

In *The Observer* editorial they begin by saying, "Are there no tactics to which a disgraced and unpopular Prime Minister will not sink in his desperate attempt to cling on against the odds? For Boris Johnson it would seem not."

They go on to say in a long editorial, "Everything Johnson and his government are now doing is driven by panic and narrow political interests. **Nothing is sacred, everything is fair game.**"

William Keegan in *The Observer* likens him to Falstaff. He writes about "Henry V in Shakespeare's *Henry IV, Part Two* in addressing Falstaff: 'I know thee not old man. Fall to thy prayers/ How ill white hairs become a fool and jester'".

And in another long article in *The Sunday Times* he quotes a parliamentary aide as saying, "At some point in politics you always lose the benefit of the doubt and I think that this might be the time for him. **That ability to glide through scrapes has gone.**"

****

On it goes I'm afraid. We know that the Treasury has said that it is not even going to try to claw back the billions of pounds lost in fraudulent claims and during the furlough scheme.

And so Lord Agnew, a Treasury minister, this afternoon resigned from the dispatch box saying that the Treasury "appears to have no knowledge or little interest in the consequences of fraud to our economy or our society," adding that a mix of "arrogance, indolence and ignorance freezes the government machine." He added that, "Downing Street could cut 1p off income tax if it tackled Covid fraud properly."

If that is not enough for one day it has also been discovered that **Boris Johnson had a birthday party in Number 10 on 19th June 2020.** About 30 people attended this party organised by his wife. They sang 'happy birthday' to him. **This was at a time when children's birthdays were cancelled and choirs were told they could not sing.**

It is obviously one long party in Downing Street.

Defending his position Boris says that he was only there for 10 minutes and they were all work people. What........his wife and their interior decorator?

Would you like some more stories? Well it is only 9.30 pm so I am sure that before the evening is over more revelations will be winging their way to the media outlets. I will let you know!

****

25TH JANUARY
Well nothing new last night, but this morning............we hear **that the Met police are now investigation all these parties.**

This could mean that Sue Gray's report is now delayed.

So Boris Johnson our Prime Minister is now under a police investigation.

Labour have asked for an urgent question in the Commons this afternoon.

****

But this afternoon we hear that the Met have no objections to the report by Sue Gray continuing and so her report could be published imminently. The PM could be making a statement to the House after PMQs tomorrow.

We know the truth already but it will be interesting to see what is said. We already hear some very strange statements from those trying to defend the indefensible.

****

26TH JANUARY

Well we are still waiting for the Sue Gray report. We were told it would be here this afternoon but no sign of it yet.

PMQs was the usual shambles full of bluster and bravado from this Prime Minister.

"I'd prefer to be led by a lawyer than a liar" said a Labour MP. He was forced to withdraw this remark but we all heard it and it is all over Twitter!

The Tories just don't get it.

"He's been ambushed by a cake" said someone else.

Rees-Mogg kept saying afterwards it was just a drink and some cake at his work place.

But all the stories of what was happening to people all over the UK on the various party days are heart breaking.

A young girl called Josephine wrote to the PM in March 2020 saying she had cancelled her seventh birthday party to help keep people safe. He wrote back saying, "Well done! You are setting a great example".

Which just shows how much more mature a seven year old is than the 56 year old Prime Minister.

****

Why does he smirk all the time and shake his head and make ill-conceived jokes, which encourages all his back benchers to laugh uproariously? They treat it all as a game.

And the lies the PM told at PMQs today are quite extraordinary. He must know everything he claims can all be checked out, but he spits it all out at top speed, bluster, bluster, bluster, and presumably hopes that no-one will notice.

He said that ours was the fastest growing economy in the G7.

Not true. Although the economy grew over the past year between the third quarter of 2020 and the second quarter of 2021 this is because the GDP fell dramatically during the pandemic. But we are fifth and well behind France and Germany if you compare the third and second quarters.

He said that Sir Keir Starmer had wanted to take us all into lockdown over last Christmas.

Not true. He had welcomed the further restrictions so long as there was support for schools and businesses.

He said there were 400,000 more people on the pay roll.

Not true. There are 500,000 fewer people in work than before the pandemic. The figures to which he always refers to do not include the self-employed.

He said that Labour wanted to abolish Universal Credit. How can he say that? **Not true, not true, not true**. It was the Tories who abolished the £20 uplift to Universal Credit and who are now saying that if people on benefits have not found work within four weeks instead of three months they have to take any job available **even if it is outside their work experience or miles away from where they live**. Labour want to over-haul the Universal Credit system so that the low income workers can earn more before having their welfare benefits cut.

He said they had got all the big calls right.

Which ones were those Prime Minister? Have I sent you a copy of my book 'Beneath the Bluster. A Diary of Despair?' No I don't think I have. It will be in the post forthwith. I think I know your address ....for now.

How is he allowed to get away with this in Parliament? Members are not allowed to call him a liar but he can lie in the Commons with impunity over and over again.

****

27TH JANUARY

Theresa May has broken her silence on the shenanigans at No 10 in a letter to her local newspaper the *Maidenhead Advertiser*.

She wrote that, "**I have said previously that it is vital that those who set the rules, follow the rules. Nobody is above the law. This is important for ensuring the necessary degree of trust between the public and Government. Like so many, I was angry to hear stories of those in Number 10, who are responsible for setting the coronavirus rules, not properly following the rules. If there is** evidence of deliberate or premeditated wrongdoing, I expect full accountability to follow."

****

And then late this evening we are hearing from *The Independent* that a heavily censured version of the Sue Gray report is to be presented to Boris Johnson "shortly". Apparently a source close to the investigation team said that in line with the request of Scotland Yard, the report will be stripped of details which the Metropolitan Police fear could compromise their separate inquiry into **potential criminal behaviour.**

The police also say that they will conclude their report as soon as possible.

So it does look as though there are serious consequences ahead.

But the confusion and uncertainty and lack of clarity has already caused a lot of disquiet and accusations of cover-ups, corruption and whitewash. As someone asked on Twitter how long before we are officially called a failed state?

It is like living through a nightmare. So many of my friends do not watch the news any more. I just feel that the whole country is ground down. We are ground down by the pandemic, by this government, by grief and bereavement, by the bureaucracy of Brexit, by the long waiting lists for operations, by long Covid, and by the spiralling rise of the cost of living.

The pain of yesterday, the confusion of today and the uncertainty of tomorrow. We desperately need to do better than this.

****

30TH JANUARY

You might remember the name Jennifer Arcuri. She was the mistress of Boris Johnson when he was London Mayor and she was given access to foreign trade missions led by him, and sponsorship for her events business raised concerns about conflicts of interest. She received £126,000 of public money in the form of grants for her technology business and event sponsorship, and received access to three foreign trade missions led by Johnson.

The Greater London Authority is overseeing two separate investigations into their affair. Arcuri is cooperating fully and has handed over hundreds of pages of notes and documents. **Johnson is facing a potential criminal offence for misconduct in public office.**

****

Reports in the Sunday papers today are saying that **Number 10 is a security risk** as secret documents have been left all over the flat for anybody to see. The PM is now banned by his aides from taking top-secret documents to the flat. There was one time when a senior political aide saw Carrie Johnson and her friends relaxing while the red box sat open, and highly classified "strap" documents were left lying around. These are easily recognised as they are printed on pink paper.

There is also concern about Johnson's relaxed attitude towards the security of the red box. A Downing Street official said that when the PM was working at weekends, "It would be outside the flat in the morning and still there in the evening. He wouldn't have touched it."

And when he was Foreign Secretary under Theresa May it was claimed that she had to order some intelligence to be withheld from him after he earned a reputation for letting things slip out.

Lord Blunkett, David Blunkett a previous Home Secretary has said that **Boris Johnson is a security risk.**

****

31ST JANUARY
11.21 am. Well, well, well, here we go. An 'updated' report has been handed to the PM by Sue Gray. We are all wondering what exactly the word 'updated' means.

Here is the statement from a Cabinet Office spokesperson: *We can confirm that Sue Gray has provided an update on her investigations to the prime minister.*

Andrew Sparrow of *The Guardian* writes that "the description of the report as an "update" implies that Gray definitely does not see it as the finished version (she has had to leave out the most incriminating material at the request of the police), and perhaps that she does envisage publishing a final version once the police inquiry is over. The use of the word "update" rather than report may also imply that the document coming today is even more minimal than anticipated."

Her report is expected to be made public within hours and the PM is likely to make a statement to the Commons at about 3.30 pm which will then be followed by questions from MPs.

Well the PM is on a visit to the Tilbury Docks this morning in his usual hard hat and high-vis jacket. Apparently he has three photographers on his pay roll paid for by the tax payer. Is this usual for a PM?

I think most people are expecting this bit of the report to be a complete whitewash. There are rumours that it has been cut down from 25 pages to 5.

****

2 PM
Well we have now all read the Sue Gray report.

I have this report in front of me and although it is 11 pages long the actual findings take up about a page and a half.

She investigated 16 parties of which 12 are being investigated by the police.

This is the crux of what she says.

Some of the behaviour surrounding these gatherings is difficult to justify.

At least some of the gatherings represent a serious failure to observe not just the high standards expected of those working at the heart of Government but also of the standard expected of the entire British population at the time

She said that *there was a distinct lack of leadership and judgment by different parts of Number 10 and the Cabinet Office at different times.*

There was a culture of excess drinking which is not appropriate in any professional workplace at any time.

The parties were in breach of Covid regulations and was not what was expected in the rest of the country.

A number of the parties should not have taken place and others should not have been allowed to continue.

Some staff wanted to raise the alarm but didn't feel able to do so.

These parties and this culture was spread over a period of 20 months.

She investigated 16 parties of which 12 are now being investigated by the police.

The police have said that they have been handed over 300 photographs and 500 documents.

****

So what happened in the Commons this afternoon?

The PM made a very hurried statement full of his usual bluster in which there was "I am very sorry" in there somewhere.

Sir Keir made an impassioned statement which was the best I have ever heard from a leader of an Opposition.

Ian Blackford leader of the SNP accused the PM of lying four times and three times Blackford was asked to withdraw his remarks. After the fourth refusal to withdraw his remarks the Speaker then ordered him to leave the Common as he was duty bound to do.

So you are kicked out of Parliament if you tell the truth but can stay in with impunity if you lie. Watching him leaving the building we saw people lining up to shake his hand and congratulate him.

Then in one of Johnson's rants he accused Keir Starmer of being responsible, when he was head of CPS, for **failing to prosecute Jimmy Savile**. I have no idea what that was about or what the relevance was.

But we then hear from Nazir Afzal, a former chief Crown prosecutor, for the North west that, "It's not true. I was there. Keir Starmer had nothing to do with the decisions taken. On the contrary, he supported me in bringing 100s of child sex abusers to justice." He calls the PM a disgrace.

Why does Johnson get away with lying in the Commons? Every time he opens his mouth there are fact checkers who check out every statement he makes. And what on earth was he doing talking about Jimmy Savile?

As the afternoon went on the Tory benches got emptier and emptier. I just hope they were sending letters into the 1922 committee.

He cannot survive this surely. And there is a by-election on Thursday at Leigh on Sea. **I will be there!!** Well in theory anyway!!

****

Meanwhile tensions are rising on the **Russian- Ukraine border**. The PM had to cancel a call to President Putin because he was defending the indefensible in PMQs.

And Liz Truss has been trashed by the Russia's foreign ministry spokesperson for **not knowing the difference between the Baltic and the Black Sea. It came as another senior Kremlin official dismissed British diplomacy as "absolutely worthless".**

****

3RD FEBRUARY

1.45pm and we hear that Boris Johnson has backed down over his false claim about Sir Keir Starmer. Having refused to withdraw his comments many MPs, and also victims of Jimmy Savile, rounded on him in disgust at these remarks. He is now admitting that Sir Keir had nothing to do with those decisions. He is in Blackpool today and when asked, he told the television cameras, "Let's be absolutely clear, I'm talking not about the Leader of the Opposition's personal record when he was DPP **and I totally understand that he had nothing to do personally with those decisions."** I think he will have to apologise to the House of Commons. We hear that more letters are being sent in.

****

Oh my word what is going on? There have been **four resignations** from No.10.

First out of the door was Munira Mirza, who had been with the PM for 14 years all through his time as Mayor of London. She is highly regarded by Tory colleagues and is extremely clever and very effective in everything she does. Apparently she had asked Johnson to apologise for his scurrilous remarks about Sir Keir Starmer and when he refused to do so she had had enough. She made her resignation email public and it is seen as an absolutely shocking criticism of the PM.

But then three others chose to leave or to "fall on their swords" as they had been involved in the party-gate scandal.

Jack Doyle, communications director, Martin Reynolds, Principle Private Secretary and Dan Rosenfield, chief of staff, all walked out of the door of No 10.

Well Johnson said he would clean up his office but this is all exceedingly quick!

I believe some are staying until replacements can be found but who on earth would want to go into the poisonous and shambolic atmosphere of Downing Street?

We wait to see what tomorrow brings.

****

4TH FEBRUARY

Well it brings another resignation! Elena Narozanski has followed Munira Mirza out of the No 10 policy unit.

It is only 9am so I will let you know if anyone else goes during the course of the day.

Meanwhile there was a by-election yesterday in Southend West which was called because of the fatal stabbing of Sir David Amess when seeing his constituents in his surgery. This was a shocking and brutal attack on a much loved and respected MP and out of respect for this situation the main opposition parties stood aside.

It was inevitable therefore that the Tory candidate would win which she did with 86% of the vote.

However the turnout was only 24% which is reportedly the lowest turnout since 1945.

There were 1,083 spoilt papers with many messages for Johnson scrawled all over them.

One sad "Boris do a Brexit –get out" whilst another said "Get Boris out".

Will he get the message? Well I can tell you now that he won't. He will smirk and joke and say, what people want is for me to get on with the job of coming through Covid and making this the best country in the world. **Because he is in a Parallel Universe.**

****

But yesterday we saw Rishi Sunak, our Chancellor, walking gently up to the post of Prime Minister. For be in no doubt, that is where he wishes to be.

He distanced himself from the PM's remarks about Starmer. "Well I would not have said that" he said whilst just stopping short of saying that the PM should apologise. He spoke very well and looked very smart against the blue background of the press room. Exceedingly polite to the Press. He always wears a black mask, the only Tory I think to do so these days. He is watching and waiting and biding his time. I could be wrong but time will tell.

But he is not for me. I remember when Sir Kevan Collins, the education tsar appointed by the PM to ramp up our schools and colleges, resigned when the Chancellor refused to give him the money he asked for. **Our children are never the priority of this government and this was a disgraceful decision by the Chancellor.**

****

6TH FEBRUARY

A Tory donor is demanding today that the Conservatives give him his money back. Telecoms businessman Mohammed Amersi **wants £200,000 returned to him after complaining that he was excluded from elite political events and was never given auction prizes he had bid for at fund- raising dinners.**

He had won a breakfast with the PM, a Japanese meal with Jeremy Hunt (who has a Japanese wife) and a "magic show" with Penny Mordaunt. (What?)

All this came to £150,000 and he had paid £50,000 for membership of the Tory donor club the Leader's Group. He had had none of these prizes and is very cross. He criticises the Conservative party co-chairman, Ben Elliot and says, "You cannot ask donors for support, expect them to purchase auction prizes, keep their money and then, like rubbish collectors, consign them to the wastepaper bin."

Well this is Boris Johnson's Conservative party we are talking about.

I say to everybody who has a few thousands of pounds to give away, please, please, please give it to a children's charity. Maybe you do as well of course but just give all of it and let the political parties receive the minimum. I promise you the rewards will be far greater than any 'special' meeting with a senior Tory.

Actually the thought of breakfast with the Prime Minister is too horrible to contemplate.

****

Also reported today is the **collapse of a scheme which was announced by Boris Johnson when he was Mayor of London.** It was a flagship £1.7 billion scheme for Chinese investors to transform east London docks into the capital's third financial district. It was the biggest commercial property deal he had announced during his time as mayor and he pledged it would be, wait for it, "a beacon for eastern investors". It would create thousands of jobs and bring in billions of pounds of investment for the UK economy.

Well there has been no significant work on the site over the last two years and the scheme appears to be on the brink of collapse. The Greater London Authority confirmed last week that a "final termination notice" had been served on the developer because of delays.

Caroline Pidgeon, a Lib Dem London assembly member, said, **"Boris Johnson's record as mayor of London often seemed as though he thought that vital rules of fairness and procurement and setting of contracts were something he could ignore. His record.... should be examined as closely as his record as Prime Minister."**

****

8TH FEBRUARY

There was the most appalling behaviour last night outside Westminster after a mob of anti-vaccers surrounded Sir Keir Starmer and shouted abuse at him and David Lammy who was walking with him at the time. They pushed and shoved and shouted **"traitor" and "Jimmy Savile" and "paedophile"**. This was a direct consequence of the Prime Minister's remarks in the Commons last week when he falsely accused the Leader of the Opposition of failing to prosecute Jimmy Savile when head of the CPS. The police had to bundle Sir Keir into a police car and drive him to safety.

Labour and others are accusing the PM of inciting the mob to violence.

On the radio this morning we heard from the husband and the sister of Jo Cox, the MP who was murdered so brutally in 2016. The Speaker also issued a statement and they were all saying that words have consequences and the poisonous and toxic atmosphere in the Commons spreads down throughout the whole of society.

The PM had said these words in the very week that there was the by-election because of the fatal stabbing of an MP in his constituency office.

The PM has refused to apologise saying that he has "other stuff" to be getting on with.

I was speaking to Sir Keir's office this morning and they said that their inbox was absolutely full with support for him.

It is difficult to know how low Boris Johnson has to go before he can be got rid of.

****

9TH FEBRUARY

John Armitage, who has given over £3.1 million to the Conservative party over the years, is another voice suggesting that Boris Johnson should resign.

He told the Tories that he would not be giving the party any more financial support as things stood. He said that he thought that the Prime Minister was "past the point of no return". He added: **"I find the lack of honour inherent in modern politics incredibly distressing."**

So do we all.

****

10TH FEBRUARY

50 people in Downing Street, including the PM and his wife, are being questioned by the police over lockdown breaching parties beginning in a few days' time. They will be sent questionnaires which will have "formal legal status", in other words as though they are under caution. That means that they have to tell the truth. That will be a novel experience for our Prime Minister.

****

Scotland Yard are also saying today that Labour lawyers have asked them to investigate the **funding of the Downing Street flat** over concerns that there was "reasonable suspicion" it had broken anti-bribery laws. I covered this at length in my first book and it is still clouded under a distinct lack of transparency. Scotland Yard have said that they will make "an appropriate response in due course."

****

And this evening we hear that Dame Cressida Dick the Met Commissioner has resigned. I was delighted when she was appointed as the first woman to hold that position but was not impressed when I heard her speak at an AGM of the Howard League. She seemed to have no idea of the League's ethos and was very dismissive of young offenders. So I am glad that she is going.

****

13TH FEBRUARY

There is an article in *The Observer* today by Nick Cohen which should be required for every member of the Conservative party. Nearly every paragraph begins with the same identical sentence. **"This is a government that lies."** Two begin with **"It lies because..."** and the last paragraph ends with, **"It lied last week as it lies every week. It lies to the Queen. It lies to Parliament. It likes to the electorate. It lies to itself. It lies as a matter of policy. It lies as a matter of course. It lies when it doesn't need to lie. It lies because it doesn't know what else to do. It lies because it is all it can do. This is a government that lies."**

And we all know that this is so true. So why is this government still in power? Why does the Speaker of the House not call it out? Why do the few honest and decent Tory MPs put up with it? How far down the road to corruption and degradation do we have to be dragged before someone somewhere calls "time"?

****

23RD FEBRUARY

And so, as Russia continues to make preparations to invade Ukraine and in actual fact has already crossed the border in two areas, we watch our Prime Minister and Foreign Secretary in dismay and disbelief.

Liz Truss did the media rounds this morning and the PM took PMQs as usual and both tried to distance themselves from Russian money in the Conservative party.

****

24TH FEBRUARY...............RUSSIA INVADES UKRAINE

A few sanctions are put in place but much more needs to be done. Ukrainians are putting up a massive fight, the Russian people are protesting throughout Russia, China has abstained from approving this invasion and we are all hoping that Putin has made a massive miscalculation.

But I will continue to write about the actions of our government so that they do not get away with hiding behind a war in Europe.

****

25TH FEBRUARY

Today we hear that the UK Statistics Authority has once again accused **Boris Johnson of lying in Parliament**. Amongst all his bluster and babbling he continues to boast that, "there are **430,000 more people in employment** than there were before the pandemic."

Every time he spouts this, and I have heard it so often, I scream at the television "RUBBISH. UNTRUE"

He is, in fact, only counting people on payrolls. Once you include the self-employed and off-payroll workers the real total is **600,000 fewer** than before the pandemic. **The fact-checking charity 'Full Fact' said this was the seventh time he has made this claim.** And Downing Street failed to correct the false claim today despite saying this week that the Prime Minister "corrects the record when appropriate."

When exactly is that then? I have never once heard him "correct the record" or, in layman's terms, apologise for telling a lie.

****

19TH MARCH

In a speech to the Conservatives spring conference in Blackpool, Boris Johnson **compares the war in Ukraine with Brexit**. It is the most disgusting thing I have ever heard. Just when you think he can't go any lower he says something like this. He also says that Labour would have flown the white flag by now. Someone has to stop his man. **Please.**

****

29TH MARCH

The Metropolitan Police **issued 20 fixed penalty notices** today to people in Downing Street who had broken the law by attending illegal gatherings during lockdown. Apparently they do not have to disclose the names of those who have been fined.

Some ministers are saying that Johnson must sack them but at the moment our PM is finding it very difficult to actually utter the words "broken the law".

Interesting to just note that these fines are for £50 which I think compares badly with, just one example, the £200 fines issued to those who attended the silent vigil held outside under strict Covid rules for Sarah Everard.

****

Also today it was the **first anniversary of the National Covid Memorial Wall** which is a memorial to all those who have died of Covid. Every death is represented by a hand-painted red or pink heart which is placed there by a relative. This wall is outside St Thomas's hospital on the South Bank of the Thames opposite the Houses of Parliament and is a third of a mile long. Hundreds of grief-stricken relatives gathered there today to pay tribute and remember them.

I would have thought that it would have been appropriate for Boris Johnson to have gone and paid his respects. Or any minister for that matter. But no. Today our Prime Minister had invited all 360 Conservative MPs to a dinner at the Crown Plaza Hotel just down the road from Westminster. After a photo shoot they all ambled along and walked in front of the many bereaved relatives who stood there holding up photos of their dead loved ones. Not one spoke to them or even looked them in the eye. "Going to another party are you then?" one of them shouted out. "Shame on you" shouted another.

Oh my goodness no it wasn't a party. Michael Fabricant was laughing and grinning and said, "No it is a dinner. It will be loads of fun." And Andrea Leadsome said the same. No wonder they were all booed. But Johnson, Patel and Sunak went by car and entered through a back entrance. I wonder why.

But it is interesting to remember that on this day last year **Sir Keir Starmer visited the mural which he described as a "remarkable memorial".** He then called on Johnson to visit it and to engage personally with the families of the deceased. Johnson later visited the wall for "quiet reflection" without meeting bereaved families, which a co-founder of the group said was "a late evening visit under cover of darkness … a cynical and insincere move that is deeply hurtful".

****

30TH MARCH

PMQs today was shambolic. If I was feeling generous I would say that the Tories were all hungover from the party last night but sadly this is their normal behaviour.

I was so angry that I dashed off the following email to the Speaker.

I am very perturbed by the quality of debate and behaviour at PMQs. How is it that the PM is allowed to call the leader of the opposition "Captain Hindsight" rather than the Honourable Member for Holborn and St Pancras?

How is the PM allowed to lie every single PMQs without being held accountable? Yesterday he said that over 200,000 children had been lifted out of poverty when the truth is that over 100,000 children have fallen into poverty.

He also keeps saying there are more people in employment than before the pandemic. This is also a lie.

And is it acceptable to comment on the leader of the SNP in the way he does by referring to his weight?

He never answers the question but just trots out the same old insults and untruths to the opposition.

The braying and jeering from the Conservative benches is disgusting.

The whole session is a complete shambles and an insult to the British public.

It is shameful and I ask you to please hold them to account and try to instil some order and dignity and intelligence to the whole procedure.

Well I just have to do something!

****

31ST MARCH

Well, well we are used to Johnson's screeching U-turns when he is in a spot of bother but today he has excelled himself and **done a double U-turn.**

We all need to concentrate to follow this one.

In last year's Queen's speech Johnson **promised to ban gay conversion therapy** -- whose adherents claim can change someone's sexual orientation or gender identity – but which has been proved to be extremely harmful, especially to young people.

But last night ITV broke the news that he **was going to ditch this promise,** giving the excuse that they had to cut down on legislation.

Oh dear that did not go down at all well. Just hours later **he changed course at top speed** after a furious backlash from campaigners, MPs and the media although apparently the latest proposals won't cover Trans people.

Questions are being asked about Johnson's judgement and the state of the Downing Street operation.

I think the answers are there in full view and if you have read this book together with the previous book you will know what they are.

****

Johnson hosted a canape and champagne reception for party donors at Claridges today.

******

3RD APRIL

We are getting news that there were yet **more parties** actually on the terrace and in the bars of the House of Commons which were attended by ministers, MPs and their staff during lockdown.

In fact there appears to be a drinking culture in the Commons to the present day. Guidance has been handed out to MPs warning them not to fall asleep in their offices because they have had too much to drink and so miss the last train home. The Speaker is launching a crackdown on the excessive intake of alcohol as **several senior politicians and their staff have recently had to be escorted from the premises because of raucous behaviour and drunkenness.**

No wonder we are in such a mess. There is no governance going on at all. A party at the Crown Plaza, a party at Claridges and a party every night in the House of Commons.

They are now all off on their holidays presumably having parties wherever they go. **It is obviously the only way they can all deal with the fact that they have a PM and a Cabinet who are completely out of it: ignorant, incompetent, immoral and idiotic.**

****

There is more. Helen MacNamara was the **director general for propriety and ethics in the Cabinet Office** between 2018 and 2020. Yes you read that correctly. **This government had someone in charge of propriety and ethics.**

She has just apologised after receiving a fine from the police for attending a party in the Cabinet Office during lockdown. *The Telegraph* reported that it was a leaving do and it had become a **"raucous" karaoke party at which there was a drunken brawl.** This had taken place on the evening before the funeral of the Duke of Edinburgh when singing by the small congregation was not allowed.

****

Oh but wait a moment, Jacob Rees-Mogg has just been interviewed by James O'Brien of **LBC**. He was asked if he thought the PM had broken any rules and he said that, no, he didn't think so and we need to look carefully at the rules. He wants to tear up the rules and if poor Boris was given incorrect information about parties then he did not deliberately mislead Parliament. We need to contextualise all of this he said. There is a dreadful war going on in Europe and this is not the most important issue in the overall scheme of things.

Well the member of the public who was asking him questions was not impressed and he recounted his experience of looking at his grand-father through a glass screen when he was very sick. "Stop taking the British public for fools" he said.

They will never ever admit that they broke the law and will say anything to keep Johnson in power. All of them are liars.

James O'Brien put his head in his hands at one point and kept saying, "you couldn't make it up."

Basically they are concerned, worried and actually sure that the PM will get a fixed penalty fine and so they are rehearsing his and their defence. He, Johnson, will attempt to shrug off any fine as he did with all his student parking fines collected years ago which he always refused to pay. But a fine will confirm that he broke the law. If he is allowed to continue in the highest post in the land we will all be tainted by the immorality of this government.

****

12TH APRIL
BREAKING NEWS!

2.45pm and we have just heard that Boris Johnson, Rishi Sunak and Carrie Johnson are all being given fixed penalty notices by the Metropolitan police for breaking lockdown rules.

This is the first time a serving Prime Minister has ever been found guilty of breaking the law.

There is so much anger from other party leaders not only about the breaking of the rules but also about his lying to Parliament.

Sir Keir Starmer said: "Boris Johnson and Rishi Sunak have broken the law and repeatedly lied to the British public. They must both resign."

Also calling for their resignations are Ed Davey, Nicola Sturgeon and Ian Blackford.

'Bereaved Families for Justice' are also very angry once more. There is an article in *The Guardian* today by Fran Hall, who is the CEO of the Good Funeral Guide and who lost her husband during lockdown. She was invited with others to go to meet the PM at Downing Street and they were each given a few minutes to talk about the people they had lost.

" I've told my story to so many, and it's so shocking it never fails to affect people, but I could see no flicker of compassion or hurt behind Boris Johnson's eyes." she writes. "For whatever reason, these politicians and advisers thought they were untouchable by the virus and public opinion"

There are calls for the recall of Parliament as they are all on the Easter Recess at the moment.

6pm and we have just heard Boris Johnson read out a statement in which he apologises profusely but lists everything he had to do that day, working flat out from 7.30 in the morning, (I don't think so) popping in to this 'gathering' for 10 minutes for one drink and some birthday cake (it was his birthday) and **he really did not think he was breaking the law. But the police have just confirmed that he had.**

Michael Fabricant, MP, enthusiastically pointed out, it was just like nurses and teachers stopping off in a staff room for a cup of tea with their colleague at the end of a busy day.

Well nurses and teachers have reacted angrily to that one and Pat Cullen the General Secretary and Chief Executive of the Royal College of Nursing has written a strong letter to Mr. Fabricant with a copy to the chair of the Conservative party, Oliver Dowden.

As she says towards the end of her letter, "There isn't a site in England that would allow alcohol on the premises for any professional to consume during working hours."

She goes on to say, "As frontline professionals, still dealing with the implications of the pandemic – **understaffed, underpaid, overworked, exhausted, burnt out and still holding it together while doing the best we can for our patients, it is utterly demoralising— and factually incorrect-- to hear you suggest that our diligent, safety critical profession can reasonably be compared to any elected official breaking the law at any time."**

As she says at the end of a busy day often well beyond their paid shift, nurses stripped, showered and struggled home exhausted before collapsing into bed.

Also, Mr. Fabricant, most schools actually remained closed at that time (19th June 2020) and did not reopen before the summer holidays. It was **LOCKDOWN. That is the whole point.** And head teachers and teachers unions are venting their anger on Twitter today.

How dare he say something so stupid and ignorant.

The BBC went to Yorkshire to ask the public up there what they thought of these fines.

Well you needed to block your ears if you were a Johnson supporter.

They don't mince their words in Yorkshire!

****

13TH APRIL
Neither Johnson nor Sunak will resign.

Questions are being asked about the amount of the fines being issued. **Only £50?**

Chris Bryant, Labour MP for Rhonda, says that a university constituent of his was fined £2,100 for attending a party.

Someone is also saying that if they had known it would cost them just them £50 in order to visit their dying father for 10 minutes they would have visited him and paid up.

Then we see an old clip of Priti Patel talking to camera and saying, **"We will be introducing a new £800 fine for those attending house parties which will double for each repeat offence to a maximum level of £6,400. These fines will apply to those illegal gatherings of more than 15 people in homes. The science is clear. Such irresponsible behaviour poses a significant threat to public health. Not only to those in attendance but also to our wonderful police officers who attend these events to shut them down."**

Well, well that is very interesting. Boris Johnson, Rishi Sunak and all the other party-goers in Downing Street obviously didn't get the memo.

****

This evening we hear about the **resignation of Lord Wolfson, a Minister of Justice in the Lords.** He has resigned over "the scale, context and nature" of breaches of Covid regulations in Downing Street. He said he was quitting not only over the events themselves, or the Prime Minister's own conduct but also "the official response to what took place."

So one Tory minister with some integrity. Are there any others?

****

14TH APRIL

Well there is another resignation but it can't be counted it as ethical.

Imran Ahmad Khan, the Conservative MP for Wakefield, has just resigned after being found guilty of sexually assaulting a 15-year-old boy. This of course means that there will have to be a by-election.

Wakefield is a Red-Wall seat so it will be a really interesting to see what happens here.

****

19TH APRIL

Parliament reconvenes today after the Easter recess. Johnson is due to make a statement to the House of Commons this afternoon about the fine he has had to pay to the Metropolitan police because he broke the lockdown laws.

He should be saying that he will resign. What he will no doubt say that is that he is **hugely sorry but he honestly thought it was OK at the time.**

Well I was right. That is exactly what he said. He spent 2 minutes apologising before going on to talk about Ukraine.

He then spent an hour responding to questions and pleas for him to resign. To each and every question he said words to the effect that 'I fully apologise and am very sorry for my mistakes.'

Sir Keir Starmer gave the performance of his lifetime. He slated the PM and he was listened to in absolute silence, especially when he talked about a constituent of his who could not go to see his dying father.

But the Tories are all playing down the importance of this fine and likening it to a speeding ticket. Really not that serious at all. To which Sir Keir said, **"The last minister who got a speeding ticket and then lied about it ended up in prison. I know because I prosecuted him."**

****

20TH APRIL

Today, we hear that at the 1922 meeting last night, straight after this performance in the Commons to which all Tory MPs were told to attend, it was absolute pandemonium. There was the banging of desks and the PM immediately launched into an appeal for unity.

Sir Roger Gale was interviewed by Kay Burley of *Sky News* and he said he could only stay in the room for 3 minutes because he did not like the tone of the meeting. It was all **bluster and pantomime**.

Then we had PMQs. It is just a circus. The PM does not answer a single question but blusters and prevaricates and repeats and repeats and repeats lie after lie after lie. It is a complete waste of everyone's time.

BBC correspondent Adam Fleming made an interesting point just beforehand. He said that yesterday a hugely important bill should have been being discussed but it had to be curtailed because the debate on the lockdown fines went on for so long. **This whole episode is eating into democratic discussion and debate.**

****

21ST APRIL

Sir Keir Starmer has called for an investigation by the Privileges Committee to decide **whether the PM's conduct amounts to**

contempt of Parliament. It is being debated and voted on today. The Conservatives all went to a meeting last night after PMQs and they were all told that there would be a **three line whip for this vote.**

Well there has been a rather sudden change of heart. The three line whip has been withdrawn and they are being allowed a free vote. Wait a minute, the Tory benches are getting very empty. Oh they have now been told they can go home and they do not have to vote at all. So this means that the investigation will be approved.

I have been listening to the debate and the standard of debate has been higher than for a very long time. This could have something to do with the fact that the PM is in India miles and miles away. There have been excellent statements from the opposition parties but also some staggering ones from the Tories who are still around.

William Wragg Conservative MP for Hazel Grove Greater Manchester said that he knows that Tory MPs are "struggling at the moment" as the party "bears the scars of misjudgements of leadership".

There are few Conservatives who can "truly enjoy" being an MP at the moment, and he says **it is "utterly depressing" to be asked to "defend the indefensible"**

"Each time, part of us withers," he states.

Steve Baker, senior Tory and former Brexit minister, had said earlier in the week that he had been "deeply moved" by the PM's apology in the Commons and wanted to forgive him.

He repeats that sentiment today, but says "that spirit of earnest willingness to forgive lasted about 90 seconds" into a meeting Boris Johnson held with his backbenchers later the same day. (Tuesday) [It was] an orgy of adulation, a great festival of bombast, and I cannot bear it," he said.

"I have to say now the possibility [of forgiveness] has gone... and for not obeying the letter and the spirit, the Prime Minister now should be long gone.

The prime minister should just know the gig's up."

Well, it is **4.30pm** and the debate has just been concluded. As there were no cries of "No" from the Conservative benches it has gone through, on the nod, without a vote.

So to be clear the Privileges Committee **will** be investigating whether or not the PM knowingly lied to Parliament.

Conservative Andrew Mangnall, MP for Totnes, says he still has a letter of no confidence in the Prime Minister in with Sir Graham Brady of the 1922 Committee.

He says he welcomes the motion and looks forward to its findings, adding: "I look forward to making sure that those who do come after the Prime Minister in many years to come will also learn from this that the conventions of the house must be respected".

Conservative MP Peter Aldous tells the Commons that "this situation is completely unprecedented".

Indeed it is. Johnson in India says this is not a problem as he has absolutely nothing to hide.

Good. So everyone is happy then.

****

22ND APRIL
"When not if."

These words are music to my ears as Tobias Ellwood speaks to the *Today* programme this morning. Mr. Ellwood is chairman of the Commons Defence Committee and he went on to say, "**The challenges just won't go away. I predicted a steady trickle of letters, of resignations, and that is now happening."**

And "The absence of discipline, of focus, of leadership" had led to a "breach of trust" among the public.

He says that using the war in Ukraine as a reason for not having a leadership election is just a "fig leaf."

****

2ND MAY

Local elections coming up in three days' time. Boris is surfacing which is very dangerous for the Conservative party. Today he was up in the north of England saying how lovely it was to be **in Teesside**. He tweeted a photo of himself eating an ice-cream. The only trouble was he was actually **in Tyneside** which is 40 miles way. The tweet has been deleted.

He really does not have a clue either about where he is, or what he is doing, or what he should be doing wherever it is that he is.

****

3RD MAY

And today Boris Johnson was interviewed by *Good Morning Britain* on ITV at 8am. This is the first interview with them for five years. Lorraine Kelly one of presenters said **yes we have finally got him out of the fridge**!! This refers back to when he hid in a fridge in Leeds on the eve of the General Election when he was being pursued by a Good Morning Britain presenter who wanted to interview him. He wanted to ask him about his "promise to talk to Piers (Morgan) and (Susanna Reid). Well Johnson obviously didn't want to be questioned about anything so he hid in a conveniently placed fridge. He really did.

But today Susanna Reid got him in the chair at last, although he kept her, and all of us, waiting for half-an-hour. She gave him a tough time.

The very first question was, "**Are you honest Prime Minister?**" to which he replied "Yes". So that was the first lie within seconds.

And of course there were more to follow.

But the stand-out story is the one about a woman called Elsie. She is 77 and lives on her own and **her heating bill has gone up from £17 a month to £85 a** month. She cannot afford to heat her council flat so she gets on a bus at 9.30am using her freedom pass and rides on a bus all day long.

Susanna Reid asked what else Elsie could cut back on?

The PM said that actually **he** had introduced the 24 hour free bus pass.

"Oh, so she should be grateful to you for her bus pass then" said Ms Reid. He had no answers and Susanna Reid is being praised for a brilliant interview.

And there has been a fact check on Johnson's claim to have introduced the freedom bus pass. Yes he extended the pass to 24 hours when he was Mayor of London but the pass was initially brought in 1973. But then Transport for London banned its use before 9.30am due to budget restraints caused by the pandemic.

At the end of the interview Ms Reid said that they had to stop because Lorraine was coming next. You could see the panic in Johnson's eyes as he thought someone else was coming to interview him further. "Who's Lorraine?" he asked. Lorraine Kelly is a household name, well known by everyone, and was about to do another presentation.

Not a good look for a PM trying to get "down with the people".

****

4TH MAY

On the *Today* programme this morning the presenter Nick Robinson said that they had interviewed the leader of every political party over the last few days, apart from the Conservatives, but he had asked Boris Johnson to be interviewed today. **He declined to do so**. What a coward. He's back in his fridge.

****

5TH MAY. BY-ELECTIONS DAY.

The Tories are really worried. There are notices from Conservative councils saying please don't punish us for the mistakes in Westminster. They are calling themselves "Local Conservatives" to try to distance themselves from the main party and there were notes pinned up everywhere saying **"To Tory voters: Stay at home; Save Lives; Protect the NHS."**

We see Boris Johnson walking to the polling station with his dog but no Carrie. Where is Carrie I wonder?

We wait to see what tomorrow brings.

****

6TH MAY

Wow, Labour has won Westminster, Wandsworth and Barnet. London has gone red and Westminster has never had a Labour council before. So No 10 is under a Labour council for the first time in its history!

Other results trickle in during the day. Interesting that the media are saying that it has not been that amazing for Labour which I find a bit difficult to understand. Yes the so-called 'red wall' has not returned fully to Labour but elsewhere it has been good. Southern cities have lost to Labour, and in the Midlands they have done well. However the Lib Dems have exceeded themselves and have picked up more seats than any other party. The Conservatives have been well and truly trounced.

We will get a better over-all situation tomorrow.

****

7TH MAY

The Tories are really worried. There are smear stories going round, starting in *The Mail*, about Sir Keir. They are saying that 'new evidence' has emerged about his working meeting in Durham on the 30th April 2021 to imply that actually it was a 'party'. Durham police have been asked (by whom?) to look into it. You might remember Durham police. They are supposed to be investigating Dominic Cummings about his trip up there whilst suffering from Covid during a tight lockdown. We are still waiting to hear about that one.

However just let us look at those results again.

Labour has won more seats in England than all of the other parties put together.

Labour	2,265
Con	1,075
Lib Dem	712
Ind	145
Greens	116
RA	51

The Conservatives lost nearly 500 seats. There are now no Tory councils in Wales. In Scotland the Tory vote plummeted into third place having been overtaken by Labour and in Northern Ireland Sinn Fein secured the most seats for the first time ever pushing out the DUP.

This, to me, looks like a spectacular defeat for the Conservative government and a huge kick in the teeth for all of those in power and how anyone can say well it's not so bad is beyond me. **Sinn Fein is committed to the re-unification of Ireland, the SNP is committed to another referendum on Scottish Independence, so**

Boris Johnson, having taken us out of the EU, looks as though he is set on destroying the UK.

I keep on saying that Johnson is a dangerous man.

Oh wait a moment what is this? *The Mail* is now saying that just before that disastrous interview with Susanna Reid, Johnson had had food poisoning. What?

I put this in because we really do need a laugh now and again. Except that actually I find it all very depressing.

Medics are saying that actually food poisoning does not generally impair cognitive function or reasoning to which I add or behaving like an intelligent, wise and empathetic human being.

****

10TH MAY

Yesterday afternoon Sir Keir Starmer made a statement to the press on television saying that no rules were broken at his work meeting but of course he will co-operate with the police and if they think otherwise and he inadvertently did break the law **then he would resign.** It was a calm, dignified, articulate statement and he came across as an honest and decent person.

The Tories do not know what to say to this. He has played a blinder and is a win, win situation. If he does get a fixed penalty notice and resigns it makes Johnson and Sunak look even worse than they already do. If he is cleared it makes him stronger.

It is interesting to note that the person who **took the photograph of Sir Keir drinking beer at the meeting through a closed window is the son of James Delingpole. He was a contemporary of Johnson's at Oxford University in the 1980's and is a journalist.** He has written for the *Mail, Spectator* and *Telegraph.* But he is also a former executive editor for Breitbart, London. Breitbart is an **American far-right** syndicated news, opinion and commentary website and much of its content has been called misogynistic, xenophobic, and racist by liberals and traditional conservatives alike. It was a rallying spot for Donald Trump's presidential campaign in 2016.

I just think you need to know that.

It is also interesting to note that many of the allegations against Sir Keir are gradually being eroded. The take-away restaurant is saying that the order was actually quite a small one. There are WhatsApp messages which suggest that they all worked until after 1am.

He is a lawyer for goodness sake. He abides by the rules.

****

19TH MAY. BREAKING NEWS.

11.30 am. The Metropolitan Police have just announced further fines for Downing Street and have said that **that concludes their investigation. 126 fixed penalty notices have been issued all together.** Some people getting more than one.

But this is odd. Neither Johnson nor Carrie have received a further fine.

He attended six illegal parties but only the junior staff get fined.

He is looking at this as "good" outcome. He is "pleased" he says. Pleased for what? That he hasn't got more fines? That the investigation is over? That there is no way that he is going to resign?

Some are comparing this outcome with a young girl who got fined £2,000 for meeting two others outside. But there are so many stories like this one.

The entire investigation cost the tax payer £460,000.

BUT, now we can see the Sue Gray report.

****

20TH MAY

Well there is a huge backlash over the fact that the PM has not received another fine. It would appear that only junior staff, and more women than men, have received fines.

All the parties investigated were attended by the PM and it is being said that he encouraged everyone to let their hair down.

Carrie has not been fined either for her Abba party in No.10.

It is also noted that the Deputy Assistant Commissioner of the Met police just happens to be Bas Javid, brother of Sajid Javid our Health Minister.

I couldn't possibly comment.

It is being said that Boris lives to see another day. It won't be the parties that will bring him down in my opinion. It will be the economy. The Partygate issue just reinforces the fact that Johnson is the most unsuited politician ever to hold a position which involves representing people in a constituency.

****

Sue Gray is working on her report this weekend and hoping to publish it next week. We are hoping that it will be published in full with no holds barred and no watering down.

****

21ST MAY

We are hearing that there was a secret meeting between Sue Gray and the PM some weeks ago but no-one really knows what was discussed.

We just hope that the report is not heavily redacted but..... he **is** her boss.

So I quote Robbie Haddon who is a builder and who has written in *The Guardian* today.

He says that, "Johnson just doesn't seem to be a proper politician. He's a journalist: he cares about how to play a game with the news; the idea there's a story one day and if you just let it rumble on it'll disappear. So we have Partygate and they talk about Rwanda. Or streaming the civil service. It's just distraction after distraction."

Mr Haddon was unable to visit his dying father.

And I would also like to quote the final paragraph of Matthew Parris in *The Times* today. He sums up Boris Johnson perfectly.

"The only story in town........is the Rasputin-like survival in office of a weird windbag entertainer. And yet again he dodges the bullet. Amazing! It's theatre! It's cinema! It's a movie! In office still! But what's he going to do with the office? Ah that's not theatre; that's government. **And of government, we have very little.**"

Exactly. All Johnson wants to do is to stay in power. To him it is a game. For us it is disaster.

****

22ND MAY
Cronyism from the top.

At the moment people are being interviewed by Priti Patel for the job of **director general of the National Crime Agency.** This is Britain's equivalent of the FBI. Two highly qualified police chiefs have been interviewed already but Johnson is trying to push forward a friend and mate of his, Lord Hogan-Howe.

Now you might remember him as the person who oversaw the Operation Midland investigation which was set up by the Met in 2014 to examine allegations of child sexual abuse and homicide. It was a dreadful investigation which destroyed the lives of many innocent men in public life.

It was based on false claims by Carl Beech, who called himself "Nick", and actually everyone with half a brain could tell it was completely false.

Harvey Proctor whose life was ruined by malicious claims said that appointing Hogan-Howe to this post would be "outrageous". He said, **"He presided over the worst police operation in this country for decades."**

But Johnson forged a close friendship with Hogan-Howe during his time as Mayor of London and he had his Tory leadership bid endorsed by him.

Look away now if you value your sanity.

Hogan-Howe has just posted a video on Twitter where he says, "I found him (Johnson) to be loyal, honourable and he did what he promised to do."

Well he hasn't got the job yet but it I think it is important to know what goes on **behind the headlines.**

****

23RD MAY
The Tory MP Imran Ahmed Khan has been jailed for 18 months for sexually assaulting a 15 year old boy.

****

24TH MAY

There has been a lot of anguish about the secret meeting between Sue Gray and Johnson but it has now transpired that it was Number 10 who requested the meeting and that the PM asked her to ditch the report. **"After all it's all out there now, nothing more to add," he is reported to have said.**

Well yes it is all out there now, as last night ITV news published a photograph showing the PM at a leaving 'do' on the 13th November 2020. He is standing beside a table laden with bottles of wine, champagne, gin surrounded by empty glasses and holding up a glass himself obviously giving a toast. There are many other people there including the photographer. No masks and a red box in the corner. Aah so maybe that turns it into a 'work event'.

This photo is on the front page of every newspaper this morning except, of course, *The Daily Mail.*

People are demanding to know why the PM didn't get a fine for this as someone who was at this event **did** get fined. So it **was** an illegal party then. They are demanding more transparency from the Met. And on Twitter they are saying so it's OK to be a Prime Minister at a boozy party in Downing Street during lockdown **but not a small woman at an outdoor vigil.**

This is referring to the **Sarah Everard vigil**, and the image of a young slim woman, with beautiful red hair, staring into a camera as she was manhandled to the ground by two enormous burly police officers, before being handcuffed and arrested, which will be burned on our minds for ever.

We also see clips of the Commons when last December the Labour MP **Catherine West asked Johnson whether there had been a party on the 13th November to which the PM said "No".**

On this day, just to be clear, there were 157 deaths from Covid and 38,351 new cases.

We now await the results of the **House of Commons Privileges Committee who** are investigating whether or not the PM has misled Parliament.

So a lot of money is being spent on trying to determine whether our Prime Minister lies or not. Three reports. For goodness sake what planet are we all on?

****

25TH MAY

Today the **Sue Gray report is published** and we see it at last. It actually doesn't tell us much more than we already know.

We hear of a culture of alcohol, raucous behaviour, partying till 4 in the morning, rudeness to cleaning and security staff who had to clear up red wine and vomit, an altercation i.e. a fight, between a couple of individuals, and senior staff inviting others more junior to 'bring your own booze.'

They knew it was illegal because one party was immediately after a press conference telling us to stay indoors and only meet one person outside. So they were told to go in the back door and to be careful not to bump into any camera crew or journalists who might be about.

And Martin Reynolds, PPS to the PM, sent an email after the party which said "**We seem to have got away with it.**"

In her scathing report, which looked at 16 events in Whitehall during the pandemic, Ms Gray wrote: "The events that I investigated were attended by leaders in government, many of these events should not have been allowed to happen. It is also the case that some of the more junior civil servants believe that their involvement in some of these events was permitted, given the attendance of senior leaders.

"**The senior leadership team at the centre, both political and official must bear responsibility for this culture.**"

So will he? No.

We hear his bluster in PMQs and compare it with a beautifully crafted speech from Keir Starmer.

We hear a previous justice minister Robert Buckland and from Tory MP Tobias Ellwood calling on him to resign. But I have forecast his demise so often and been so wrong that I am not falling into that trap again.

His spineless and corrupt back benchers will keep him in power for as long as possible. A criminal who has been happy to have excessive alcoholic 'gatherings' in his work place which is a sacking offence in every other professional place of work. Someone who made the rules but doesn't seem to understand them and so someone who is totally unsuitable for any form of high office whatsoever. There is complete lack of trust in government.

But we are also hearing that Number 10 had sight of the report yesterday and after Sue Gray insisted on a 'ministerial direction' she watered it down slightly and didn't name certain senior civil servants.

****

The 'Good Law Project' has taken the first formal steps **in further judicial review proceedings against the Metropolitan Police** over its failure to investigate the Prime Minister in respect of three gatherings on the 13th November 2020 the 17th December 2020 and the 14th January 2021.

These were all leaving parties. **People who attended these parties were sent questionnaires but not the Prime Minister.**

Former senior police officer Lord Paddick says that, "If the Met is to avoid further deterioration in public trust and confidence, they must explain why they failed to even question the Prime Minister about his attendance at these events. We are simply asking the Met to either explain or investigate further, and if necessary we will ask the Courts to force the Met to do so."

As Jo Maugham says, "**It was only after 'Good Law Project' began judicial review proceedings in January that the Met agreed to investigate at all.** And we will not hesitate to commence further proceedings to ensure it investigates them properly.

"For the rule of law to operate it must operate fairly, without favour to the powerful. We will do what we can to ensure it does."

We all owe the 'Good Law Project' an enormous debt. They function on charitable giving.

****

But also today hiding behind the Sue Gray report I find this:-

A group of Conservative staffers have written a letter to the Prime Minister, Oliver Dowden the Conservative party Chair and to Sir Lindsay Hoyle the Commons' Speaker. This letter has been seen by *The Guardian* and it is reported by their political correspondent Aubrey Allegretti.

It is about the fact that any complaints about the serious sexual abuse of some MPs is treated as "mere gossip."

They urge Boris Johnson and party HQ to do more to tackle the problem.

"Change must come from the top," they say. "MPs must call out their colleagues' behaviour and end this constant cycle of scandal that tarnishes all of us."

"In any other workplace, things would never have been allowed to get this bad. It is shocking that those most involved in the governance of our country have overseen such a denigration of standards."

Oliver Dowden is my MP. I will write to him about this.

****

27TH MAY

But just when you think it couldn't get any worse we hear this. Boris Johnson has **just re-written the preface of the ministerial code** which is published today.

Ministers who are found to have breached the ministerial code will no longer have to resign or face the sack.

Anneliese Dodds shadow secretary for Women and Equalities said, **"What do integrity, objectivity, transparency, and honesty have in common? They're all words Boris Johnson just deleted from his foreword to the ministerial code."**

Well, well, well could this have anything to do with the fact that he is about to be under investigation by the Privileges Committee for knowingly lying to Parliament?

The new changes have been met with derision by opposition parties, who have accused the PM of "watering down the rules to save his skin".

To me it is an admission of guilt.

But there we go. We have seen over and over again that if this Prime Minister doesn't like the rules he will either break them with alacrity or change them with impunity.

The trouble is we don't have a written constitution. It is solely up to the Prime Minister of the day to decide on such things as the ministerial code. As Johnson did when Priti Patel was found to have been bullying her staff and should have resigned then as it was in breach of the code. But no, Johnson decided she could remain in post.

Labour have just asked for a vote in the Commons and I have just signed a petition to introduce an independent body to enforce the ministerial code on ministers.

****

29TH MAY

Boris Johnson is not only incompetent, dishonest, and uncaring but he is incredibly lazy and shambolic. There is a long article in *The Sunday Times* today about the PM and I pick out just two points that shock me.

One is that the 8.30am cabinet meeting of senior staff had to be moved to 9am because the PM was always late for it. People came in from miles away to get there well before 8am but, "he couldn't be bothered to walk down two flights of stairs to get there on time."

And the other is that Martin Reynolds (the former PPS who organised the 'bring your own booze' party) used to pretend the PM was in a meeting to cover for him while he was having an afternoon nap.

The whole atmosphere in Downing Street is shambolic and Lord Sedwill, the former cabinet secretary, told allies he left No 10 amid concerns about the "frat house" atmosphere.

You could not imagine this sort of dysfunctional behaviour under any other PM.

****

30TH MAY

Well you might not believe this but at last it would seem that the Tory Party is beginning to see Boris Johnson as an election liability. One Tory MP is quoted today as saying, **"He doesn't seem to have an idea of what he's doing or who he is or what we are. The domestic stuff has no direction."**

You just cannot accuse them of being quick to understand the on-going problem that's for sure.

What is the big announcement at the moment? The PM has announced that to celebrate the Queen's Platinum Jubilee he will bring back Imperial measures. And let's get the crown symbol back on the pint glass he says.

You see? He doesn't even know that the crown symbol was never **off** the pint glass. EU laws permitted it so long as it didn't overlap the CE symbol.

He is completely unaware of all the problems mentioned in this book. He doesn't care and he doesn't know.

But one of his MPs apparently said in an interview this morning something along the lines of "Oh yes the Imperial measures debate comes up regularly on the doorstep."

Idiots everyone.

****

2nd June Lord Geidt, Boris Johnson's ethics adviser, has threatened to resign over the Downing Street parties' scandal after concluding that there were "legitimate" questions about whether the Prime Minister breached the ministerial code.

If you remember his previous ethics adviser, Sir Alex Allan, **did** actually resign over the Priti Patel bullying incident.

It really would not look good for a second one to go.

****

Also today we see an interview Johnson had with Justine Roberts founder of 'Mumsnet'. He obviously thought that this would be an easy ride but possibly changed his mind pretty quickly after the very first question.

"Why should we believe anything you say when it has been proven you're a habitual liar?" Ms Roberts asked.

He answered with his usual bluff and bluster.

She then asked him what books he reads to his children at bedtime.

Well that was a difficult question. Again he couldn't answer and just said something about **his** favourite book as a child which was Dr Seuss apparently. Obviously doesn't read to his children.

It's all just about him.

****

3RD JUNE
It is the Platinum Jubilee weekend celebrating 70 years on the throne of the Queen.

Today it is the service in St Paul's cathedral. As Johnson and his wife, Carrie walked up the steps there were boos from the crowd. In the interest of fairness I could hear some cheers but the boos seemed to be dominant.

Once this long weekend is over it is being said that more Tories will turn against Johnson.

****

6TH JUNE
And they have! Just after 8 this morning Sir Graham Brady announced that the threshold of 54 letters has been reached and there will be a vote of confidence in the Prime Minister between 6 and 8 this evening. Win or lose he will be hugely damaged.

****

7TH JUNE

The result was: **211 voted for the PM and 148 voted against**. So this looks like a win for the Prime Minister.

However.........it seems he has won the vote but lost his authority as this was a far greater rebellion than anyone had anticipated. It was worse than Theresa May's result and she was out within months. It was worse than Thatcher and she resigned within weeks. Three quarters of his back benchers want him to go.

These are the headlines this morning:

"A wounded victor", says *The Times*

"Hollow victory tears Tories apart" says The *Daily Telegraph*

"Party's over, Boris" proclaims *The Mirror*

"PM clinging to power after vote humiliation", from *The Guardian*.

"Wounded Johnson in peril" is *The i's* front page.

"The party is over Boris" says *The Metro*

Inside the papers we read:

"It may be weeks, it may be months but Boris is toast" from John Crace in *The Guardian*

"Revolt makes the PM's position unsustainable – he must spare his party and the country further agonies. He should look for an honourable exit" from William Hague in *The Times*.

This result "seems to place the prime minister in the critically wounded category," says Sean O'Grady of *The Independent*

And if you are still unsure about the strength of the PM's position other remarks heard today are "dead man walking" a "lame duck" "limping on" and my favourite of all "**should be gone by the autumn**".

But if you are a Johnson supporter or, of course even Johnson himself, you see this as a fantastic win and a mandate to get on with the job. You also see it, as an MP said in an interview by the BBC this morning, as a witch-hunt by the BBC and all the media, who do not recognise the Prime Minister's achievements and abilities to get things done.

Hmmm. Don't think he has read my book.

Interesting to hear that this is thought to be the best result for the Labour party.

So he is still there, for the moment. But there is a lot of in-fighting going on and a lot of blaming each other which is never a good look. It is definitely now when not if.

****

15TH JUNE
Lord Geidt, the government's ethics minister, has just resigned. This is the second ethics minister to resign in the two years of Johnson's premiership.

It doesn't surprise me and if you have read through this book it won't surprise you either.

'Ethics' and 'Boris Johnson' are words which do not sit lightly in the same sentence. We are waiting for Lord Geidt's resignation letter to be published in full which as yet has not happened.

****

16TH JUNE
Aha. Here it is. It is a long and detailed letter which he ends like this:-

"This week, however, I was tasked to offer a view about the Government's intention to consider measures which risk a deliberate and purposeful breach of the Ministerial Code. This request has placed me in an impossible and odious position. My informal response on Monday was that you and any other Minister should justify openly your position vis-à-vis the Code in such circumstances. However, the idea that a Prime Minister might to any degree be in the business of deliberately breaching his own Code is an affront. A deliberate breach, or even an intention to do so, would be to suspend the provisions of the Code to suit a political end. This would make a mockery not only of respect for the Code but licence the suspension of its provisions in governing the conduct of Her Majesty's Ministers. I can have no part in this.

Because of my obligation as a witness in Parliament, this is the first opportunity I have had to act on the Government's intentions. I therefore resign from this appointment with immediate effect."

Well that sounds pretty damaging to me. It means that the PM is looking for his third ethics advisor in under 18 months. Who on earth would want to take on this role I wonder?

****

17TH JUNE
Well that is a question on everyone's lips today. And the PM is obviously thinking it might be difficult because it is being said that he might decide not to have an ethics minister at all.

But there is a backlash in Westminster about that and out on the broadcast round earlier today John Penrose, the Tory MP and Johnson's former corruption tsar who recently resigned, said that it was "pretty clear" that the PM had broken the ministerial code on Partygate, and that it was "important" that some sort of successor is found for Geidt.

****

15.30 BREAKING NEWS!

We are just hearing that Boris Johnson has pulled out of a major red wall conference which should be taking place this afternoon. This was very last minute and he was due to meet Tory MPs, councillors and business leaders in Doncaster.

According to Sky News the reason for this will be revealed in the next couple of hours.

Could it be, could it possibly be?????

16.00

No, no it couldn't! **He is on a surprise visit to Ukraine.** Business leaders in Doncaster are said to be furious. They were told he was on the train to Doncaster this morning and one of them was saying it will be so good to talk to the PM and he was sure that Johnson would listen to them.

Well actually that would have been a first.

Interesting that yesterday the EU leaders visited Ukraine. Did he feel left out?

He is running away again when things are bad here. Another photo shoot where no-one will boo?

****

19TH JUNE

This story needs a very careful read. I have only just caught up with it and the names you need to remember are **Carole Cadwalladr and Arron Banks**. Banks is a British business man and a political donor. He was one of the largest donors to the UKIP party giving them £100,000 and he was co-founder of the Leave EU campaign. His wealth has been estimated at £250 million. It was reported that he had had multiple meetings with Russian embassy officials as well as having been offered business opportunities in Russia in the run up to the Brexit referendum. However he denied any wrong doing and the Electoral Commission conceded he did not break electoral law.

But Carole Cadwalladr is a journalist of courage, integrity and determination and she had been investigating the role of social media in the leave campaign, and in particular Facebook, and it led to record fines. It also found that Bank's leave campaign had indeed broken the electoral and data laws. But it was the associations with the Russian government that was reported by her in *The Guardian* which really hit a nerve with Banks.

So when she spoke at a Ted's conference in 2019 and uttered these words to the audience: ... **"and I'm not even going to get into the lies that Arron Banks told about his covert relationship with the Russian government**," he hit the roof and decided to sue her.

It has been a long and ugly journey for her and a lesser being would have given up years ago. She was only able to persevere with her case because of the generosity of her legal team and the kindness of strangers. 28,887 people contributed to the astonishing sum of £819,835 to her two crowd-funds.

It was just last week after a six month wait that she learned that she had won the libel case against her. It has been three years of intense stress and as she says she is not so much relieved as completely numb. She says that if she had not pursued this case some key facts about the political movement that changed our country for ever –Brexit- could have been rewritten. **"The ability to report on the Kremlin's involvement with leading individuals in the Brexit campaign would have been stifled for ever. The record could have been changed."**

She goes on to say that, **"Boris Johnson's government came to power on the coat-tails of Brexit.** It has refused to investigate Russia's continuing attacks on western democracy and our information systems. Johnson personally intervened to delay publication of the Intelligence and Security Committee's Russia report. **He continues to refuse its demands for an inquiry."**

She finishes her article in *The Observer* today by saying, **"There were at least four meetings between the main funder of the Brexit campaign and the Russian government. There are reasonable grounds to believe there were many more. Fact."**

This has been such an important case and Carole Cadwalladra is to be congratulated on her tenacity and bravery. **This is probably the most important story in this book.**

****

We hear of another story today on a completely different level but of interest never-the-less.

In the first edition of *The Sunday Times* today there was an article about Boris Johnson and Carrie Symonds. Apparently when he was Foreign Secretary Johnson tried to get Carrie a job worth £100.000 as his chief of staff. Well this didn't happen as his allies told him it would not be a good look.

The strange thing is that in all later editions the story wasn't there. It had been pulled. No 10 are denying the veracity of this story but the journalist who wrote it, Simon Walters, is standing by it.

Now I have no idea whether it is true or not, although it is a bit concerning that one minute it is there and the next it has gone, but the issue for me is that at this time 2018, Johnson was still married to his second wife and Symonds was his mistress. I think he had just given up his affair with Jennifer Arcuri. Not only that, but his wife was undergoing treatment for cancer. That tells me all I need to know about the character of this man.

****

23RD JUNE
Today is by-election day. Just to remind you there is a by-election in Tiverton Devon because their Conservative MP, Neil Parrish, resigned

as he was found guilty of watching pornography twice on his phone during debates in the House of Commons. There is also a by-election in Wakefield Yorkshire because their Conservative MP also resigned as he was found guilty of sexually assaulting a 14 year old boy.

Tiverton has a 24,000 Tory majority and has always been Conservative but the Lib Dems are mounting a huge campaign there in order to try to overturn them if at all possible.

Wakefield was Labour but voted for Johnson in the last election and is known as one of the 'red wall' seats. Labour is working hard here to try to win them back.

This is the chance for people to send Boris Johnson a message and we have our fingers crossed that the Tory party is well and truly trounced tonight. But we will see. The PM is in Rwanda today and for the next few days at a Commonwealth meeting so is well out of the way. But at the moment Tiverton are saying it could be neck and neck.

****

24TH JUNE
Conservatives have lost both seats! Not only that but the swing to the Lib Dems in Tiverton was almost 30% on a turn-out of 53% to secure a majority of 6,144. **It is the worst by-election defeat in history**. It is also the first time they have been anything but Conservative since 1923.

In Wakefield there was a swing to Labour of 12.7% with a majority of 4,925.

No sitting prime minister has lost two by-elections in one day since John Major in 1991.

Then we hear that my MP, Oliver Dowden, sent a resignation letter at 5.35 am to Johnson to say **he is resigning as Conservative party chairman**.

My cup runneth over.

Johnson was supposed to be being interviewed on the BBC this morning but obviously cancelled.

So we waited for the deputy PM, Dominic Raab to take his place but he didn't show up. In fact BBC Breakfast finished without any spokesperson from the Tories. The Conservative candidate for Tiverton has locked herself into a room and has refused to speak to anyone!

****

Just in case Boris Johnson or any Ministers try to say that losing by-elections mid-term is par for the course we need to remember what happened when Tony Blair was Labour Prime Minister.

He fought 28 by-elections and won every one.

****

26TH JUNE
So what have they all been saying?

Well **Suella Braverman** said, "It's disappointing to see that there's actually a dishonest pact between the Lib Dems and Labour and that's more worrying." Just to remind you that Suella Braverman is the Attorney General and actually, no Ms Braverman, what is much more worrying than any of that is the fact that you appear to have absolutely no knowledge or understanding of the law.

A **nameless Tory MP** said of Neil Parish, the cause of the Tiverton by-election, said that, "He should have just gone away with his wife for a few weeks and then come back to the job. I don't know why the girls had to speak out like that."

I just have to leave that one with you but yes, always a good idea not to forget the wife.

Boris Johnson said that he understood he should take the blame but it is obviously time for the media to stop all this negative reporting and let him "get on with the job." I presume he means the job of completely destroying the country.

He also said that he hears what we say and he is now preparing to lead the country into a third term.

What? He is only half way through his first and only term and if he heard what we said he would resign tomorrow.

So par for the course, always, always blame others.

But some are not happy.

One Tory source said the PM is "completely delusional" and **another said** he is "showing increasing signs of a bunker mentality and that never ends well."

One leading rebel said "The next leader of the Conservative party needs integrity, courage, and to show leadership. That rules out all of the current Cabinet."

It is also being rumoured that about six Conservative MPs are thinking of deflecting to Labour but we won't know the truth of this one until PMQs in three days' time.

And then it is being said that more and more letters are going in to the 1922 committee. Well strictly speaking there cannot be another vote of confidence for a year but the Tories are very good at changing the rules to suit them so we are watching this space.

****

Then there is this story today. **Apparently Boris Johnson wanted to build a tree house for 2 year old Wilf in the garden estate at Chequers**. Well how lovely is that except that actually Chequers is not owned by him and as someone says he is only squatting there whilst he is PM. But then he was told it would be a security risk as it would be able to be seen from the road. It would therefore need bullet-proof glass.

Where on earth are we going with this one?

It would cost £150,000 that's where.

Not a good look Prime Minister when people in some parts of the country pay this much for a house to live in or when you refuse to extend free school meals for young children.

He had apparently asked Lord Brownlow (once again) if he could find some money.

It didn't happen.

****

30TH JUNE
I promise you it does get worse.

If you look back to the second story on the 19th June you will be reminded of the story in the first edition of *The Times* which was later withdrawn. We are grateful to *Private Eye* magazine for investigating the reason for this.

Well I am not sure that grateful is quite the correct word here actually **and maybe those of you with a sensitive disposition should look away now. There is some sexual content here.**

It seems that they were worried that the rest of the story would come out.

The reason Johnson was offering Carrie a £100,000 salaried job as his chief of staff was because she was his mistress at the time. And the reason we know she was his mistress at the time, beyond all reasonable doubt, was because an MP, who was used to entering Johnson's office without knocking, walked in one morning to find Carrie performing oral sex with Boris Johnson, on the sofa.

This was at his place of work, whilst he was still married to his wife who was undergoing chemotherapy at this time.

OK you can look back now.

It won't come as a surprise to anyone when I say that there has been no coverage of this story anywhere on mainstream media. No surprise either that it is all over social media!

I think we also need to explain Boris Johnson's behaviour a little more just in case you have missed some of it. Carrie was not his only mistress during his marriage to Marina Wheeler. His mistresses apparently include Petronella Wyatt who had a terminated pregnancy, Helen Macintyre who had a daughter, Jennifer Arcuri who received a grant of £126,000 in the form of grants for her business and event sponsorship and Anna Fazackerley. This is all documented in *The Times* by Stuart Heritage.

I think this must go some way to explaining the PM's dismissive attitude to the following story.

****

Because later today we hear this.

The Deputy Chief Whip is an MP called Chris Pincher. This evening he has written a letter of resignation to Boris Johnson because he says that last night when he was in the Carlton Club he had too much to drink and became an embarrassment to himself and others.

The Carlton Club is a private members club in London originally founded for Conservative members.

So what had he done that was so embarrassing? **He had 'groped' two men.**

Actually people are saying, call it what it is which is he sexually harassed two men.

Well Johnson has accepted his resignation as deputy chief whip and accepted his apology and has said 'matter closed'.

Hmmm, some are not happy about that.

****

1ST JULY
Definitely not happy.

There is a huge back story coming out about this man who has apparently been involved in sexual allegations in previous years. It is becoming increasingly worrying as to why he was appointed deputy chief whip in the first place.

He was investigated in 2017 when he had to resign. But in January 2018 he was cleared of wrong doing and it was then that he was appointed as deputy chief whip.

After the election in 2019 he got the job back again in February 2022.

People are asking how much Johnson knew about these indiscretions when he appointed him and want to know why he has not had the whip withdrawn.

Well this evening the PM has bowed to pressure and withdrawn the whip but everyone is saying that he should have done this much sooner.

But this is how he acts. Does nothing hoping it will go away until forced to act.

Of course he doesn't want him to be suspended and found guilty because that will mean another trashing at a by-election.

And we are hearing that maybe Johnson closed his ears to Pincher's wrong doings because he was supported by him all through party-gate and beyond.

But two sources have said that they heard the PM refer to Chris Pincher many years ago as **"Pincher by name and Pincher by nature."** Now obviously I can't really verify that remark but knowing Johnson as we do I think we can believe that that that is how he talks.

I don't think this story is going away anytime soon.

****

4TH JULY
It certainly isn't. Back bench MPs are furious with the way in which he has dealt with the Pincher scandal and are planning to promote Tory MPs who are not in favour of his leadership on to the 1922 committee when they have new elections in a weeks' time.

Already we are seeing names being bandied about as possible new leaders. And if a significant number of MPs write more letters of no-confidence the men in grey suits could be having a quiet chat with him.

****

5TH JULY
Oh my word things are hotting up. Ministers have been appearing on the media saying that so far as they know the PM knew nothing about any specific allegations about Chris Pincher at any time. Therese

Coffey, Will Quince and then this morning Dominic Raab, all saying the same thing.

But today there is a letter from Lord McDonald published on Twitter saying that when the PM was Foreign Secretary he, Lord McDonald, was told that an **official had met the PM face to face to brief him about the allegations.** It seems there are always, always lies about everything and the attempted cover up is almost worse than the original stories. This is beginning to sound really serious.

Pincher has to resign now and there has to be a by-election at Tamworth.

****

11TH JULY

And today we hear about **yet another discredited Tory MP,** who shall be nameless so far as this book is concerned.

He has been found guilty of crashing his car and then walking away from the accident without reporting it to the police. He crashed into a lamp-post at one o'clock in the morning but phoned his father to come and take him home. The car was left in a dangerous position. This man had declared himself to be trans- gender to the House of Commons, which was a very brave thing to do. But this was a grave dereliction of duty and as the judge said he made some very bad decisions.

I expect he was a bit embarrassed actually, because when the police did catch up with him, when he was in bed later that night, they discovered he had been wearing a black leather mini-skirt, tights, high heel shoes and a pearl necklace.

What is it with Tory MPs?

****

I look back to the beginning of this chapter and I try to count the number of times that I say that this must be the end of Johnson. I read over and over again the words of eminent people deploring his lack of honesty and his unsuitability for high office.

I just say this: we are sleep-walking into a place of danger and corruption. We are standing by, looking but not seeing, hearing but not listening, denouncing but not acting.

****

So, in order to preserve my sanity and also very probably to preserve yours dear reader, I am bringing this book to a close and I will just leave you with my thoughts as to how the UK is progressing on many issues discussed in my two books. The Prime Minister's answer to everything is that the British public just want him to carry on and to get on with the job and that is what he is going to do.

So let us see how well he and his government have done.

****

JOB DONE PRIME MINISTER?

July 2022

MINISTRY OF DEFENCE

You might remember that in '**Beneath the Bluster**' I mentioned in the chapter on **Money** that the Ministry of Defence had spent £5.5bn on a fixed price contract for 589 Ajax armoured vehicles and that only 14 had been delivered.

Well now, a year later, only a further 12 have been received and none of them are fit for purpose.

These vehicles are useless. They can't go more than 20 mph, they cannot fire whilst moving, reversing over objects higher than 20 cm is impossible and they vibrate so much that soldiers driving them suffer from tinnitus, get sick and have aching joints.

A Parliamentary committee has said that the MOD need to either fix or scrap the Ajax programme or risk compromising national security.

Would they get any of the money back? Probably not.

But the most worrying issue at the moment is the lack of funding and investment in our defence budget.

At a recent land warfare conference we heard that at Russian rates of fire we would run out of artillery shells in just two days.

In an article in *The Times* by Edward Lucas he writes that our plight stems from shocking complacency. As he says "politicians have little interest in the unglamorous and costly business of keeping stocks for just-in-case contingencies."

Ben Wallace, the Defence Secretary, has written to the PM asking for an increase of 20% in the defence budget to meet shortfalls in military capabilities.

But last November Boris Johnson said that the era of big tank battles in Europe was over. Obviously, as Mr. Lucas says, Putin did not get that memo.

So, although I understand that the first priority of a Prime Minister is to ensure the safety of its population I am not confident that Johnson is the correct person to do so.

Job definitely not done.

****

SEWAGE IN RIVERS AND LAKES

In October 2021 this Conservative government succeeded in **voting down an amendment designed to stop private water companies from dumping raw sewage into the UK's waterways.** Their reason was that the water companies know best what to do about this.

In the past two years, the charity 'Surfers Against Sewage' has received more than 640 reports of illness, including ear and eye infections and diarrhoea, from people who have been swimming in the sea or rivers.

Last weekend a Thames water boss admitted that the company is not sure when it is discharging untreated sewage or not.

Job definitely not done.

****

THE ENVIRONMENT
George Eustace is to scrap the EU law Habitat Directive which protects Natura Zone sites of which there are 900 in the UK.

Richard Benwall Chief Executive of Wild life and Countryside Link said it was a retrograde and deregulatory directive. He said that these laws, "remain the most effective protection for nature on the UK statute book, providing a rigorous defence for internationally important wildlife, in a way that gives certainty and confidence to businesses and ecologists alike."

He went on to say that there were ways in which the regulations could be improved, including more flexibility for climate change, wider application to harmful projects and even stronger protection from damaging developments.

"But simply stripping away the habitats regulations on the misguided assumption that other domestic laws can do the job alone would be a serious step backward in nature protection, as well as creating costly delay and uncertainty," he said.

You definitely need to sort that out Prime Minister.

****

BREXIT OF COURSE
I would just like to remind you of what **Boris Johnson said after the referendum in 2016:**

"British people will still be able to go and work in the EU; to live; to travel; to study; to buy homes and to settle down.....and there will continue to be free trade and access to the single market"

And this is James O'Brien in *The Mirror.*

"Every crisis the UK currently faces is being made worse by Tory determination to torch our decades-old "Welcome " mat and become the first country in history to impose economic sanctions on itself.

There is a shortage of doctors, nurses, lorry drivers, fruit pickers, vets, cabin crew, baggage handlers, hospitality staff and many, many more."

"Project Fear" he says, "is now Project Here"

And Iain Martin writes in *The Times* (8th June) that sooner or later, **"we will need to talk about Brexit."** Indeed if we want to survive we absolutely will.

He goes on to say that, "For our own economic good, and to foster better relations with our nearest neighbours, the emphasis must shift from hostility and denial to improving trade and making exporting to the EU easier."

The trouble is that the present right-wing government is incapable of ceasing hostilities with the EU.

In *The Observer's* editorial on 12th June it finishes by saying, "As Britain looks set to rediscover its role as the sick man of Europe, a closer economic relationship with the EU is starting to feel like an inevitability, no matter how long it takes."

And on the same day in *The Times* William Keegan writes that Brexit is reversible. He says, "It is no good Lord Mandelson advising the Labour party that its effects can be 'mitigated'; or believing that Labour if elected, can 'make Brexit work'.

Brexit isn't working, and it is not obvious that it can ever work"

Job definitely not done.

Oh no wait what is this I am hearing? Boris Johnson speaking on German TV says, **"The sooner Brexit vanishes into the background and we leave Brexit behind us the better it is."**

He thinks it is done.

****

NHS

Do you remember the pledge made by the Prime Minister in 2019 **to build 40 new hospitals by 2030?**

Would it surprise you to know that NHS leaders are concerned that some of these works will never get off the ground because of wrangling between what one source described as the "toxic triangle" of No 10, the Treasury and the Department of Health?

Six projects that predate Johnson's premiership have started construction and one, just one –a £35 million cancer centre in Cumbria -- has been completed.

All the others are still waiting for decisions on funding. Delay after delay after delay. And of course many of the 'new hospitals' will be alterations or refurbishments and not rebuilds at all.

But let's just look at one.

The Queen Elizabeth hospital in King's Lynn is having to use 1,500 steel and timber supports to hold up its roof in 56 separate areas. The hospital is due to come to the end of its life in 2030 **and so far no money has yet been confirmed for a rebuild.**

And let us just suppose these hospitals were indeed built the question is who will staff them?

Today (6th June) the general secretary of the Royal College of Nurses, Pat Cullen, will warn of nurses' growing concerns over patient safety.

A survey found that only a quarter of shifts have the planned number of registered nurses on duty.

She will say, **"Don't ever think that it is normal to not have enough staff to meet the needs of patients. It is not.**

"The patients and those we care for have had enough. We are tired, fed up, demoralised, and some of us are leaving the profession because we have lost hope."

But Boris Johnson says that struggling public sector workers should brace themselves for a meagre pay rise this year.

Well yes Prime Minister that should sort it out.

But listen to this: **The Independent National Audit Office is to launch an official inquiry into the claim by the PM that 40 new hospitals will be built by 2030.**

They are concerned that this is another case of over-promising and under-delivering.

Job definitely not done.

****

PUBLIC INQUIRY.
We have been asking for this for months. Finally (June 28th) the Covid-19 Bereaved Families for Justice have decided to seek a judicial review about the delay. They are very concerned that vital documents could have been lost because of the unprecedented delay of 6 months since the appointment of a chair person. The chair was appointed in December 2021 and normally inquiries start within a few weeks. **They are saying that this a breach of the Inquiries Act.**

Oh wait a minute. **Today (June 29th) the PM has said he accepts all the extra terms of reference and the inquiry will start today.**

Job not done yet.

****

ASYLUM SEEKERS

This will be ongoing of course but sadly this Home Office has no idea how to help refugees fleeing from war.

Priti Patel has refused to meet with the Home Affairs Committee before the summer recess, to discuss serious failings in her asylum programme.

And David Neale who is the chief inspector of borders and immigration has just produced a damning report on the failings of an "ineffective" and "inefficient" response by the Home Office to the security procedures and the safety of migrant children who come across the channel in small boats. **After three years the Home office system for dealing with the "crisis" was "clearly overwhelmed" he says.**

David Neale came into this job 18 months ago and has written to the Home Secretary many, many times asking to meet her. She has not agreed to a meeting so he has never seen her.

Rwanda? They have just said (23rd July) that they can only take 200 refugees. That will work out at about £600,000 for each refugee.

Job not even begun here and definitely no signs whatsoever of getting done.

****

GRENFELL

I wrote about the horrors of the Grenfell fire in my book '**Beneath the Bluster'** on page 128 in January 2021. I mentioned the lack of urgency by the government to remove the dangerous cladding on other buildings.

The Fire Brigades Union has just written to the government to demand that it rethinks its decision to reject a key Grenfell Tower Inquiry **recommendation on the evacuation of disabled residents of high-rise buildings.**

The inquiry recommended "that the owner and manager of every high-rise residential building be required by law to prepare personal emergency evacuation plan" for all disabled residents. The government had promised to implement the Grenfell Tower Inquiry phase one recommendations "in full", of which this is one.

So what has the government done? **They have rejected the recommendation and revealed downgraded plans, which have been roundly criticised by Grenfell campaigners and disability rights campaigners.**

Sadiq Khan, mayor of London says that this is just one example of inaction by the government. He says that, "Major reforms to fix a broken system are nowhere to be seen and **to its shame the government has so far failed to complete a single recommendation directed at ministers from the first phase of the enquiry**—a disgraceful dereliction of duty that is leaving too many at risk".

It really is unbelievable. **The Grenfell fire was in 2017 and here we are in 2022 still asking the government to take some action to ensure nothing like this can ever happen again.**

Job definitely not done.

****

THE ECONOMY

This is not looking good. The Organisation for Economic Co-operation and Development says (8th June) that Britain will have the slowest growth in the developed world next year. **UK growth will fall to zero percent driven by double-digit inflation.** They say that compared with other wealthy countries the UK is battling with high inflation, higher taxes and rising interest rates.

They urge the government to ease the pace of its financial proposals which include raising the tax burdens and they also call on the government to address the growing food crisis.

Their chief economist Laurence Boone says, "The outlook is sobering".

A report by the 'Resolution Foundation' on the 22nd June says "Brexit will keep wages down and make the UK poorer in the decade ahead."

Job definitely not done.

****

CHILDREN'S 'CARE' HOMES.

Of all the things I have written about in this book, and in my previous book, this is the one that shocks and upsets me the most. The fact that no-one seems to be doing anything at all to improve the situation displays criminal negligence.

This month there has been a shocking report on a secure children's home in South Gloucestershire called Calcot Services. The report, on the 9th June, says that there are serious and widespread failures which means that children and young people are not protected and their welfare is not promoted or safeguarded.

The BBC has seen leaked company records and confidential local authority briefings. They have also spoken to a dozen current and former Calcot employees. Their findings are extremely concerning and I do not understand why these homes are still open. **There are stories of children being groomed for sex, allegations of child-on-child sexual abuse and alcohol being readily available.**

The BBC has also learnt that two homes in Doncaster, run by a different company, maintained their good Ofsted ratings until their closure was announced - despite more than 100 reports of concern having been made since 2018 to the local council and regulator. Police are now investigating allegations of abuse at the homes operated by the Hesley Group, which says it is co-operating fully with the authorities.

All these homes are making massive profits and are being given thousands of pounds by local authorities.

The Children's Commissioner for England, Dame Rachel de Souza, said she was "appalled" and she said that, "The entire system needs radical reform."

But this is what they say every year. I was writing about it all this time last year.

Today (12th July), the findings of the inquiry into child sexual exploitation in Telford have at last been published. The inquiry was set up in 2019 after a report by *The Sunday Mirror*. **It finds that more than 1,000 children had been abused.** Evidence was ignored. Key agencies dismissed exploitation as 'child prostitution'. Children were blamed rather than the perpetrators. Teachers and youth workers were discouraged from reporting exploitation.

I do not have sufficient words to adequately express and convey my horror.

Nothing is ever done about this, Prime Minister. In fact I don't suppose you are even aware of any of it.

****

CANNABIS OIL FOR EPILEPSY
I wrote about this in my first book on page 53, January 5th 2021. Medical cannabis can change the lives of children with epilepsy, but

in spite of its authorisation being granted by the then Home Secretary three years earlier in 2018, it is still very difficult to obtain.

Mrs Charlotte Caldwell, whose son suffers from epilepsy has said that, "While I am delighted that there is now a route to affordable and reliable medical cannabis treatment in the UK **it remains a complex and at times opaque process"**.

She said it is estimated that up to 60 paediatric epilepsy patients are unable to get NHS-funded medical cannabis and some are reportedly paying up to £2,000 a month to access it through private healthcare.

About 1.4 million people are using black market cannabis to treat a medical condition.

Why is it so difficult for the government to do the right thing?

Job not done satisfactorily.

****

PMQS
This continues to be the usual bear garden. Even when Johnson is away it is noisy, unruly, disrespectful and vacuous.

We saw the deputy prime minister Dominic Raab opposite the shadow deputy Angela Rayner. It really was appalling.

First he berated the nurses and railway workers for having the audacity to ask for a pay rise. **We won't give way to such militant action he said at which all those behind him cheered and clapped.**

We were **applauding** key workers during the pandemic.

Some number crunching from *Private Eye* is interesting to note.

7% is what railway workers are asking for when inflation is 9% and which Grant Shapps calls "extreme".

7% is what the chief executive of tax payer subsidised 'FirstGroup', Britain's largest train operator received last year when inflation was below 1%.

Then just to explain the complete idiocy of Dominic Raab in all its transparency he has a go at Angela Rayner. She was photographed drinking champagne at Glyndebourne over the weekend and he sneeringly called her a champagne socialist.

So if you are working class you should know your place and do not think of attending something posh or classy.

To which Angela Rayner replied by explaining to him the story of "The Marriage of Figaro" which tells of a working class young girl who gets the better of a dim-witted baron. Indeed as someone pointed out Mozart would be delighted that she was there.

The job of making PMQs a respectable and intelligent debating environment is not even on the PM's agenda.

****

THE PRIVILEGES COMMITTEE.

This has just begun its investigations into whether or not Boris Johnson knowingly mislead Parliament about party-gate. They plan to finish it by the autumn. The interesting thing is that the PM and his allies are already dismissing it and saying it will be a 'kangaroo' court, and it will just be based on hearsay with no hard evidence.

My question to the PM is, just suppose in the unlikely event that they find you innocent, will you still question its veracity and call it a 'kangaroo' court? It sounds to me as though you believe yourself to be guilty.

Job not done yet.

****

THE ARTS.

Well we know that this Tory government has no interest in the arts whatsoever and sneer at those who do. Instead of criticising Angela Rayner for enjoying the opera it would be good to see a minister at the theatre or ballet or opera.

Orchestras are still finding it difficult to tour abroad without the necessary visas and without foreign hauliers able to move freely between Europe and the UK.

The bookings of UK musicians to play at EU summer festivals have dropped by 50% due entirely to Brexit red tape.

Help always promised but never given.

Job not done.

****

A SUMMER OF DISCONTENT.

It is not looking good.

Travel disruption is forecast to continue throughout the summer.

Rail workers are on strike and Aslef, the train drivers union, are also balloting on strike action. Criminal barristers are on strike and postal workers are striking this month. The British Medical Association has said that unless its demands are met, the union will prepare for a ballot of junior doctors in England for industrial action by early 2023 at the latest.

Teachers are also balloting to decide whether to take industrial action in the autumn.

Dockers at Felixstowe are to go on strike and there is now talk of a general strike by the autumn.

Motorists are 'going slow' on many motorways to protest against the rising cost of fuel. They do leave the 'fast' lane free for emergency vehicles but Priti Patel wants them all to be arrested and put in prison.

Imagine her surprise when she realises that police forces are over-stretched, all criminal barristers are on strike and the prisons are full and falling down.

Job not done.

****

THE NORTHERN IRELAND PROTOCOL

The European Union is restarting legal action against Britain today (15th June) over breaches of the Brexit Withdrawal Agreement.

Rafael Behr sums it up perfectly in *The Guardian.*

As he says, the real meaning of the protocol is nothing to do with customs checks or the existence of a border down the Irish Sea. "It will not shock Brussels into concessions, or persuade anyone who thinks Johnson is a feckless Prime Minister that he is anything else. **It is the inevitable degeneration into absurdity of government defined by Brexit**. It is a doctrine that makes an enemy of reality. If that foe will not yield to rhetoric, it must be suppressed by law."

Job not done

****

OUR CHILDREN

This is a quote from Socrates that is in *The Times* Education Commission which has just been published. He told his pupils that, **"Education is the kindling of a flame not the filling of a vessel."**

And I also like this one: "No one can teach, if by teaching we mean the transmission of knowledge, in any mechanical fashion, from one person to another. The most that can be done is that one person who is more knowledgeable than another can, by asking a series of questions, stimulate the other to think, and so cause him to learn for himself."

Socrates died in 399 BC. And we are still teaching to the test.

Job definitely not done and will not be under this PM.

****

BROKEN BRITAIN

Now just let's look a little more closely, once again, at the people keeping Johnson in power.

THE CABINET:-
Dominic Raab: "The barrister's strike is irresponsible and disappointing." He said this at the Annual Dinner of Judges at the Mansion House this month. The judges booed him. I will just write that again. **The judges booed the Justice Minister.**

Nadine Dorries: "My long-standing memory is that 2003 drop-goal." The Culture and Sport secretary talking at a Rugby League World Cup event in St Helens. Only trouble was that the goal was in a Rugby Union match.

Jacob Rees-Mogg: "Brexit has saved our economy billions." "Brexit turned the UK into a democracy." Our Brexit secretary on *BBC Newsnight*. And "I will not serve under another Prime Minister." Well that's a relief.

Grant Shapps: "The rail strikes are unnecessary and are a result of trade union leaders gunning for a fight." Our Transport Secretary decides not to even try to negotiate.

Michael Gove: "Removing the Prime Minister now would be bonkerooney." Our Levelling-Up Secretary after the two disastrous by-elections. Yes they really do talk like that.

Nadhim Zahawi: "The Prime Minister is committed to building up the UK's position as a Science Superpower." Our Education Secretary. Horizon? Erasmus? There is a huge brain-drain of British scientists.

Therese Coffey: "I am not aware of any individual conversations. I don't know anything. I haven't read the Sunday papers and I don't follow Twitter." Our Work and Pensions Secretary talking to *Sky News* about sex allegations of Chris Pincher.

Savid Javid: "There are more doctors and nurses in the NHS than ever before." Possibly true, but Health Secretary, there are 110,000 posts unfilled and the NHS is on its knees. There is a shortage of nearly 40,000 nurses and nearly 10,000 doctors.

Priti Patel: The work of this government is to deter illegal crossings and illegal entry." Sorry Home Secretary there is no such thing as an illegal asylum seeker.

Rishi Sunak: "The economic situation is extremely serious. The next few months will be tough but I stand ready to act." No new specific details and it won't be tough for him.

Liz Truss: "I am rushing back to take control" cutting short her trip to an international conference in Indonesia.

Boris Johnson: The PM says at PMQs that, "Nothing and no-one" will stop him from getting on with the job and delivering for the British people and remaining as Prime Minister.

Really Prime Minister? Do you think that maybe it would be a good idea to get hold of a dictionary and look up the meaning of the word **democracy?** Also look up the word **delivering.**

****

But to fully understand this Prime Minister we can look at three excellent articles written this month which sum him up brilliantly.

One is Chris Blackhurst of *The Independent*. He says "We are truly living in a **parallel universe** at present. Boris Johnson and his sycophantic supporters in their world; and the rest of us in ours, the one based on reality".

He goes on to say in a long and critical article, "On three key criteria we're down: domestic expenditure is suffering as inflation kicks in and real incomes fall; exports are tough, not least because we've removed our ability to trade freely and easily with the huge bloc on our doorstep and have not replaced that loss with the promised trade deals; and investment is stalling as businesses take stock and try and assess what the post-Brexit, post-Covid, post-war, post-energy shortages climate looks like."

"A legacy of Covid is that around half a million people have dropped out of the labour force. Their return would ease inflationary pressures and boost output. But there is no pot of gold at the end of the rainbow."

****

Another article is written by Jonathan Freedland of *The Times*.

Like many of us he is appalled at the cavalier attitude of Johnson and the law. His headline is:

"For 800 years, traditions and statute have protected citizens from tyranny. This PM will trash it all."

He mentions all of the laws Johnson has broken that have been written about in my books. It started of course with the illegal prorogation of Parliament. Then there are the fines for breaking the lockdown laws, the Northern Ireland Protocol, the sending of asylum seekers to Rwanda, and the resignation of Lord Geidt due to the fact that Johnson has, in his view, knowingly broken the ministerial code.

He talks about the rule of law.

"It's so basic, we take it for granted. **It's the notion, spelt out in Magna Carta in 1215, that even those in power do not enjoy unlimited or unfettered authority, but are constrained by rules; that even the sovereign – the state – is subject to the law of the land.** Only then can citizens feel relatively safe from the threat of arbitrary power, safe from a king – or prime minister – doing whatever the hell he likes."

He closes his article by saying, "Yet the rule of law is anything but the preserve of the elite. It is the last, most precious protection of the weak against the whims of the strong. It is what stands between us and tyranny. Our prime minister poses a grave threat to it – and it's not deranged to say so."

****

The third is by Patrick Cockburn of *the i*. He writes that, "This is a government that feeds off crises of its own making which it hopes will divert attention from its latest scandal and failure. Raw gobbets of nostalgia are served up to stimulate memories of supposedly better times, but over-all there is a lack of seriousness exemplified by Johnson himself and his cabinet of mediocrities, opportunists and fanatics."

How can people keep him in power when they read these words?

****

We have a corrupt, immoral and incapable Prime Minister and an inadequate and vacuous Cabinet.

As I bring this book to a close rumours are getting stronger about the demise of them all. Britain is being talked about as a failed state as Ministers are continually prepared to go out and lie to the media, to journalists and to all of us.

The summer recess is nearly upon us and by the autumn we hope to see a completely different political landscape.

****

Oh no!! What is this that I am hearing?

Things are about to explode and I need to write another chapter!

****

THE END GAME

5TH JULY: 6PM:
Boris Johnson is giving an interview to the BBC saying that he is so sorry about appointing Chris Pincher to deputy chief whip because actually yes, he remembers now, he **did** know about his previous behaviour and investigations for sexual misconduct. Oh goodness he is always so busy doing so much stuff that sometimes these things slip his mind. So actually when he told ministers to go out and defend him by saying he hadn't known, they were in fact all telling a lie.

Some of them appear to be unhappy about that.

Breaking news. During this interview the strap-line said, **"Sajid Javid has resigned."**

We hardly had time to draw breath when a second strap-line came up which said, **"Rishi Sunak has resigned."**

Oh my goodness, during the biggest NHS crisis the Health Secretary goes and during the worst ever cost of living crisis the Chancellor of the Exchequer goes.

AT LAST........and not before time, the Cabinet, or at least some members of the Cabinet, are finding their spines.

I find it inexplicable though that they are resigning over lies about a sex scandal rather than any of the issues covered in this book.

But you will be relieved to hear that Nadine Dorries, Dominic Raab, Priti Patel and Ben Wallace are all still supporting the PM.

****

6TH JULY
AM.

More resignations this morning. In fact so far there have been **18 further resignations from junior ministers.**

PMQs was the usual shambles but Sir Keir got in a few good lines: "They look like the charge of the light-weight-brigade" was one and, "It must be the first ever recording of the sinking ship deserting the rat" was another.

It has also just been confirmed that Michael Gove has seen the PM to tell him he has to go and Liam Fox has written a letter to him with the same message.

Nadhim Zahawi has been appointed Chancellor and Steve Barclay is the new Health Secretary.

So we now have the fourth Education Secretary in three years as Michelle Donelan, a junior education minister, takes over this important role. Important, that is, to all of us, but not I'm afraid to this government. Nadhim Zahawi was there for one year and achieved nothing.

Education is just seen as a stepping stone to higher things.

I have just been watching this Prime Minister first at PMQs and then at his two hour grilling at a liaison committee this afternoon and I honestly think he is seriously unhinged. I don't think this is a medical term but it is all that I can come up with.

When asked this afternoon whether he is considering resigning he blustered and shouted and said he had a huge mandate from the

British people in 2019 and when times get tough he must keep going and continue to deliver his manifesto to the people.

As others, who know the constitution better than he have been saying, actually the British people do not vote for a Prime Minister they vote for their own MP and for a party. He is not a president he just happens to be leader of the party which got the most votes.

Then we hear more about the story of Johnson and his meeting with the former **KGB agent Alexander Lebedev.** This story has been in the news for a while now, albeit never reported, so far as I know, by the BBC, but was in fact first highlighted in *The Observer* in 2019.

Johnson was asked about it directly and he actually admitted, for the first time, that when he was Foreign Secretary in 2018 he stayed in a villa in Italy owned by Lebedev's son, and whilst there he had meetings with Lebedev senior, an ex-KGB officer, without officials or security and with no records kept. **This meeting came straight after NATO's Secretary General had convened a meeting in Brussels for all the foreign ministers to discuss security and in particular the Kremlin's chemical attack on Salisbury.** There is worry that Johnson might have had documents with him from this meeting.

Carole Cadwalladr, the brilliant journalist whom I have already written about, has written a long and extremely damaging article for the Observer. (17th July). In it she describes **Johnson as being a possible cause of a fundamental breach of our national security.** A breach that potentially endangered not just our country but the entire NATO alliance.

Johnson was seen and photographed at Perugia airport by a *Guardian* reader the weekend after his stay in Lebedev's villa. **He was alone without any luggage, in a dishevelled hung-over state "looking like he had slept in his clothes" and "struggling to walk in a straight line."** The photo is in the *Observer.*

There is so much more in her article which is extremely concerning but I will just conclude by saying that in the early hours of 13th December 2019 Johnson won a landslide victory and later that same day he attended a **vodka and caviar party at Evgeny Lebedev's London home to celebrate his father's 60th birthday. It was then a year later, that Evgeny Lebedev was elevated to the House of Lords by Johnson.** So he is now Baron Lebedev of Hampton in the London Borough of Richmond upon Thames and of Siberia in the Russian Federation.

I cannot begin to say how appalling I find all of this together with the further stories of parties and media people who are all bound up with it. We don't forget that the Lebedevs own *The Evening Standard* and *The Independent*. And Amol Rajan, the media editor of the BBC and now working on the *Today* programme, has also been involved with the Lebedevs' newspaper group. **And as Putin himself has said, there is no such thing as an ex-KGB agent.**

But what is MI5 doing? Surely these Russian allegations should be investigated.

And whilst we were watching Johnson drowning at the liaison committee there were more and more resignations from Ministers.

At the last count it was up to 39. These are mostly Parliamentary Private Secretaries, Trade Envoys and junior ministers in various departments.

A senior civil servant has just said that meetings tomorrow have had to be cancelled as there are no ministers left.

We have a dysfunctional government. In fact there is no governing going on at all.

As he returns to No 10 after the liaison committee a group of MPs are going in to tell him to quit. These appear to be Grant Shapps, Simon Hart, Priti Patel, Kwasi Kwarteng, Brandon Lewis and Nadhim Zahawi.

Hang on. Who? Zahawi was only appointed Chancellor last night. **Someone has just remarked that that is the quickest backstabbing in history.** But I am hearing that he has been planning for months for the leadership campaign.

Wait a moment. I thought he was Education Minister and was planning the future of the education of our children.

6PM: Graham Brady chair of the 1922 committee has just walked in to No 10. They are bringing forward the votes for a new committee from next Wednesday to Monday of next week. (Today is Wednesday). It is being said that if Johnson refuses to go they will change the rules and have another confidence vote which he would lose.

All quiet at the moment and TV newscasters are having a hard time filling in outside No 10!

Resignations gone up to 43.

9PM: OH MY WORD WHAT ON EARTH IS THIS?
Boris Johnson has just sacked Michael Gove over the phone and referred to him as a 'snake'.

Now whatever you think of Gove most people would agree that he is possibly the only cabinet minister with a functioning brain. He has been a close colleague of Johnson's for a great many years and is the most senior cabinet minister.

The PM has finally completely lost it.

Apparently the story is that Gove said this morning that if Johnson hadn't gone by 9pm he, Gove, would resign. So Johnson called him at 8.59 and fired him.

So now it would appear that there is no-one in the Department of Housing and Levelling-up.

A paralysed government.

What will happen tomorrow? Do we have another Trump or will he go?

******

7TH JULY
There are now 53 resignations in total at the last count.

Oh my goodness we hear that Michelle Donelan the new education secretary has resigned after precisely 36 hours in the job.

However there has been no communication whatsoever from Downing Street this morning and Chris Mason, BBC political editor, is trying to work out what they are doing behind that famous door. "This is unprecedented" he says.

The *Today* programme is continuing after the news at 9am for the first time ever this morning and ....oh my word......... 9.10am and Chris Mason has just received a call to say that **the Prime Minister is resigning today.**

I have to stop here for a moment to gather my senses, take a few deep breaths and spread the news.

******

AT LAST

The news that I have been predicting for a couple of years has finally come to pass.

We need to celebrate this news in the moment because it is being said that he has resigned as leader of the Conservative party but will stay on as Prime Minister until the autumn when a new leader will have been elected.

There is a huge amount of discussion going on as to whether this is sustainable or not. Very many MPs are very angry at this thought and the idea of him making big policy announcements and carrying on as normal is anathema to all of them.

But he is busy forming a new government and some new appointments have just been issued.

Greg Clarke will replace Michael Gove.

Kit Malthouse will be the new Duchy of Lancaster

James Cleverly is the new Education Secretary (I've stopped counting)

Robert Buckland (Former Justice Secretary and a Welshman) is the new Welsh Secretary (just for three months he says).

How can these people agree to serve under Johnson a disgraced PM?

12.30PM
Boris Johnson has just come to the lectern outside No 10, to give his resignation statement.

I have to say that he spoke as though there was absolutely no problem and certainly not with him.

There was no remorse, no apology, no humility, no contrition, and he seemed to blame the Conservative MPs for their "eccentric" decision to remove him. He actually said that, "as we've seen at Westminster the herd instinct is powerful and when the herd moves it moves."

It was a very graceless speech and he never used the word "resign". He really can't quite believe it is all up for him.

He said what we had been expecting him to say, which was that he would be staying on as PM for the next few months until a successor has been found.

However it is the 1922 committee who decides the time table for all of this and Graham Brady has just announced that he wants the leadership contest to be down to two people by the beginning of the summer recess on 21st July.

A reporter for *The Times* is forecasting that Dominic Raab will be caretaker Prime Minister by the end of the day! There are too many angry MPs out there to let him continue for another day.

We will see.

Also the Labour party have said that if Johnson doesn't go today they will trigger a no-confidence motion in the House of Commons. If they win this it would mean a general election. Well the Tories don't want that as many of them would lose their seats including Johnson.

****

Sir John Major has written to the 1922 committee to say that Boris Johnson should go without delay.

I watched all the new members of the Cabinet walking into No 10 for a Cabinet meeting this afternoon. Amazing how they have all signed up for this. But it must be easier to appoint a new Cabinet than to find replacements for the 50 or so junior ministers who have resigned. Who on earth can replace them?

But surely Johnson cannot be allowed to make any policy decisions now.

****

8TH JULY
Well that is exactly what people are asking this morning. He has not yet seen the Queen and until he does so he has not resigned as PM.

There is a frightening article in several papers this morning by his ex-girlfriend Petronella Wyatt who says she knows him well and he is "bereft of humility" and will NEVER resign. In short" she says "I wouldn't be at all surprised to wake up next year and find that Boris is still Prime Minister."

Oh my goodness. You have been warned!

****

12.30PM
Good news!

Durham police have cleared Sir Keir Starmer and Angela Rayner of breaking lockdown rules. **"There is no case to answer."**

This has been a huge waste of tax-payers money and police time. This work event was investigated last year and he was cleared then. It was only re-started because the *Daily Mail* launched a huge campaign against Starmer trying to make out that he was just as bad as Johnson. There were huge headlines on their front page every day for two weeks about this ridiculous 'currygate' story, and of course Johnson and his cronies mentioned it at every opportunity.

But then none of them would recognise integrity or decency or honesty if it hit them in the face with a wet fish as James O'Brien says in his brilliant analogy on LBC.

****

9TH JULY

Simon Case, the cabinet secretary, has written to civil servants to tell them to "focus on delivering the agenda it has already agreed" in order to limit what Boris Johnson is able to do in his remaining time in office. Some are just a little bit worried about what he might do in his role as 'caretaker.'

Names are being hurled about, with some people I have never heard of putting themselves forward for the role of PM. And of course the knives are out for them all from members of their own party. That **is** something the Tories are good at.

But the 1922 Committee is talking a lot of sense at the moment. They are planning to speed up the election process considerably. Nominations will close on Tuesday 12th and they hope to get the selection numbers down to four by the 14th and down to two by the 21st, which is the start of the summer recess. Then the two names go out to all Conservative members in the UK to vote for their preferred candidate. **They hope to have the new Prime Minister installed by the 5th September when Parliament returns from the summer recess.**

****

One of the new ministers in the Department of Education was seen yesterday walking past a group of protesters outside Downing Street.

They were booing her a little and one person was holding up a photo of her deceased husband. She 'gave them the finger.' This has gone viral on Twitter and people are asking for her resignation. If any teachers did this they would instantly be sacked. Just how low do we all go?

****

Well she has written a letter in her defence. No apology, just excuses as seems to be the norm with Tory MPs. It is full of grammar and punctuation mistakes and I have just seen it on Twitter with a load of corrections in red ink!

****

10TH JULY

This is going to be the dirtiest campaign in history. The knives are out in the Conservative party and if you know what that is like you will already have taken cover.

I have just seen a digital document which has been handed to Labour by a Conservative MP and it is a list of 40 Tory MPs and beside each name is an allegation of inappropriate behaviour. Well-known names are all there and most of the behaviour is of sexual misconduct. It is said to have come from the whip's office and could be used at any time to keep them in check. It is dreadful. Some very deviant practices are there.

Even Nadine Dorries says **"The hounds of hell have been unleashed. People will shred each other to pieces...It will be a bloodbath."**

Of course most of the Sunday papers are full of it all and are writing about Johnson in various degrees of disgust.

Andrew Rawnsley's headline in *The Observer* is, **"Boris Johnson plumbed the depths of degeneracy in his shabby carnival of** misrule." He says that, "he was ultimately undone by his amorality, his arrogance, his indiscipline and his duplicity."

Or to put it another way a former Tory cabinet minister said, "The trouble with Boris is he's not very interested in governing. He's only interested in two things. Being World King and shagging."

Johnson thrived on chaos. But again as Andrew Rawnsley says, "One of the unfortunate side-effects of his chaos theory of the premiership was that it killed a lot of people."

So as Will Hutton of *The Observer* says, "Exit Johnson -- leaving behind a mess for others to clear up."

Nearly every contender for leadership is tainted with the Boris effect. And nearly every contender has already been targeted with allegations of inappropriate behaviour. These people all supported Johnson for three years or so, they kept him in power when he should have resigned, and they came out onto the media every morning to defend the indefensible.

Eleven have thrown their hat into the ring at the moment. Here they are:

Rishi Sunak. He is the bookies favourite but Johnson is determined to stop him in his tracks. He was fined by the police for breaking lockdown rules.

Nadhim Zahawi. He is currently being investigated by HMRC over his tax returns although he says he has nothing to hide.

Sajid Javid. September 2020: Raising the National Insurance tax "is the act of a responsible government." September 2022: "It's time to scrap the National Insurance tax rise."

Penny Mordaunt. She had to redo her campaign video. She had included a disabled Olympic champion who is not a Conservative and who was furious when she saw the video. She was trying to talk about the greatness of Great Britain. She is an ardent Brexiteer. She lied in 2016 about Britain not being able to stop Turkey joining the EU. She was moved on from being Defence Minister after only 85 days.

Liz Truss. Mad, bad and dangerous to know. Thinks of herself as the new Margaret Thatcher. She is being supported by Jacob Rees-Mogg and....... wait for it.......Nadine Dorries. "She is probably a stronger Brexiteer than both of us." Says Nadine.

Grant Shapps. Had a second job as a "multi-millionaire web marketer" under the pseudonym Michael Green. Will rule out a general election if he becomes prime minister. Just said that we have an embarrassment of Conservative talent. Embarrassment is the word

Kemi Badenoch. Never actually heard of her. Only held one junior ministerial position.

Suella Braverman. Attorney general who is not up-to-date with the law. She advocates leaving the European Court of Human rights.

Rehman Chishti. Never heard of him. Wants fresh ideas, a fresh team and a fresh start.

And two who have not been in the present cabinet and so are not tarred with the Boris brush.

Jeremy Hunt. Former Health Secretary. Just said he will make fox-hunting legal.

Tom Tugendhat. Formerly in the military. Just said he will expand the Rwanda plan.

And we thought these two were relatively sane.

I now write the most chilling and terrifying sentence in this book.

Priti Patel is thinking about putting her name forward to be our next Prime Minister, supported by Jacob Rees-Mogg.

So there we have it. The most right-wing selection of MPs that we could possibly have, all offering more of the same.

****

Nurses and teachers are 'ready to quit' if pay rises are delayed any longer. Unions are warning the new cabinet ministers that settling wage deals for public sector workers cannot be held up by the chaos in Downing Street.

But Nadhim Zahawi, our recent Education Secretary and who advocated a 9% pay rise for teachers is now the Chancellor and is saying that **"nurses and teachers have to be disciplined about pay rises."**

****

Millions of people across the UK are facing delays of up to two weeks for the cost of living payments promised by the government. A government spokesman said that the £326 payment will not be handed out in one tranche and will instead be staggered across several weeks and placed in people's bank accounts "ad hoc" depending on how much "the system can cope with." **The government is accused of being too "busy fighting among itself" to ensure support for the poorest households.**

The incompetence goes on.

****

12TH JULY (TUESDAY)
Yesterday the new 1922 Committee members met to decide on the rules for the election of a new Prime Minister. Each candidate will have to have the support of 20 MPs in order to be nominated by

6pm today and they will then enter the ballot tomorrow. The second ballot will be on Thursday when they will each have to have 30 MPs to support them. If needed, further ballots will be held to whittle it down to two by the 21st July. These two will then go out to all members of the Conservative party who will vote for their preference and the new PM will be announced on the 5th September.

This means that it will be up to about 160,000 mainly elderly, retired and reasonably well-off people to choose the new Prime Minister. A very unrepresentative group and in fact, of course, mostly those who chose Johnson.

****

Labour is calling for a vote of no confidence in the government and Boris Johnson today, with the vote taking place tomorrow. People are concerned that this disgraced PM is still in office and judging by a headline in *The Times* today we really do need to be sure that he goes. **"Johnson not ruled out making comeback"** they say.

It will probably fail because if it passes it will mean a general election and the Tories do not want that.

But if they do vote against this motion they will be accused of hypocrisy by supporting Johnson.

****

THE ERG
How much do you know about this group? I have to confess that although I knew of its existence and the fact that it was a right-wing group of the Conservative party I did not know much more than that. So as I enlighten myself I hope to enlighten some of you as well.

Its definition on Wikipedia says the European Research Group is a secretive research support group of Eurosceptic Conservative Members of Parliament of the United Kingdom.

In the period leading up to the EU referendum ten members of the ERG acted in an official capacity for **Vote Leave.**

In February 2017 they sent a letter to the Prime Minister Theresa May setting out their hard-line Brexit demands.

On 11th September 2018, members of the ERG met in Westminster to discuss plans to bring down the Prime Minister. This was the year when the chairman was Jacob Rees-Mogg.

On 15th April 2019 the Press Association reported that, "Critics...... accuse it of acting as a 'party within a party' running its own whipping operation in support of its objectives of a so-called 'hard' Brexit, if necessary leaving without any deal with Brussels."

Many of the new Conservative MPs elected in the 2019 general election joined the group.

And I am sure that you will be interested to know that tax payers' money is being used to fund this group.

So let us look at just some of the names who are here.

First the candidates for the new PM:

Penny Mordaunt, Suella Braverman, and Sajid Javid.

Then some others picked out at random:

Steve Baker, Andrew Bridgen, James Cleverly, Therese Coffey, David Davis, Iain Duncan-Smith, Charlie Elphicke, Liam Fox, Michael Gove, Andrea Leadsome, Brandon Lewis, Peter Lilley, Kit Malthouse, John Penrose, Chris Pincher, and Jacob Rees-Mogg.

The chairman is Mark Francois, and the deputy is Andrea Jenkyns, she of the middle finger.

An interesting past member is **Daniel Kawczynski who resigned on 8th April 2019,** stating that "I can no longer be a member of a caucus which is preventing WA4 (a fourth vote on the Brexit withdrawal agreement) from passing."

So it would appear that what I have been suggesting all along is actually officially true. This government is not the Conservative party of old. It is the UKIP/ Nationalist party, and it is very dangerous.

In July 2019 a tribunal declared that the ERG's research must be made public.

****

Oh my word after all that we need some good news. Priti Patel has just pulled out of the leadership contest.

However we need to be clear for the reason for this. It is so that the right-wing vote is not split in too many ways. She is supporting Liz Truss. In fact, be in no doubt, this is the ERG in action here.

****

6PM
The deadline for nominations has passed. Grant Shapps has already pulled out and so has Sajid Javid and Rehman Chishti leaving eight for the next ballot tomorrow. All eight are about to face a grilling from MPs shortly.

****

And we have just heard that Boris Johnson has blocked the vote of no confidence which Labour wanted for tomorrow. I must admit I wasn't aware that he had the power to do this. Labour is furious. However he has apparently called for a confidence vote in the Commons for next Monday. This is a bit odd but I am sure all will be revealed.

****

13TH JULY

PMQs was complete uncontrollable chaos. There were some cheers, would you believe, for Boris Johnson when he entered the Chamber. But before the session could start there was shouting and jeering and booing and so much noise that nothing could happen. The ineffective Speaker had absolutely no control and twice told them all to "**shut up**". For those who are not familiar with the protocol, the correct phrase is "**order, order.**" I say bring back John Bercow. The Tories didn't like him because he **was** able to shut them up but I thought he was brilliant.

Two members of the Alba party (ex SNP) were escorted out of The Chamber and have been suspended from Parliament.

Boris Johnson was as up-beat as ever spouting the same lies. When asked what he could do about the fact that **all 10 ambulance trusts have declared critical incidents** he said it was because there were too many bed-blockers so people aren't moving out of hospital but, he said, isn't it marvellous that he has restored the social care system?.

I hope you can understand the logic here.

He then made a sort of farewell speech and said although his leaving was not of his timing he said "I can leave with my head held high."

I was so angry that I immediately banged out a tweet.

"How dare you prime minister. He says he will leave with his head held high. What about all those unnecessary deaths due entirely to you for not locking down early enough? Do you remember those? No I don't suppose you do."

I have to let off steam somehow!

Hopefully that means that he won't appear next week, but why not and who will take his place? He wants to stay in power **but can't be bothered to do the job.**

****

And there are others who can't be bothered to do their job at the moment.

One is Priti Patel. She was required to appear before a Home Office Select Committee which she is bound to do but didn't show up. She blamed "unprecedented changes" to government but MPs said she should have prioritised the committee hearing. They were due to ask questions about record passport backlogs, soaring Channel migrant crossings, her stalled Rwanda policy and violence towards women. The Chair said she expects her to appear next week, which will be the last opportunity before the recess. But she doesn't.

And **Dominic Raab** has postponed **his** evidence session at the UK Parliament Human Rights Committee scheduled to take place next week.

The new Health Secretary sent a junior minister to answer questions in the House about the failing ambulance service.

And someone else not doing their job?

One thing that came out of the Sue Gray report was **the lack of respect that No 10 had for the cleaners who worked there.**

So the industry body who represents them asked to meet the Cabinet secretary Simon Case to discuss this.

However they have had no reply to these requests and so no agreement to a meeting.

The chairman of the British Cleaning Council, Jim Melvin says, "Given the lack of anything substantial in response to our request for a meeting, **we can only assume that the ministerial statements and apologies over the way cleaning staff were treated were merely empty rhetoric."**

Yes that sounds about right.

And then there is this MP who also cannot be bothered to do the job he was elected to do.

Mark Pritchard MP for The Wrekin in Telford was criticised by Tom Crowther QC who wrote the report on the child abuse scandal, **for failing to contribute to the inquiry and for his lack of engagement.**

Then we hear very disturbing news from the **Met police who have just admitted they did not send questionnaires to Boris Johnson for two parties he attended during lockdown. Others who attended these same parties received fines.** These details have been released as part of a judicial review brought by the Good Law Project. As they say "The Met's actions have raised grave concerns about the deferential way in which they are policing those in power." **So The Met are not doing their job.**

And now I hear of Michael Ellis MP and Cabinet Office Minister who has declined to give evidence on government policy for adapting the UK's infrastructure to resist climate change. The Joint Committee on National Security Strategy has just held its last session and are concerned that he cancelled his attendance with only a week's notice. He said he was only the "convening" minister rather than a minister with responsibilities for the policies in question. This is extremely worrying and the committee said that there **"appeared to be no minister responsible for the strategy for CNI climate resilience which suggested a major hole at the centre of government."**

Grant Shapps Transport Minister has just confirmed that he's not willing to sort out the rail dispute. **Yet another minister not doing his job.**

And the candidates? How are they doing?

Well it is interesting to note that this afternoon there was a special **climate briefing meeting** hosted by the All Party Parliamentary Climate Change Group and Peers for the Planet. The government's chief scientific advisor **Sir Patrick Vallance was a speaker. Not one candidate for the PM's job attended.**

Chaos and irresponsibility everywhere you look.

****

14TH JULY
Covid deaths have now reached 200,000.

****

Peter Oborne wrote the book "The Assault on Truth" which is about the rise of populist politics as seen with Johnson and Trump, or, as he says, "the emergence of a new moral barbarism."

He has just written a fascinating article, about politics in Britain today, for the *Middle East Eye*. This is a digital magazine founded in April 2014 and chiefly covers stories in the Middle East and North Africa.

However its headquarters are in London and it encourages stories from wider afield and reports have been referenced by many international bodies. Several journalists have been recognised for their writing for MEE and Peter Oborne is one of them.

In this column he compares the politics of the 1970s when it was "all beer and sandwiches at No 10", with the politics of today when "access to the prime minister is for sale to billionaires."

It is a long and detailed article and at the end we are in no doubt that as he says, **"It's the fiscal rich. They own this Tory government."**

He mentions Ben Elliot MP who is Co-Chairman and fund raiser for the Conservative Party. "He is the "umbilical cord which links the Tory party to its financial backers."

"He has done business offshore, jointly owning a filming financing business that cropped up with Pandora papers."

Pandora papers are the 11.9 million leaked documents from 14 companies in offshore tax havens with details of ownership of 29,000 offshore companies and trusts from Vietnam to Singapore.

He goes on to say that the **"Thatcher system she championed has degenerated into an obscene system of governance by and for the super- rich."**

He compares the present lot unfavourably with Mick Lynch the General Secretary of the Maritime and Transport workers. **He is "loyal, decent, stands up for his people, pays his taxes and isn't based off-shore."**

We know Mr Oborne, we know.

We have watched him and listened to him over the past few weeks as he appeared on news items and chat shows making the case for his workers who have voted for strike action. We all think he is brilliant and we approve of his straight talking.

So we hear that the 14 front runners in the leadership campaign had secured £307,000 in donations over the last 12 months. And the "limit on spending on the leadership campaign has been quietly lifted to £300,000."

They are not exactly short of money.

****

15TH JULY

No they are not. Today we hear that the Home |Office's most senior civil servant was given a bonus of between £15,000 and £20,000 last year. This is on top of his annual salary of £185,000. His deputy was given a bonus of between £10,000 and £15,000. But of course all the rest of us have to be disciplined and patient.

.

******

16TH JULY

Last night I watched a television debate with the remaining five candidates. It was not so much a debate actually, as answering questions from an audience of floating voters. As only a very few watching have any vote you could say it was a bit pointless but we did get to see them all in action and as I knew very little about three of them, and had never heard them speak before, it was interesting.

The main subject was tax and the only person who talked remotely knowledgably about that was, as you might expect, the former Chancellor, Rishi Sunak.

But when asked if they thought Johnson was an honest man, yes or no, the only person who gave a straight answer, "No", was Tom Tugendhat.

As an ardent feminist it pains me to say this but the three women were distinctly underwhelming. The two men did have functional brains but Tugendhat is too far behind and so the only one with any qualifications for the highest office in politics is so far as I am concerned, is Rishi Sunak. But this is from a low bar.

Matthew Parris former Conservative MP and columnist for *The Times* obviously believes that they are all inadequate apart from Sunak as he begins his article today by writing, "**Have we gone bonkers?"**

He finishes it by writing "We need experience. I'm in deadly earnest when I say this, and Tories had better understand it: **there may be only a few days left to save the Conservative Party."**

I agree. I actually think they are in free fall and that there will have to be a general election very, very soon after September 5th.

****

18TH JULY

But be in no doubt, the most serious issue at the moment is the relationship between the Conservative party and Russian money. In an article in *The Times* today Edward Lucas writes that, "**We are now perilously close to being a country run by the dodgy rich for the dodgy rich."** Not only Russians of course, but London is seen as the money-laundering and reputation-washing centre of the world" and, as he says "The worst people in the world steal many billions of pounds, dollars and euros every year from the poor."

He also says that, "**Deterring Russia necessarily mean closer ties with Europe."**

"**We cannot defend ourselves or our friends alone."**

But there is absolutely no hint of the urgent need for better ties with Europe in any way from any of the current prospective would-be leaders of the Conservative party.

Every televised debate gets worse and worse and at the moment the best contender for the premiership in my view, is Sir Keir Starmer.

****

19TH JULY

The televised debate due to have taken place on Sky this evening has been cancelled. Rishi Sunak and Liz Truss had such an ill-natured spat during the last one that they decided to withdraw and the Tory HQ decided that they were all doing so much harm to the Conservative party that it should be stopped. **"Running Scared"** is the phrase doing the rounds at the moment or, as *The Times* editorial puts it, "**Stage Fright**". As they also say, "Important issues are at stake. **An election conducted behind closed doors risk delivering a leader with no mandate and little chance of delivering effective government."**

And speaking of **Liz Truss**, it is important to check the veracity of what she says. During the last debate she emphasised the fact that whilst Sunak went to a famous public school, she said the reason she became a Conservative was because she went to a school in a "red wall" seat. She saw "kids at my school being let down in Leeds, perhaps not getting the opportunities you had at your school Rishi." She said that she saw, **"children who failed and were let down by poor expectations."**

Well this school is Roundhay School in Leeds. A member of my family knows it well. So do many other people. It is in a very wealthy and leafy part of Leeds and is definitely not a "red wall" seat. Its alumni includes a concert pianist, judges, several knights, a Victoria cross recipient, an Arch-deacon of Cambridge , a neuroscientist, an editor of the Sunday Telegraph, MPs, Professors of surgery and many more.

And during the time Truss was there it was a Conservative led authority. Why does she feel that she has to lie?

****

I also watched part of the confidence debate in the Commons yesterday.

The reason for this vote, called by Johnson, is so that he can give his second valedictory speech in which he says what a fantastic job he has done and how everything is going absolutely swimmingly.

He is in his usual unkempt state and he starts by saying that he doesn't know why on earth this debate was called by Starmer as we could be discussing something much more serious and this is just a waste of time. **The Speaker then intervened to say that actually Prime Minister it was you who called for this debate.**

Some are saying that he appeared drunk or worse as he blustered his way through an interminable and incomprehensible speech.

Of course he is going to win this vote. If they don't, it results in a general election and none of them want that. Nearly all of them would lose their seats. As we know, turkeys don't vote for Christmas. And turkeys are what they are. Every one of them as they all voted yes to having confidence in the government. As Keir Starmer says they should re-read their resignation letters of last week. He read some of them out.

Deranged, deluded and dishonest. All of them.

****

Wait a minute. I am wrong here. There were a few who voted against. There were also a few who couldn't be there but who managed to 'pair' with someone. **However, one MP could not attend because he was in Moldova at the time before going on to Ukraine in his role as Chairman of the Commons Defence Committee.** So the PM has removed the whip from him. His name is Tobias Ellwood.

He said in a statement that he had been "unable to secure return travel due to unprecedented disruption both here and in the UK."

He goes on to say, "I am very sorry to lose the whip but will now continue my meetings **in Ukraine promoting the prime minister's**

ABOUT THE AUTHOR

Sue Wood was born and brought up in a medical family in Coventry. She was educated in Leamington Spa and Maria Grey Froebel College in Twickenham. She worked as a Primary school teacher in Coventry and Cambridge and then took a break from teaching and worked as Director of Public Relations at Coventry Cathedral. After her wedding there she moved with her husband, first to Abu Dhabi and then to Aberdeen. She is now settled in Hertfordshire with her husband, and has two children and two grand-children.

She returned to teaching, first in Bushey and then in Elstree. On retiring she became a Speaker for Save the Children. She has always been concerned about those whom she feels are being treated unjustly and has been a member of the Howard League for Penal Reform for over 25 years.

She started writing at the age of 10 when her American aunt gave her a 5 year diary and has written five books for friends and family. Her first published book for the general public, "Beneath the Bluster. A Diary of Despair. Ignorance, Incompetence, Confusion and Lies" was published in October 2021.

She has always been interested in news and politics; the entire premiership of Boris Johnson is recorded for future generations in these two books.

****

efforts here and specifically seeking to secure the opening of Odessa port – so vital grain exports can re-commence."

So it would appear that the only Tory MP doing any really important, significant work is punished by the Prime Minister.

Why is that do you think? Could it be because Mr. Ellwood, a former member of The Royal Green Jackets, argued with him about tank warfare and cuts in defence spending, and also said we could re-join the single market very quickly? He is that rare breed, a decent hard-working, sensible Tory. He is also the person who ran towards danger when a policeman was stabbed to death outside Parliament in 2017 and he tried to resuscitate him. Three other people died in that terrorist attack and at least 40 people were injured. Sounds like the sort of chap you want on your side.

****

20TH JULY

Yesterday was the hottest day on record with temperatures reaching over 40 degrees in some places. Fires broke out all over the country and major incidents have been declared by five fire brigades including London with 10 separate blazes across the capital. Even today fires are continuing to break out including one on the 17th floor of a block of flats in Greenwich.

****

Today was the last ever PMQs with Prime Minister Boris Johnson. And that is a sentence I have been wanting and waiting to write for two and a half years. He carried on his usual fashion of bluster, bombast and lies. He truly thinks he has been a fantastic PM. He is completely delusional. He is extremely rude to Starmer and Blackford and the Speaker doesn't pull him up. But most bizarre of all is the nature of his going.

"Hasta La Vista baby" was his closing phrase and he leaves to a standing ovation from the very MPs who were responsible for his demise. All, that is, except for Theresa May who stood with her arms folded. It really does beggar belief.

They then all leave the Chamber to go and vote for the final two who are competing for his job.

And they are.................Rishi Sunak and Liz Truss.

****

So those are the two final candidates.

They both display a below average intellect.

They will both lie about Brexit if they discuss it at all.

Neither has a plan for the NHS, for our education system, for the criminal justice system or for climate change.

Present strike action and future possible industrial action is met with aggression and threats.

They both support the unworkable and illegal Rwanda plan for refugees.

The inevitable slide into recession and the number of people in poverty does not seem to worry them unduly.

They are both trying to appeal to the Tory right wing.

Liz Truss is the favourite at the moment.

They have both been members of Johnson's cabinet over the last two and a half years.

We now have to listen to them fighting it out over the next six weeks.

****

Together, with my last book 'Beneath the Bluster', I have now kept a daily record of the entire premiership of Boris Johnson.

It is a record of what I believe to be the most shameful period in our history. A time when our leader was dishonest, incompetent, ignorant, and dangerous. A leader who surrounded himself with those of inadequate and third rate talent whose only requirement was that they would support him whatever and keep him in power. There will be more neglect and incompetence as we move towards the winter and I urge you to call it out whenever you see it.

There is a worrying report in the *Financial Times* which states that there is a disturbing **lack of talent amongst all western democracies just now**. I am sure that is true but I do think that, to coin one of Johnson's most often used phrase, **we** are actually **"world beating"** at that.

So we await the results of the two inquiries, the Covid-19 inquiry and the Privileges Committee inquiry. It has been confirmed by the Speaker that should Johnson be found guilty of misleading Parliament by the Privileges Committee he would have to resign his seat and there would be a by-election. I think that that is a slightly cheering note on which to end this book.

For end it I must.

Some say that maybe the history of Johnson's premiership will be re-written and he will be seen to have been "not really that bad."

So I finish by a quote about the department that has probably been one of the worst affected: my beloved NHS.

Rachel Clarke is a palliative care doctor. She has written a long article about the PM of which this is just a small part:

"There were – as of yesterday, but still counting- 197,635 reasons why he makes every doctor and nurse I know seethe with stone-cold fury. We watched patients plead and gasp and fade and die, over and over again."

She writes about his failure to lock down in time so resulting in so many deaths.

"Their deaths should stain his conscience –if it exists- for ever," she writes. "We ran out of beds, we ran out of ambulances, we ran out of ventilators and we watched and wept as they suffocated. It's a monstrous legacy. Thank God he is gone."

Never let anyone get-away with saying that Boris Johnson got the big calls right.

****

WE NEED A GENERAL ELECTION AND WE NEED ONE NOW.

****

ACKNOWLEDGEMENTS

I want to say a huge thank you once again to all journalists and columnists everywhere. The accurate and fearless reporting of news is more important than ever before.

My thanks go to:

The Times	ITV
The Sun	The Mirror
The Sunday Times	Channel 4
The Financial Times	The Daily Mail
The Guardian	The Good Law Project
Sky News	The I
The Observer	Care4Calais
LBC	Politics home
The Independent	Twitter
BBC	HuffPost
The Evening Standard	The Express

Many, many people, charities and protest groups have been credited throughout this text and if I have left anyone out, I apologise. But without all of you this book could never have been written.